COME UP HITHER TO Zion

COME UP HITHER TO
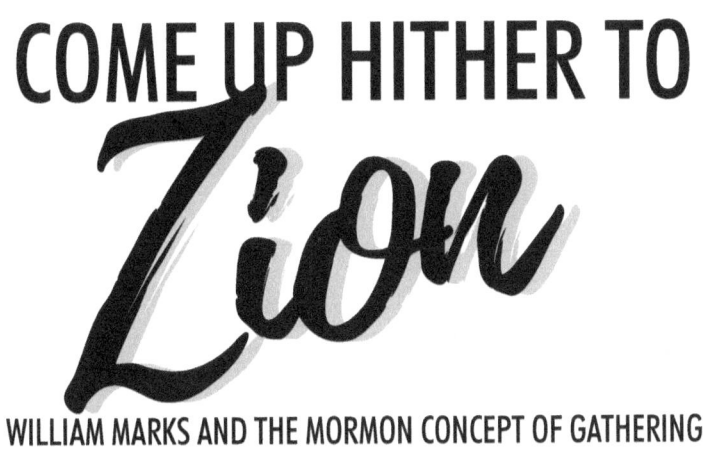

WILLIAM MARKS AND THE MORMON CONCEPT OF GATHERING

CHERYL L. BRUNO
JOHN S. DINGER

Greg Kofford Books
Salt Lake City, 2024

Copyright © 2024 Cheryl L. Bruno and John S. Dinger.
Cover design copyright © 2024 Greg Kofford Books, Inc.
Cover design by Loyd Isao Ericson and Cheryl L. Bruno.
Cover portrait by Christina Freeman. Used with permission.
Inside front cover image by Jonathan Streeter. Used with permission.

Published in the USA.

All rights reserved. No part of this volume may be reproduced in any form without written permission from the publisher, Greg Kofford Books. The views expressed herein are the responsibility of the authors and do not necessarily represent the position of Greg Kofford Books.

ISBN 978-1-58958-802-8 (paperback)
Also available in ebook.

Greg Kofford Books
P. O. Box 1362
Draper, UT 84020
www.gregkofford.com
facebook.com/gkbooks
twitter.com/gkbooks

Library of Congress Control Number: 2024938046

Contents

Preface	ix
Introduction: They Shall Be Gathered In	xiii
1. Ordained to Preside Over Kirtland	1
2. Missouri, the Land of My People	25
3. Commerce: Suited for the Saints	37
4. Nauvoo Municipality	53
5. The Ties that Bind	71
6. A Viper on the Wall	97
7. Succession and Shoulder-Rounding	111
8. James J. Strang: Claims and Clashes	135
9. Charles B. Thompson's Gathering Committee	155
10. The Weary Wanderer	175
11. Reorganizing Zion	185
Conclusion: Quiet Cornerstone	207
Appendix A: William Marks—Letters	219
Appendix B: William Marks—Publications	251
Bibliography	265
Index	293

William Marks photograph on Scoville silvered copper plate, circa 1850–1860. Courtesy of Community of Christ Library and Archives.

Preface

Like-minded acolytes have often felt a desire to band together into supportive communities that would strengthen their faith and serve as a central location for expansion. The metaphysical concept of Zion as a center of spiritual consciousness and a place of unity has been contemplated in different ways in a variety of religious organizations. This book explores the meaning of the principle of "gathering to Zion" within the movement founded by Joseph Smith Jr., as illuminated by the life of one of his most loyal converts, William Marks. Marks, who became an important leader in the Latter Day Saint church, was both drawn to this principle and present through its early development from 1830 to 1844. After the death of Smith, several groups claiming the right of succession attempted to gather followers into a religious or philosophical organization, as well as to a physical location termed "Zion," where they were to follow a communal lifestyle. Consequently, Marks not only experienced gathering as conceptualized by Smith, but he encountered it again four other times: in Brigham Young's call to move the Saints west; in James Strang's community at Voree, Wisconsin; in Charles Thompson's Congregation of Jehovah's Presbytery of Zion; and in the reorganization group eventually led by Joseph Smith III.

Marks's position in the top echelons of leadership in these groups involved him in defining moments in Mormonism. The banking crisis in Kirtland, Ohio, the ejection of the Saints from Missouri, the building of a religious "kingdom" in Nauvoo, Illinois, the clandestine practice of plural marriage, and the predicament of who would lead the church after Joseph Smith's death are all watershed Mormon issues that are profitably studied alongside the biography of Marks. These moments all intersect to some extent with the Latter Day Saints' distinctive idea of gathering.

Furthermore, Marks can be seen as an example of actions often paired with gathering: boundary maintenance of who is to gather with the select company, or the expulsion of those who don't fit. His life thus encapsulates two main themes. The first, gathering, is seen in his continued desire to find the true church he is seeking. The second, excommunication, is something he experienced from both ends through his own excommunication from Presbyterianism to join the Mormons, a major calling on the Kirtland High Council where he dealt with polygamy through excommunications, his expulsion from Nauvoo after the death of Smith, and his participation with James Strang in excommunicating Young and other Mormon apostles. Perhaps the most striking event in this vein was Marks's role in the excommunication of Sidney Rigdon, as Marks stood up for established rules and processes even when he was penalized for it.

Records detailing Marks's daily life and thoughts are scarce. He kept no journal, and his personal contemplations and beliefs are limited to brief statements published in a few church newspapers, as well as a series of letters written to a friend in later life. These are important, however, as they describe some of the major controversies in Mormonism from an insider's point of view. Marks wasn't a dynamic speaker or writer, though minutes of high council and city council meetings in Nauvoo offer glimpses of careful actions he took and measured decisions he made. He was quiet, thoughtful, and considerate of the expertise of others, thus winning the respect and admiration of his fellows. He was successful and esteemed in both spiritual and temporal pursuits, though at times he found himself involved in grueling power struggles with those in leadership. In the diaries of acquaintances, contemporary religious journals, and histories of the various ecclesiastical groups with which he was affiliated, Marks is thus described as everything from a "mean conspirator" to "the noblest of men."

Through careful analysis of existing documents, the authors of this book have come to view Marks as a sincere seeker who was devoted to Joseph Smith and the movement he founded. It is evident that Marks struggled with Smith's most divisive doctrines while remaining committed to the overall cause. After the death of the charismatic leader, Marks faced weighty issues along with the rest of Smith's followers. Questions foremost in his mind emerged as these: Would Mormonism continue as the true, restored religion Joseph Smith described? Were the Saints to gather as one body? Where? Under whose direction? How was belonging in the Latter Day Saint tradition to be defined? Marks's struggle with these queries is representative of so many early Book of Mormon believers.

This manuscript uses the 1830 capitalization and punctuation of "Latter Day Saint" that was carried over into the James Strang, Charles Thompson, and Reorganization movements. We also use the terms "Mormon," "Mormonism," and "Mormon church," all of which were ubiquitous in the time period we discuss, used by member and nonmember alike. Likewise, the terms "Reorganization" and "Reorganized church" are used to reference the now Community of Christ (formerly Reorganized Church of Jesus Christ of Latter Day Saints) beginning with its initial planning meetings in the 1850s. With due respect, we generally refer to people by surnames, except when first names are needed to distinguish between family members. In quotations we replicate the spelling and punctuation of the original manuscripts. When we add letters or words for clarification, we use [brackets]. When a word is crossed out in the original, we use ~~strikethrough~~. When letters or words are added above the line, we use ^carets^.

The authors wish to thank Rachel Killebrew at the Community of Christ Library and Archives for her valuable assistance in searching for and providing scans of documents, Robin Jensen for reading and commenting on our treatment of succession, John Hajicek for suggestions and insights both on succession and the James Strang movement, Holly Welker for her suggestions, editing, and sometimes scathing commentary on the manuscript, and Loyd Isao Ericson and Raistlyn Camphuysen of Greg Kofford Books for close and caring oversight while preparing this book for publication.

In this biography, we welcome each interested reader to explore key Mormon doctrines and early church history through the intriguing and poignant wanderings of William Marks.

INTRODUCTION

They Shall Be Gathered In

"The gathering, not polygamy, was Mormonism's oldest and most influential doctrine," wrote historian William Mulder.[1] William Marks, descendant of Puritan founders of New England[2] and convert to Mormonism, was shaped by both. Marks joined his fortunes to Joseph Smith's young, upstart religion at a pivotal time in its early history, when the principle of gathering was beginning to be preached and practiced. Marks's life was characterized by the many gatherings that he participated in—gatherings that were often being broken and scattered because of polygamy.

According to Smith, in September 1827 he received a set of golden plates from the angel Moroni, a resurrected being who had lived on the American continent over a millennium earlier. These plates were divinely translated by Smith and published in 1830 as the Book of Mormon. With Smith's Church of Christ being established one month later in April, it could be argued that doctrines like gathering, which are contained in the Book of Mormon, precede Mormonism itself.

The Book of Mormon purports to be a record of groups of Israelites who migrated to the Americas. It contains the writings of prophets who descended from them and includes an account of Christ's visit to those people. Many of the prophets in the Book of Mormon speak of the gathering of Israel. The prophet Nephi, who lived around 560 to 545 BC, quoted Isaiah and told the people that God would "gather together the dispersed of Judah from the four corners of the earth" (2 Ne. 21:12). Jacob, another Book of Mormon prophet who was active at the same time, made clear that the gathering was to be a physical event. He prophesied that Christ would "come among the Jews" who would reject him, leading to destruction and pestilence. However, after they would repent and be-

---

1. William Mulder, "Mormonism's 'Gathering': an American Doctrine with a Difference," 249.

2. For example, William's great-great-grandfather, Abishai Marks, was married to Martha Cornwall, descendant of William Cornwall, Puritan founder of Middletown, Connecticut, who came to America before 1633. William and Cornwall/Cornwell became family names for many generations to follow. See Edward E. Cornwall, *William Cornwall and His Descendants: A Genealogical History of the Family of William Cornwall, One of the Puritan Founders of New England, Who Came to America in or before the Year 1633, and Died Middletown, Connecticut, in the Year 1678*, iii, 2–3.

lieve in Christ, "they shall be gathered in from their long dispersion, from the isles of the sea, and from the four parts of the earth" (2 Ne. 10:3–8).

The Book of Mormon also records the prophesying of Christ who visited the Americas after his death and told believers he would "remember the covenant which I have made with my people; and I have covenanted with them that I would gather them together in mine own due time, . . . [in] the land of Jerusalem, which is the promised land unto them forever" (3 Ne. 20:29). Christ described a "New Jerusalem" to be established in the Americas. There, his people would be "gathered in, who are scattered upon all the face of the land . . . and I also will be in the midst" (3 Ne. 21:23–25).

William Marks and the early Saints read these words in the Book of Mormon and discussed the promises associated with the gathering of the Lord's people—as both a physical event and a philosophical concept rooted in the Bible.[3] The principle was also taught by the new prophet Joseph Smith, who often provided revelation from God on the matter and preached that the time had come for the prophesied gathering to begin.

In September 1830, just six months after the formation of the church and right before a church conference, Smith received a revelation dealing with the gathering of God's people. While this revelation was given to a small group of people, "Six Elders of the Church & three members," they were commanded that they "are called to bring to pass the gathering of mine elect." Further, they were told that "wherefore the decree hath gone forth from the father that they shall be gethered [sic] in unto one place upon the face of this land to prepare their Hearts & be prepared in all things against the day of tribulation & desolation." There was some need for immediacy as "the hour is nigh" and "they that do wickedly shall be as stub[b]le & I will burn them up."[4] At the conference held after this revelation was received, Colesville branch president Newel K. Knight recorded that it was discussed and the Saints were instructed "to begin the gathering of Israel, and a revelation was given to the Prophet on this subject."[5] While the gathering was to be "one place upon the face of this land," it was not disclosed where this place was to be.[6]

Smith received another revelation in December 1830 that specifically told him and all the Saints "that it is expedient in me [the Lord] that they

---

3. See, e.g., Deut. 30: 3–5; Isa. 11, 14:1–2.
4. "Revelation, September 1830–A [D&C 29]," 37, JSP.
5. "Newel Knight autobiography, circa 1871," 268–69, CHL.
6. "Revelation, September 1830–A, as Recorded in Hyde and Smith, Notebook [D&C 29]," 30, JSP.

should assemble together at the Ohio." At the time, Smith was working on a translation of the Bible. The revelation went so far as to tell him to put it off until the gathering: "I say unto you that it is not expedient in me that ye should translate any more until ye shall go to the Ohio."[7] Revelations like this emphasized the importance and priority of gathering among the early Saints.

Months later, other revelations spoke of gathering and provided additional context. At this point, the concept of gathering took a second form. Originally, it was a physical assembling of the faithful to a location, but additional revelations expanded the effort by calling certain elders to go out and gather others to the fold through missionary work. In February of 1831, church members were told to "go forth baptizing with water . . . Until the time shall come when it shall be revealed unto you from on high, when the city of the New Jerusalem shall be prepared." Gathering thus started to include proselytizing, with an overarching purpose "that ye may be gathered in one."[8]

Mormon settler Solomon Hancock described his experience traveling to Jackson County, Missouri, a land that was "very rich and productive abounding in much wild fruit and honey and game," which made it "lovely and desireable for settlers." Hancock considered the county "a home for the Saints, a land of zion and a place of gathering . . . and we began to preach for the Saints to gather to Jackson County Missouri the land of Zion to learn more of the ways of the Lord."[9]

While the Saints gathered in both Ohio and Missouri, revelations and instructions continued to come forth on the subject. In March 1831, Smith again received revelation instructing members "with one heart and with one mind, gather up your riches that ye may purchase an inheritance which shall hereafter be appointed unto you." The New Jerusalem was to be "a land of peace, a city of refuge, a place of safety."[10] In July 1831, Missouri was appointed and consecrated for gathering: "Wherefore it is wisdom that the land should be purchased by the saints." Local leaders were to assist families to "plant them in their inheritance" in the land that the Lord had "appointed & consecrated for the gethering of the Saints."[11]

---

7. "John Whitmer, History, 1831–circa 1847," 4, JSP. See also Elizabeth Maki, "'Go to the Ohio,'" 70–73.

8. "John Whitmer, History, 1831–circa 1847," 13, JSP.

9. "Charles B. Hancock autobiography, circa 1882," CHL.

10. "History, 1838–1856, volume A-1 [23 December 1805–30 August 1834]," 108, JSP.

11. "Revelation, 20 July 1831 [D&C 57]," 93, JSP.

When Smith proclaimed that Jackson County was Zion, the "New Jerusalem," his followers were eager to begin building the city in preparation for the coming of Christ.[12] Smith painted a vivid picture of Jackson County as the place where the first humans, Adam and Eve, lived after leaving the Garden of Eden and before the great flood shifted biblical history to the Middle East. Here, Adam had blessed his posterity, and in the end times the great progenitor would return to this consecrated spot that Smith named "Adam-ondi-Ahman," or "Adam in the presence of God."[13] Believers who assembled in that place would witness the Second Coming of Jesus Christ and a grand council where the Savior would collect back the keys of the kingdom that had been distributed to Adam and other stewards of gospel dispensations.

In late summer of 1831, the Latter Day Saints, as they were known, began flooding into the county, which, since its incorporation in 1826, had already been occupied by settlers who perceived the Mormons as a threat. By the end of 1833, the county's first settlers had violently forced about 1,200 "obnoxious" Mormons into neighboring counties.[14] Early Mormon convert John Corrill wrote to Oliver Cowdery, the Second Elder of the church, at church headquarters in Kirtland, Ohio, expressing his belief that the governor of Missouri would support the Saints in moving back into their homes but could not help further unless there was a military force that could stay and protect them.[15] The response came in the form of a revelation to Smith in which the Lord summoned both young and middle-aged men—"all the strength of mine house . . . warriors . . . [to go] straightway unto the land of my vineyard, and redeem my vineyard; for it is mine" (LDS D&C 101:55–56). Although the Saints in Missouri were told that this affliction had come upon them to chasten them for their sins, they were assured that Zion would "be redeemed."[16] "It is better, in the eyes of God," Smith wrote them, "that you should die, than that you should give up the land."[17]

---

12. "Revelation, 20 July 1831 [D&C 57]," 93, JSP; "Revelation, 6 June 1831 [D&C 52]," 87–89, JSP.

13. Orson Pratt interpreted the name to mean "Valley of God, where Adam dwelt." Orson Pratt, "Daniel's Vision," February 25, 1877, *JD*, 18:343.

14. "History, 1838–1856, volume A-1," 322, JSP.

15. John Corrill, "From Missouri," *EMS*, 126.

16. "History, 1838–1856, volume A-1," 361, JSP.

17. "History, 1838–1856, volume A-1," 394, JSP.

Church representatives Parley P. Pratt and Lyman Wight made an arduous winter journey back to Kirtland, arriving on February 22, 1834. A letter they bore from W. W. Phelps, assistant president of the church in Missouri, reiterated that the governor was willing to restore the Saints' property, but the state constitution gave him no power to enforce such an action. Phelps warned, "The mob swear, if we come [back] we shall die!"[18]

Two days after they arrived in Kirtland, Pratt and Wight were commanded through revelation to assemble at least one hundred (and optimally five hundred men) as a military force to return with them to Missouri.[19] This enterprise would come to be known as "Zion's Camp." On Wednesday, February 26, Smith left his home in Kirtland "to obtain volunteers for Zion, in compliance with the foregoing revelation."[20] Through this trip, William Marks would meet the Mormons.

On their way east, Smith and Pratt passed through Ohio, Pennsylvania, and then several western New York townships and settlements. At Perrysburg, they "called the church together, and related unto them what had happened to our brethren in Zion." Smith prophesied mightily, and consequently, "with all readiness, the young and middle aged volunteered for Zion."[21] On Saturday, March 8, they held a meeting in Farmersville, New York, and arranged for another to be held March 10 in Freedom Township, where they had been invited to stay at the home of Oliver Cowdery's brother, Warren.

Though Warren had been aware of the Book of Mormon since 1830 and was sympathetic to the difficulties of the Saints in Missouri, he was not a member of the church at that time. Warren, his wife Patience, and their eight children lived in a fine brick home in Freedom. On the property adjoining their farm lived another big family: Samuel Miles, his wife, Prudence Marks Miles, and their brood of seven. Having heard of Mormonism from Warren, Samuel and some of his older sons had traveled nine miles to attend the meeting in Farmersville on Saturday. "After the meeting closed," Samuel's son later recounted, "a few proceeded to a nearby stream where the ice was cut, it being mid-winter, and some baptisms were tended to." The Miles family, Warren Cowdery, and several other families in Freedom became interested in what Smith and Pratt were preaching.

---

18. "History, 1838–1856, volume A-1," 398, JSP.
19. "History, 1838–1856, volume A-1," 440, JSP.
20. "History, 1838–1856, volume A-1," 441, JSP.
21. "History, 1838–1856, volume A-1," 445, JSP.

Thus, on Monday, March 10, 1834, Smith and Pratt preached "to an overflowing house." After the evening meeting, Smith proposed that "if any wished to obey, and would make manifest, we would stay and administer to another meeting." A young man from the Methodist church was typical of many who listened to the Zion's Camp recruiters. He stood and proclaimed his faith in the fullness of the gospel. He wished to be baptized. Smith and Pratt accordingly "appointed another meeting for the next day," a Tuesday, and baptized the ardent Heman T. Hyde.[22]

"In a few weeks," Samuel Miles Jr. related, "our town was visited by Elders John Murdock, Orson Pratt, and others. A large branch was raised up."[23] A local history captures some of the consternation the residents of Freedom felt at the "humbug" the Latter Day Saint missionaries were promoting:

> [T]he quiet precincts of Fish Lake neighborhood were invaded by Joe Smith, Sidney Rigdon, John Gould, and Parley Pratt. . . . Meetings were held, daily and nightly, in barns and dwelling-houses, and a prodigious excitement pervaded the minds of many people in that immediate vicinity. . . . 30 men and women were induced to join the Mormons, and emigrated with them to Kirtland, Ohio. Some came back and renounced their faith in Mormonism, while others continued with them to the end of their lives.[24]

Samuel and Prudence Marks Miles and several of their children were among those baptized.[25] Prudence's brother, forty-two-year-old William Marks, visited Freedom at this time and attended meetings. "He became a convert to the truth of the gospel and was shortly afterward baptized," along with over forty people in the area.[26] Warren Cowdery was set apart as president of the Freedom branch.[27]

---

22. "History, 1838–1856, volume A-1," 446, JSP.
23. "Samuel Miles autobiography, circa 1904," 2, CHL.
24. Franklin Ellis, ed., *History of Cattaraugus: Illustrations And Biographical Sketches Of Some Of Its Prominent Men And Pioneers*, 399.
25. Prudence Marks Miles and some of her children crossed the plains to Utah with the Ezra T. Benson company in 1849.
26. Converts included the Israel Calkins family, the Lyman Calkins family, the Aaron and Mehitable Cheney family and Aaron's brother Hurd, Warren and Patience Cowdery, Isaac and Harriet Decker, Ira and Wealtha Hatch, The Heman and Polly Hyde family, the Tilton and Eunice Hyde family, Thomas Graven, Dimon McPherson, the Rufus and Adelia Metcalf family, the Samuel and Prudence Miles family, Nehemiah and Lucy Sparks, and Benjamin and Eliza Wheeler.
27. "Samuel Miles autobiography, circa 1904," 2, CHL.

An account by Dr. B. W. Richmond, quoted and paraphrased in the *Deseret News* in 1875, establishes William Marks's urbane reputation in the neighborhood of Oak Hill, near Portage, New York, while simultaneously describing the folksy and devout ways of the visiting Mormon preachers. Claiming to be a close associate teaching near Marks's residence in 1833, Richmond identifies Marks as a wealthy farmer of strict integrity. That year, the "strange sect" came into the neighborhood teaching that "theirs was a new and glorious dispensation under the head of a prophet anointed by God." Five or six priests stayed in town for the winter and "drew many respectable persons into the church." Richmond describes "wild scenes of hubbub" such as speaking in tongues, prophesying, visions, and giving revelations and interpretations.[28]

Because of the Mormon leaders' interest in healing, an impoverished old woman named Mrs. Simmons was brought to Marks's home, perhaps shortly before he joined their movement. There, she was provided with "a good bed, comfortable room, cheerful fire, and good nurses," a testament to the Markses' wealth and good grace. The woman was described as a "nervous and susceptible female" with pale skin and large, intense black eyes. Around her bed "were ranged the [Mormon] priests gifted with heal-

---

28. "The Prophet's Death," *DN*, 11. This article was originally published in the *Chicago Times* on November 20, 1875. It was reprinted with the same title in *Deseret News* on December 8, 1875. The *Deseret News* explains: "Half a century ago there lived in New York, in the vicinity of Palmyra, where Joseph Smith first became known to fame, a young man named B. W. Richmond, who afterward studied medicine and acquired the title of doctor. He formed Joseph's acquaintance there, and was familiar with the 2 circumstances attending his self-announcement as a prophet. In later years he saw him in Ohio, and observed his course with interest. Still later, he met him in Nauvoo, and was an accidental witness of the scenes incident to, and consequent upon, his tragic death at the hands of an Illinois mob. Ten years afterward, partly in compliance with a request of the prophet, made just prior to his assassination, he wrote a full account of the affair, intending to publish it in book form. Various causes combined to delay the publication, and in 1864, twenty years after the occurrence of the events which he had committed to writing, Dr. Richmond died, leaving the manuscript in the hands of his widow, Mrs. Lucinda Richmond, now residing in McGregor, Iowa, by whom it has been carefully treasured until the present time. Thus The Deseret News does not have all the sub-headings, and prefaces this article with, 'The following, from the Chicago Times, which is in the main correct as concerning the tragedy which is the burden of the article, will be perused with much interest by our readers, coming as it does from a disinterested source—'."

ing, some with hands on her bed, others clasping her hands in theirs, or reverently laying them on various parts of her person, and uttering earnest prayers." They did this three or four times a day while feeding her nourishing food. "Mr. Marks had a large, fine, red young rooster which THEY SLEW IN THE NAME OF THE LORD and the invalid was nourished most tenderly with the broth. Hope beamed into her soul, and, as her care and food became better, her faith increased and added to the earnest prayers of the faithful." In two weeks, the emaciated old lady regained her strength and walked for the first time in months. Richmond remarked, "My friend Marks and myself could never agree whether the benediction of the priests or the nursing and the flesh and broth of the slain chanticleer had most to do with the remarkable recovery of this most helpless case of neglect and debility."[29]

The Mormon priests earnestly believed they had worked a miracle, and when others were similarly healed, local women "began to fear that the Lord was among the Saints, and to escape the fearful penalties denounced against unbelievers, hastened to join them. . . . Among the persons who joined them in this region were many of good minds and well educated."[30] Richmond's account seems to ridicule both the earnest Mormon priests and the intimidated females who joined them, while at the same time wondering at the religion's appeal to the more informed and sophisticated residents such as William Marks.

When Parley P. Pratt came back through Freedom on his way to Kirtland, he was impressed by the branch that had been formed in just a few weeks. Heman T. Hyde went with Pratt back to Kirtland and participated in Zion's Camp. William Marks, father of a large family of sturdy children, remained in the area for the time being to become one of the most stalwart and reliable members in the New York branches. However, throughout the rest of his life, his personal quest for Joseph Smith's concept of Zion would lead him to physical and philosophical places he never could have imagined.

---

29. "The Prophet's Death," *DN*, 11.
30. "The Prophet's Death," *DN*, 11.

CHAPTER 1

Ordained to Preside Over Kirtland

William Marks was born on November 15, 1792, in Rutland, Rutland County, Vermont, nine months almost to the day after his parents were married on February 13. Cornwell Marks and his wife, Sarah Goodrich, hailed from Glastonbury, Hartford County, Connecticut, a shipbuilding town located on the Connecticut River. In 1785, Cornwell moved to Pawlet, Vermont, as a young man of sixteen. However, he must have maintained ties in Glastonbury, for he returned there to marry Sarah in the Eastbury Church.[1] He brought his bride back to Pawlet, where they raised a family of six children in this compact industrial town in the Taconic mountains.[2] Cornwell was known as a "kind hearted and exemplary man." Sarah "was a skillful nurse, and devoted much of her time to attendance on the sick."[3] A history of Pawlet mentions that she was baptized into the Mormon church by Joseph Smith Sr. when he visited and preached in town.[4] Perhaps this occurred in 1836, when Joseph Sr. went on a mission to the Eastern States with his brother John Smith. Cornwell and Sarah both remained in Pawlet and died there in 1857, at ages 88 and 87 respectively.

Their son William Marks married Rosannah Robinson on May 2, 1813, in Pawlet. The young family soon moved to Nunda (later Portage), Allegany County, New York, where they had nine children between the years of 1814 and 1832. Rosannah's sister Polly and her husband Prosper Adams had been early settlers of the town. Adams established the first tavern just south of the current "Deep Cut." Located where the Genesee Valley Canal was cut through the high land, it served as the main hub for business in the town. Around 1821, Adams sold the tavern to his brother-in-law William Marks, who managed the tavern for about fifteen

---

1. Henry Ernest Woods, ed., *The New England Historical and Genealogical Register*, 387.
2. His children and the year they were born: William, 1792; Prudence/Paulina, 1795; Elisha, 1797; Electa, 1800; Elizabeth, 1802; Ira, 1805.
3. Hiel Hollister, *Pawlet for One Hundred Years*, 213.
4. Hollister, 150. Sarah Marks is not found in Susan Easton Black's *Membership of the Church of Jesus Christ of Latter-day Saints, 1830–1848*; nor is it found in her *Early Members of the Reorganized Church of Jesus Christ of Latter Day Saints*.

years. Canal workers frequented the establishment, and meetings of various types were held on its premises.

On December 5, 1819, the Reverend Elihu Mason formed a Presbyterian church in Nunda. Six charter members included Richard W. Robinson and his wife Charlotte, who exhibited letters that they were members in good standing from their church in Pawlet, Vermont. These six admitted five additional members, including Richard's cousin Rosannah Robinson Marks.[5] Her husband, William Marks, was examined and received into the church on April 19, 1822.[6] From 1820 to 1832, all nine of the Marks children were christened at the Oakland Presbyterian church. One can surmise that the family participated regularly in this church, as the records demonstrate the practice of excommunicating members when they did not attend public worship and partake of the Lord's Supper.

Though the church had one hundred members by 1828, it had no church building proper. Meetings were held in the local school and even in members' barns. On Friday, May 9, 1834, and again on May 20, a general session of the church leadership was held at the Marks home for the purpose of considering an accusation of "the habitual intemperate use of ardent spirits" by their fellow church member, Daniel D. Wells. Both William and Rosannah testified that Wells had purchased "bitters" from them too often, and that they had seen him take too much drink.[7] It is the first record available where William Marks participated in the judgment of another for their religious behavior. He would find himself called to do this frequently in his future ecclesiastical roles.

William and Rosannah Marks joined the Latter Day Saints at some point in the six months between May 20 and November 3, 1834. The Oakland Presbyterian church kept particular records of when members were admitted and when they left the congregation. It was common that a member was taken off the rolls either by death or by requesting a letter of good standing to present to the next Presbyterian church they intended to affiliate with. In a few cases, members left to join other churches. The records betray the Presbyterians' opinion of these churches. When the parishioner switched their allegiance to Methodism, the records state simply: "joined the Methodists" or "went to the Methodists."[8] In several other

---

5. Richard's father, Richard Robinson, and Rosannah's father, Ephraim Robinson, were brothers.

6. "Records of the Oakland Presbyterian Church, 1819–1871," 1–7.

7. "Records," 93–94, 96–99.

8. "Records," n.p.

cases, the records report that members "absconded to Episcopalians," a sect more dissimilar in doctrine. A conversion to Mormonism was even more intolerable.

In the minutes of November 3, 1834, the Presbyterian deacons and elders expressed concern that some of their members had been baptized by the Mormons.[9] On November 21, the council, or "session," named the four members who had united with the Mormons: William and Rosannah Marks, Polly Adams, and Mehitabel Bennett.[10] Thereupon they held a "consideration" of the subject. They resolved that these individuals be called before the session to answer the following charges:

> The violation of their covenant obligations by joining the sect commonly called Mormons.
>
> The treating of the ordinance of baptism in this church as though it had no validity, & consequently with contempt.
>
> The promotion of division among the professed prophet ^of God^ in withdrawing from the church.
>
> The treating of the church as if it were not the church of Christ, & in fact rejecting it, by meeting with a sect which profess not to fellowship us as a church.
>
> Representations of this import, that ignorance & prejudice are the grand reason why the members of session & the other members of the church do not become Mormons.
>
> A belief in the following erroneous sentiments or delusions. 1. That some of the Mormons have the gift of unknown tongues. 2. That the Mormons have immediate revelations from God. 3. That some of the Mormons have the gift of healing, & of prophecy. 4. That some of the Mormons have the gift of the interpretation of tongues. 5. That the extraordinary gifts of the Holy Spirit are essential to the purity & perfection of the church. 6. That all wicked things among the Mormons are brought to light by immediate revelation from God.[11]

This written consideration illuminates how some of the early teachings of the Latter Day Saint church were perceived by other sects, and why join-

---

9. "Records," 104.

10. At their meeting on December 4, 1834, the session decided that since "Mehitabel Bennett is in a degree deranged," her trial could be postponed. Mehitabel died not long after.

11. "Records," 104–6.

ing the Mormons was viewed differently from joining—or even "absconding"—to other churches.

A trial was held on December 12, 1834, at which the accused did not appear. The moderator of the session testified that he had heard a Mormon preacher say "that the Mormon church is the only church built on the true foundation, & that all other churches are built on foundations of mere human wisdom." It was also reported that "Mormons do not fellowship other churches." Mr. and Mrs. Marks and Mrs. Adams had given similar representations and were heard to state "that they had united with the Mormons & been baptized by them."[12] These bold sentiments were unacceptable to the conservative Presbyterians. After Elder Caldwell and Deacon Totten unsuccessfully visited the three miscreants to admonish them to repent, the session met again on January 1, 1835, and suspended them from the sacraments of the Presbyterian church.[13] On April 18, the session performed the final rite of excommunication of Polly Adams and William and Rosannah Marks.[14]

What would induce this forty-three-year-old, staid, and settled Presbyterian merchant to join the rough-and-tumble, disparaged Mormons? Marks did not leave a written record, but his actions in the second half of his life show devotion to an innovative and aspirational religion. His search for a utopia—a latter day "Zion"— took him from his comfortable surroundings into a maelstrom of frontier life, unique religious doctrines, and charismatic leaders, all with their own versions of "the gathering" to Zion.

During Marks's break with the Presbyterian church, events were occurring two hundred miles down Lake Erie in Kirtland, Ohio, which would have important repercussions in his life and in the future of Mormonism. A call went forth on a momentous St. Valentine's Day, 1835, for all those who had participated in Zion's Camp to assemble in the Kirtland schoolhouse along with "as many more of the Brethren & Sisters as felt disposed to attend." A year earlier, the Camp's march to defend the Saints in Missouri had been unsuccessful, disbanding in late July 1834 during a cholera outbreak and in the face of an overwhelming force of Missouri militia men who prevented the Mormons' arrival into Jackson County.[15]

---

12. "Records," 108.
13. "Records," 110.
14. "Records," 117–18.
15. For information on the members of Zion's Camp, see Milton Vaughn Backman, Jr., Keith Perkins, and Susan Easton Black, *A Profile of Latter-day*

After a scripture and prayer, "the Bretheren [*sic*] who went to Zion, were requested to take their seats together in one part of the house by themselves." The Prophet Joseph Smith addressed them, assuring these faithful Saints that their trials and sufferings during the march to Missouri had not been in vain, but that "those who went to Zion, with a determination to lay down their lives, if necessary . . . should be ordained to the ministry and go forth to prune the vineyard for the last time." They would be endowed with power from on high to assist them in their ministry to prepare for the Second Coming, "which was nigh, even fifty six years, should wind up the scene."[16]

Smith, in his characteristic rousing manner, stirred the congregation to a great excitement for the coming evangelistic work. He called upon those of the Camp of Israel to rise to their feet, which they enthusiastically did. The rest of the assembly was asked if they would sanction the ordinations and endowments, and they all raised their right hands in affirmation. With that, the congregation sang one of the hymns made popular during the march:

> Hark! listen to the trumpeters!
> They sound for volunteers!
> On Zion's bright and flowery mount
> Behold their officers;
> Their garments white, their armor's bright
> With courage bold they stand,
> Enlisting soldiers for their King,
> To march to Zion's land.[17]

After a one-hour recess, the conference recommenced with a prayer by Joseph's brother Hyrum Smith. Joseph then called forward Oliver Cowdery, David Whitmer, and Martin Harris, who were known as the three witnesses to the Book of Mormon. At the book's publication, they testified in writing "unto all nations, kindreds, tongues, and people," that the Book of Mormon was of divine origin and that they had "beheld and

---

Saints of Kirtland, Ohio and Members of Zion's Camp, 1830–1839: Vital Statistics and Sources.

16. "Minutes, Discourse, and Blessings, 14–15 February 1835," 147–49, JSP.

17. Reuben McBride, "Reuben McBride reminiscence," 2, CHL. The hymn was a version of a Methodist piece which had appeared in hymnals since at least 1811. Stith Mead, ed., *A General Selection of the Newest and Most Admired Hymns and Spiritual Songs Now in Use*, #d40.

saw the plates" from which Joseph translated the work.[18] The growth of the new church across several states necessitated visits from trusted church authorities who could handle administrative issues and perform ecclesiastical ordinances. Therefore, prior to the conference, the three witnesses had been asked to prayerfully choose twelve men "as Apostles to go to all nations, kindred toungs [sic] and people."[19] After the First Presidency blessed the three witnesses by the laying on of hands, they chose Lyman Johnson, Brigham Young, Heber C. Kimball, Orson Hyde, David W. Patten, Luke Johnson, William E. McLellin, John F. Boynton, Orson Pratt, William Smith, Thomas B. Marsh, and Parley P. Pratt to serve in the newly established Quorum of the Twelve Apostles.[20]

Over the next two days, the three witnesses laid their hands upon each new apostle's head and individually set him apart for his ministry with remarkable words of instruction and blessing. For example, Brigham Young was told that he would "do wonders in the name of Jesus . . . cast out Devils, heal the sick, raise the dead, open the eyes of the blind." As he went forth "from land to land and from sea to sea," the heathen nations would "even call him God himself, if he did not rebuke them."[21]

Lyman Johnson was blessed with faith "like unto Enoch,"[22] while his brother Luke was told he would "bear testimony to the kings of the earth."[23] Angels would "waft" Heber C. Kimball "from place to place," and he would "come into the presence of God."[24] Orson Hyde was blessed to "have power to smite the earth with pestilence, to divide waters and lead through the Saints" and would "be like unto one of the three Nephites."[25] David W. Patten was to "have power over all diseases" and "be able to tear down priest-craft like a Lion."[26] William McLellin would be "a prince and a saviour to God's people," and John F. Boynton was blessed to "lead the

---

18. See "The Testimony of Three Witnesses" included with each edition of the Book of Mormon.
19. A revelation had been given in Fayette, New York, in June 1829 relative to the choosing of twelve apostles. See "Book of Commandments, 1833," 38, JSP.
20. "Minutes, Discourse, and Blessings, 14–15 February 1835," 149, JSP.
21. "Minutes, Discourse, and Blessings," 150, JSP.
22. "Minutes, Discourse, and Blessings," 149, JSP.
23. "Minutes, Discourse, and Blessings," 152, JSP.
24. "Minutes, Discourse, and Blessings," 150, JSP.
25. "Minutes, Discourse, and Blessings," 151, JSP.
26. "Minutes, Discourse, and Blessings," 152, JSP.

Elect triumphantly to the places of refuge."[27] William Smith was told that he would "be preserved and remain on the earth, until Christ shall come to take vengeance on the wicked."[28] Parley P. Pratt, Thomas B. Marsh, and Orson Pratt were not in Kirtland yet, and received their blessings later.

On February 27, 1835, Joseph Smith met in council with the Twelve to give them instructions. During this meeting, he clarified their role as follows:

> They are the twelve apostles who are called to a travelling high council to preside over all the churches of the saints among the gentiles where there is no presidency established. They are to travel and preach among the Gentiles until the Lord shall ~~shall~~ command them to go to the Jews. They are to hold the keys of this ministry— to unlock the door of the kingdom of heaven unto all nations and preach the Gospel unto every creature. This is the virtue power and authority of their Apostleship—Amen.[29]

At the time, there was a presiding, or "standing," High Council of Zion located in Missouri, and an additional high council located in Kirtland, each composed of twelve men.[30] The apostles, or traveling high council, were to have jurisdiction to regulate and set in order those areas of the church which were not presided over by an acting high council.[31] They had "no right to go into Zion or any of its stakes where there [was] a regular high council established, to regulate any matt[e]rs pertaining thereto."[32] Little did anyone know the importance this sentence would hold at the death of Joseph Smith regarding the question of who would succeed him as leader of the church.

On the evening of March 12, 1835, at the next meeting of the Twelve, Smith proposed a first mission for them in the Eastern States, holding

---

27. "Minutes, Discourse, and Blessings," 153, JSP.
28. "Minutes, Discourse, and Blessings," 154, JSP.
29. "Record of the Twelve, 14 February–28 August 1835," 4, JSP.
30. John Dinger, *The Nauvoo City and High Council Minutes*. Joseph Smith put together the first permanent council at his home in Kirtland, Ohio, on February 17, 1834. He called it "the high council of the church of Christ" (LDS D&C 102:1). The high council "of the seat of the First Presidency of the Church" was to be the primary governing body for the church, as well as the appellate court for other high councils that would be organized.
31. The traveling high council, composed of the Twelve Apostles, was initially subordinate to the High Council of Zion. This is evidenced by the presiding High Council of Zion at Far West voting on and filling vacancies in the Quorum of the Twelve in 1838.
32. "Record of the Twelve, 14 February–28 August 1835," 6, JSP.

conferences in the existing branches of the church and "regulateing [sic] all things necessary for their welfare." It was decided that the Twelve Apostles, as a traveling high council, would leave Kirtland on Monday, May 4, 1835, and visit several New York branches of the church.[33]

When the Twelve reached Freedom, New York, on May 22, 1835, they organized the "Freedom Conference," which included the New York branches of Freedom, Portage, Grove, Burns, Rushford, Geneseo, Avon, Java, Holland, Aurora, Greenwood, and Niagara. The presiding elder, Warren Cowdery, reported sixty-five members in good fellowship in the Freedom Branch. William Marks, a member of the Portage branch, was in attendance at this conference. Having been associated with the church for some months, he had already attained the office of priest, and seemed to be held in high regard, as he reported on behalf of three branches.[34] The branch in Portage, he said, followed most expectations to be in good fellowship but did not generally obey the Word of Wisdom.[35] The church in Grove was in the same condition as last reported, and the church in Burns consisted of thirty members in good standing.[36]

The Monday morning after the conference at Freedom concluded, a large company consisting of William Marks, Jonathan Hale, and eight of the Twelve traveled the twenty-one miles east to Portage and arrived that evening at the Marks home. The company stayed for two days before departing for the rest of their circuit.[37] No record of the events of these two days exists, but it was not insignificant that Marks was spending time with leaders of the new church who had associated with Joseph Smith. His ma-

---

33. "Record of the Twelve, 14 February–28 August 1835," 4, JSP.

34. At a conference held a month earlier, April 4, 1835, at Freedom, the Portage branch of twenty-six members—which had been "raised principally by brother Squires"—represented by William Marks, priest. W. A. Cowdery, "Freedom, April 3, 1835," *MA*, 101.

35. Apparently this was an issue with other branches as well. At a May 9, 1835, meeting organizing the Westfield (New York) Conference, the Laona branch was described as being "rather low in spirit in consequence of a neglect to keep the 'word of Wisdom,'" a code of health given as a February 27, 1833, revelation. The code restricted the use of tobacco, wine, "strong drinks," and "hot drinks," and recommended a diet of herbs, wheat, grains, and fruits while consuming meat sparingly. See "Record of the Twelve, 14 February–28 August 1835," 9, JSP; "Word of Wisdom," JSP.

36. "Record of the Twelve, 14 February–28 August 1835," 11, JSP.

37. "Jonathan H. Hale reminiscences and journals, 1837–1840," 6, CHL.

ture age, commodious property, reliable leadership, and social connections would propel him quickly to leadership positions in the fledgling church.

On March 3, 1836, at the age of forty-three, Marks became an elder, an ecclesiastical office authorizing Latter Day Saint men to preach the gospel. His certificate reads as follows:

> To whom it may concern.
>
> This certifies that William Marks has been received into the church of the Latter ~~day~~ day Saints, organized on the sixth of April, in the year of our Lord, one thousand eight hundred & thirty, & has been ordained an Elder according to the rules & regulations of said church, & is duly authorized to preach the gospel agreeably to the authority of that Officer. From the satisfactory evidence which we have of his good moral character, & his zeal for the cause of righteousness, & diligent desire to persuade men to forsake evil & embrace truth we confidently recommend him to all candid & upright people as a worthy member of society. We therefore, in the name & by the authority of this church, grant unto this, our worthy brother in the Lord, this letter of commendation as a proof of our fellowship & Esteem: praying for his success & prosperity in our Redeemer & Causes. Given by the direction of a conference of the Elders of said church assembled in Kirtland, Geauga County, Ohio, the third day of march, in the year of our lord, one thousand, eight hundred & thirty six.
>
> Joseph Smith Jr. Chairman.
H.G. Williams Clerk.
Kirtland, Ohio, June 1, 1836[38]

Marks's name also appeared in the *Latter Day Saints' Messenger and Advocate*, a Mormon newspaper, along with the 243 others who were elders of the "church of the Latter Day Saints."[39]

Previous to a second push to gather in Missouri, church members and leaders were encouraged to assemble in Kirtland, the site of their temple, commonly called the "House of the Lord." The edifice was dedicated by Joseph Smith on March 27, 1836, and the ceremony was repeated days later.[40] Here, they received temple "endowments" of spiritual power to enable them to perform successful missionary work. Warren Cowdery wrote an account that described a theophany and visitation from three Old

---

38. "Kirtland elders' certificates, 1836–1838," 127, CHL.

39. Thomas Burdick, "List Containing the Names of Ministers of the Gospel," *MA*, 336.

40. Church members in Kirtland increased from 150 on June 25, 1833, to 900 by late 1835, with 200 more living close by. "Journal, 1835–1836," Historical Introduction, JSP.

Testament prophets to his brother Oliver and Joseph Smith in the temple on April 3, an Easter Sunday that coincided with the Jewish Passover. During this vision, "Moses appeared before them and committed unto them the Keys of the gathering of Israel from the four parts of the Earth and the leading of the ten tribes from the Land of the North."[41]

This was an exciting but unsettling time in the history of the young church. Elders were preaching the gospel and making new converts, many of whom moved to Kirtland and the surrounding areas to join their fellow Saints. The displaced members frequently lacked adequate means to set up in their adopted city. An awkward accumulation of small hovels sprang up along the Chagrin River south of the temple. Church leaders struggled to pay debts incurred from the building of the temple, to purchase large contracts of land for immigrating members, and to support widespread missionary work. In a sermon on April 6, 1837, Smith mentioned "the embarrassments of a pecuniary nature that were now pressing upon the heads of the church."

> He [Smith] observed they began poor, were needy, destitute, and were truly afflicted by their enemies; yet the Lord commanded them to go forth and preach the gospel, to sacirfice [sic] their time, their talents, their good name and jeopardize their lives, and in addition to this, they were to build a house for the Lord, and prepare for the gathering of the saints.[42]

Other church members, watching the new population arrive, fervently engaged in land speculation and became precariously prosperous.[43]

Leaders scrambled to meet the demand for a system of exchange in such a situation. In 1836, the Ohio state legislature twice denied church leaders' requests for a bank charter. On January 2, plans for the bank were revised to form a joint stock company called the Kirtland Safety Society Anti-Banking Company.[44] Feeling that it had been "instituted by the will

---

41. "Journal, 1835–1836," 193, JSP.

42. "Discourse, 6 April 1837," 487, JSP.

43. "We were much grieved . . . on our arrival in Kirtland, to see the spirit of speculation that was prevailing in the Church. Trade and traffic seemed to engross the time and attention of the Saints. . . . Some men, who, when I left, could hardly get food to eat, I found on my arrival to be men of supposed great wealth; in fact everything in the place seemed to be moving in great prosperity, and all seemed to be engaged to become rich." Orson F. Whitney, *Life of Heber C. Kimball*, 111.

44. For a thorough overview of the Kirtland Safety Society, see Jeffrey N. Walker, "The Kirtland Safety Society and the Fraud of Grandison Newell: A

& revilations [sic] of God," many members of the community responded to Smith's invitation to fund the bank by purchasing stock in the company.[45] The Smith family was the largest investor, and Joseph issued and signed bank notes as treasurer. At first, it seemed that the company bolstered the financial health of Kirtland. However, its capital structure was fragile. As one historian has explained, "The Society would issue notes to land owners and receive in return a mortgage on the land. This mortgage then became an asset against which additional notes could be issued."[46] The situation prompted one of the church's enemies, Grandison Newell, to "drive about the country and buy up all the Mormon money possible, and next morning go to the bank and obtain the specie" in an effort to drain the bank capital.[47] In March 1837, Joseph Smith and Sidney Rigdon were charged with illegal banking. A trial was held in October 1837, and the two were found guilty of illegal banking under the 1816 Act (no longer in force in 1837) and were fined $1,000 each. They appealed the decision but were forced to flee Ohio before another trial could be held. Additionally, a national bank crisis known as the Panic of 1837 developed in May of that year. Overspeculation and the inability of banks to easily convert their assets into cash caused hundreds of banks to fail and added to the pressure placed upon the Society.[48] Smith and Rigdon ceased issuing bank notes, focusing on collecting loans that were due as April 1837 arrived. John Johnson, a wealthy Latter Day Saint investor, withdrew his considerable property from the Society, which dealt a considerable blow to the institution in May. Disaffection from the church became rampant throughout the community.

William Marks moved to Kirtland during a time of heated dissent. As Joseph Smith began to withdraw from many of his Kirtland enterprises, he surprisingly transferred his financial interests to the newcomer.

Legal Examination," 32–148.

45. "Articles of Agreement for the Kirtland Safety Society Anti-Banking Company, 2 January 1837," 443, JSP; "Minutes, 3 September 1837," 236, JSP.

46. Scott H. Partridge, "The Failure of the Kirtland Safety Society," 440.

47. Arthur B. Deming, "James Thompson's Statement," 3.

48. Church leaders made an effort to make the Society a branch or subsidiary of the already chartered Bank of Monroe, Michigan, by effecting a merger or acquisition, as permitted by Ohio law. The owners of the Bank of Monroe sold their controlling interest and Oliver Cowdery was appointed a director and vice president of the Monroe Bank. However, the Panic of 1837 caused its temporary closure. Cowdery resigned as director and returned to Kirtland. Walker, "The Kirtland Safety Society," 53, 54.

In April 1837, Joseph Smith named Marks proprietor of the Kirtland Printing Office, previously owned by Smith and Sidney Rigdon. The shop dealt in books, stationery, letter and wrapping paper, as well as printed cards, blanks, handbills, checks, notes, drafts, labels, books, and blank books; it also published the *Latter Day Saints' Messenger and Advocate* newspaper. Although Marks was the legal owner of the shop, Smith and Rigdon, "by power of attorney from said Marks," were to "act as his agents for the time being," and Warren Cowdery continued "in charge of the editorial department, to whom all communications, by mail relative to the business of the office, should be addressed."[49] In June, Warren wrote an editorial in which he blamed "the principal remote causes of distress in our community" on over-trading, the "deranged state of the money market abroad," and "inflated paper circulation at home." He further stated that these calamities were "common to our whole country."[50] The *Messenger and Advocate* was printed for five months under Marks's proprietorship. The month of August was its last printing, after which the paper gave way to a new publication, *The Elders' Journal*.

On April 10, 1837, Joseph Smith and his wife, Emma, conveyed the Kirtland Temple property to Marks for a consideration of $500. The grantor reserved "the Market house occupied by Whitmer, Rich & Co. which stands on the above described lot of land."[51] Joseph conveyed six additional tracts of land in Kirtland for $3,800, and Sidney Rigdon conveyed one tract of land for $1,500, all to Marks, and all on the same date.[52] Smith and Rigdon likely transferred ownership of the press, the temple, and other lands to separate the assets of the church from their personal property while undergoing legal proceedings.

It is not clear why Smith and other church leaders chose Marks to transfer their interests to. Marks had been a member of the church for

---

49. "Notice," *MA*, 496.
50. Warren Cowdery, "The Change of Times," *MA*, 522.
51. Geauga County Deed Records, book 23, p. 536.
52. Marks was active in buying and selling real estate in the Kirtland area during this time. Between the purchases from Smith and Rigdon, Marks also obtained lots no. 17, 18, 19, 29, 30, and 31 of block 99, as well as small parcels of other land. The purchases were significant as lot no. 30 was 144 acres. Geauga County Deed Records, book 23, pp. 535–39. Marks obtained other land as well—he also sold lot no. 15 of block 99 to Oliver Granger for $25 and lots 1, 2, 3, and 4, of block 111 for $2,000 to Oliver Granger. "William Marks deed, 1837 August 7," 1, CHL.

three years, an elder for barely a year, and had not completed traveling missionary service. He had just arrived in Kirtland and seemingly only had passing contact with Joseph Smith. However, he was loyal, and may have seemed more stable than many of the Kirtland Saints who were chafing under Smith's direction. He was a man of means and was competent in business and managing people. Marks was also able to fill this role, as he had not invested in the Safety Society. Thus, he avoided both the loss of his capital and any susceptibility to lawsuits.

Once Smith and Rigdon had transferred ownership of the *Messenger and Advocate*, the Kirtland Temple, and several tracts of land to Marks, they pulled out of the Kirtland Safety Society. Following the last ledger entries on June 2, 1837, Smith and Rigdon resigned.[53] Warren Parrish, a prominent church member, and Frederick G. Williams, a member of the First Presidency, became disaffected from the church and assumed control of the Society. For a short time, they continued to make loans by issuing more banknotes, resulting in Parrish being accused of forgery and embezzlement. There are many questions surrounding Joseph Smith's actions in regard to the Safety Society and the pending lawsuit. Some contemporaries were confused and angry that a banking enterprise conceived and operated by a person who professed to be a prophet of God would fail. They felt betrayed that Smith removed himself from responsibility for the venture.[54] In a conference talk on September 3, 1837, Smith countered

---

53. Joseph Smith's history records, "Some time previous to this [7 July] I resigned my office in the 'Kirtland Safety Society' disposed of my interest therein, and withdrew from the institution… almost all banks throughout the country one after the other have suspended specie payment and gold and silver have risen in value in direct ratio with the depreciation of paper currency." "History, 1838–1856, volume B-1 [1 September 1834–2 November 1838]," 764, JSP. On June 8, Smith and nine other stockholders transferred their holdings to Oliver Granger and Jared Carter. D Paul Sampson and Larry T. Wimmer, "The Kirtland Safety Society: The Stock Ledger Book and the Bank Failure," 428.

54. Warren Parrish claimed: "I have listened to him with feelings of no ordinary kind, when he declared that the audible voice of God, instructed him to establish a Banking-Anti Banking institution, which like Aaron's rod should swallow up all other Banks (the Bank of Monroe excepted,) and grow and flourish and spread from the rivers to the end of the earth, and survive when all others should be laid in ruins." Parrish, M. [*sic*, W.], "Kirtland, Feb. 5, 1838, To the Editor," *PR*, 3. Wilford Woodruff wrote: "I also he[a]rd President Joseph Smith Jr. declare in the presence of F. Williams, D. Whitmer, S. Smith, W. Parrish & others in the Deposit Office that he had receieved that morning the Word of the Lord

that he "had always said that unless the institution was conducted on righteous principles it would not stand."⁵⁵ Smith's supporters laid the blame at the feet of Williams and Parrish. One author even suggests the possibility that Smith withdrew to keep his followers from continuing to invest once disreputable agents took control of the Society.⁵⁶

Smith's financial predicament was not the only cause of disillusionment among his followers. By 1837, rumors were flying about Kirtland that Emma Smith had caught her husband in a compromising position with their young housemaid, Fanny Alger. Talk was so pervasive that it seems likely Marks would have heard the rumors. As a newcomer to Joseph Smith's complexities, he may not have believed them, whether they suggested adultery or polygamy. There is no evidence that the incident affected his relationship with the prophet or the church at this time. But this was not the case with all Kirtland residents.

On a Sunday in August 1837, when Joseph Smith was out of town, anger and frustration among thwarted investors and disheartened devotees boiled out of control. Warren Parrish, Apostle John F. Boynton, and a group of malcontents armed with pistols and bowie knives staged a takeover of the seat of Mormon power and worship—the Kirtland Temple. Unsuspecting of their plans, the venerable Joseph Smith Sr. rose from his place on the Melchizedek Priesthood pulpits on the west end of the temple to open Sabbath services. Parrish and company, occupying the Aaronic Priesthood pulpits on the east end of the room, loudly and rudely interrupted the speaker. The commotion was so disruptive that Smith Sr. called for the police in an effort to keep order. Eliza Snow reports that at this, the malcontents "rushed down from the stand into the congregation; J. Boynton saying he would blow out the brains of the first man who dared to lay hands on him." The crowd milled about in great agitation, and some even "tried to escape from the confusion by jumping out of

---

upon the subject of the Kirtland Safety Society. He was alone in a room by himself & he had not ownly the voice of the spirit upon the subject but even an audable voice. He did not tell us at ^that^ time what the LORD said upon the subject but remarked that if we would give heed to the Commandments the Lord had given this morning all would be well." "Wilford Woodruff Journal, 1833 December–1838 January.," January 5, 1837, CHL.

55. "History, 1838–1856, volume B-1 [1 September 1834–2 November 1838]," 771, JSP.

56. Walker, "The Kirtland Safety Society," 57.

the windows."⁵⁷ Since few contemporary journals or letters survive from this jarring period in Kirtland, only late reminiscences describe the awful scene, and we do not know if Marks was present during the brawl. But as the financial owner of the temple, he was closely involved in the incident and its aftermath.

This fraught, potentially deadly melee in the temple was only a scraping of an iceberg that included disaffected members of every quorum of the church. Parrish, Boynton, and Apostle Luke Johnson gathered thirty other leading citizens and formed a group they styled the "Old Standard, or the Church of Christ." The breakoff sect believed Smith was a fallen prophet and rejected the Book of Mormon and the concept of a restored priesthood. In the seven months leading up to June 1838, fifty leading members of the church were excommunicated, and an estimated two to three hundred Kirtland residents left Mormonism.⁵⁸

This apostasy was Marks's first experience with large-scale schism in the church. His faithfulness to the prophet at this challenging time advanced him into leadership, which he would staunchly maintain until the end of Smith's life.

At a conference held on September 3, 1837, in Kirtland, the church surveyed its losses. Seven men on the high council and traveling high council (apostles) were removed, including John Johnson and Martin Harris, who had left the church, and an eighth, John Smith, who had been called to another position. Marks was one of the men chosen to fill the vacated spots on the high council. Each member customarily drew a number to represent the position he would represent in council, and Marks drew number five.⁵⁹ Another high councilor chosen at the time was Oliver Granger, a former Methodist preacher from New York. The following week the council gathered in their assigned numerical arrangement.⁶⁰

---

57. Eliza R. Snow Smith, *Biography and Family Record of Lorenzo Snow, One of the Twelve Apostles of the Church of Jesus Christ of Latter-day Saints*, 21.

58. "John Smith letter, Kirtland, OH, Jan. 1, 1838," CHL.

59. "Oliver Granger, Henry G. Sherwood, William Marks, Mahew Hillman, Harlow Redfield, Asa[h]el Smith, Phineas Richards, & David Dort, were chosen to fill the place of those objected to, and the seats in the Council which were vacated by reason of Thomas Grover having moved to the west John Smith having been chosen one of the Presidents of the church." "Minute Book 1," 237, JSP.

60. "History, 1838–1856, volume B-1 [1 September 1834–2 November 1838]," 772, JSP.

The business transacted by this first high council attended by Marks included the withdrawal of the hand of fellowship from Uriah and Lydia Ann Hawkins "for unlawful matrimony, deceiving, and unchristianlike conduct."[61] This foreshadowed many such councils Marks would eventually preside over, dealing with a different sort of "unlawful matrimony." The following day, September 10, 1837, the Kirtland High Council met to discuss rules of the temple and excommunicate members of the Twelve. Marks, a Presbyterian excommunicate himself, was now on the other side of the table.

On September 17, an assembly of the Saints gathered at the Kirtland Temple. Newel K. Whitney, the bishop of the church in Kirtland, addressed the congregation and reminded them of a revelation given five years previous, in September 1832. Whitney felt that the time had arrived that he should travel to other branches as mentioned in the revelation, and he nominated Marks to officiate as "Agent to the Bishop" and transact the business of the bishop at Kirtland in Whitney's absence. Although Marks was a seasoned man at age 44, he was still new to church service and not readily distinguished from the other members of the high council. However, the nomination was unanimously approved. Sidney Rigdon made some remarks on the duties and responsibilities of the bishop, his agent, and counselors. He called upon them to "stand forth immediately" to dignify their office.

That evening a conference of elders was held in the temple. Duties of the different quorums relating to the gathering of Zion were laid out by Joseph Smith, who remarked that Kirtland was "at this time crowded to overflowing" and that "it was necessary that there be more Stakes of Zion appointed in order that the poor might have a place to gather to." It was "moved, seconded, and carried by vote of the whole" that Smith and Rigdon would select new stakes and places of gathering and give the elders certificates as to where they would be appointed, signed by the clerk of the church. This action demonstrates that early in the history of the church, gathering in smaller groups and in various places was seen as legitimate. There were 109 elders present at the conference who were "in a situation to travel."[62] These were counted out beginning on the south side of the room and moving to the north. Then they were divided by number into eight companies and assigned in turn to travel east, southeast, south, southwest, west, northwest, north, and northeast. If an elder desired to travel in a different direction, he could exchange his assignment with an-

---

61. "Kirtland, Sept. 9th, 1837," *MA*, 574.
62. "Minutes, 17 September 1837–B," 243, JSP.

other elder. The different divisions were charged to meet together to make further arrangements for their journeys.

Also at this meeting, Marks was called upon to officially accept the appointment made to him that morning. He rose and said "that he would comply with the request of the Church & the Lord being his helper he would discharge the duties thereof to the best of his abilities."[63] Because this appointment put him in charge of managing local affairs, Marks did not travel with the other elders.

For the next few months, high council meetings were held almost every Sunday and usually once or twice more during the week. They were often held at the Kirtland Temple or at Marks's home, and generally "at early candle lighting."[64] On Sunday, October 8, at 4:00 p.m. in the temple, the high council chose some new members to substitute for those of their company who would be absent in the coming winter.

On a Wednesday night, October 11, 1837, the council met at Marks's home for an evening of prayer and "instructive conversation some of which was animating and encourageing." It was enjoyed so much by the members that they agreed to meet again on Wednesday evenings of each week and invite the presidents of the different quorums of the church to meet with them.[65] Though they did meet on the following Wednesday, October 18, and then again on November 1, the prayer and conversation meetings did not appear to become consistent.

Since the high council had been organized in 1834 "for the purpose of settling important difficulties which might arise in the church, which could not be settled by the church, or the bishop," they sat in judgment of several different offenses, some mundane and some interesting. On October 30, a hearing was held at the Marks home concerning ten-year-old [James] Colin Brewster who claimed he saw the angel Moroni. This claim was taken seriously enough to be debated by the highest tribunal then existing in the church. John P. Green dramatically declared "that Moroni that appeared to Collin was the Devil in-deed." Many of the high councilors agreed. "Brother Marks thought it was a spirit that was not of God, and therefore could not be right."[66] Notwithstanding the high council's disapproval, the boy continued his claims and at least some towns-

---

63. "Minutes, 17 September 1837–B," 243, JSP.
64. "Minute Book 1," 250, JSP.
65. "Minute Book 1," 250, JSP.
66. "Kirtland High Council minutebook, Conference A, 1832–1837," October 30, 1837, CHL.

Kirtland home of William Marks, undated. Courtesy LDS Church History Library.

people were interested. On November 20, 1837, charges were preferred against Colin, his parents, and nine other people for "giving heed to revelations said to be translated from the book of Moroni by Collin Bruister [*sic*]."[67] Shockingly, it came out in the meeting that Moses Norris, one of the rank-and-file members of the church, had laid his hands upon Colin and ordained him to be a prophet. Some of the accused manifested a "hard spirit" against the president of the church and the high council and were determined to pursue their own course "whether right or wrong."[68] Others were repentant and acknowledged that they may have erred. John Smith, who was presiding over the meeting, told the accused that the council would withdraw fellowship from those who persisted in this disorder.

By January 1838, Marks was the owner of many lots of land in Kirtland, some of which he sold at a profit. For instance, he purchased lots 17, 18, and 19 in block 99 of Kirtland for $500, and later sold just lot 18 to John Smith for $500.[69] He owned a comfortable home and managed many of the financial affairs of the church in his position as agent

---

67. These were "Z.H. Bruister[,] Jane Bruister[,] Collen Bruister[,] T.H. Austin & wife[,] Moses R. Norris & wife[,] Eliza Norris[,] Samuel Barnet[,] Jonnana Butler[,] O. Duel Butler[,] Roxana Repshill." "Minute Book 1," 261, JSP.

68. "Minute Book 1," 262, JSP.

69. Richard Lyman Bushman, Ronald K. Esplin, Dean C. Jessee, eds., *The Joseph Smith Papers, Journals, Volume 1: 1832–1839*, 390–91; Geauga County Deed Records, book 23, pp. 535–39, and book 24, p. 189.

for the bishop. He served as a judge in Israel over his fellow Saints as a member of the Kirtland High Council. Most of his contemporaries were not so snug. The Twelve and many of the elders of the church were laboring "without purse or scrip" in the mission field. The scattered Saints in Missouri had been provided a segregated county of their own in which to settle and were beginning to gather in Caldwell County, in and around the town of Far West. Joseph Smith and Sidney Rigdon were facing lawsuits and civil action from aggrieved bank investors. On January 12, with the local sheriff planning to arrest him for banking fraud[70] and accusations of his improprieties with Fanny Alger becoming more strident, Smith told his family that he had received a revelation. "Thus saith the Lord Let the presidency of my Church take their families as soon as it is pra[c]ticable and a door is open for them and move on to the west as fast as the way is made plain before their faces and let their hearts be comforted for I will be with them," the revelation directed. "Verily I say unto you the time [has] . . . come that your laibours are finished in this place, for a season."[71]

In "the dead hour of night" and the cold of winter, Smith climbed into a box nailed on an ox sled and made his escape with Rigdon.[72] At a safe distance from Kirtland, they climbed on horses and rode fifty miles south to Norton, Ohio. Their families joined them there, and they started for Missouri on January 16. A few days later, Marks, John Smith, and Reynolds Cahoon were "elected and ordained to preside over Kirtland" as the presidency of the stake.[73] Due to the conditions and the efforts to elude pursuers, Joseph and Emma Smith and their children did not arrive in Far West until March 17, 1838.

While on the road, the prophet had a vision of Marks, the new stake president. In the vision, Marks was being closely pursued by "an innumerable concource of enimies [sic]." They seemed about to devour him when a chariot of fire intervened. "The Angel of the Lord put forth his hand unto Br. Marks & said unto him thou art my son come here." Immediately he was caught up in the chariot, and he rode away triumphantly out of the

---

70. Richard Lyman Bushman, *Joseph Smith: Rough Stone Rolling*, 340–41; Fawn McKay Brodie, *No Man Knows My History: The Life of Joseph Smith, the Mormon Prophet*, 207.

71. "Revelation, 12 January 1838–C," 1, JSP.

72. Lucy Mack Smith, *Biographical Sketches of Joseph Smith, the Prophet, and His Progenitors for Many Generations*, 216.

73. "Historical Department journal history of the Church, 1838," January 19, 1838, CHL.

midst of his enemies. The Lord said to Marks, "I will raise th[ee] up for a blessing unto many people." Smith wrote the vision in a letter to the presidency of the church in Kirtland on March 29, 1838, in order that they might know "that the hand of the Lord would be on his behalf."[74]

Hopefully Marks was comforted by this vision as he labored for the absent prophet's interests. Money was so scarce that on January 16, 1838, the Kirtland printing office was "taken and sold for Joseph's and Sidney's debts" to someone Phebe Woodruff identified as Nathaniel Milliken and John Smith described as "black legs." These dissenters from the church celebrated their acquisition by drinking so much that either by arson or simply through their carelessness, the building caught fire and was destroyed, along with all its contents.[75] Marks sold eight other Kirtland properties for the church. Furthermore, he and a few others "turned out their farms," mortgaging them to pay debts left by Smith and Rigdon. As stake president, Marks did his best to liquidate church assets and assist those who were now leaving to gather in the Mormon Zion in Missouri, arranging

---

74. "Letter to the Presidency in Kirtland, 29 March 1838," 25, JSP. The historical introduction to this letter in the Joseph Smith papers states: "About two weeks after JS's arrival in Far West, Missouri, he wrote the following letter to the presidency of the church in Kirtland, Ohio: William Marks, president, and John Smith and Reynolds Cahoon, assistant presidents. In the letter, JS recounted the difficulties of the journey from Kirtland in the middle of winter, his safe arrival in Far West, and information regarding Rigdon and his family, who had stopped traveling for several days because of illness. JS and his family had pushed on, arriving in Far West on 14 March. George W. Robinson, Rosannah Marks's younger brother and Rigdon's son-in-law, arrived two weeks later, on 28 March, with news that Rigdon would probably arrive soon.

Joseph Smith's letter to the Kirtland presidency also reported that the problems with William W. Phelps and John Whitmer, former members of the Zion presidency, had been recently 'a[d]justed' by apostles Thomas B. Marsh and David W. Patten in collaboration with the high council. JS conveyed expressions of friendship for those in Kirtland and relayed a vision he had seen of Marks, which JS interpreted as an indication that God would deliver Marks from his enemies. JS requested that the Saints migrating to Missouri bring seeds for vegetables, fruit trees, and hay and bring well-bred cattle and horses. With the letter, JS enclosed a copy of the 'Motto of the Church of Christ of Latterday Saints,' which he had composed for the church upon arriving in Far West."

75. "Printing Office, Kirtland Township, Ohio," JSP; "Letter, Vinalhaven, Maine, to Wilford Woodruff, Castline, Maine, March 1, 1838," CHL; "John Smith letter, Kirtland, OH, Jan. 15, 1838," CHL.

for them to purchase land that would be ready when they arrived. But the value of property was severely depressed in Kirtland, as expressed by Stephen Burnett in a letter to the former Apostle Lyman Johnson on April 15, 1838. "I was told Luke [Lyman's brother, also a former Apostle] offered his house And Lot for $100 Cash, and could not get that— . . . you state in your letter that you have lost six thousand dollars Kirtland paper."[76] William Cahoon and his father Reynolds left for Missouri in the spring of 1838. Cahoon wrote: "I left behind me a good lot all paid for, for which I labored very hard to get, also a good seven-room house well-furnished and owned by myself. . . . I could not dispose of it, so I turned the key and locked the door and left it, and from that day to this, I have not received anything for my property which is in the hands of strangers. However, we left it and went on our journey, pitching tents for a house."[77]

As Smith's agent, Marks had to do more than simply disposing of property; he also had to insert himself into the legal affairs of Smith, Rigdon, and the church. For example, in early 1837, Samuel Rounds initiated multiple lawsuits against the officers of the Kirtland Safety Society, including Smith. Using an Ohio statute, he won judgments against them, as they had acted as officers of an unauthorized bank. The fines against Smith and these men were paid by Marks as he acted as agent for the church.[78] Marks also had to act as agent in the case *Patterson and Patterson v. Cahoon, Carter & Co. and Rigdon, Smith & Cowdery*, in which Smith, Rigdon, and Cowdrey had not paid a debt. Certain land was seized and auctioned to satisfy the debt. Marks intervened, purchasing the seized lots and taking title of them.[79] Handling Smith's legal and business affairs in the wake of the Safety Society was no small task, and it highlighted Marks's leadership and business ability.

During these spring months of 1838, many loyal Saints who remained in Kirtland left for Missouri when they had the means to do so. But the poorest and those with various disabilities lingered behind. Church leaders struggled to know how to support these members. Hyrum Smith suggested bringing them to Missouri by steamboat. A few were able to do this, but others felt stranded. A non-member observer describing the Kirtland Saints' condition wrote:

---

76. "Letterbook 2," 65, CHL.

77. Stella Cahoon Shurtleff and Brent Farrington Cahoon, eds., *Reynolds Cahoon and His Stalwart Sons: Utah Pioneers*, 85.

78. "Assignment of Judgment, 1 March 1838 [Rounds qui tam v. JS]," 1, JSP.

79. "Docket Entry, Costs, circa 5 June 1837 [Patterson and Patterson v. Cahoon, Carter & Co. and Rigdon, Smith & Cowdery]," 54, JSP.

When their bank failed, all their imaginary wealth vanished; their money was gone; their teams were gone; their provisions were gone; their credit was gone; their store of goods disappeared. No community could be left in more destitute circumstances, and the only alternative was for them to leave—leave their temple, their homes, all that they had held dear, and go to, they knew not where. And how to go was a serious problem.[80]

The high council tried to come up with a plan, but despaired, turning the responsibility over to the Seventy. Zera Pulsipher and about four others of the Presidents of the Seventy were still meeting regularly in the temple. One Sunday during their deliberations they had a notion that if they put all their property together it might be sufficient to finance the eight-hundred-mile journey. "When we had made that calculation we felt a great flow of the spirit of God, not withstanding the great inconvenience we labored for want of means," they explained.[81] When others heard of this plan to pool resources, they asked to join the group, until over five hundred Saints had covenanted to go together in one company to Missouri. The Presidents of the Seventy realized that such a large undertaking could only be effected with divine help and the power of the priesthood. The men assembled Tuesdays through Saturdays from March 6 through March 20 to lay an administrative and behavioral framework for what came to be known as "Kirtland Camp."[82] As they prayed one day in the temple, Pulsipher saw a divine messenger "like an old man with white hair down to his shoulders." He spoke in approval of their plan to leave town, saying, "Be one and you shall have enough."[83]

Marks supported the undertaking to the best of his ability. On the day the company departed Kirtland, July 6, 1838, he accompanied the ungainly group of five hundred fifteen people, twenty-seven tents, fifty-nine wagons, ninety-seven horses, twenty-two oxen, sixty-nine cows, and one bull on the first leg of their journey—a distance of seven miles down the old Chillicothe road until they reached the town of Chester. There he blessed the leaders of the camp in the name of the Lord and left a blessing with the members in general, "covenanting to uphold them by the prayer of faith."[84]

---

80. Christopher B. Crary, *Pioneer and Personal Reminiscences*, 35.

81. "Zerah Pulsipher's History," 5, CHL.

82. Gordon Orville Hill, "A History of Kirtland Camp: Its Initial Purpose and Notable Accomplishments," 10–11.

83. "Zera Pulsipher's History," 6, CHL.

84. *Journal History of the Church*, July 6, 1838, CHL. It is likely that some people joined the group soon after departing Kirtland. An official account of

Kirtland Temple, ca. 1900. Courtesy of LDS Church History Library.

During the early summer of 1838, a scaled-back Elders' Quorum met in the Kirtland Temple, where on June 3 and June 10, Marks attempted to fill vacant administrative positions.[85] But on July 11, after the departure of the Kirtland Camp and the Presidents of the Seventy, he finally bowed to the inevitable and transferred ownership of the temple, or "House of the Lord," to Mead, Stafford & Company of Buffalo for goods purchased in 1836.[86]

Kirtland Camp written by Elias Smith mentions 529 persons in the camp. John Pulsipher put the count at 515 and added other details. "John Pulsipher Journal Vol. 1 (March 1835–October 1874)," 4.

85. Kirtland Elders Quorum Record 1836–1841, CCLA. "President [William] Marks Made some remarks that Elder [John] Mortons Abilities and understanding the business of the Quorum qualified him for this office In Preference to Any other one And had the spirit of prophecy to that effect that Elder Morton should hold the office of President of this Quorum." The office of Elder's Quorum President was soon to be vacated by Reuben Hedlock, who was moving to Missouri with Kirtland Camp.

86. "Deed, William and Rosannah Robinson Marks to Mead, Stafford & Co., 11 July 1837," 212, JSP. The temple property was to revert to Joseph Smith, Jr., Sidney Rigdon, Oliver Cowdery, Hyrum Smith, Reynolds Cahoon, and Jared Carter upon their repayment of several promissory notes in the amounts of $1377.00, $1464.54, and $1552.22.

CHAPTER 2

Missouri, the Land of My People

The same week the Kirtland Camp departed on its way to Missouri and William Marks relinquished ownership of the temple, Joseph Smith was writing a letter that would become part of the Mormon scriptural canon (LDS D&C 117). From Far West on July 8, 1838, Smith dictated a directive from the Lord that Marks and Ohio Bishop Newel K. Whitney should "settle up their business speedily" and journey to Missouri before winter. The missives Smith wrote in the name of the Lord often came with pointed warnings and rebuke, and this one was no exception. "If they tarry it shall not be well with them," the letter cautioned, while instructing the men to "repent of all their sins & of all their covetous desires before me."[1] Despite the fact that such language was characteristic of Smith's revelations, the words must have stung.

Marks had been directed to remain in Kirtland as stake president and had been asked to liquidate church assets in a difficult market. He had carefully followed these directions to minimize church deficit, even when it came at a personal cost. Now, Smith's letter charged that the properties of Kirtland "be turned out for debt," for "what is property unto me, Saith the Lord. . . . Let them go . . . & whatsoever remaineth let it remain in your hands."[2] To Marks's business-minded head, this might have seemed rash.

Whitney had been called as bishop in Kirtland and had been administering to the temporal needs of the Saints there. He was known for his personal service to the impoverished as exemplified by a "sumptuous feast" he held at his home for three days in 1836, at which he furnished refreshment from his own pocket for "the lame, the halt, the blind," and "all in the vicinity of Kirtland who would come."[3] Notwithstanding his service to the church in Kirtland, Smith's letter scolded Whitney for associating with "the Nicholatins & of all their secret abominations" and for "all his littleness of soul before me."[4] This term, drawn from Revelation

---

1. "Letter to William Marks and Newel K. Whitney, 8 July 1838," 1, JSP.
2. "Letter to William Marks and Newel K. Whitney," 1, JSP.
3. "History, 1834–1836," 171, JSP. Elizabeth Ann Whitney, "A Leaf from an Autobiography," *WE*, 83.
4. "Letter to William Marks and Newel K. Whitney," 1. The "Nicholatins" was a reference to a group mentioned in Revelation 2:6 and 2:15 whose deeds and doctrine the Lord said he hated.

2:6 and 2:15, likely referred to the many members who left the church in Kirtland. Heber C. Kimball later recalled: "those who apostatized sought every means and opportunity to draw others after them. They also entered into combinations to obtain wealth by fraud and every means that was evil."[5] Alternately, Smith's mention of Nicolaitans could have alluded to Freemasonry, an organization which was known as a "secret combination." Whitney had been a local Freemason since 1817 and was, by 1838, a Royal Arch Mason as well. If Smith had Masonry in mind when warning Kimball, the passage may be an early indication that Smith considered contemporary Freemasonry an apostate organization.[6]

Oliver Granger, a third man mentioned in the letter, had recently traveled from Kirtland to Far West, and was conscripted to carry the letter back to Ohio and deliver it to Marks and Whitney. The letter compliments Granger, saying that "his name shall be had in sacred remembrence [*sic*] from generation to generation for ever & ever" and gave him authority to "contend earnestly" to settle certain debts of the First Presidency.[7] Smith later stated, "As I was driven from Kirtland without the privilege of settling up my business, I had previous to this employed Colonel Oliver Granger as my agent, to close all my affairs in the east."[8] The flattering praise of Granger, when compared to Marks and Whitney, highlighted and commended his move to Far West. Granger was told to return as soon as possible, and the remaining Saints in Ohio were to make every effort to go to Missouri "this Summer."[9]

"Is there not room enough upon the mountains of Adam ondi awman & upon the plains of Obashinihah or Oleashinihah or in the Land of

---

5. Orson F. Whitney, *Life of Heber C. Kimball*, 101.

6. See Cheryl L. Bruno, Joe Steve Swick III, and Nicholas S. Literski, *Method Infinite: Freemasonry and the Mormon Restoration*, 13–14, 117–20.

7. "Letter to William Marks and Newel K. Whitney, 8 July 1838," 1, JSP; "Authorization for Oliver Granger, 13 May 1839," JSP; "History, vol. C-1 Addenda," 11–12, JSP; Letter of Introduction from Thomas Griffith and John Seymour, October 19, 1838, in "Letterbook 2," 40, JSP; Letter of Introduction from Horace Kingsbury, October 26, 1838, in "Letterbook 2," 40, JSP; and Letter of Introduction from John Howden, October 27 1838, in "Letterbook 2," 41, JSP.

8. "History, 1838–1856, volume B-1 [1 September 1834–2 November 1838]," 837, JSP.

9. "Letter to William Marks and Newel K. Whitney, 8 July 1838," 1, JSP. On May 4, 1839, at a conference in Quincy, Illinois, Oliver Granger was sent back to Kirtland again to preside over the general affairs of the church and to take charge of the temple. Granger died in Kirtland on August 25, 1841.

where Adam dwelt that you should not covet that which is but the drop & neglect the more weighty matters[?]" the letter asked rhetorically. Here Smith was using words from his efforts to restore the "pure language" spoken by Adam in the Garden of Eden, for Smith taught his followers that Jackson County, Missouri, was the location of the Garden of Eden. The time had come when all the Saints were to gather there. Having personally experienced the pushback of non-Mormon Missouri settlers to the waves of Mormon immigrants into the state, Smith called for reinforcements to cement their position. "Come up hither unto the Land of my people[,] even Zion," the revelation entreated.[10]

Those who were still in Kirtland were to do all they could to close out their business affairs in Ohio. "If they cannot sel[l] their property let them turn it out on the debts & when the Lord lift us all up they will rise with the rest," the letter counseled. Once they arrived in the idyllic spot, they need not fear. Smith promised "there are provisions or will be in great abundance of all kinds indeed there is a plenty now neither has there been a scarcity at any time since we come." However, those who had "turned out" all their property may have hesitated when they read "but let none think to get property whenever they get <come> here for there is none for them at present but there will be."[11]

Nothing was as important as joining with the Saints. Although Marks and Whitney were reprimanded, they were also promised that they would retain their church authority in the new location. Marks was to "preside in the midst of my people in the City Far West" and Whitney would "be a bishop unto my people" in the land of "Adam Ondi Awman."[12]

The Whitney and the Marks families both left Kirtland in the fall of 1838, though not in the same company.[13] After being apprised of the mobbing and persecution of the Saints in Far West, the Whitneys went on to St. Louis and waited there for further word. Marks, his wife Rosannah, and

---

10. "Letter to William Marks and Newel K. Whitney, 8 July 1838," 1, JSP.
11. "Letter to William Marks and Newel K. Whitney, 8 July 1838," 2, JSP.
12. "Journal, March–September 1838," 58, JSP. Earlier that year, David Whitmer, W. W. Phelps, and John Whitmer had been removed from church leadership in Missouri.
13. Elizabeth Ann Whitney, "Leaf from an Autobiography, Continued," *WE*, 91. A letter from William Perkins dates Marks's departure to before October 29, 1838. "Letter from William Perkins, 29 October 1838," 2, JSP. Marks's daughter Mary Eliza and her husband, John Skidmore, had already moved to Missouri, where their daughter Rosana was born in 1837.

eight of their children ages 6 to 24 traveled to Missouri with a group of about thirty families. Still more than one hundred miles east of Far West, they met Isaac Russell, a colorful British immigrant who had joined the church in Toronto, Canada. The Russells had recently arrived in Missouri from Kirtland, and it is likely that Marks was already acquainted with them. Smith had sent Russell down the Mississippi to assist the Saints coming into the state.[14] However, when he met the Marks company, Russell asserted the right to preside over them and told them he had been sent to stop them from going to Far West.[15] Though Marks outranked Russell in terms of church leadership, he seems to have acquiesced to this appropriation, perhaps conceding to Russell's greater knowledge of the landscape. On November 1, 1838, at a place close to Huntsville, Missouri, the group met a company consisting of brothers Chandler and Noah Rogers and their families. The two companies traveled together until November 6, when they stopped to camp for ten days. During this time, Marks took his team and went up to Far West with the intention of getting Russell's family and bringing them back. Chandler Rogers described the conditions of the camp while Marks was gone: "There came a severe snow storm and then a rain which melted the snow so the watter [sic] ran in the Tents and wet the beds so when they arose they had to dip the water from them." Despite the cold and drenched conditions, Russell forbade the camp members to leave the ground, telling them, "you are to suffer so much any way." When a few of the families opted to set off on their own, Russell "cursed them for it." On November 16, the group moved on in the midst of a snow storm. By the following day, they were within four miles of the town of Louisiana, Pike County, Missouri, where they camped for four days. "Russel[l] said they must not part nor leave the stait [sic] as it was the place of Zion."[16]

Russell felt called to lead a separatist group to minister to the "Lamanites," a people prominently mentioned in the Book of Mormon as progenitors of the modern Native Americans. Months previous, while leading a company of the Toronto Saints from Kirtland to Missouri, he had betrayed his interests when he stopped at Indianapolis. John Taylor (who a month later would join the Quorum of the Twelve) and his wife, Leonora, visited with them there. The Taylors observed Russell stirring his group into an emotional

---

14. "William Dawson statement, 1888 December 22," CHL. William Dawson claimed that Joseph Smith had sent Russell "back to the Mississippi river to meet and hurry up a company of emigrants before the mobs closed in upon them."

15. "Chandler Rogers statement, 1845 September," 1, CHL.

16. "Chandler Rogers statement, 1845 September," 1–2, CHL.

frenzy: "they began leaping up at the campfire, shouting, dancing, speaking in tongues, screaming in ecstasy." The Taylors heard Russell claim he had been chosen of the Lord to lead the Mormons to Missouri, where they would join with the Lamanites for mutual redemption.[17] Perhaps Russell now wished to add the Marks company to his adherents.

Seeking a location for the exhausted group to locate, Russell "went ten miles above Louisiana [Missouri] on the Missi[ssip]pi River." There, he "found a place on the Spanish Claims," a portion of Missouri that had been granted to settlers by the Spanish government. "This," said he, "is the plais [place] God has shown me and you must go there."[18] Only twelve of the families went with Russell to his chosen spot, including the families of Marks, Chandler and Noah Rogers, Silas Smith, John Sweet, Hugh Snively, Joseph Carlton, and Joel Harvey.[19] There, they built log shanties to shelter them throughout the frigid, snowy Missouri winter. In these penurious circumstances, six-year-old John Aikens Smith, the son of Silas and Mary Smith (and Joseph Smith's first cousin), died.[20] Perhaps to keep more families from leaving, Russell taught the group that he was the chosen of the Lord and that Joseph was a fallen prophet and instructed them to sell their teams and wagons, "for he said when you leave here you will have to go on foot and take nothing with you." One wonders how that claim resounded with the bereaved Smiths.[21]

Less than two months later, Russell would begin a secret correspondence with a branch of the church in England that he had raised up while serving a mission there in 1837. He wrote his friends and converts that

---

17. Samuel W. Taylor, *The Kingdom or Nothing: The Life of John Taylor, Militant Mormon*, 37.

18. "Chandler Rogers statement, 1845 September," 2, CHL.

19. "Mormontown: The History of a Little Understood Settlement in Pike County, Illinois," 6, CHL.

20. The Silas Smith family had been traveling with the Chandler and Noah Rogers brothers when they met up with the Marks company. "Jesse N. Smith autobiography and journal, 1855 October–1906 June," CHL.

21. "Chandler Rogers statement, 1845 September," 2, CHL. George W. Russell, Isaac's son, wrote a letter to A. M. Musser on November 7, 1879, saying "at the time Boggs Army came to Far West, my father was down at DeWitt in Carroll County, having been sent by Joseph the Prophet to assist some emigrants, who had been stopped by the mob, and some of whom were shot down in his presence." "George W. Russell letter to A. M. Musser," CHL.

the day of the Lamanites had come and they were now to be "visited with the Gospel."[22]

"The Lord has directed me with a few others," Russell wrote, "to go into the wilderness where we shall be fed & directed by the hand of the Lord until we are purified & prepared to minister to the Lamanites." He claimed he had been sent before to "prepare a Zion" and implied that in the due time of the Lord he would send for the faithful among them and they would join him in the "place of Refuge." Russell directed them to make a covenant not to reveal this to the world or to the rest of the church and that if they should hear "that I am apostatized, believe it not, for I am doing the work of the Lord."[23]

Russell was an example of the appeal that unique Mormon doctrines held for those who had a tendency to extremism. In this case, Russell seized upon the doctrine of gathering and tweaked it for his own purposes. Other Latter-day Saints were drawn in to his enthusiasm and in many cases did not realize the difference between Russell's and the authorized version until much later. The Marks family may have been deluded for a time as well.

Marks reached Far West immediately following the apogee of the Mormon Missouri War. In the face of harsh invective on both sides, as well as numerous armed and sometimes fatal skirmishes, Governor Lilburn Boggs of Missouri penned Missouri Executive Order 44. Known as the "Mormon Extermination Order," it was issued on October 27, 1838, and ordered all Mormons to leave Missouri or be "exterminated or driven from the state." On November 1, Major General Samuel D. Lucas, commander of the state militia, used the executive order to gather 2,500 troops to Far West. He set the terms for a surrender, then arrested and conveyed Joseph and Hyrum Smith, Sidney Rigdon, Missouri Bishop Edward Partridge, and other Mormon leaders thirty miles away to Richmond to await trial. After the trial, they were convicted and brought in a large heavy wagon to jail in Liberty, Jackson County, Missouri.

Hundreds of Latter Day Saints left the area immediately. Their best options to find housing and employment nearby were the urban centers of St. Louis, Missouri, and Quincy, Illinois. Those who did not have the means to leave spent a miserable winter in Far West, where fugitives fled from other Mormon settlements and mobs continued to raid their supplies.

---

22. "Willard Richards, Letter, Alston, England, to Joseph Fielding and William Clayton, Manchester, England," 2, CHL.

23. "Willard Richards, Letter," 2, CHL.

The church's First Presidency, Joseph and Hyrum Smith and Sidney Rigdon—as well as Parley P. Pratt of the Quorum of the Twelve and other leaders—remained in Liberty Jail throughout December. The church desperately needed leadership, and the Missouri High Council stepped in to fill the void. The high council met on December 13, 1838, and filled vacancies in its ranks. Brigham Young led a resolution to assist poor and destitute Saints without means to travel to leave the state of Missouri.[24] A committee was appointed to gather and distribute the Saints' available means and property to assist in this effort.

During the confusion, Marks met with leaders of the church, then returned to find his family and the rest of the company. He arrived back from his trek to Far West just before Christmas in 1838. Marks did not bring the Russell family back to Pike County with him. Instead, he informed Russell that the authorities of the church had sent for him. Russell started off to Far West before the first of the year, and Marks took charge of the camp.[25]

During the winter on the Spanish Claims in Pike County, Bishop Edward Partridge and George Robinson came to visit the Marks group. Partridge had been in jail about three or four weeks in Liberty with Joseph Smith. After he was released, he took his family to Pittsfield, Illinois, and then to Quincy. Those who remained at the camp with Marks and his family soon followed, moving to Illinois in late February, 1839.[26] Marks himself may have traveled ahead of the rest of the company, because he was in Quincy by the first of the month.

Silas Smith's son Jesse Nathaniel Smith wrote that the group left their log-cabin camp on February 21, 1839, crossed the Mississippi River into Illinois the following day, and reached Pittsfield, the county seat of Pike

---

24. "Far West Committee minutes," CHL.

25. Joseph Smith had received a revelation that the Twelve Apostles would depart from the Far West temple site on April 26, 1839, for a mission to England. When Smith was imprisoned and the Saints had to leave the state, Russell thought the revelation would not be fulfilled. However, Brigham Young and other apostles returned to the Far West temple site under cover of night to fulfill the revelation on the appointed day. While on the temple grounds, church authorities excommunicated Isaac Russell, his wife, and thirty others of his party from Canada. This group stayed in Far West when the others left. "Far West, Missouri, 1839 April 26," 1, CHL.

26. "Chandler Rogers statement, 1845 September," 2, CHL; "Affidavit, 1839 May 15," 2, CHL.

County, Illinois,[27] on February 23. A resident named Thomas Edwards, who lived a few miles east of town, made them "some advantageous offers to settle upon and occupy his land, [and] they all concluded to do so."[28] Joined by several other Mormon refugees, they built cabins on both sides of the road and dug wells. Edwards joined the church, and the settlement became a branch, with Silas Smith as branch president.[29] A school and church building were constructed, evidence of the Mormons' industriousness. Nearby residents christened the place "Mormontown."[30] Marks and his family landed in Pittsfield proper, where the youthful Abraham Lincoln started a law practice the same year.[31] There they lived during most of 1839.

On February 1, 1839, Marks was chosen to preside over a meeting held in Quincy to consider a new location for settlement. A land agent, Isaac Galland, had made an offer to the Latter Day Saints to sell them twenty thousand acres of land lying between the Mississippi and Des Moines rivers near Montrose, Iowa, for two dollars an acre. A committee including David W. Rogers had examined the land and found it well suited as a gathering place for the Saints. Marks "was altogether in favor of making the purchase," but he hesitated to see gathering as the will of the Lord, since the Saints had continually been driven from places where they

---

27. It is somewhat confusing that the two states of Missouri and Illinois both had counties named Pike. Pike County, Missouri, was established in 1818 and covered the entire northeast border of Missouri. Pike County, Illinois, was established in 1821 and included the then-small village of Chicago.

28. "Jesse N. Smith autobiography and journal, 1855 October–1906 June," 7, CHL.

29. In October 1842 a conference was held here, at which Brigham Young and Heber C. Kimball preached. The branch grew to over three hundred members before it disbanded in 1845.

30. Members of the church referred to this settlement as "Pittsfield" or "Pike Town," but surrounding residents called it "Mormontown." It was located fifty miles southeast of Quincy, Illinois, where many of the Saints relocated after being ejected from Missouri. It grew to comprise about three hundred inhabitants at its peak, but disbanded with the Mormon migration by 1845.

31. See Heber C. Kimball, "Epistle," *TS*, 860. In this letter, Kimball tells of visiting Pittsfield, "where President Marks resided," and the next day going "about four miles to another town where your Uncle Silas Smith resided." He "arrived a few days after his death," on September 13, 1839, which helps to date the location of the Marks family to late 1839.

Isaac Galland. Courtesy of LDS Church History Library.

tried to congregate. Marks asked the brethren to "speak their minds; the Lord would undoubtedly manifest His will by His Spirit."[32]

Each participant then voiced their thoughts on purchasing the land and proceeding with a gathering protocol. Israel Barlow answered Marks's concerns by opining that perhaps the Saints had been scattered because they had not built "according to the pattern." If they were to do it correctly, gathering might be perfectly appropriate. He was in favor. Wandle Mace then spoke eagerly "in favor of an immediate gathering." Partridge, on the other hand, felt that it would be more acceptable to God to let the people scatter into different places, and provide for them wherever they might be; that "it was not expedient under the present circumstances to collect together." Partridge's skepticism dampened enthusiasm for gathering. Those who spoke later, such as Judge Elias Higbee, who had been in favor at first, gave up the proposition. The committee agreed that it was not advisable to purchase the lands at that time.[33]

---

32. "Far West Committee minutes," February 1839, CHL.

33. "Far West Committee minutes," February 1839, CHL; Wandle Mace, "Journal of Wandle Mace." The RLDS *History of the Church* misconstrues Marks's position on the issue of purchasing the Galland lands, seemingly mistaking Marks for Partridge: "After the church was driven from Missouri, Elder Marks, with others, believed it unwise to again settle in a body, and advocated the propriety of scattering abroad and building up homes individually, where each one should

Leaders of the church continued to ponder the prudence of gathering for the traumatized bodies of Saints, who were then spread from the Eastern States to Missouri, and in branches on many continents. Albert Rockwood wrote plaintively: "It is thought by some we shall not gather again in large bodies at present, still we do not know[.] [O]ur leader is gone, we have none to tell us what to do by direct Revelation."[34] But revelation was soon to come. Joseph Smith wrote letters to the Saints in Quincy on March 20 and 22, 1839, which addressed the issue.[35] Mary Fielding Smith called them "Epistols to the Church," and read them several times. "They seem like food for the hungrey [sic] we have taken great pleasure on perusing them."[36]

Smith noted in his letter of March 20 that he could not counsel the Saints as he could if he were present with them, and he left church leaders to decide for themselves whether they would accept Galland's offer.[37] In his second epistle, however, Smith made it clear that "the church would do will well to secure to themselves the contract of the Land which is proposed to them by Mr. Isaac Galland and to cultivate the friendly feelings of that gentleman." It had been deeply impressed upon Smith's mind, he said, "that the saints ought to lay hold of ev[e]ry door shall that shall seem to be opened for unto them to obtain foot hold on the Earth."[38]

Smith suggested that those who understood the spirit of gathering should "fall into the places of refuge and saf[e]ty that God should open unto them betwean [sic] Kirtland and Far West," and he told those from the East and West and from other countries to "fall in some where betwean [sic] those two bound[a]ries in the most safe and quiet places they can find." This was his counsel "until God shall open a more effectual door

---

choose." Heman C. Smith and F. Henry Edwards, *History of the Reorganized Church of Jesus Christ of Latter Day Saints*, 3:721.

34. Dean C. Jessee and David J. Whittaker, "The Last Months of Mormonism in Missouri: The Albert Perry Rockwood Journal," 34.

35. The second letter is undated, and could have been written between March 21 and April 6, 1839. Editors at the Joseph Smith Papers project find it most likely that Smith wrote the letter on March 22, the same day he composed a letter to land speculator Isaac Galland, and sent it with a package of letters that Alanson Ripley picked up from the jail on that date.

36. "Mary Fielding Smith letters to Hyrum Smith, 1839, 1842," April 11, 1839, 3, CHL.

37. "Letter to the Church and Edward Partridge, 20 March 1839," 10, JSP.

38. "Letter to Edward Partridge and the Church, circa 22 March 1839," 1, JSP.

for us."³⁹ Smith also cautioned the Saints not to organize "upon common stock principals in property or of large companies of firms untill the Lord shall signify it in a proper manner."⁴⁰

Smith's words recommended scattering such as Partridge had described, but only temporarily. The Mormon prophet was counseling his people to lay low for the time being. The key words in the revelation, "our brethren scattered abroad who understand the spirit of the gathering," made it clear that although they should hunker down in safe and quiet places, gathering should remain their future goal.⁴¹ While in Kirtland, Marks had been reprimanded for tarrying too long and "neglect[ing] the more weighty matters" of gathering.⁴² This was a message he was not likely to miss a second time.

Tellingly, the same day he counseled the Saints not to gather yet, Smith dictated a letter to Galland asking him to hold the land in reserve and stating his intention to purchase it upon his release from prison.⁴³

---

39. "Letter to Edward Partridge and the Church, circa 22 March 1839," 4–5, JSP.
40. "Letter to Edward Partridge and the Church, circa 22 March 1839," 5, JSP.
41. "Letter to Edward Partridge and the Church, circa 22 March 1839," 4, JSP.
42. "Letter to William Marks and Newel K. Whitney, 8 July 1838," 1, JSP.
43. "Letter to Isaac Galland, 22 March 1839," 56, JSP.

CHAPTER 3

Commerce: Suited for the Saints

On the auspicious date of April 6, 1839,[1] Joseph Smith and his fellow prisoners were transferred from Liberty to Gallatin, Missouri, to be investigated by a grand jury on the charges of murder, treason, burglary, arson, theft, and larceny. The venue chosen for the investigation was in Boone County, Missouri. The prisoners, escorted by the sheriff and four guards, were transported by horseback and escaped en route. Joseph and Hyrum Smith and the rest of the fugitives—Lyman Wight, Alexander McRae, and Caleb Baldwin—arrived in Quincy, Illinois, on April 22.

Joseph Smith wasted no time before contacting land agent Isaac Galland. Smith spent a few nights with his wife and children, who had been taken in by Judge Cleveland after relocating to Quincy from Far West. Then Smith and a selection committee traveled to Commerce on April 25 to survey the area for several days. On April 30, 1839, Galland sold three parcels of land including a house, ferry rights, and hotel privileges to the church for the sum of $18,000.[2] Acting for the church, Oliver Granger and Vinson Knight also purchased from Galland seven parcels of land across the river in Iowa, consisting of about 18,000 acres, for close to $50,000.[3] By mid-August, church leaders acquired two substantial pieces of additional land on credit from Horace Hotchkiss.[4] While the Saints

---

1. April 6 was enshrined among the early Saints as the day the church was formally organized in 1830. Later, tradition held that April 6 was the true date of the Savior's birth.

2. Lyndon Cook, "Isaac Galland—Mormon Benefactor," 270–74. See this article for many details of this purchase. One of these parcels included 47.17 acres that Galland had purchased from Alexander White's estate on May 2, 1837, for $2,000. Cook cites the Hancock County Deed Book G, pp. 247 and 388. The land was deeded to George W. Robinson on behalf of the church. Robinson was to deed the land back to the church when it had been paid for. See also "Alanson Ripley Statements, circa 1845 January," CHL. Ripley's statement gives another account of the purchase, which was followed in *History of the Church* 3:342, 378, but the purchase prices given are contradicted by the Hancock County and Lee County deed books.

3. Cook, "Isaac Galland," 271–74.

4. "Hotchkiss Purchase, Commerce, Illinois," JSP; "William White Purchase, Commerce, Illinois," JSP; Alanson Ripley, "Keokuk, Lee County, Iowa Territory," *TS*, 24.

were cash poor, they intended to pay these debts by transferring abandoned plots in Missouri and lands from recently arrived converts from Pennsylvania and New Jersey.[5]

Shortly after Smith's purchase, on May 4, 5, and 6, 1839, Marks was present at a general conference of the church held at an old Presbyterian camp-meeting ground near Quincy, Illinois.[6] It was the first conference since Smith had returned from jail, and much business of consequence was accomplished. Accompanied by Smith, Sidney Rigdon was appointed to go to Congress in Washington DC and present petitions of redress that the displaced Mormons had collected against the state of Missouri. Kirtland was to serve as a stake of Zion for the Saints who remained in the Eastern States.[7] Then, with an eye to the future, members of the church at general conference sanctioned the purchase of land in Commerce and across the river in Iowa. Smith had not given up his plans for Jackson County as a "new Jerusalem" that would play a major role in ushering in the second coming of Christ. But until conditions were more amenable, the Saints would gather elsewhere. The Commerce purchase was an ideal place to plant a new "cornerstone of Zion." Located on a bend of the Mississippi River and beside an established portage trail, it had potential for commercial success.

At the May conference, it was resolved "that Elder Marks be hereby appointed to preside over the Church at Commerce, Illinois."[8] Marks's appointment demonstrates Smith's intention to transfer the Mormon utopia to this new gathering place without delay. Marks was to go immediately to Commerce, along with Bishop Newel K. Whitney, who was, from that base of operations, to act in unison with the other bishops of the church. Provisions were made for the families of Marks, Whitney, and Oliver Granger to be kept among the Saints at Quincy until arrangements could be made for their relocation.[9] Smith and his family, for their part, moved

---

5. Cook, "Isaac Galland," 277–80; "Erastus Snow Journal, 1838 January–1841 June," March 29, 1841, 105, CHL; "Authorization for Hyrum Smith and Isaac Galland, 15 February 1841-B," 1, JSP; "History, 1838–1856, volume C-1 [2 November 1838–31 July 1842]," 1222, JSP.

6. "Wilford Woodruff Journal, 1838 January–1839 December," April 27–May 4, 1839, CHL.

7. "History, 1838–1856, volume C-1 [2 November 1838–31 July 1842]," 934, JSP.

8. "History, 1838–1856, volume C-1 [2 November 1838–31 July 1842]," 935, JSP.

9. See Heber C. Kimball, "Epistle," *TS*, 860.

First house in Commerce (James White), from early 1900s Nauvoo postcard collection. Courtesy of LDS Church History Library.

into one of the few houses in Commerce on Friday, May 10, 1839.[10] Others were slower to make this move—Marks and his family were still residing in Pittsfield in mid-September, and it is not certain that they ever stayed in Quincy before relocating to Nauvoo.

Though ordered to move to and preside over Commerce, Marks continued to deal with the liquidation of property in Kirtland. However, it seems that Smith wanted Marks to focus on Commerce and Oliver Granger to focus on Kirtland. In that same conference, it was resolved that "Elder Grainger be appointed to go to Kirtland and take the charge and oversight of the House of the Lord, and preside over the general affairs of the Church in that place." Days later, Marks executed a power of attorney to Granger dealing with certain properties in Kirtland.[11]

Construction of homes and businesses in Commerce began without delay. The city's rudimentary orientation square to the shore was realigned east-to-west and modeled upon Joseph Smith's 1833 "plat of Zion" city plan.[12]

As the city developed, it followed "a simple gridiron" pattern with "150 squares of about four acres, each divided into four equal lots."[13] By October

---

10. "Journal, 1839," 1, JSP.
11. "History, 1838–1856, volume C-1 [2 November 1838–31 July 1842]," 934, JSP; "Williams Marks power of attorney, 1839 May 7," CHL.
12. "Plat of the City of Zion, circa Early June–25 June 1833," JSP.
13. Robert B. Flanders, *Nauvoo: Kingdom on the Mississippi*, 42.

5, 1839, enough members of the church had moved to the new city to hold general conference there. Smith spoke about "the situation of the Church, the difficulties they had had to contend with, and the manner in which they had been led to this place." He stated his opinion that the area in which they were now situated was "a good place and suited for the saints." Smith then asked the brethren to state "whether they wished to appoint this a stake or not."[14] Establishing such a large ecclesiastical unit as a stake in this spot was significant. It indicated that the church was committed to a more permanent presence in Illinois. However, it also meant abandoning their hopes for a Zion in Missouri, at least for the present.

The voice of the people was unanimous—not only that a stake should be built, but that Commerce and its surrounding communities should be appointed a place of gathering for the Saints. Three wards and their leaders were delineated on the Illinois side of the river. Whitney was to be bishop over "Middle Ward," Edward Partridge was appointed bishop over "Upper Ward," and Vinson Knight was assigned as bishop over "Lower Ward." Marks was to lead these wards as their stake president,[15] and a high council consisting of twelve men was to be organized under his leadership. Another branch of the church was established on the Iowa side of the river. Joseph Smith's uncle, John Smith, was called as branch president, with Alanson Ripley as bishop, and twelve men to form an Iowa High Council. During the weekend of the conference, Joseph Smith and officers under his direction performed baptisms and confirmations, ordained elders, raised funds, and gave instructions for preaching the gospel abroad. Mormon leaders set the stage for a massive influx of Mormons and a building effort such as never had been seen in the Midwest United States.

During a season of sickness and misery caused by standing water in the lowlands, the Saints labored to clear and drain the swampy land. By September 1839, Joseph Smith was calling the new Mormon gathering place "Nauvoo," which, he taught his followers, was the Hebrew term for "fair," "beautiful," or "delightful plantation."[16] An observer described the area as "a situation of surpassing beauty." It was composed of "rolling and fertile prairies" with "natural parks and fields of flowers which the hand

---

14. "Minutes and Discourses, 5–7 October 1839," 30, JSP.

15. Counselors in the Nauvoo Stake presidency were first appointed on March 30, 1841. "Minutes, 1840 March 8–1842 May 20," 26–27, CHL.

16. J"Letter to Isaac Galland, Sept. 11, 1839," JSP. The name of the city was not officially changed until April 1840, when the Commerce post office was renamed Nauvoo. "Letterbook 2," 135, JSP; Alanson Ripley, "Nauvoo," *TS*, 122–23.

of the Creator seems to have originally planted there for the inspection of his own eye." The cabins of the Saints began to dot the countryside "in the most enchanting perspective, either on the borders of the timbers, or beside the springs and streams of living water, which are interspersed on every hand."[17] Marks chose a plot near the Mississippi River on the corner of Water and Granger streets, across from what would become Smith's Red Brick Store.[18] Here he would eventually build a sturdy, spacious brick home, but in March 1841, Marks was still living in a makeshift cabin with his wife, Rosannah, and his four youngest children.[19]

For the first two years, Nauvoo lacked a civil government with elected officials. Instead, a church body—the high council, with Marks at its head—took on this role after being sustained at the October 1839 general conference. Marks, as stake president and head of the high council, thus became instrumental in the initial development and management of the city.[20]

The high council met for the first time after its initial formation on October 20, 1839, at Dimick Huntington's shop, and they made plans to meet there at sundown each Sabbath evening. It was at this first meeting that the civil affairs of Nauvoo were discussed, along with matters of an ecclesiastical nature.[21] Because the city lacked its own criminal code or a manner to punish lawlessness locally, the high council used its ability to determine the members' church standing to influence behavior.[22] The council's first order of business was to consider an "imprudence of conduct" on the part of Harlow Redfield, a former member of the high

---

17. John A. Clark, *Gleanings By the Way*, 221–22.

18. Marks bought this lot (lot 4, block 149) on November 5, 1841. "Deed to William Marks, 5 November 1841," 116, JSP.

19. The 1840 census of Hancock County was taken by Thomas H. Owen in March 1841. Three other sons were living elsewhere in Nauvoo, and two married daughters remained in Missouri. The Henry McHenry family and the John Skidmore family are both enumerated in the 1840 Blythe, Caldwell County, Missouri, census.

20. "Minutes and Discourses, 5–7 October 1839," 30, JSP. The first Nauvoo high council consisted of William Marks, president; Austin Cowles and Charles C. Rich, counselors; Samuel Bent, Henry G. Sherwood, George W. Harris, Thomas Grover, Newel Knight, Lewis D. Wilson, Aaron Johnson, David Fullmer, Alpheus Cutler, William Huntington Senior, William Allred, and Leanord Soby.

21. "Minutes, 1839 October 20–1840 May 2," 1, CHL.

22. Nauvoo did not have its own criminal code at this time and was subject to the Illinois criminal code. Nauvoo did not have the authority to pass laws until the passage of the Nauvoo Charter in 1841.

council in Far West, who had been disciplined at conference. Because he confessed his wrongdoing and "had no evil intention," the council "motioned and voted to forgive & restore him to his former standing of fellowship" in the church. On the other hand, it was resolved that the high council would disfellowship any member of the church "that shall ferry or carry over the river people or freight—to injury of the ferry," as well as those who let their animals destroy the crops of others.[23] While the high council could not impose a legal punishment, disfellowshipping provided a way for them to combat lawlessness.

Marks and the high council structured the financial affairs of the city in their council minutes the following day. Smith was unequivocally recognized as the treasurer in the business of the church, but because he was often traveling or involved in ecclesiastical activities, assistants were needed to carry out quotidian financial duties. The council established James Mulholland as the "sub-Treasurer," a clerk position wherein he would "attend to the land contracts and other business as may be needed." Henry G. Sherwood was assigned the task of showing, contracting, and selling lots in Nauvoo, with the caveat that Sherwood should "lay it before Joseph Smith Jun & Hiram Smith ^for their approval^" and that they would assist him in pricing the lots.[24] While Joseph Smith seemed set on retaining responsibility for the city finances, it soon proved to be an excessive burden. By June 20, 1840, the high council acted to "relieve him from the temporalities of the Church" in order that he could "engage, more particularly, in the spiritual welfare of the Saints; and also, to the translating of the Egyptian Records[,] the Bible[,] and wait upon the Lord for such revelations as may be suited to the condition and circumstances of the Church."[25] The council appointed Sherwood to act as clerk and to take full responsibility for business transactions in Nauvoo. Alanson Ripley was appointed steward "to see that all the necessary wants of the First Presidency be sup[p]lied" and "to aid President Joseph Smith in his important work."[26]

---

23. "Minutes, 1839 October 20–1840 May 2," 1, CHL.
24. "Minutes, 1839 October 20–1840 May 2," 3, CHL.
25. "Minutes, 1840 March 8–1842 May 20," 9, CHL.
26. "Minutes, 1840 March–1842 May 20," 10, CHL. Due to Smith's objections to this decision, minor changes were made on July 3, 1840, leaving Smith responsible as treasurer for the city plot, but retaining Sherwood as clerk of business transactions and Ripley as steward. Funds for both the Presidency and the clerk's paid service would be raised from sources other than the city plot.

Marks and the high council fixed prices for each parcel of land in Nauvoo at between "$200 to $800."[27] Throughout the rest of 1839, the men continued to govern finances and city affairs by setting the salary of the ferryman,[28] setting the wages of the clerk,[29] building a stone boarding house,[30] building a school,[31] appointing a butcher,[32] setting prices for beef and pork,[33] running a printing office,[34] and appointing agents to continue to obtain land in and around Commerce.[35] Even before the action to relieve Smith of some of his responsibilities, it was apparent that the high council was instrumental in directing the financial affairs of the church.

However, Smith was unwilling to cede his financial power. On June 27, 1840, only a week after the high council relieved him of his financial duties, he "sent in his veto . . . to the proceedings of the Council relative to . . . the last Council."[36] While there is no scriptural precedent for the president of the church's "veto," it was nonetheless taken seriously. At the following meeting on July 3, the high council met at Smith's office where they all discussed the issue. It was agreed by all the parties that the high council would not relieve him of his duties, but "assist him, so as to relieve him from the temporalities of the Church."[37]

The council also considered trivial financial matters on its docket. On December 8, 1839, for example, it motioned and voted on a proposal that Bishop Newell K. Whitney "secure the cow belonging to Sister Orson Pratt & that it be kept [at Nauvoo] for her use when needed."[38] On the same day, Elder Thomas Grover brought up "certain embarras[s]ments" of a financial nature that were not spelled out in the minutes, but he clearly needed help of the high council. The body put off the matter temporarily to give them more time to understand, investigate, and adjust the

---

Additionally, all proceeds from the sale of lots would be given to Smith to pay down debts of the city plot.

27. "Minutes, 1839 October 20–1840 May 2," 3, CHL.
28. "Minutes, 1839 October 20–1840 May 2," 3, CHL.
29. "Minutes, 1839 October 20–1840 May 2," 5, CHL.
30. "Oliver Cowdery diary, 1836 January–March," 28, 37, CHL.
31. "Minutes, 1839 October 20–1840 May 2," 9, 11, 19, CHL.
32. "Minutes, 1839 October 20–1840 May 2," 9, CHL.
33. "Minutes, 1839 October 20–1840 May 2," 9, CHL.
34. "Minutes, 1839 October 20–1840 May 2," 12, CHL.
35. "Minutes, 1839 October 20–1840 May 2," 11, CHL.
36. "Minutes, 1840 March 8–1842 May 20," 11, CHL.
37. "Minutes, 1840 March 8–1842 May 20," 11, CHL.
38. "Minutes, 1839 October 20–1840 May 2," 9, CHL.

situation.³⁹ On April 12, 1840, Alvah Keller charged Ripley with "taking nails from his lot." Apparently the leaders counseled complainants on these small matters, because this charge was withdrawn at the same meeting "after the matter had been explained by Joseph Smith."⁴⁰ Nails were mentioned again on May 2, this time giving Ripley and Smith authorization to use "the nails formerly belonging to the city plot" as they saw fit. Anyone who had taken nails unlawfully should restore them or "render a recompense."⁴¹ This information provides insight on just how difficult it was to scrape by in the early days of Nauvoo.

Besides secular affairs, the high council also oversaw large and small projects for the church such as printing hymnbooks and copies of the Book of Mormon and deciding on who should act as chorister of the Singers of Nauvoo.⁴²

The Nauvoo High Council met at the home of Oliver Granger on December 1, 1839, and this became their practice until Granger was authorized to transact business for the church in the East. On that first day of December, the high council assigned Bishop Edward Partridge to draft an article for the Mormon-owned *Times and Seasons* "informing our brethren ^in^ the west that it is improper to remove from the west to locate in Kirtland Ohio & such as do will be disfellowshipped by this council."⁴³ This letter clarified the principle of gathering and established the environs of Nauvoo as the preferred habitation of the Saints. Members of the church in the eastern part of the United States could appropriately settle in Kirtland, but once they were gathered to the Nauvoo area they were not to move back unless authorized. On March 29, 1840, a specific case was mentioned in regard to this policy. The high council responded to a letter from Daniel Bliss requesting advice about moving back to Ohio. Bliss was referred to "the council [*sic*] given in the Times & Seasons on that subject," and it was reiterated that "if he goes back he does it without the influence of the Council."⁴⁴ Thus, by the end of 1839, Marks and the high council had made considerable progress on fashioning an impressive

---

39. "Minutes, 1839 October 20–1840 May 2," 9, CHL.
40. "Minutes, 1840 March 8–1842 May 20," 5, CHL.
41. "Minutes, 1839 October 20–1840 May 2," 22, CHL.
42. "Minutes, 1840 March 8–1842 May 20," 16, CHL.
43. "Minutes, 1839 October–1840 May 2," 7, CHL. The article appeared in December 1839 as H. G. Sherwood, "To the Saints Scattered Abroad, in the Region Westward from Kirtland, Ohio," *TS*, 29.
44. "Minutes, 1840 March 8–1842 May 20," 4, CHL.

municipality and headquarters for the orderly and organized gathering of the Latter Day Saints to the Zion they were intent on creating.

In 1840, Marks continued in his role as a city leader, searching for creative ways to deal with the lack of a court system and law enforcement. In January it was necessary to appoint committee members to settle a difficulty between members of the church. Some of the colonizers had been trespassing on church property and "cutting certain timbers wrongfully and unjustly."[45] As Hancock County consisted mostly of prairie land, there was a dearth of timber with which to build. It was "voted that H[enry] G. Sherwood be appointed to make every discovery possible of all such persons as has been trespassing [sic] on the Church . . . and to bring all Such before the authorities of the Church."[46] Sherwood was a seasoned member of the high council, having served as such in Kirtland and Missouri before his appointment in Nauvoo. He had also been part of a committee under Brigham Young to help move all the underprivileged Saints who wanted to leave Missouri by the end of April 1839. The stealing of timber made it plain that if the poor were to gather to the Nauvoo area as commanded, and build homes and shelters, they would need further assistance. The high council stepped up to help, and on January 8, 1840, "voted to loan all the monies possible for the relief of the poor saints."[47] The first instance of this charitable effort occurred on January 19, when the high council "voted that a city lot in Nauvoo be donated to Br James Hendrick," a member of the church who was shot in Missouri. A lot was also donated to Father Joseph Knight, an elderly Saint mentioned in the Doctrine and Covenants (see LDS sections 12 and 23). The high council appointed a committee of three of their members to build houses on the two donated lots.[48] Marks, through the high council, also assumed debts on behalf of the church. In January 1840, they effected a mortgage on the Iowa lands to help with the church's debt load.[49]

In an interesting case involving an absent Joseph Smith, two men appeared before the high council on January 12, 1840. Brothers [John?] Annis and [?] Fuller made a charge against George W. Harris, who had lived near Smith in Missouri and was the husband of Lucinda Pendleton Morgan.

---

45. "Oliver Cowdery diary, 1836 January–March," 42, CHL.
46. "Oliver Cowdery diary," 42.
47. "History, 1838–1856, volume C-1 [2 November 1838–31 July 1842]," 1012, JSP.
48. "Minutes, 1839 October 20–1840 May 2," 15, CHL.
49. "Minutes, 1839 October–April 1840," 17, CHL.

The council decided to postpone the case until a trial could be held with Smith present. But as soon as this decision was recorded by the secretary, the council decided to pay the amount of money owed and charge it to Smith. The parties reconciled, and Fuller dropped the charges.[50]

On February 2, 1840, the Nauvoo High Council heard the case of Francis Gladden Bishop, a visionary character whose 1826 theophany rivaled Smith's. Bishop had been suspended by a high council in Bradford, Massachusetts, in 1835 for excessive enthusiasm. He had been brought back into the church a month later in Kirtland, but was warned against "advancing heretical doctrines."[51] In Nauvoo, Bishop was again disfellowshipped, this time by a council composed of members of the Seventy. When he appealed the decision before the high council, they immediately reinstated him, as the Quorum of Seventies did not have jurisdiction over a high priest. The decision may have been hasty, as Bishop was to come before Marks and the high council again in 1842.[52] However, through Marks's encounters with renegade members of the church like Luke Johnson, Colin Brewster, Isaac Russell, and now Bishop, he was gaining valuable insight into the delicate dance of fellowship versus discipline in ecclesiastical settings.

As Nauvoo grew in size, it became necessary for Marks and his high council to begin delegating certain civil tasks to committees. When David W. Rogers was charged by Joseph Smith with "unchristianlike conduct" on March 8, a committee of three was appointed to "take up a labor with him."[53] On March 15, the ferry between Illinois and Iowa was becoming a point of contention,[54] so it was voted that a committee of three, con-

---

50. "Oliver Cowdery diary, 1836 January–March," 43, CHL.

51. "Oliver Cowdery diary," 45, CHL.

52. "Minutes, 1840 March 8–1842 May 20," 39, CHL. "A charge was prefer[r]ed against Elder F. G. Bishop by R. Cahoon. First for setting himself up as a prophet and revelator to the Church. Second for an improper course of conduct in meetings. He pled not guilty two were then appointed to speak on each side namely (1) S. Bent (2) James Allred (3) L. D. Wilson (4) and E. Higbee. The charge was sustained after which it was decided that the he be expelled from the Church by the unanimous vote of the Council."

53. "Minutes, 1840 March 8–1842 May 20," 1, CHL.

54. The location of the ferry on the Nauvoo side was near John Annis's mill. Apparently the location of the mill was affecting the ingress and egress of the ferry operations. This came to a head at the March 15, 1841, high council meeting where it was decided, over Joseph Smith's objection, that the "Mill be altogether removed." Annis was given four months to comply. Two years later, in June 1843,

sisting of the First Presidency (Joseph Smith, Hyrum Smith, and Sidney Rigdon), be appointed to superintend the affairs of the ferry.[55] On May 2, a separate committee of three was appointed "to contract for the building of houses for some of the wives of the Twelve," and "for the fencing and ploughing of the lots."[56] On June 20, 1840, another committee of three was appointed to make "an examination into the affairs of the Galland purchase and also of the Church records and make a report of the same to the High Council."[57]

Throughout the remainder of 1840, Marks and his high council continued running the city, but a majority of their time was taken up by the investigation and prosecution of trials for crimes committed in Nauvoo. Specifically, Marks presided over six cases of slander,[58] two cases of theft,[59] a case of perjury,[60] a case of fraudulent proceedings,[61] and a case of civil debt.[62] While these were criminal in nature, the high council lacked legal authority, and thus they were carried out ecclesiastically. By this time Nauvoo did have justices of the peace who could handle less serious crimes and could send more serious ones to the county court in Hancock. Daniel H. Wells was a justice of the peace in Hancock County in 1837. During

---

the city council gave Joseph Smith a "license to keep a Ferry for the term of perpetual succession across the Mississippi River." A month earlier in May 1843, Smith had bought a half interest in a riverboat, the *Maid of Iowa*. "Minutes, 1840 March 8–1842 May 20," 2, CHL; "Proceedings, 1841 February–1845 February," 175, CHL.

55. "Minutes, 1840 March 8–1842 May 20," 2, CHL.
56. "Minutes, 1840 March 8–1842 May 20," 7, CHL.
57. "Minutes, 1840 March 8–1842 May 20," 10, CHL.
58. The cases of slander included John Hicks on April 19, 1840; Moses Martin on August 8, 1840; Elijah Fordham on August 17, 1840; Oliver Walker on October 10–11, 1840; William Gregory on October 17 and 24, 1840; and Robert D. Foster between November 28 and December 20, 1840. "Minutes, 1840 March 8–1842 May 20," CHL.
59. The cases of theft were against Alanson Ripley on April 12, 1840, and Elijah Fordham on August 17, 1840. "Minutes, 1840 March 8–1842 May 20," 5, 14, CHL.
60. The perjury case was against Elijah Fordham on August 17, 1840. "Minutes, 1840 March 8–1842 May 20," 14, CHL.
61. The fraudulent proceedings case was against Ebenezer Black on June 20, 1840. "Minutes, 1840 March 8–1842 May 20," 10, CHL.
62. The debt case was against Hirum Dayton on August 29, 1840. "Minutes, 1840 March 8–1842 May 20," 17, CHL.

the Saints' time in Nauvoo, Ebenezer Robinson and Aaron Johnson were also appointed.[63] It seems, however, that Marks and the high council preferred to handle matters locally.

Nauvoo, like many cities in America, relied on William Blackstone's *Commentaries on the Laws of England*, a four-volume legal treatise discussing the development of the common law.[64] Blackstone's *Commentaries* described slander as an "injur[y] affecting a man's *reputation* or good name." He went on:

> As if a man maliciously and falsely utter any slander or false tale of another; which may either endanger him in the law, by impeaching him of some heinous crime, . . . or which may impair or hurt his trade or livelihood. Words also tending to scandalize a magistrate, or person in a public trust, are reputed more highly. . . . Also, if the defendant be able to justify, and prove the words true, no action will lie, even though special damage hath ensued.[65]

The first case of slander that Marks dealt with was brought by John P. Green against John Hicks after Hicks accused Green of stealing a horse. Marks presided over the trial, which was heard on May 2, 1840. As had become customary for high council trials, Marks appointed an equal number of councilors to defend and to prosecute.[66] In this case, there were three on each side. Hicks objected to the impartiality of Thomas Grover, but the

---

63. "Justice of the peace docket, 1837–1841," CHL; "Hancock County justice of the peace docket," CHL.

64. On June 10, 1844, the Nauvoo City Council used Blackstone's *Commentaries* as justification to declare the Nauvoo Expositor a nuisance and ordered it destroyed. Marks was present at the meeting. Joseph Smith described Blackstone as a "distinguished lawyer, who is considered authority, I believe, in all our courts, states, among other things." "History, 1838–1856, volume F-1 [1 May 1844–8 August 1844] [addenda]," 5, JSP.

65. William Blackstone, *Commentaries*, 325–26; emphasis in original. While the Saints and the Illinois legal system used the common law for general slander, the Illinois legislature did pass a specific law dealing with sexual slander in 1822. John S. Dinger, "Sexual Slander and Polygamy in Nauvoo," 1–22.

66. This was done after being directed by a revelation received by Joseph Smith on February 17, 1834. The revelation outlined the procedures that the high council should follow: "The councilors appointed to speak before the council are to present the case, after the evidence is examined, in its true light before the council; and every man is to speak according to equity and justice. Those councilors who draw even numbers, that is, 2, 4, 6, 8, 10, and 12, are the individuals who are to stand up in behalf of the accused, and prevent insult and injustice." "Revelation Book 2," 113, JSP; LDS D&C 102:15–17.

high council sustained him. They found that a "different arrangement" had been made by "parties unknown" who had donated the horse to John P. Green. While Hicks was not punished for his slander, he was made to confess and was told to publish his wrongdoing in the *Times and Seasons*.[67]

In August 1840, Marks presided over three cases of slander treated as more severe because they dealt with the slandering of church leaders. On August 8, Moses Martin was charged with assaulting the characters of high council member Seymour Brunson, High Priest Amasa Lyman, and other elders with "certain slanderous and unchristian-like expressions[,] insinuations &c derogatory [language]." Martin maintained that the church had "countenanced" the actions of these brothers, who he called "a gang of Gadianton rob[b]ers."[68] This was a reference to a lawless secret combination discussed in the Book of Mormon. Martin was threatened with excommunication, but he finally made a full "confession" and was received back into fellowship.[69]

The next case held that month was a dramatic one, heard by both the High Council of Nauvoo and the High Council of Iowa Territory, together with the First Presidency. Elijah Fordham was accused by John Patten of "libelous, slanderous and infamous reports . . . lieing [sic], burglary, and attempt to murder," and "a spirit of malevolence and high toned wickedness."[70] The case had begun as a simple dispute over a garden plot, but it escalated spectacularly. Patten included charges that Fordham falsely recommended certain medicinal "pill rostrums," played the violin for a "Negro ball," and took Patten's daughter to balls. Alongside these were important accusations that Patten made regarding church authorities. As well as accusing Fordham of trying to drive him out of the high council, Patten said Fordham declared "that the council might enter immediately" into the controversial "consecration law" and that Patten "had spoken against the proceedings of the High Council in public." Further, Fordham said Patten had accused him of saying "that President Hyrum Smith was vested with the authority of the First Presidency in the absence of the other two Presidents."[71] Patten recognized that these types of statements weakened

---

67. "Minutes, 1840 March 8–1842 May 20," 8, CHL. The confession was never published.
68. "Minutes, 1840 March 8–1842 May 20," 13, CHL.
69. "Minutes, 1840 March 8–1842 May 20," 14, CHL. Martin immediately confessed and was "received again into fellowship."
70. "Minutes, 1840 March 8–1842 May 20," 14–15, CHL.
71. "Minutes, 1840 March 8–1842 May 20," 15, CHL.

the influence of the high council. Further, the remarks about Hyrum Smith show a concern with succession authority long before the death of Joseph Smith.[72] While these claims may sound like they should most appropriately be heard in an ecclesiastical setting, Patten specifically stated all his claims fit into the "catalogue of crime and misdemeanors."[73] It was clear that the complainant viewed the council as akin to a court of law, though it had no such authority. Marks and the council members took the accusations quite seriously. Marks did not preside over this case, as Joseph Smith was in attendance, but he did take an active role. Marks and Zarahemla Stake President John Smith, as well as Hyrum and Joseph Smith, all spoke to the council, discussing the evidence and calling for resolution. In the end, the parties were reconciled without a vote being necessary.

On August 22, John Zundel preferred a charge against [Henry] Ourbough and [David?] Waggoner for "grossly Slandering the Presidency of this Church and evil speaking against this Church."[74] Both of the accused confessed but persisted in their slander. Thus, they were expelled from the church. The charge against Ourbough and Waggoner is ambiguous, but it may have been similar to the insinuations made by Moses Martin. Regardless, additional important accusations that came up in the autumn months did seem related to Martin's associating church leaders with Gadianton robbers and to thefts in and around Nauvoo.

Oliver Walker was accused of slander on October 11, 1840, for stating that in the church at Nauvoo "there did exist [a] set of pilferers, who were actually thieving, rob[b]ing, plundering, taking and unlawfully carrying away from Missouri certain goods and chattles, wares and property" and that such thieving "was fostered and conducted by the knowledge and approbation of the heads & leaders of the church, viz; by the Presidency and High Council."[75] These were serious accusations, as many in Missouri still harbored significant animosity toward the Saints.

A week later on October 17, William Gregory was also tried for slander for similarly stating "that much pilfering, pillaging, plundering, stealing &c. is practised by members of said Church and that such practise is known to and tolerated by the heads and leaders of the church (or certain

---

72. If one member of the First Presidency held supreme authority in the absence of the other two, this would have important implications for Sidney Rigdon's claims to succession upon the deaths of Joseph and Hyrum Smith.

73. "Minutes, 1840 March 8–1842 May 20," 16, CHL.

74. "Minutes, 1840 March 8–1842 May 20," 16, CHL.

75. "Minutes, 1840 March 8–1842 May 20," 20, CHL.

of them)."⁷⁶ Walker was able to continue his trial until the following April, but Gregory lost at trial and was made to proffer "a humble confession to the satisfaction of the Council."⁷⁷

Although these high-profile slander cases were decided in favor of the plaintiffs, there were two notable cases in 1840 that came down in favor of the defendants. On September 5, 1840, Almon Babbitt was charged with slander for accusing Joseph Smith and Sidney Rigdon of extravagance. Babbitt took exception to Smith's and Rigdon's purchase of several sets of clothes when they were in Washington DC, as well as dressing their families "in profusion."⁷⁸ An additional charge hearkened back several years, when Babbitt allegedly held "secret Council in the Lord's House in Kirtland, and for locking the doors of the house for the purpose of prohibiting certain brethren, in good standing in the church, from being in the council and thereby depriving them the use of the house."⁷⁹ Two members of the high council were assigned to speak, one on each side of the case. After evidence was heard, "the charge was withdrawn by Joseph Smith Jr."⁸⁰ It seems out of character for Smith to have backed down, but perhaps after the evidence was heard, he realized his charge was a misunderstanding.

Finally, in November and December 1840, the high council heard the case of Robert Foster, who was accused "Firstly, for slandering the authorities of the Church. Secondly, for lying, profane sw[e]aring and individual abuse and for other unchristian=like conduct."⁸¹ Foster pled not guilty and two councilmen were appointed to speak on the case. Evidence was given and witnesses were examined for four separate days over the course of the next two months. On December 12 and 13, the trial continued from 10:00 a.m. until dark, with only one hour break. On December 20, 1840, "the Presidency decided that he (R. D. Foster) should be acquit[t]ed of the charges brought against him which was voted unanimously by the Council."⁸²

While it is not clear how closely these pseudo-criminal trials followed correct or just procedure and evidence requirements, they did attempt to be fair. In the midst of these trials, new rules were instituted at the high

---

76. "Minutes, 1840 March 8–1842 May 20," 21, CHL.
77. "Minutes, 1840 March 8–1842 May 20," 22, CHL.
78. "Minutes, 1840 March 8–1842 May 20," 17, CHL.
79. "Minutes, 1840 March 8–1842 May 20," 18, CHL.
80. "Minutes, 1840 March 8–1842 May 20," 18, CHL.
81. "Minutes, 1840 March 8–1842 May 20," 22, CHL.
82. "Minutes, 1840 March 8–1842 May 20," 24, CHL.

council to ensure fairness. On July 11, 1840, it was decided that defendants had the right to be present at their trial, that there should not be exparte communications, and that defendants had the right to notice.[83] Thus, it is apparent that Marks provided a way for the citizens of Nauvoo to address grievances in an orderly manner. Although these hearings led by Marks were not perfect, they filled a need until a real criminal court could be formed.

In Nauvoo, the gathering of Zion was earnestly launched, and an emphasis was placed on the community being purified and purged of those who did not belong. Minutes of the proceedings of the Nauvoo High Council portray the type of leadership William Marks offered in pursuit of this objective. Never vaunting himself, Marks worked behind the scenes to dispense justice to a religious organization striving to build a utopian community on the midwestern frontier. When needed, Marks took up the reins of leadership, speaking to and effectively persuading his fellow council members. However, he valued open discussion. Marks often called for the opinions of others and for attention to the workings of the Spirit. His style was to delegate, appoint committees, and work through established patterns laid out by his file leader, Joseph Smith.

---

83. "Minutes, 1840 March 8–1842 May 20," 12, CHL. Specifically, the new rules were, "That the Council should try no case without both parties being present, or having had an opportunity to be present," "neither should they hear one parties complaint before his case," is brought up for trial, and "neither should they suffer the character of any one to be exposed before the Council without the person being present and ready to defend him or herself."

CHAPTER 4

Nauvoo Municipality

William Marks and members of the high council had oversight of Nauvoo for more than a year before Illinois legislators ratified a city charter on December 16, 1840.¹ The document was developed and submitted by John C. Bennett (Quarter Master General of the Illinois State Militia before joining the church), under the direction of Joseph Smith. Nauvoo now possessed a civil government, which gave it political independence.² While Nauvoo's charter resembled those of other cities, it allowed for several distinctive functions that directly impacted Marks.³ These included the right to hold elections, the right of *habeas corpus*, and the right to establish a municipal and mayor's court and pass legal ordinances, as well as to create an independent militia and a university. The policies adopted in the document also gave the city a number of unique powers, including the absence of requirements for political office, and the ability of city council members to remove city officers at will. The charter was specifically created to be both inclusive and powerful. Smith wrote that he had "concocted it for the salvation of the Church, and on principles so broad, that every honest man might dwell secure under its protective influence without distinction of sect or party."⁴

---

1. "Minutes, 7–11 April 1841," 386, JSP.
2. "The City Charter: Laws, Ordinances, and Acts of the City Council of the City of Nauvoo. And also, the Ordinances of the Nauvoo Legion: from the commencement of the city to this date," 1–32, CHL.
3. Richard E. Bennett and Rachel Cope, "'A City on a Hill'–Chartering the City of Nauvoo," 21. See also James L. Kimball, Jr., "The Nauvoo Charter: A Reinterpretation," 39–45. Nauvoo's charter included thirty-nine sections from article five of the Springfield charter. Its suffrage qualifications were identical to those in the Alton charter. The right to pass any ordinance not specifically conflicting with powers granted the federal and state governments was drawn from provisions also seen in the charters of Galena, Quincy, and Springfield. In both Alton and Nauvoo, city courts possessed the authority to issue writs of habeas corpus. Lastly, there was a remarkable resemblance between the Nauvoo Legion and the Fairfield "Invincible Dragoons," an independent militia company which Bennett was instrumental in incorporating in 1837. Kimball suggests that the bulk of the Nauvoo City Charter was "based solidly on precedents" that were "not unheard-of."
4. "History Draft [1 January–31 December 1840]," 18, JSP. John C. Bennett, Quarter Master General of the Illinois State Militia before joining the church,

Though Smith gave lip service to Nauvoo's ecumenism, the principle of gathering brought a predominantly Mormon group of residents into the city. Converts from Great Britain, the eastern United States, and many other places were encouraged to immigrate, and they surged into the new gathering place. As the population grew into the thousands, it was necessary to have a municipal government as well as an ecclesiastical structure in place. With the passage of its charter, residents of Nauvoo were able to elect a mayor, city councilmen, and aldermen, enabling them to govern themselves by civil law. Nauvoo, however, was unusual because the city administration retained a theocratic flavor, even as it grew more substantial.[5] Marks was part of the overlap that existed among church and civil authorities.

On February 1, 1841, an election was held in Nauvoo that determined who would govern the city under the newly passed charter. John C. Bennett, though a recent convert, had quickly gained power and influence in the city and was elected mayor. Marks was elected an alderman, also a very powerful position.[6] Each of the four Nauvoo aldermen held a municipal rank immediately below the mayor, doubling as a justice of the peace and adjudicator in the city court. Absent the mayor, an alderman could fill in as chief justice of the municipal court. According to the Nauvoo charter, there were also nine councilmen who served on the city council. These men discussed and voted on city ordinances and were not involved with the courts.[7]

Two days later on February 3, Marks raised his arm to the square and swore the oath, "We . . . do solemnly swear, in the presence of Almighty

---

was instrumental in developing the documents, drawing upon the most liberal policies in existence then. Both Bennett and Smith claimed credit for the Nauvoo Charter. "Bennett stated, 'I wrote and procured the passage of the . . . charters.' Joseph Smith asserted, 'The city charter of Nauvoo is of my own plan and device.'" James L. Kimball, "The Nauvoo Charter: A Reinterpretation," 45.

5. The Nauvoo City Charters were presented before the church for a sustaining vote at the general conference held April 7, 1841. "Minutes, 7–11 April 1841," 386, JSP.

6. "Municipal Election," *TS*, 309. "The following ticket was elected by majorities varying from 330 to 337 votes; to wit: REGULAR TICKET. For Mayor, John C. Bennett. Aldermen[:] William Marks, Samuel H. Smith, Daniel H. Wells, [and] N[ewel] K. Whitney. Counsellors[:] Joseph Smith, Hyrum Smith, Sidney Rigdon, Charles C. Rich, John T. Barnett, Wilson Law, D[on] C[arlos] Smith, J[ohn] P. Greene, [and] Vinson Knight. The Council will be organized on Wednesday the 3rd inst."

7. "The City Charter," sec. 8–13, pp. 4–5, CHL.

Nauvoo home of William Marks, from early 1900s Nauvoo postcard collection. Courtesy of LDS Church History Library.

God, that we will support the Constitution of the United States, and of the State of Illinois, and that we will well and truly perform the duties of Aldermen of the City of Nauvoo according to law and the best of our abilities."[8] With the institution of a city council, the high council of the church took a more ecclesiastical role in governance. For example, in the first few months of 1841, the high council heard cases on "unchristian conduct" such as stealing and defrauding, dishonesty, drinking, and immoral habits. Members of the church came to the high council for letters of recommendation when they went on missions, or to petition for their membership to be restored after excommunication or disfellowshipping. In contrast, the Nauvoo City Council appointed city officials such as city marshal, city recorder, supervisor of streets, and city assessor. They organized the Nauvoo Legion and the city university. They prepared a code of city ordinances and decided upon the management and operation of city plots, roads, bridges, piers, and a canal. The city council also regulated sales of alcohol, gunpowder, and poison. By March 1841, the council had divided the city into four portions, called wards, and assigned each area an alderman and two or three councilmen.

The city and high councils worked well together to govern affairs in Nauvoo. Marks was one of several men on both councils, and occasionally the city council crossed over into matters regarding religion. On

---

8. "Oaths from Nauvoo City Officers, 3 and 8 February 1841," 1, JSP.

March 1, 1841, for example, Joseph Smith introduced a motion to assure freedom of religion, assuring "toleration and equal Privilieges [sic]" for "Catholics, Presbyterians, Methodists, Baptists. Latter-Day Saints, Quakers, Episcopalians Universalists Unitarians, Mohommedans, and all other religious sects and denominations whatever."[9] On July 12, Mayor John C. Bennett proposed and the council unanimously adopted the setting apart of a day of "fasting, Humiliation, & Prayer. <on account of the Death of Senator [Sidney H.] Little,>. as a feeble Testimonial of our high regard, & great respect, for his public Services & private Virtues, as a Statesman & Citizen."[10] The high council also crossed over into secular affairs, such as their continued oversight of the financial affairs regarding the building of the "stone school house."[11] The schoolhouse and the financial burden it laid upon the high council was discussed on four separate occasions. Finally, on September 22, the high council resolved that whereas in times past they had "of necessity and by the advice and instruction of the First Presidency, [assumed authority] to transact buisness [sic] of a temporal nature, for the Church ^&^ thereby involve itself with debts and other temporal burthens which, under other circumstances, would not have devolved upon it," they would now transfer all business of a temporal nature to the proper authorities, which were "now organized and acting in their proper places."[12] Even after this, the high council struggled to transfer the burden of the building of the schoolhouse from its docket. Additionally, issues between members of the church regarding land claims continued to be brought before the high council. Thus, temporal affairs

---

9. "Nauvoo City Council Minute Book, 1841–1845," 13, JSP.

10. "Nauvoo City Council Minute Book," 20, JSP.

11. Alpheus Cutler was given funds so he could build a schoolhouse. "Minutes, 1840 March 8–1842 May 20," 8, CHL. William Marks and Peter Haws were to procure provisions and other means necessary for the building of the schoolhouse. "Minutes," 16, CHL. The trustees of the school house were to settle with the building committee. "Minutes," 21, CHL. Samuel Bent brought up the schoolhouse on May 17, 1841, upon his return from a mission to the East. He asked for an account of the present condition of the high council relative to the building of the stone schoolhouse, wanting to "make arrangements to relieve the Council from the responsibility of all debts and obligations in which the Council was now involved." A committee was appointed to look into who had claims. "Minutes," 29, CHL.

12. "Minutes," 32–33, CHL; "History, 1838–1856, volume C-1 [2 November 1838–31 July 1842]," 1226, JSP.

in Nauvoo were never completely transferred from the ecclesiastical high council to the oversight of the city council.

A prayer by Joseph Smith opened the initial meeting of the Nauvoo City Council at the home of Amos Davis. At this meeting on February 3, 1841, Marks was appointed, along with Joseph and Hyrum Smith, to one of the council's most powerful select committees: the committee on "Vending Spirituous Liquors," which oversaw the regulation and sale of alcohol, one of the major issues faced by the city council throughout their jurisdiction in Nauvoo.[13] As a member of this committee, Marks helped form and pass multiple ordinances dealing with alcohol.[14] In fact, only days later the committee passed an ordinance decreeing that "all persons & establishments whatever, in this City, are prohibited from vending Whiskey in a less quantity than a Gallon, or other Spirituous Liquors in a less quantity than a Quart."[15] The intent of this law was to keep bars, which dispensed much smaller amounts of liquor per person, out of the city. The law was based on an 1838 state law in Massachusetts prohibiting the sale of intoxicating liquors in less than fifteen-gallon quantities.[16] This effectively made Nauvoo a dry city, prompting the *Times and Seasons* to declare it a "Great Moral Victory!" and "a glorious example to the world."[17]

Regardless of the "Great Moral Victory," Marks continued to fight against alcohol his whole tenure as an alderman, passing numerous laws on the subject and, as the stake president in numerous disciplinary councils, dealing with the effects of alcohol. At the general conference on April 6, 1841, for example, the high council discussed the case of Bishop Alanson Ripley, who drank to excess, causing him to abuse his brethren while under the influence. The high priests let Ripley's behavior slide on that occasion, but eventually he was removed from his office as bishop.[18]

---

13. "Proceedings," 5, CHL.

14. These include An ordinance in Relation to Temperance, An ordinance concerning drunks, An Ordinance to regulate Taverns and Ordinaries in the City of Nauvoo, An Ordinance to amend an ordinance entitled "An ordinance to regulate Taverns and Ordinaries, in the City of Nauvoo," An Ordinance concerning the sale of spirituous Liquors, and An Ordinance concerning Spirituous Liquors and other purposes.

15. "Minutes, 15 February 1841, Draft," 5, JSP.

16. *Encyclopaedia Britannica*, s.v. "Prohibition."

17. "A Great Moral Victory," *TS*, 320–21. The ordinance was passed unanimously.

18. "Minutes, 1840 March 8–1842 May 20," 28. On April 6, 1841, the high council minutes reported, "Objections were made to him for his drinking and immoral habits which necessaryly follows and his abusing his brethren while under

Another one of Marks's influences on the city of Nauvoo was as a member of the board of health. A board of health for the city of Nauvoo was first mentioned at the inaugural meeting of the city council on February 3, 1841. At that time, a committee composed of Joseph Smith, N. K. Whitney, and John T. Barnett was chosen to organize the board. The city of Commerce and its environs were essentially an undrained swamp, and the Saints had discovered as soon as they moved there that it was a dangerous and disease-ridden area. Despite finding it beautiful, Smith called it "a low, marshy, wet, damp and nasty place."[19] Although Nauvoo "had been objected to by some on account of the sickness that has prevailed in the summer months," Smith still promoted the area as the gathering place of the Saints and stated, "I am led to the conclusion that this must eventually become a healthy place."[20] While the board of health would not officially be formed until February 11, 1843, Marks began working to improve the health of the city almost as soon as he was elected an alderman.[21]

In addition to all the diseases bred in the swamps, Nauvoo was dangerous because of disease spread by dead bodies and improper burial. One in thirty people died every year.[22] A dedicated burial ground was therefore discussed at a city council meeting on May 1, 1841. Marks was not present, and the responsibility of obtaining a "ten acre[]" "Bur[y]ing Ground

---

the influence of Liquor. His situation and character was discussed at considerable length. After which he was approved by a majority." The *Times and Seasons* reported: "The quorums reported, that they had investigated the conduct of the persons who had been objected to, and that they had rejected Alanson Ripley and James Foster. . . . Resolved, that as Alanson Ripley, has not appeared to answer the charges prefered against him, that his bishoprick be taken from him." Robert B. Thompson, "Minutes of the general conference of the Church of Jesus Christ of Latter Day Saints held at the City of Nauvoo, Hancock Co. Ill. on the seventh day of April, in the year of our Lord one thousand eight hundred and forty-one," *TS*, 388.

19. John Butler, "Autobiography of John Butler," 21.

20. "History, 1838–1856, volume C-1 [2 November 1838–31 July 1842]," 1117, JSP.

21. Samuel Morris Brown, *In Heaven as it is on Earth: Joseph Smith and the Early Mormon Conquest of Death*, 20; see also Fred Woods, "The Cemetery Record of William D. Huntington, Nauvoo Sexton," 131–63; M. Guy Bishop et al., "Death at Mormon Nauvoo, 1843–1845," 70–83; John Dinger, *The Nauvoo City and High Council Minutes*, 157–58. Marks was appointed on this date along with Joseph Smith Jr., William Law, and Samuel Bennet.

22. Evan L. Ivie and Douglas C. Heiner, "Deaths in Early Nauvoo, Illinois, 1839–46, and in Winter Quarters, Nebraska, 1846–48," 163–74.

. . . out of the City," was given to Daniel H. Wells, Wilson Law, and John T. Barnett.[23] By September 1841, the committee had not made any progress, so Marks was added to the committee and he actively started looking for land.[24] By January 15 the next year, Marks was close to obtaining a cemetery. At this time he helped pass a resolution appointing a sexton who would "have Two Dollars for digging each Grave, & interring a Body," and would keep records such as the decedent's name, age, and cause of death.[25]

The city council gave Marks and his committee authority to "proceed forthwith & do all Acts & things that they may consider necessary, in Relation to the Burying Ground, or Grounds."[26] On June 11, 1842, Marks purchased a burial ground southwest of Nauvoo, by personally making a deed for the land, but "for the use of the city."[27] The city intended to reimburse Marks for the purchase. At the January 14, 1843, city council meeting, these payments were discussed; however, by the next meeting other debts had come up, so Marks was to be paid by proceeds of burial lots being sold.[28]

Marks was apparently never paid for the burial ground and retained the title to the cemetery. By November 1844, at which point Marks was distrusted by the Quorum of the Twelve, the burial ground was discussed at a city council meeting. George A. Smith commented, "that the lots are all sold and that some of them are paid for and others is not."[29] As late as 1869, Joseph C. Rich, a missionary serving in Illinois, wrote a letter to Bishop Edward Hunter describing the condition of the burial ground:

> There is, probably fifty tomb-stones standing. Among the number I found one to the memory of my sister. The fence around the graveyard is down and exposed. The ground was bought by the city in "Mormon" days from Wm. Marks, but no deed for it exists on record. . . . Application has been made by

---

23. "Nauvoo City Council Rough Minute Book, February–December 1841," 19, JSP.

24. "Nauvoo City Council Rough Minute Book," 22, JSP.

25. "Nauvoo City Council Rough Minute Book, January–November 1842," 7, JSP; "Motion from William Marks, 15 January 1842," 1, JSP. See also William Dresser Huntington, "Cemetery record and store ledger, 1839–1845, 1861–1866," CHL.

26. "Nauvoo City Council Rough Minute Book, January–November 1842," 13, JSP.

27. "History Draft [1 January–30 June 1842]," 17, JSP.

28. "Nauvoo City Council Rough Minute Book, November 1842–January 1844," 1, JSP; "Minutes, 30 January 1843," 5, JSP.

29. "Minutes, 9 November 1844, Draft," 3, JSP.

Barnett, Chauncey Robinson, and others to Marks for a quit claim deed to the property, in order that it might be taken care of, but he refuses to make one, although he has received his pay for the land from the old city of Nauvoo.[30]

Although the burial ground turned into a hotly contested parcel of land, Marks's dedication to its procurement and development contributed to the safety and health of the citizens of Nauvoo in significant ways.

As 1842 began, the Nauvoo City and High Councils had made much progress in defining their roles with Marks as a key player. In a meeting on January 18, he redefined the religious obligations of the high council and urged them to "set in order all things relative to their duty as Councellors." Marks asked the councilors to make a record of all who kept the Word of Wisdom, and he encouraged helping the poor. The high councilors were to oversee the bishops; thus Marks asked them to make sure members of the Aaronic priesthood were meeting together, that priests were visiting house to house, and "that there was no malice—no hardness—no difficulty in the Church."[31] Though he served as a justice on the Nauvoo Municipal Court, he nonetheless spoke against the brethren suing each other, one of the difficulties which took up considerable time for the high council to sort out. Marks himself brought such a case before the high council on November 7, 1842. He preferred a charge against Windsor Lyon, owner of a drug and variety store, for "instituting a suit at law against me" and "for other acts derogatory to the character of a christian." Though Lyon protested that he had instituted the suit "in another man's name," the council sustained the charge. Lyon was told that "unless he repent humble himself and repent, the hand of fellowship be withdrawn from him."[32]

Marks's most important and powerful role in Nauvoo was that of spiritual leader and president of the Nauvoo Stake. In this role he was subject only to the First Presidency as he "governed members, arbitrated disputes, investigated misconduct, and oversaw the ecclesiastical and religious life of Mormons within the stake's boundaries."[33] Marks's hierarchical position was demonstrated at the April 1841 general conference, when certain members with leadership positions were objected to for vari-

---

30. Joseph C. Rich, "Correspondence," *DN*, 595.

31. The authority of high councilors over bishops was reiterated by Hyrum Smith. "Minutes, 1840 March 8–1842 May 20," 34, CHL.

32. "Minutes, 1842 May 20–1843 February 19," 16, CHL.

33. D. Michael Quinn, *The Mormon Hierarchy: Origins of Power*, 59. See also LDS Doctrine and Covenants 102.

ous reasons.³⁴ One of these members was John E. Page, a member of the Twelve Apostles who had "written certain abusive letters, [in]criminating certain individuals, wrongfully." Even though Page was a member of the Twelve Apostles, he was brought before Marks and his high council to "approve or disapprove" his continued role in that calling. "After his case had been spoken on, at considerable length," Marks and the high council decided unanimously that Page should continue in his calling as one of the Twelve Apostles.³⁵

Marks's power was not limited to the high council. He also wielded significant power independently as the stake president. On May 8, 1842, the high council, with Hyrum Smith in attendance, heard a case involving members of the Pleasant Vale branch of the church. It was found out that "there had been difficulties & hardness in that branch," because of "parties" (factions), "contending about points of doctrine," "slandering," and "confusion."³⁶ While Hyrum Smith counseled the members to "drop all party feelings & animosities," Marks did something quite different. Seeing the dysfunction in the branch, Marks used his power as stake president to "desolve" and "discontinue" the Pleasant Vale Branch, and to absorb the members into the Nauvoo Stake under his direction.³⁷ Though they lived eighty miles from Nauvoo, Marks clearly wanted to keep an eye on these Saints.

Because of his activity in these many roles, Marks was well-known and respected throughout Nauvoo, though he was not predisposed to seek for honor and glory. He fulfilled his duties unobtrusively. As the church continued to send the Twelve Apostles, Seventies, and Elders out into the mission field to preach the gospel, Marks was one of the few church leaders who remained in the city, steadfastly working to improve the quality

---

34. This included John Hicks, the president of the Elders Quorum whom the high council did not believe had followed their council in May 1840; Bishop Alanson Ripley for drinking and immoral habits; John E. Page, a member of the Twelve Apostles who had written abusive letters; Noah Packard, who was a counselor in the High Priest Quorum, for rash and ignorant expressions; James Foster, a president of the Quorum of the Seventy, for a lack of faith; and Bishop Newel K. Whitney for unknown reasons.

35. "Minutes, 1840 March 8–1842 May 20," 28, CHL.

36. "Minutes," 43, CHL.

37. "Minutes," 44, CHL. Pleasant Vale was located at the site of the present-day town of New Canton. It was a branch of about 166 members and originally belonged to the Geneva Stake. See "Pleasant Vale Branch Report," September 27, 1841, CHL.

of daily life. In his positions on the councils of the church and the city, Marks had occasion to observe the reactions of those who were chastised for their behavior. Some confessed and repented, while others became violently disaffected.

John C. Bennett was one of the latter. When several of Bennett's sexual improprieties (which shall be more fully covered in the next chapter) became public, a notice was published by the First Presidency, the Twelve, and Bishops Whitney, Knight, and Miller of Nauvoo. The notice professed to "withdraw the hand of fellowship" from him, in order "to persuade him to amend his conduct,"[38] perhaps hoping that he would repent, confess his sins, and be reconciled, as others who had come before the high council had done. He did no such thing. Bennett tendered his resignation as mayor on May 17, 1842. In this document, Bennett assumed that his duties would devolve upon Joseph Smith, the "Vice Mayor."[39] Instead, the high council held a vote for a mayor to succeed Bennett. This action, which fell under civil jurisdiction, further demonstrates the influence of the church in Nauvoo. Most members of the high council probably believed as Bennett did, and simply rubber-stamped Smith's advancement. It speaks well of Marks, however, that he received one vote to Smith's eighteen in the election—the only other man suggested as mayor of Nauvoo. When the ballot was taken to replace Smith as vice-mayor, he was also represented: eighteen men voted for Hyrum Smith, one for Marks, and one for Willard Richards.[40]

Another power that Marks quietly wielded stemmed from his position as alderman on the municipal court, one of two courts set up under the Nauvoo Charter.[41] Each member of this court was paid $2.50 per day for his service.[42] One of the most important roles of the municipal court was the investigation of arrests of Nauvoo citizens through the writ of

---

38. "Notice, 11 May 1842," 1, JSP.
39. "Resignation from John C. Bennett, 17 May 1842," 1, JSP.
40. "Minutes, 19 May 1842," 28, JSP.
41. "The City Charter," sec. 17, p. 6, CHL. "The Mayor shall have exclusive jurisdiction in all cases arising under the ordinances of the corporation, and shall issue such process as may be necessary to carry said ordinances into execution and effect; appeals may be had from any decision or judgment of said Mayor or Aldermen, arising under the city ordinances, to the Municipal Court . . . which court shall be composed of the Mayor, as Chief Justice, and the Aldermen as Associate Justices."
42. See, for example, "Municipal court attendance reports, 1843–1845," CHL.

habeas corpus. Joseph Smith was introduced to this writ when he and other church leaders were incarcerated in Missouri's Liberty Jail. While there, his lawyers invoked *habeas corpus*, which allowed courts to review the evidence against a suspect and free them if the evidence was deemed to be insufficient or illegal. Under this petition, Clay County judge Joel Turnham ruled that there was not sufficient evidence to hold Sidney Rigdon, and he was released.[43] Beginning at this time, Smith became both a "student and practitioner in the use of the writ."[44] Not only did the Nauvoo Charter provide for *habeas corpus* in section 17, but it also gave the municipal court "power and authority to make, ordain, establish, and execute, all such ordinances, not repugnant to the Constitution of the United States or of this State, as they deem necessary for the peace, benefit, good order, regulation, convenience, and cleanliness, of said city."[45] This enabled the municipal court to enact further laws regulating how *habeas corpus* could be used in Nauvoo.

On June 4, 1841, Smith was arrested in Illinois upon a demand from Missouri Governor Lilburn Boggs that he be extradited to Missouri, where he had been charged with treason. Smith obtained a writ of *habeas corpus*, which was heard by Judge Stephen A. Douglas. Upon an examination of the evidence, Douglas determined that the writ to extradite Smith was expired and released Smith from custody. The incident showed Mormons the power of this legal device to protect them against what they perceived as unjust persecution. The Nauvoo Municipal Court, with Marks as a prominent participant, began to develop several expansive statutes to strengthen *habeas corpus* in their jurisdiction.

On the night of May 6, 1842, Governor Boggs survived an assassination attempt by a gunman outside his window. Smith was accused of complicity with his friend and personal bodyguard Orrin Porter Rockwell in the intended murder. Bennett, whose falling out with Smith and other church leaders was complete, wrote a letter dated June 27 to the *Sangamo Journal*, a newspaper in Springville, and promised to expose the secrets of the Saints, including their involvement with the Boggs shooting. In a sworn affidavit dated July 2, Bennett claimed, "In 1841, Joe Smith predicted or prophesied in a public congregation in Nauvoo, that Lilburn W Boggs, ex-Governor of Missouri, should die by violent hands within

---

43. Jeffrey N. Walker, "Habeas Corpus in Early Nineteenth-Century Mormonism: Joseph Smith's Legal Bulwark for Personal Freedom," 27.

44. Walker, 31.

45. "The City Charter," sec. 11, p. 5, CHL.

one year. From one or two months prior to the attempted assassination of Gov. Boggs, Mr. O. P. Rockwell left Nauvoo for parts unknown to the citizens at large. I was then on terms of close intimacy with Joe Smith, and asked him where Rockwell had gone? Gone, said he, 'GONE TO FULFILL PROPHECY!'"[46]

The Nauvoo City Council realized that Missouri was again preparing to extradite Smith. In response, on July 5, 1842, the city council met and passed an ordinance that stated, "no Citizen of this City shall be taken out of the City by any Writs, without the privilege of investigation before the Municipal Court, and the benefit of a Writ of Habeas Corpus, as granted in the seventeenth Section of the Charter of this City."[47] This was the first of seven ordinances passed by the city council dealing with *habeas corpus*. This granted the aldermen of the city, including Marks, jurisdiction over all crimes allegedly committed by Nauvoo citizens. Anyone trying to make an arrest in Nauvoo would have to obtain the permission of the municipal court.

One month later, Smith and Rockwell submitted to arrest on August 8, 1842, by the sheriff of Adams County and two assistants.[48] This arrest was based on a warrant from the state of Missouri for "assault with intent to kill" of ex-Governor Boggs. The two accused immediately exercised the power of *habeas corpus* and were brought before Marks and the municipal court. Smith asked that he might "be entitled to the privilege of showing to your honors the insufficiency of the Writ and the impossibility of utter groundlessness of the charge preferred in said Writ."[49] Marks and the other associate justices ordered Smith and Rockwell released and set a trial for the following session in September.

The arresting officers were flummoxed. They left for Quincy to obtain further instruction from Illinois Governor Thomas Carlin. Meanwhile, Marks proceeded to a hastily called city council meeting where he helped pass another supplementary *habeas corpus* law, expanding his power as

---

46. John C. Bennett, "Further Mormon Developments!! 2d Letter From Gen. Bennett," *SJ*, 2.

47. "Ordinance, 5 July 1842–A, as Published in the Wasp–B," 3, JSP. See also John S. Dinger, "Joseph Smith and the Development of Habeas Corpus in Nauvoo, 1841–44," 135–71.

48. "Illinois vs. Joseph Smith and O. P. Rockwell, on habeas corpus, 1842 August 8," 1, CHL.

49. "Illinois vs. Joseph Smith and O. P. Rockwell," 1.

an associate judge in the municipal court.⁵⁰ In addition to allowing inquiry into the procedures utilized in obtaining an arrest warrant, the new Nauvoo ordinance authorized the municipal court to hear the merits of the entire case. If the court determined that the warrant had been issued "either through private pique, malicious intent, religious or other persecution, falsehood, or misrepresentation," they could invalidate the warrant.⁵¹

In December 1842, after much back and forth regarding this case, Carlin's successor, Governor Thomas Ford, advised Joseph Smith that he should "submit to the laws and have a Judicial investigation of your rights." US District Attorney Justin Butterfield agreed and wrote to Smith that "the judges [of the Illinois Supreme Court] were unanimously of the opinion that you would be entitled to your discharge under a habeas corpus to be issued by the Supreme Court, but felt some delicacy in advising Governor Ford to revoke the order issued by Governor Carlin." He further advised Smith to "come here without delay," and told him he would "stand by you, and see you safely delivered from your arrest."⁵²

Smith accordingly traveled to Springfield, Illinois, on December 27, with Marks and several other trusted associates.⁵³ When they arrived, Smith's attorney petitioned Judge Nathaniel Pope, of the District Court of the United States for the State of Illinois, for a writ of *habeas corpus*. Pope issued the writ and set a time for a hearing on January 2, 1843. The trial was held on January 4. Marks was one of the witnesses called on behalf of Smith.⁵⁴ An affidavit was filed stating Smith was not in Missouri at the time of Boggs's assassination attempt. It stated that "these deponents Hiram Smith, Willard Richards, & William Marks were with the Said Smith at his dwelling house, in Nauvoo, on and during the evening of the

---

50. "Proceedings," 98–99, CHL.

51. "Ordinance, 8 August 1842," 2, JSP. In regard to his arrest, Smith stated, "It is absolutely certain that the whole business is—another glaring ^instance^ of the effects of prejudice ^against me as a religious teacher^ and that it proceeds from a persecuting spirit, the parties have signified their determination to have me taken to Missouri, whether by legal or illegal means." "History, 1838–1856, volume D-1 [1 August 1842–1 July 1843]," 1364, JSP.

52. "Journal, December 1841–December 1842," 215, JSP.

53. Richard Lyman Bushman, *Joseph Smith: Rough Stone Rolling*, 479.

54. "Account of Hearing, 4 January 1843 [Extradition of JS for Accessory to Assault]," 50, JSP.

fifth day of May last."⁵⁵ This was the same day that Marks, with others, administered the endowment ceremony to Joseph and Hyrum.⁵⁶

The day after the trial, Pope ruled that the warrant was improper and ordered that Smith be discharged. Marks then accompanied the prophet back to Nauvoo. Although Marks's testimony was immaterial due to the warrant being ruled improper, his staunch loyalty was evident. After returning home from Springfield, on January 11, Smith invited all his most trusted friends to "a dinner party at my house on Wednesday next, at 10 in the morning" to show his appreciation.⁵⁷

Regardless of the District Court's findings, cases involving Smith and the shooting of Boggs continued to be pressed by Missouri. In his capacity as an associate justice of the Municipal Court of Nauvoo, Marks was frequently involved. Because Smith invoked *habeas corpus* whenever he was arrested, he would be brought before the Nauvoo Municipal Court to hear the case first. On one of these occasions, the municipal court convened on June 30, 1843, with Marks serving as president *pro tempore*.⁵⁸ Joseph H. Reynolds, a law enforcement officer from Jackson County, Missouri, had arrested Smith the previous week. Still acting as the presiding judge on July 1, Marks heard testimony from Hyrum Smith, Parley P. Pratt, Brigham Young, George W. Pitkin, Lyman Wight, and Sidney Rigdon. These witnesses stated that Joseph Smith had not committed treason or murder in Missouri.⁵⁹ However, Smith addressed a technicality in the warrant, which was directed to "Joseph Smith, Junior." Smith had been using the title "Joseph Smith, Senior" ever since his father had died in 1840, and said the warrant was not addressed to him. Both arguments seemed persuasive to Marks and the other members of the court. They ordered that "the said Joseph Smith Senior be discharged from the said arrest and imprisonment complained of in said Petition." Smith was released "for

---

55. "Wilson Law and Others, Affidavit, 4 January 1843, Willard Richards Copy [Extradition of JS for Accessory to Assault]," 29, JSP.

56. Devery S. Anderson and Gary James Bergera, *Joseph Smith's Quorum of the Anointed, 1842–1845, A Documentary History*, 7–11.

57. "History Draft [1 January–3 March 1843]," 8, JSP.

58. "Nauvoo Mayor's Court docket book, 1841 October–1843 February," 55, CHL.

59. See, for example, the testimony of Brigham Young before the municipal court: "Judicial Proceedings: Municipal Court, Brigham Young, testimony, 1843 July 1," 4, CHL.

want of substance in the Warrant upon which he was arrested as well as upon the merits of said Case," and allowed to leave without delay.[60]

The Nauvoo Municipal Court eventually passed seven expanded and powerful *habeas corpus* ordinances in Nauvoo. There were provisions in these ordinances meant to protect their citizens and present major hurdles for arresting officers. One imposed a penalty of between five hundred and one thousand dollars or an imprisonment of between six and twelve months for attempting "through any false pretext to take or intimidate any of the inhabitants of this City."[61] One provision addressed double jeopardy, stating: "No Person or Persons Who have been discharged by Order of the Municipal Court on a habeas Corpus, shall be again imprisoned, restrained, or kept in custody for the same cause."[62] A penalty of "one thousand Dollars" could be placed upon anyone who arrested or detained a prisoner for a writ the court had already discharged.[63] The municipal court hoped that this would end Missouri's attempts to arrest Smith and Rockwell because the evidence had already been reviewed and found wanting.[64] Imprisonments or penalties could be imposed upon officers who attempted to avoid the jurisdiction of the municipal court. However, Smith continued to be harassed by "vexatious law suits" founded upon these same charges.[65]

The situation came to a climax when Daniel Avery, who was convicted of stealing a horse in Missouri, returned to Nauvoo after several days of being detained in Missouri. He told a horrific tale of being abducted from Illinois at the point of guns and bowie knives and being chained in jail

---

60. "Judicial Proceedings: Municipal Court; People vs. Joseph Smith, on habeas corpus, 1843 June 30, 1843 July 1," 26, CHL. While this may seem a dishonest ploy to some, it should be noted that the last time he signed a letter with Jr. was in July 1840. Of the forty-three known letters written by Joseph Smith or directed to be written by Joseph Smith after July 1840, he never signed or used Jr. See Dean C. Jesse, *Personal Writings of Joseph Smith*, 515–635.

61. "Nauvoo City Council Minute Book, 1841–1845," 122, JSP.

62. "Nauvoo City Council Minute Book, 1841–1845," 125, JSP.

63. "Nauvoo City Council Minute Book, 1841–1845," 127–28, JSP.

64. This ordinance did contain exceptions under which a person could be retried. If more evidence subsequently came to light, or if a defendant was let go on a technicality ("discharged for any illegality in the . . . Process" or neglect of "any of the forms required by law"), the suspect could be detained a second time if the process and forms were redone properly.

65. "Nauvoo City Council Minute Book, 1841–1845," 191, JSP.

while his son was forced to testify against him under duress.[66] Fearing that Smith would easily be susceptible to the same treatment, the city council called a special session on December 8, 1843, to prepare "for any invasion from Missouri." The court passed an extremely harsh "Special Ordinance in the Prophet's Case, vs. Missouri," stating:

> if any person or persons shall come with process, demand, or requisition, founded upon the aforesaid Missouri difficulties, to arrest said Joseph Smith, he or they so offending shall be subject to be arrested by any officer of the city, with or without process, and tried by the Municipal Court, upon testimony, and, if found guilty, sentenced to imprisonment in the city prison for life: which convict or convicts can only be pardoned by the Governor, with the consent of the Mayor of said city.[67]

The fear and frustration of the city council is evident in its proceedings of this day. Area newspapers vigorously criticized the "Special Ordinance," as well as other *habeas corpus* acts passed by Marks and his fellow councilmen, to the point of calling for repeal of the Nauvoo Charter.[68] After several weeks of reflection upon the undue severity and probable unconstitutional nature of a life imprisonment sentence for an arresting officer, the council did repeal the ordinance on February 12, 1844.[69]

While most of the cases heard by the municipal court involved *habeas corpus*, Marks also presided over cases involving other ordinances passed by the Nauvoo City Council. Just as he had as the leader of the high council, he heard many cases dealing with slander in the municipal court. On November 30, 1842, Joseph Smith brought a complaint before Marks, claiming that Amos Davis did "at Divers other times previous to that time, and before the commencement of this Suit, make use of ^indecent,

---

66. "Affidavit from Daniel Avery, 28 December 1843," 1–10, JSP.
67. "Nauvoo City Council Minute Book, 1841–1845," 192, JSP.
68. See the *Davenport Gazette* 3, no. 23, Whole No. 127 (Jan. 25, 1844): 2. "The Mormons have recently, held a meeting at Nauvoo, at which they resolved that Joe Smith is not guilty of any charge made against him by the State of Missouri. The city of authorities have passed an ordinance, directing the imprisonment for life, of any person who shall come within the corporate limits of Nauvoo, with a legal process for the arrest of Joe Smith, for an offense committed by him in this State during the Mormon difficulties. The prophet Joe has also considers it his duty, as Lieut. General of the Nauvoo Legion and of Militia of Illinois, to enforce said ordinance." This same paper also in regard to Smith's untouchable status stated he was "protected by that immaculate body the Nauvoo Municipal Court." *Davenport Gazette* 2, no. 52, Whole No. 104 (Aug. 17, 1843): 3.
69. "Nauvoo City Council Minute Book, 1841–1845," 203, JSP.

unbecoming, abusive and ridiculous^ language concerning the Acts and Character of Deponent, contrary to the Ordinances of said City."⁷⁰ Marks served as the president *pro tem* of the municipal court for the trial. Multiple witnesses were examined and cross examined, and Amos Davis was found guilty by the court, whereas he was "fined, to pay a sum of fifty Dollars, and full Costs ^of suit^ and that he also enter into a recognizance in a sum of Two hundred Dollars, to keep the peace and be of good behavior."⁷¹

Marks thus helped pass and enforce the laws of the new city in his roles as municipal court judge and alderman on the city council. He helped govern the church in his role as stake president and member of the high council. Another group with which Marks was affiliated took part in making and executing laws in the city: the Nauvoo Court Martial, consisting of the Nauvoo Legion's commissioned officers.

The Nauvoo Charter had authorized the creation of a military body or militia when it was adopted in December 1840. Thus, the Nauvoo Legion was formed to defend the city "against misrule[,] anarchy[,] and mob violence." By forming their own militia, the Saints sought "to control the county's existing militia structure to preclude a recurrence of the violence experienced three years earlier at the hands of the Missouri militia."⁷² Under the Nauvoo Charter, the Nauvoo Legion's Court Martial was similar in many respects to other local militias, serving as judge and sometimes as jury. One unique provision in the Nauvoo Charter was the authority it gave the court martial to operate as a law-making unit. "The commissioned officers of the Legion, who comprised the court, used this legislative right regularly."⁷³

Marks was not a part of the court martial, but he did hold an officers' position in the Nauvoo Legion. In July of 1841, twelve assistant chaplains were appointed, with six to each cohort. Eleven of these assistant chaplains were drawn from the Quorum of the Twelve, and the remaining one was Marks.⁷⁴ These chaplains held the rank of Major and were commissioned

---

70. "Complaint, 30 November 1842 [City of Nauvoo v. Davis for Slander of JS–C]," 1, JSP.

71. "Docket Entry, between 30 November and circa 3 December 1842 [City of Nauvoo v. Davis for Slander of JS–C]," 13, JSP.

72. Richard L. Saunders, "Officers and Arms: The 1843 General Return of the Nauvoo Legion's Second Cohort," 141.

73. John Sweeney, Jr., "A History of the Nauvoo Legion in Illinois," 13.

74. "Officers of the Nauvoo Legion," 1, CHL; Sweeney, "A History of the Nauvoo Legion in Illinois," 48. Members of the Twelve assigned as assistant

officers.⁷⁵ There were an abundance of officers who formed the Nauvoo Legion, and their military obligations were fairly demanding, necessitating time commitments for drills, parades, and mock battles, which were held frequently. Fines were levied for those who did not attend. At a court martial on October 21, 1843, one of the participants motioned that "every officer who wishes to withdraw may be allowed to do so." The motion was seconded, but the chair, Major General A.P. Rockwood simply ruled, "No."⁷⁶

In addition to his other heavy church and civic responsibilities, Marks was appointed a regent of the University of Nauvoo,⁷⁷ a small board that ran the public education system in Nauvoo at the university, seminary (high school), and common school levels.⁷⁸ Impetus for developing a comprehensive school system likely came from John C. Bennett, who had already incorporated medical schools, universities, and a Christian college in the states of Virginia, Indiana, and Ohio. His unorthodox methods (such as awarding "mail order" degrees) won him criticism, but his experience in inaugurating educational organizations when he arrived in Nauvoo is undeniable. As one of twenty-three men on the board of regents, Marks gained valuable experience in setting up a broad and comprehensive system for hiring, certifying, and compensating teachers, planning curriculum, and developing structure for delivering education to a majority of Nauvoo's population.

William Marks was one of Joseph Smith's most reliable and trustworthy associates throughout the Nauvoo years. His experience as the bishop's agent, high council member, and stake president during the gathering period in Kirtland made him an adept leader during Nauvoo's expansion. He assisted the immigrants in settling into their new homes and helped to keep order as the city boomed. More work was ahead for this staunch devotee, as he began to be drawn into the exclusive network of Smith's closest followers.

---

chaplains were Brigham Young, Heber C. Kimball, Parley P. Pratt, Orson Pratt, Orson Hyde, John Taylor, Wilford Woodruff, William Smith, Willard Richards, John E. Page, and George A. Smith. William Marks was chosen as the twelfth assistant chaplain instead of Apostle Lyman Wight, the newest member of the Quorum who had been ordained in April 1841.

75. Saunders, "Officers and Arms," 149–50; Sweeney, "A History of the Nauvoo Legion in Illinois," 198.

76. "Proceedings, 1842–1844," 42, CHL.

77. Dinger, *Nauvoo Minutes*, 7; "Nauvoo City Council Proceedings," 4, CHL.

78. Susan E. Black, Harvey B. Black, and Sarah Allen, "The University of the City of Nauvoo, 1841–1845," 5–8.

CHAPTER 5

The Ties that Bind

William Marks was a mature forty-eight years old and had established a home in Nauvoo by the time of the 1840 United States census. His wife Rosannah was forty-five, and their children ranged in age from mid-childhood to adulthood. Still at home were Llewellyn, 8; William Jr., 10, Sophia, 11; and Ira Goodrich, 15.[1] Henry and Ephraim were young men of nineteen and twenty-two respectively, and they had remained with the family in their migration to Missouri and Nauvoo. Lafayette, twenty-four, had married in New York, but he and his wife Martha had also stayed with the family during their travels. They were living in their own household in Nauvoo. The Markses' oldest daughter, twenty-six-year-old Lucy Ann, married Henry McHenry in 1832, before the family became acquainted with the church. Daughter Mary Eliza, now seventeen, married John Skidmore at a very young age while still in Kirtland. Both married daughters moved to Caldwell County, Missouri, with their husbands before the rest of the Marks family and remained there after the Mormon expulsion.[2] William was beginning to see the scattering of his family.

Some of the poignant feelings of seeing loved ones die or move away must have been shared by Marks's leader and prophet. Joseph Smith was younger than Marks by over a decade, but he had experienced the loss of several children. The disaffection of many of his trusted followers pained him. Smith now engaged in building a theology that took gathering a step

---

1. "United States Census, 1840," Hancock Co., Illinois, entry for Woodrum Marks. This census was taken in March 1841 in Nauvoo. The Marks family is also enumerated in a list of church members living in the Fourth Ward in Nauvoo on February 12, 1942. William and Rosannah Marks were living with five of their children: Ephraim, Goodrich, Sophia, William, and Llewellen. This home was located close to the river, across the street from the Joseph Smith family residence. Nauvoo Fourth Ward, Record of Membership, 1842.

2. "United States Census, 1840," Caldwell Co., Missouri. The Henry McHenry family and the John Skidmore family are both enumerated in the 1840 Blythe, Caldwell County census. John Skidmore was the new Caldwell County sheriff in March 1839. "Introduction to Boosinger v. JS et al. and Boosinger v. O. Cowdery et al.," JSP. Henry McHenry was in Missouri by October 21, 1838, when he was witness to arson. See "Indictment, circa 10 April 1839 [State of Missouri v. Gates et al. for Arson]," 4, JSP.

further—to bind close friends and family together in life and after death. Marks became part of a complex system of fraternal, ecclesiastical, and civil organizations uniquely crafted to encourage loyalty and affection, not only among their members, but specifically to their charismatic leader.

The Nauvoo Legion was one of these organizations. In many ways, it still retained ties with the "Daughters of Zion," or Danites, a quasi-military group that bound its members with secret tokens and oaths.[3] Drawing its name from several scriptural references,[4] the group had protected the Saints in violent vigilante fashion throughout the Missouri period. Though Smith retained plausible deniability, it is evident that he and other top Mormon leaders were the driving force behind the Danites' existence.[5] Smith con-

---

3. Sampson Avard gave testimony that "it was stated by Joseph Smith, jr., that it was necessary this band should be bound together by a covenant, that those who revealed the secrets of the society should be put to death. The covenant taken by all the Danite band was as follows, to wit: They declared, holding up their right hand, 'In the name of Jesus Christ, the Son of God, I do solemnly obligate myself ever to conceal and never to reveal the secret purposes of this society, called the Daughters of Zion. Should I ever do the same, I hold my life as the forfeiture.'" *Document Containing the Correspondence, Orders, &c, in Relation to the Disturbances with the Mormons; and the Evidence Given Before the Hon. Austin A. King*, 97.

4. The Old Testament uses "daughter of Zion" symbolically to refer to the covenant people. In Micah 4:8–13, the daughter of Zion is delivered from her enemies and told to "arise and thresh . . . and thou shalt beat in pieces many people." For more information on the provenance of the various appellations of the Danites, see Cheryl L. Bruno, Joe Steve Swick III, and Nicholas S. Literski, *Method Infinite*, 202–10.

5. Though he rejects Eli Norton's accusation about Danites in the city council meeting, Smith takes credit for their name and existence as a defensive force: "The Danite system alluded to by Norton never had any existence; it was a term made use of by some of the brethren in Far West and grew out of an expression I made use of when the brethren were preparing to defend themselves from the Missouri mob in reference to the stealing of Macaiah's images (Judges chap: 18,) if the enemy comes the Danites will be after them, meaning the brethren in self-defence." "History, 1838–1856, volume E-1 [1 July 1843–30 April 1844]," 1853, JSP. See also the crossed-out entry in Joseph Smith's journal entry for July 27, 1838. "They have come up hither Thus far, according to the ord[e]r of the Dan-Ites, we have a company of Danites in these times, to put to rights physically that which is not righ[t], and to cle[a]nse the Church of verry great evils which hath hitherto existed among us, inasmuch as they cannot be put to rights by teachings & persuaysons, This company or a part of them exibited on the fourth

ferred top leadership ranks in the Legion to men who were known Danites in Missouri. For example, Hosea Stout, clerk to the high council, was an active Danite vigilante. In the Nauvoo Legion, Marks was both colonel and captain of a battalion company, to whom Stout taught a particular maneuver known as "the old Missouri Danite drill."[6]

Freemasonry, the quintessential oath-bound organization, was another way Joseph Smith could forge binding ties with his brethren in the church.[7] On December 29, 1841, eighteen Mormon Freemasons in the city of Nauvoo, including Hyrum Smith and John C. Bennett, met to elect officers for a Masonic Lodge in the city. By the time of its official installation on March 15, 1842, the incipient lodge had brought together over forty men who had previously been raised Master Masons in other places—a core group that already surpassed the membership of any other lodge in the state. Smith maintained a high level of interest and activity in the Nauvoo Lodge in the remaining years of his life. His brother, Hyrum, was Master of the Lodge from November 1842 until his death, presiding over the initiation of hundreds of Mormon Freemasons.

William Marks and his son Ephraim were in the first group to petition for membership in Nauvoo Lodge U. D., along with other community leaders.[8] Marks was initiated, passed, and raised on April 20–22, 1842. He attended three meetings of the lodge in May, then again on January 31 and February 1, 1843, the dates of a trial for his brother-in-law George Robinson's Masonic membership. Similarly, Marks's twenty-one-year-old son, Henry, petitioned the lodge on May 19, 1842, received degrees on June 14–18, 1842, and attended six additional meetings in June and July 1842.

---

day of July[.] They come up to consecrate, by companies of tens, commanded by their Captain over ten." "Journal, March–September 1838," 61, JSP.

6. Juanita Brooks, ed., *On the Mormon Frontier: The Diary of Hosea Stout, 1844–1861*, 1:141, 197.

7. See a discussion of this in Bruno, Swick, and Literski, *Method Infinite*, 362–63.

8. Apostles Brigham Young and William Smith, Bishop Vinson Knight, Alderman and Justice of the Peace Samuel Smith, City Marshall Dimick B. Huntington, and others were in the first group of petitioners. On December 30, 1841, and February 3 and 17, 1842—all dates which occurred before the official installation—the Nauvoo Lodge accepted fifty-seven petitions for membership into the Masonic order. Most of these were rewritten into a second, official minute book under the later date of March 17, 1842. Ephraim's name was not included on this second list, even though he had petitioned, been investigated and cleared, and was balloted for and accepted for membership. This gives insight into when the recopying was done; probably after the date of Ephraim's death on April 7, 1842.

Tragedy struck the Marks family when William and Rosannah's son Ephraim died at age twenty-four on April 7, 1842. Joseph Smith spoke at Ephraim's funeral and seemed moved by the sad event, which reminded him of his own brother's death eight months earlier. Don Carlos Smith, who was the same age as Ephraim, had succumbed to malarial fever. "It has been hard for me to live on earth & see those young men upon whom we have leaned upon as a support & comfort taken from us in the midst of their youth. . . . When we loose [sic] a near & dear friend upon whom we have set our hearts we can never feel the same afterwards," said Smith. Reflecting upon his own mortality, he stated: "It may be the case with me as well as you. Some has supposed that Br. Joseph could not die but this is a mistake." Although at times he had been promised he would live to complete certain tasks, "having accomplish[ed] those things I have not at present any lease of my life & am as liable to die as other men."[9]

Sidney Rigdon spoke next, saying "that the death of this young man had made a vacancy in his heart that nothing could fill up till it was filled by restoring the society of the same person in eternity." Rigdon also preached on happiness, remarking, "when we see a principle that makes us the most Happy if we will cultivate that principle & practice it ourselves it will render others Happy for that course of conduct that pleases you will please others."[10] Smith would seemingly ponder upon these remarks and write his own "happiness letter" a short while later.[11]

Ephraim Marks's body was conveyed to the grave in solemn silence. As each person passed by, they dropped a branch of evergreen into the grave.[12] The dropping of an evergreen branch, representing the sprig of acacia in the Hiram Abiff legend, was a cherished part of Masonic funerals. It accompanied a recitation found in the closing sentences of the monitorial lecture of the Third Degree: "This evergreen is an emblem of our faith in the immortality of the soul. By this we are reminded that we have an immortal part within us, which shall survive the grave, and which

---

9. "Wilford Woodruff Journal, 1838 January–1839 December," April 9, 1842, CHL.

10. "Wilford Woodruff Journal," April 9, 1842, CHL.

11. "6th Letter From Gen. Bennett," *SJ*, 2. See also "Discourse, 5 January 1841, as Reported by William Clayton," 7–8. Susan Staker discusses Smith's language of happiness in Susan Staker, "A Matter of Many Wives: Joseph Smith's Courting in Secret Nauvoo," 11n15.

12. "Discourse, 9 April 1842, as Reported by Wilford Woodruff," 145, JSP.

shall never, never, never die."[13] Mourner Helen Mar Kimball Smith later remembered that Don Carlos Smith's funeral also contained military and Masonic elements.[14]

* * *

In the early 1840s, several of Joseph Smith's followers began to learn about another plan he had for cementing earthly and eternal relationships: celestial plural marriage. It is not clear exactly when Smith began to experiment with marital relationships. Certainly there were already rumors connecting Mormons' ideas about community property with sexual relationships as early as Kirtland (as mentioned in chapter 1).[15] Smith's

---

13. From the Master Mason funeral service. Waldemar Malmene, *The Freemason's Hymnal: A Collection of Original and Selected Hymns, Odes, and Songs for the use of Lodges, Chapters, and Commanderies*, 56. The elements of Masonic funeral services present at Ephraim Marks's burial argue strongly that he had received at least the first degree of Entered Apprentice before his death.

14. Helen Mar Whitney, "Scenes in Nauvoo," *WE*, 42. "A few days after their return to Nauvoo the Prophet's brother Don Carlos died, and being an officer in the legion as well as a Freemason he was buried with Masonic and military rites. Those of the Masonic fraternity marched next to the family to the grave which was in a little grove at the foot of the hill southwest of the temple." What Helen remembers as the Masonic fraternity may have been the Nauvoo Legion, since the Masonic Lodge had not yet been organized at the time of Don Carlos's funeral. However, there were many Freemasons in Nauvoo already, so it is possible. Additionally, Masonic elements could very well have made up parts of the ceremony, as they did Ephraim Marks's.

15. The 1835 Doctrine and Covenants 101:4 states: "Inasmuch as this church of Christ has been reproached with the crime of fornication, and polygamy: we declare that we believe, that one man should have one wife; and one woman, but one husband, except in the case of death, when either is at liberty to marry again." "Statement on Marriage, circa August 1835," 251–52, JSP. This statement denies the allegation but demonstrates that rumors were already circulating. For earlier accusations see Levi Lewis's affidavit citation concerning Eliza Winters in 1827–1829. Lewis said that he was "acquainted with Joseph Smith Jr. and Martin Harris, and that he has heard them both say, [that] adultery was no crime. Harris said he did not blame Smith for his attempt to seduce Eliza Winters." E. D. Howe, *Mormonism Unvailed*, 268. Clark Braden (b. 1831) in a debate with RLDS missionary E. L. Kelly fifty-two years later stated: "In March 1832, Smith was stopping at Mr. Johnson's, in Hiram, Ohio, and was mobbed. The mob was led by Eli Johnson, who blamed Smith for being too intimate with his sister Marinda."

romance with Fanny Alger was discussed in high council meetings in Far West, Missouri, while Marks was still in Ohio. At that time, Smith seemed successful in discrediting the whistleblower, Oliver Cowdery, calming the high councilors' concerns for a time.[16]

Marks did not directly confront the issue of polygamy among fellow church members until 1841. On February 6 of that year, Theodore Turley, a married man with seven children, was brought before the high council with shocking allegations. Turley was accused of "romping and kissing the females and dancing" while at sea on a ship bringing a group of converts to the United States from England.[17] Further, he was charged with "sleeping with two females coming up the Lake and on the road to Dixon's Ferry." Turley allegedly said "that Brother Joseph would not hear any thing" the accusers said against him, "for he [Joseph] was of the same spirit and . . . the same Priesthood."[18] The case was sufficiently serious that six councilmen were appointed to speak, three on each side. The charges were sustained. Marks told Turley that if he wanted to retain his membership, he must confess publicly as well as to the high council. After Turley

---

Marinda was actually Eli's sixteen-year-old niece, daughter of John Johnson. Edmund L. Kelley and Clark Braden, *Public Discussion of the Issues between the RLDS Church and the Church of Christ (Disciples) Held in Kirtland, Ohio*, 202.

16. On November 7, 1837, Smith first told members of the high council who brought up "a matter between Oliver Cowdery, Thomas B. Marsh and myself" that "our settlement of the affair should be sufficient for the Council." "History, 1838–1856, volume B-1 [1 September 1834–2 November 1838]," 775, JSP. For more on Fanny Alger, see "History, 1838–1856, volume B-1 [1 September 1834–2 November 1838]," 775, JSP; Oliver Cowdery, letter to Warren A. Cowdery, January 21, 1838, HHL; Thomas B. Marsh, "Dear Brother, We Lament that Such Foul and False Reports Should Be Circulated," *EJ*, 45–46; Oliver Cowdery, letter to Joseph Smith, January 21, 1838, HHL; History, 1838–1856, volume B-1 [1 September 1834–2 November 1838]," 775, JSP; "Minute Book 2," April 12, 1838, 118–26, JSP.

17. "Minutes, 1840 March 8–1842 May 20," 25, CHL.

18. "Minutes, 1840 March 8–1842 May 20," 26, CHL. Turley and Joseph Smith were close friends. In 1841, the Turleys lived three doors down from Smith, next to his mother, Lucy Mack Smith. "United States Census, 1840," Hancock County, Illinois, taken in March 1841. Note that Turley researcher Mary Ann Clements finds this early connection with Theodore Turley and polygamy tenuous, and considers that the more serious charge against Turley by the high council had to do with mismanagement of money on the trip.

made his confession to the council, he boldly said "that he would rejoice in the opportunity of making the like confession before the publick."[19]

The situation of one of the women named in the Turley case, Mary Clift, became more complicated in August 1842, when her ward teacher, Elisha Everett, discovered she was pregnant. Before the high council, Everett accused Gustavus Hills, another married man and a professor of music at Nauvoo University, of "illicit intercourse" with Clift. Hills had asserted "that the heads of the Church practised such conduct & that the time would come when men would have more wives than one." On September 4, minutes state that the high council read Clift's affidavit, in which she testified that Hills offered to provide money for an abortion and that "the authorities of the Church countenanced and practiced illicit connexion with women & said there was no harm in such things provided they kept it secret."[20] Church member Esther Smith also gave evidence that Hills "told her it was lawful for people to hold illicit intercourse if they only held their peace" and that this was the practice of some of the leading men and heads of the church.[21] The high council unanimously disfellowshipped Hills, though he was soon restored to fellowship and he continued to serve on the Nauvoo City Court. Mary's father, Robert Clift, sued Hills in a paternity suit in September, and the city court ordered Hills to pay child support for the first three years of Mary's child's life.[22] The baby, Jason, was born in October 1842, but died a year later. Turley, one of the earliest polygamists, likely married Mary Ann Clift and her sister Sarah Ellen, on April 26, 1844, within Joseph Smith's lifetime. Turley later married a third sister, Eliza Clift.[23] In a family record book, Turley recorded his 1846 sealing to Mary in the Nauvoo Temple and identified her child as "Jason Turley."[24]

---

19. "Minutes, 1840 March 8–1842 May 20," 26, CHL.

20. "Nauvoo Stake High Council papers, 1840 October–1842 November," 53, 55, 57, CHL.

21. "Minutes, 1842 May 20–1843 February 19," 8–10, CHL.

22. "Paternity suit of Mary Clift vs. Gustavus Hills, Robert Clift agent for Mary Clift, September 15, 1842."

23. If this date is correct, it makes Turley's the first Mormon polygamous marriage after Joseph Smith's. See Mary Ann Turley Clements, "Mary Clift Turley," transcribed in Ann Laemmlen Lewis, "Death of Mary Clift Turley, wife of Theodore, 30 March 1850, Salt Lake City."

24. See a scan of this family record in Lewis, "Death of Mary Clift Turley."

On April 22, 1842, Jesse Turpin appealed his conviction from the Quorum of Seventies for "having married another man's wife." The high council heard the case and ruled that the evidence was only circumstantial. Turpin was "restored to his former fellowship and official standing in the Church."²⁵

By this time, allegations were circulating in Nauvoo and throughout Illinois that Smith and the mayor, John C. Bennett, were involved in polygamy and running a brothel.²⁶ Smith had indeed married between seven and twelve women and had taught the principle of plural marriage to several others.²⁷ However, he carefully denied his involvement in "illicit immorality." On May 14, 1842 the Nauvoo City Council, with Marks present, passed "An Ordinance concerning Brothels and disorderly Characters," which criminalized not only prostitution but also adultery and fornication. Specifically, it stated that for every proven act of adultery or fornication (with the individual's own acknowledgment admissible as evidence), "the Parties shall be imprisoned Six Months, and fined, each, in the Sum of from five hundred to fifty thousand Dollars."²⁸ Adultery and fornication were not defined by the statute, but they did have a common definition at the time. Adultery was "the unfaithfulness of any married person to the marriage bed," while fornication was "incontinence or lewd-

---

25. "Minutes, 1840 March 8–1842 May 20," 41–42, CHL. Besides appealing to the high council, Turpin had written a letter to LDS Apostle Wilford Woodruff "wishing to [ap]peal his case to the Twelve for a rehearing as he had been cut of[f] from the Church." "Wilford Woodruff journal, 1841 January–1842 December," October 11, 1841, CHL.

26. While there is no evidence tying Joseph Smith to a brothel, the same cannot be said for John C. Bennett. Years later, Francis Higbee testified that Bennett had introduced him to "a woman on the hill," with whom Higbee had sex. "Municipal Court," *TS*, 538–40. Further, in testimony in the famous Temple Lot Case, John Taylor (not the LDS church president) testified that Bennett had run a brothel in Nauvoo and that the authorities had pushed it off a cliff into a gully. However, this is probably confused with later legends of a grocery-store "grog shop" that was destroyed in 1841.

27. George D. Smith, *Nauvoo Polygamy: "…but we called it celestial marriage,"* 621–22; Brian C. Hales, *Joseph Smith's Polygamy, Volume 1: History,* 259; Gary James Bergera, "Identifying the Earliest Mormon Polygamists, 1841–44," 1. George D. Smith found that Joseph had married twelve women at this time, while Brian Hales believes the number is seven or eight. Gary Bergera finds he had married ten women by this date.

28. "Ordinance, 14 May 1842–A," 77, JSP.

ness of unmarried persons . . . [or] . . . the criminal conversation of a married man with an unmarried woman."[29]

Smith explained that the ordinance was intended "to suppress houses & acts of infamy in the city; for the protection of the innocent & virtuous & [for the] good of public morals" and said he demonstrated "clearly that there were certain characters in the place who were disposed to corrupt the morals & chastity of our citizens."[30]

Belying his efforts to preserve morality in the city, Smith was implicated in several cases brought before the high council by Bishop George Miller in May. These closely followed John C. Bennett's resignation as mayor on May 17, 1842.[31] In a hearing beginning May 20, Chauncey Higbee was accused of "unchaste and un-virtuous conduct with the widow [Sarah] Miller and others." Twenty-six-year-old Sarah and sisters Margaret and Matilda Nyman testified that Higbee had seduced them with a story that Smith had taught him that "free intercourse" was right "if it was kept secret." The women also claimed Higbee "taught that Joseph Smith autherized [sic] him to practise these things."[32] The accusation is believable when juxtaposed with a public sermon Smith preached in November 1841:

> God will not accuse you. If you have no accuser, you will enter heaven, and if you will follow the Revelations and instructions which God gives you through me, I will take you into heaven as my back load. If you will not accuse me, I will not accuse you. If you will throw a cloak of charity over my sins, I will over yours—for charity covereth a multitude of sins. What many people call sin is not sin; I do many things to break down superstition, and I will break it down.[33]

However, Smith had also spoken against sexual immorality to the Nauvoo Choir of Singers, which Sarah Miller belonged to. In her testimony, which was edited and published in the *Nauvoo Neighbor* two years

---

29. Noah Webster, *Noah Webster's first edition of an American dictionary of the English language*, s.v. "adultery." There was no American legal dictionary in print at the time this statute was passed.

30. "History, 1838–1856, volume C-1 [2 November 1838–31 July 1842]," 1331, JSP.

31. "Letters from John C. Bennett and James Sloan, 17 May 1842," 1, JSP.

32. "Minutes, 1842 May 20–1843 February 19," 1, CHL. At the end of the evidence, Hyrum Smith motioned that Chauncey "be expelled from the Church and the same be made publick." The high council followed Hyrum's motion and Chauncey was cut off.

33. "History, 1838–1856, volume C-1 Addenda," 20, JSP.

later, Miller explained that as a result of "brother Joseph Smith's teachings to the singers,"[34] she had become alarmed at the situation Higbee had led her into. He had reassured her "that Joseph now taught as he did through necessity, on account of the prejudices of the people, and his own family particularly, as they had not become believers in the doctrine." But she now publicly claimed that she realized "all of Chauncey's teachings had been false and that he had never been authorized by any one in authority to make any such communication to me."[35]

The Nyman sisters' testimonies were also edited and published in the *Nauvoo Neighbor*. They are remarkably formulaic, seemingly included in the local paper with the purpose of clearing Smith of any association with the affair.[36] Contemporary sexual slander laws in Illinois could have in-

---

34. Sarah Miller was part of a choir which met and rehearsed at the Joseph Smith home.

35. "Chauncy L. Higbee," *NN*, 3.

36. "Chauncy L. Higbee," *NN*, 3. Margaret Nyman stated, in part: "During the evening's interview, he [Chauncey], (as I have since learned) with wicked lies proposed that I should yield to his desires, and indulge in sexual intercourse with him, stating that such intercourse might be freely indulged in, and was no sin: That any respectable female might indulge in sexual intercourse, and there was no sin in it, providing the person so indulging, keep the same to herself; for there could be no sin, where there was no accuser—and most clandestinely, with wicked lies, persuaded me to yield by using the name of Joseph Smith: and as I have since learned, totally false and unauthorised; and in consequence of those arguments, I was influenced to yield to my Seducer, Chauncey L. Higbee. I further state that I have no personal acquaintance with Joseph Smith, and never heard him teach such doctrines, as stated by Chauncey L. Higbee, either directly or indirectly. I heartily repent before God, asking for the forgiveness of my brethren." Matilda Nyman testified: "During this spring Chauncy L. Higbee kept company with me from time to time and, as I have since learned, wickedly, deceitfully, and with lies in his mouth, urged me vehemently to yield to his desires; that there could be no wrong in having sexual intercourse with any female that could keep the same to herself—most villainously and lyingly stating that he had been so instructed by Joseph Smith, and that there was no sin where there was no accuser:—Also vowing he would marry me, Not succeeding he, on one occasion, brought one, who affirmed that such intercourse was tolerated by the heads of the Church. I have since found him also to be a lying conspirator against female virtue and chastity, having never received such teachings from the heads of the church; but I was at the time partially influenced to believe in consequence of the source from whom I received it . . . I repent before *God* and my brethren and ask forgiveness. I further testify that I never had any personal acquaintance with Joseph Smith and

fluenced the participants in this case to withdraw their accusations that Smith's teachings were invoked in Higbee's courting of the women. The Illinois Legislature passed a law in 1823 dealing with sexual slander that stated, "If any person shall falsely use, utter, or publish words, which in their common acceptation shall amount to charge any person with having been guilty of fornication, or adultery, such words so spoken shall be deemed actionable, and he, she or they, so falsely publishing, speaking or uttering the same shall be deemed guilty of slander."[37] This law, intended to protect female victims, used gender neutral language that allowed Smith to file a complaint against Higbee before Justice of the Peace Ebenezer Robinson on May 24, 1842.[38] Sarah Miller, Margaret J. Nyman, and Matilda Nyman were subpoenaed, and they attended the hearing and testified. The charge against Higbee was upheld.[39] This lawsuit would have had a deterring effect on those in Nauvoo who knew of Smith's involvement with polygamy.

While Smith's lawsuit on sexual slander was pending, Marks and the high council heard the other cases brought by Bishop George Miller. On May 25, 1842, Catherine Warren was charged with "unchaste and unvirtuous conduct with John C. Bennett and others."[40] Warren gave "the names of several others who had been guilty of having unlawful intercourse with her[,] stating that they taught the doctrine that it was right to have free intercourse with women and that the heads of the Church also taught and practised it."[41] The men she told the high council about

---

never heard him teach such doctrine as Higbee stated either directly or indirectly." These testimonies are remarkably similar to Clarissa Marvel's recanting before the Relief Society.

37. *The Revised Code of Laws of Illinois: Enacted by the Fifth General Assembly*, 521.

38. "Docket Book of Ebenezer Robinson," CHL. Though the affidavit is no longer extant, Robinson's docket book records that Higbee did "slander and defam[e] . . . the said Joseph Smith, and Emma Smith his wife, at sundry times, in the City of Nauvoo and county of Hancock." There is no evidence that Higbee ever slandered Emma, but she was probably included in the suit to win sympathy considering the paternal nature of the courts in Illinois regarding the sexual slander law.

39. Higbee was ordered to answer the lawsuit at the October 1842 term of the Hancock Circuit Court at Carthage, Illinois. However, there is no record of this suit appearing before that court. For more information on this case and others, see John Dinger, "Sexual Slander and Polygamy in Nauvoo," 1–22.

40. "Minutes, 1842 May 20–1843 February 19," 2, CHL.

41. "Minutes, 1842 May 20–1843 February 19," 3, CHL.

were John C. Bennett, Chauncey L. Higbee, Darwin Chase, Lyman O. Littlefield, Joel S. Miles, and George W. Thatcher.

Even though no evidence had been necessary at her trial because "she confessed to the charge . . . and did repent before God for what she had done and desired earnestly that the Council would forgive her," Warren wrote a heartbreaking testimony regarding the case. She stated that Bennett promised that if she became pregnant, "he said he would attend to that. I understood that he would give medicine to prevent it."[42] She also confessed that she had "unlawful connexion" with Higbee about five or six times, Higbee having "made propositions to keep me with food if I would submit to his desires." An extract of this testimony clearing Smith of directly teaching free intercourse was published in the *Nauvoo Neighbor*.

After the naming of names by Warren, charges were brought by the high council against Littlefield, Chase, and Miles on May 27, 1842, for unvirtuous conduct and teaching false doctrine. The clerk of the Nauvoo High Council, Hosea Stout, was circumspect in recording the details of these trials. He simply wrote that Littlefield and Miles "plead not Guilty," the charges were sustained, and the accused were disfellowshipped.[43] Wilford Woodruff, who filled in on May 27 for an absent high councilor expounded:

> The first Presidency The Twelve & High Council & virtuous part of the Church are making an exhertion abo[u]t these days to clense the Church from Adulterors fornicators & evil persons for their are such persons crept into our midst. The high council have held a number of meeting[s] of late & their researches have disclosed much iniquity & a number [have] been Cut off from the church. I met with the High Council to day on the trial of L[yman] O. Littlefield[,] Joel S Miles & Darwin Chase. The two former were cut of[f] for Adultery & the case of D[arwin] Chase was put of[f] till tomorrow.[44]

---

42. Catherine Warren, "Catherine Warren statement," dated May 25, 1842. This claim was supported by testimony of other deponents. For example, Sarah Miller testified regarding a possible pregnancy that "Chauny [Higbee] said there was no Danger <& that> Dr Bennt understood it & would come & take it away if there was any thing." Hyrum Smith also made these claims, but he was probably recounting what he learned at these hearings: "He [John C. Bennett] would give them medicine to produce abortions, providing they should become pregnant." Hyrum Smith, "Affidavit of Hyrum Smith," *TS*, 870–72.

43. "Minutes, 1842 May 20–1843 February 19," 3–4, CHL.

44. "Wilford Woodruff journal, 1841 January-1842 December," May 27, 1842, CHL.

Years later as a witness in the Temple Lot Case, Littlefield testified that although he never spoke of free intercourse with Smith personally, "the doctrine was talked of between myself, and a great many other parties, and always with the understanding that it had its origin, with Joseph Smith the prophet, himself."[45]

Chase's trial, held the next day, raises questions for the careful historian. In his case, the charge of unvirtuous conduct and teaching false doctrine was "not sustained":

> The President decided that he should be restored to full fellowship which was carried by a majority of 8 to 4. After which the case [was] spoken on by different ones of the Council to show further light on the subject and showing reasons why they did not aceede to the Presidents decisions. The President again called on the council to sanction his decision which was done unanimously.

It is difficult to ascertain who "the President" was in this case. Marks, serving as President of the High Council, was usually referred to simply as "President." Yet Smith often presided over the meetings and was named by his title, "President" of the church. Even President Hyrum Smith participated in high council meetings and could have been presiding in this case. This passage also raises the question of why "the President" did not sustain the charges against Chase, and why four of the councilors did not agree.

In studying the high council minutes, the reader can only speculate over the participants' discussions over the troublesome issue of polygamy. We do not know if Marks and the others on the council suspected that Smith had permitted or directed the defendants to engage in questionable sexual practices. Perhaps in an effort to protect Smith, the high council had publicly warned members against going to court with fellow Saints.[46] But the problems continued.

During this time there was additional tension between Marks and Smith over financial issues. On Monday, April 4, 1842, Smith's journal history states that he "closed a settlement with William Marks in the counting room. And paid him off, principal and interest to the last farthing for all that myself or the Church had had of him."[47] The use of the phrase "to the last farthing" seems to reveal some animosity on Smith's

---

45. "United States testimony 1892," 149, CHL.

46. "The High Council of the Church of Jesus Christ, to the Saints of Nauvoo, Greeting," *TS*, 700.

47. "History, 1838–1856, volume C-1 [2 November 1838–31 July 1842]," 1313, JSP. See also "History Draft [1 January–30 June 1842]," 8, JSP.

part, as well as evidence that Marks had been pressuring the prophet for the repayment of a debt during a time when ready cash was difficult to come by. Apparently Smith had not been as prompt in his repayment of that debt as Marks would have liked.[48] Following the large land purchases the church and its leaders made in Illinois and Iowa, ready cash was hard to come by for several years. A letter from Smith to Horace Hotchkiss, one of the sellers, illuminates the situation.

On August 25, 1841, Smith reminded Hotchkiss of his verbal agreement not to charge interest on the property for five years. Smith revealed that even though he knew that the land was inhospitable—a "deathly sickly hole"—he had "been keeping up appearances, and holding out inducements to encourage immigration, that we scarcely think justifiable, in consequence of the Mortality that almost invariably awaits those who come from far distant parts." In order to meet the payments, Smith and other church leaders were strongly promoting gathering to Nauvoo, with as much a mercenary motive as a spiritual one. Smith berated Hotchkiss for goading him "to meet the payment of the extortionate sum, that you exacted for the land we had of you."[49] He felt the same about Marks's insistence that he pay back the smaller debt owed him.

Even in Nauvoo, Marks had not lost his business acumen. At times, his tendency to place financial concerns first and foremost may have placed him in a questionable spot for a religious leader. On February 17, 1842, for example, the city council resolved that members of the council could resign their pay to "a poor Fund, to be appropriated hereafter for the benefit of the Poor of the City of Nauvoo." Many of the council members made the choice to do so, but Marks declined.[50] Nonetheless, Marks was widely respected for his foresight and financial success.

---

48. Robert D. Hutchins, *President William E. Marks . . . A Man Forgotten*, 17.

49. "Letter to Horace Hotchkiss, 25 August 1841, Copy," 2, JSP. See also "Letter to the Saints Abroad, 24 May 1841," 434, JSP.

50. "The Vice Mayor, Councillors B[righam] Young, W[illard] Richards, H[eber] C. Kimball & W[ilford] Woodruff Assigned their Fees as Councillors for the City, in favor of the City, until further Notice. Ald[er]m[a]n [Samuel H.] Smith resigned up his Fees for the past Year. Co[unci]l[o]r Wilson Law resigned his Claim to pay [compensation], as a City Councillor, up to this time, in favour of the Blind Inhabitants of the fourth Ward of this City, to be equally divided amongst them. Co[unci]l[o]r W[illia]m Law resigned his pay as Co[unci]l[o]r for the time past, and the present year, except any Fines which may be levied on him." "Nauvoo City Council Proceedings," February 17, 1842, 59–60, CHL.

Another source of tension was John C. Bennett—once Smith's closest friend and confidante, but now a bitter enemy after Smith openly discredited him. When Bennett first arrived in Nauvoo, he boarded with the Smith family for thirty-nine weeks and during that time claimed to have known "Joseph better than any other man living for a[t] least fourteen months!"[51] Beginning June 10, 1842, Bennett began publishing a series of articles in the *Sangamo Journal* accusing Smith of "spiritual wifery," among other things.[52] Although he was able to name many of Smith's wives in his exposés, it is difficult to know exactly where the teachings he described originated. Bennett may have been spreading a different and unauthorized form of the principle than Joseph Smith was practicing and teaching by 1842. Historian Gary Bergera concludes, "the stealth with which Smith propounded his doctrine of multiple wives facilitated the rise of rival teachings and independent interpretations."[53] However, it is also likely that Bennett, a trusted friend and associate, knew more than he is given credit for. Late in life when Marks was asked if "Joseph was in polygamy," he answered, "Yes he and Dr. Bennett were the first that went into it."[54] After being exposed, Smith may have made changes and an earlier form of sexual experimentation evolved into celestial plural marriage, with a religious ceremony required.

It seems impossible that Marks could have read Bennett's accusations in the *Sangamo Journal* and heard all the many testimonies in high council regarding Smith's sanction of illicit intercourse without having questions. He must have agonized over what Smith's position was on the issue. In his articles, Bennett specifically called on Marks to join him in "expos[ing] the corruptions of the impostor." Marks and others had "been taken in as

---

51. Andrew F. Smith, *The Saintly Scoundrel—The Life and Times of Dr. John Cook Bennett*, 56. William Law, who later became assistant president of the Mormon church, agreed with Bennett's assessment of his relationship with Smith. According to Law, Bennett "was more in the secret confidence of Joseph than perhaps any other man in the city." William Law, letter to Thomas B. H. Stenhouse, November 24, 1871, quoted in Thomas B. Stenhouse, *The Rocky Mountain Saints*, 198.

52. The term "spiritual wifery" was used early and only later was credited with the connotation of unauthorized intercourse.

53. Gary James Bergera, "'Illicit Intercourse,' Plural Marriage, and the Nauvoo Stake High Council, 1840–1844," 59.

54. Mark Hill Forscutt, Journal, May 24, 1867. For a contrary view, see Brian C. Hales, *Joseph Smith's Polygamy*, 1:566–73, in which he argues Bennett was not a polygamy insider.

blind to deceive the people," Bennett claimed. "Marks has a very strong squinting at apostacy."[55]

> If Sidney Rigdon will suffer a base attempt on his daughter's chastity; Orson Pratt another on his wife; and William Marks will look tamely on at these disclosures, and say nothing, I am much mistaken in the man. The public look to Rigdon, Pratt and Marks and other kindred spirits, to speak at this eventful crisis—they have *seen and heard,* and FELT in their own families,[56] the corruptions of this Smith, that soul-damning impostor.[57]

Marks responded to Bennett by defending Smith in a statement dated July 26, 1842, and published in the *Times and Seasons*:

> Inasmuch as John C. Bennett has called upon me through the Sangamo Journal to come out and confirm the statements which he has made concerning Joseph Smith and others, I take this opportunity of saying to the public, that I know many of his [Bennett's] statements to be false, and that I believe them all to be the offspring of a base and corrupt heart, and without the least shadow of truth, and further that he has used my name without my permission. I believe him to be a vile and wicked adulterous man, who pays no regard to the principles of truth or righteousness, and is unworthy [unworthy of] the confidence of a just community. I would further state that I know of no Order in the Church which admits of a plurality of wives, and do not believe that Joseph Smith ever taught such a doctrine, and further, that my faith in the doctrines of the Church of Jesus Christ of Latter Day Saints, and in Joseph Smith, is unshaken.[58]

Two months later, on October 1, 1842, the *Times and Seasons* also published an affidavit by nineteen prominent women in the community, most of them members of the Relief Society. In it, they certified that "we know of no system of marriage being practised in the church of

---

55. John C. Bennett, "Gen. Bennett's third Letter," *SJ*, 2.

56. While many of Bennett's allegations are less than trustworthy, this could be interpreted as further evidence that Smith attempted to marry Marks's daughter.

57. John C. Bennett, "Gen. Bennett's third Letter," *SJ*, 2.

58. "Certificates of William and Henry Marks," *TS*, 875. The same issue of the *Times and Seasons* published an affidavit sworn by Marks and the members of the city council before Daniel H. Wells, Justice of the Peace, regarding a council meeting of May 19, 1842. In this meeting, Bennett confessed his sexual wrongdoing and testified "concerning Joseph Smith's innocence, virtue and pure teaching." Council members stated "that John C. Bennett was not under duress at the time. . . . His statements that he has lately made concerning this matter are false; there was no excitement at the time, nor was he in anywise threatened, menaced or intimidated." "Affidavit of the City Council," *TS*, 869–70.

Jesus Christ of Latter Day Saints save the one contained in the Book of Doctrine and Covenants." This referred to the revelation, "On Marriage," which declared that "we believe, that one man should have one wife; and one woman, but one husband."[59] This was added to Restoration scripture in 1835, but the Utah-based church removed it from their 1876 and subsequent editions of the Doctrine and Covenants, believing it had been superseded by Joseph Smith's revelation on polygamy. "We give this certificate to the public to show that J. C. Bennett's 'secret wife system' is a disclosure of his own make," declared the women, who included both Rosannah Marks and her daughter, Sophia.[60]

In January 1843, the man who William and Rosannah Marks defended so stoutly publicly started taking more of an interest in their family, specifically their teen-aged daughter, Sophia—the only Marks daughter who was still unmarried and living at home. Having been christened in Livingston, New York, on August 20, 1828, Sophia was just fourteen years old when she unaccountably became a charter member of the Relief Society. She attended that first meeting on March 17, 1842, likely with one or more of her extended family, several of whom were present.[61] Because of the many women with ties to Joseph Smith's polygamy joining the Relief Society, it can be regarded as yet another of the organizations Smith created to bind his followers together with bonds of secrecy. Rosannah Marks, possibly due to her feelings regarding plural marriage, did not join the Nauvoo Relief Society until its very last day of its existence, when Emma Smith was reading the "Voice of Innocence" at every meeting and many sisters were vowing opposition to polygamy.[62]

On January 13, 1843, perhaps motivated by the recent death of another of the Markeses' young adult sons, Henry,[63] Joseph Smith went to the

---

59. "Doctrine and Covenants, 1835," 251, JSP.

60. "We the undersigned members of the ladies' relief society," *TS*, 940.

61. Members of Sophia Marks's family who were present at the charter meeting of the Relief Society were Sophia Robinson, her maiden aunt and namesake; Athalia Rigdon Robinson, daughter of Sidney Rigdon and wife of Sophia's uncle George W.; and Nancy Rigdon, Athalia's sister.

62. "The Voice of Innocence from Nauvoo, 1844, March 9," CHL. This document repudiates polygamy and the spiritual wife system and was read and approved in the final four Nauvoo Relief Society meetings. For more information on this, see Cheryl L. Bruno, "Keeping a Secret: Freemasonry, Polygamy, and the Nauvoo Relief Society, 1842–44," 158–81.

63. Henry had been voted in as constable in an election held August 1, 1842, and had a promising future.

Marks home "to see Sophia who was sick." The Marks family lived across the road from the Smiths. While visiting the now fifteen-year-old Sophia, Smith "heard her relate the vision or dream of a visit fr[o]m her two brothers who were dead.—Touching the associati[o]ns and relations of anoth[e]r wolrd [sic]."⁶⁴ The following day, with Sophia still on his mind, Smith convened a "special council in the chamber—to pray for Sophia Marks."⁶⁵

According to Joseph H. Jackson, Smith was contemplating a relationship with Sophia at the time. Jackson wrote, "[Joseph Smith] had endeavored to seduce the daughter of [William] Marks, and she had informed her parents who were very wrathy, and Joe dreaded their influence."⁶⁶ While Jackson's claims are often viewed with skepticism, others corroborate his allegation. Eliza Jane Churchill Webb wrote in a letter in 1876, "William Marks[,] an influential man in the church, left because Joseph was determined to have his daughter Sophia Marks sealed to him."⁶⁷ Further, in an 1884 public discussion, Clark Braden stated, "Did space permit we could give the sworn statements of Orson Pratt's wife, Wm. Law's wife, Dr. Foster's wife, Wm. Mark's daughter, Nancy Rigdon, Martha Brotherton, Melissa Schindle, and a score more of as respectable women as ever lived in Nauvoo, that Smith tried to seduce them into spiritual wifery."⁶⁸

A possible courting of Sophia and others who refused him may explain a period of about seven months when Smith did not contract any new marriage alliances. (The last person he married during this period was Martha McBride in August 1842.) In March of 1843, he started marrying again, including many teenagers who were similar in age and status to Sophia.⁶⁹ An original poem that Sophia wrote in an autograph book

---

64. "Journal, December 1842–June 1844; Book 1, 21 December 1842–10 March 1843," 129, JSP.

65. Editors of the Joseph Smith Papers speculate that "the 'chamber' here might refer to the upper room in JS's store—or to the second floor in JS's home, where JS and close associates had held special prayer meetings in the past." "Journal, December 1842–June 1844; Book 1, 21 December 1842–10 March 1843," 130, JSP.

66. Jackson, Joseph H., *A Narrative of the Adventures and Experience of Joseph H. Jackson in Nauvoo*, 22.

67. Eliza J. Webb [Eliza Jane Churchill Webb], letter to Mary Bond, April 24, 1876, CCLA.

68. E. L. Kelley and Clark Braden, *Public discussion of the issues between the Reorganized church of Jesus Christ of Latter day saints and the Church of Christ (Disciples)*, 202–3.

69. Partridge was nineteen years old, Woodworth sixteen years old, Kimball fourteen years old, and Walker seventeen years old.

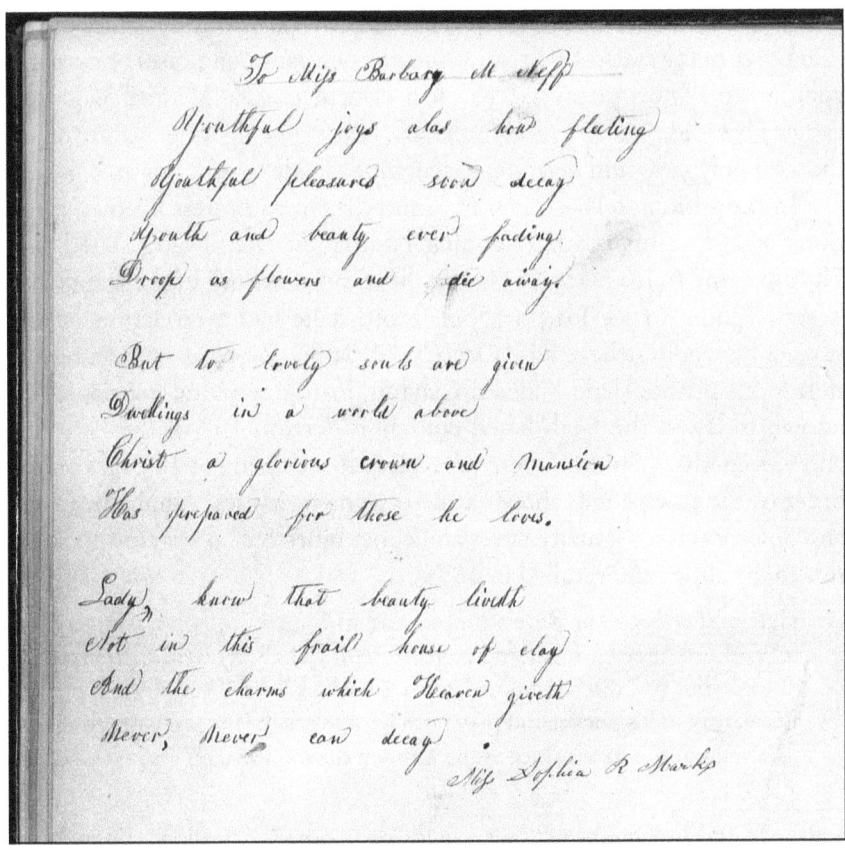

Sophia Marks in Barbara Neff Moses Autograph book. Courtesy of LDS Church History Library.

for Barbara M. Neff laments the transient nature of youth, which, at her tender age, she was already beginning to recognize:

> Youthful joys alas how fleeting
> Youthful pleasures soon decay
> Youth and beauty ever fading
> Droop as flowers and die away.

Beauty, Sophia wrote, does not dwell in "this frail house of clay," but in the glorious crown and mansion Christ prepares for those he loves. Whether Sophia had a personal encounter with the new doctrine of celestial plural marriage or not, her sentiments mysteriously echo those of other Nauvoo girls whose youth was curtailed in service to their religious commitments.[70]

---

70. For example, Helen Mar Kimball, said to be age fourteen at the time of her marriage to Joseph Smith, wrote a poem describing herself as "a fetter'd bird

Before William Marks was clued in to Smith's polygamy doctrine, he presided over many cases of polygamy, pseudo-polygamy, and cases of marriage contrary to Illinois marriage law.[71] It is evident that, as Wilford Woodruff earlier observed, Marks put considerable effort into fighting against unauthorized polygamy and defending accusations made against Smith.

In the spring of 1843, Hyrum Smith began to express his own questions regarding his brother's conjugal activities. Marks later stated that Hyrum came to his place saying that he did not believe in polygamy, but he was "going to see Joseph about it and if he had a revelation on the subject he would believe it."[72] On July 12, 1843, Joseph dictated a revelation to his private clerk, William Clayton, justifying plural marriage, and known today in the Utah-based church as Section 132 of the Doctrine and Covenants. Clayton "wrote a Revelation consisting of 10 pages on the order of the priesthood, showing the designs in Moses, Abraham, David and Solomon having many wives and concubines &c."[73] Clayton spoke of this many times and recalled in 1874,

> Hyrum then took the Revelation, to read to Emma . . . [who] was very bitter and full of resentment and anger. Joseph quietly remarked [to Hyrum], "I told you, you did not know Emma as well as I did." Joseph then put the Revelation in his pocket and they both left the office. The revelation was read to several of the Authorities of the Church during the day.[74]

---

with wild and longing heart" that would "daily pine for freedom and murmur at thy lot," but because there was "glory in obeying this high celestial law," her obedience would "bring eternal joy" and make her progenitors' "crown[s] more bright." "Autobiography, 30 March, 1881," CHL.

71. These included the cases of Henry Wilson on January 21, 1843; Henry Cook on January 21, 1843; Sarah Miller and John Thorpe on January 21, 1843; John Annis on January 21, 1843; Charity Thorpe and Thomas Prouse on January 21, 1842; John Bleazard and Elizabeth Poole on January 28, 1843; James Reed and Mary Powell on January 28, 1843; John Wells on January 28, 1843; Job Green on March 4, 1843; Jordan Hendrixson on April 1, 1843; and Elizabeth Rowe on July 22, 1843. For a thorough analysis of these cases, see Bergera, "'Illicit Intercourse,'" 59–90.

72. "Minutes, meeting of the First Presidency and Quorum of Twelve," 11–12, CCLA.

73. George D. Smith, ed., *An Intimate Chronicle: The Journals of William Clayton*, 110.

74. "Revelation on celestial marriage, 1874 February 16," 6, CHL. See also "Affidavit of William Law," *NE*, 2. "I hereby certify that Hyrum Smith did, (in his office,) read to me a certain written document, which he said was a revelation

One month later, on August 12, 1843, concerns about polygamy arose during a high council meeting. Hyrum Smith responded by reading the revelation to the Nauvoo High Council.[75] Thomas Grover, a member of the high council, recalled that after Hyrum read the revelation he declared, "Now, you that believe this revelation and go forth and obey the same shall be saved, and you that reject it shall be damned."[76] Official notes of the meeting only state, "Teaching by Pres[iden]ts Hiram Smith & William Marks."[77] This cryptic note suggests that Marks may have known about the revelation before it was presented to the council. The majority of council members accepted the teaching, but Stake President William Marks, Councilor Austin Cowles, and Leonard Soby objected.[78]

Years later, Marks explained his reaction to the revelation and the position this put him in:

---

from God, he said that he was with Joseph when it was received. He afterwards gave me the document to read, and I took it to my house, and read it, and showed it to my wife, and returned it next day. The revelation (so called) authorized certain men to have more wives than one at a time, in this world and in the world to come. It said this was the *law*, and commanded Joseph to enter into the *law*.—And also that he should administer to others. Several other items were in the revelation, supporting the above doctrines. Wm. Law."

75. "Affidavit of Austin Cowles," *NE*, 2; "Affidavit of Leonard Soby," 378–79. "On or about the 12th day of August, 1843, in the city of Nauvoo, in the state of Illinois, in the county of Hancock, before the High Council of the Church of Jesus Christ of Latter Day Saints, of which body and council aforesaid he was a member, personally appeared one Hyrum Smith, of the first presidency of said church, and brother to Joseph Smith, the president and prophet of the same, and presented to said council the Revelation on Polygamy, enjoining its observance and declaring it came from God; unto which a large majority of the council agreed and assented, believing it to be of a celestial order, though no vote was taken upon it, for the reason that the voice of the prophet, in such matters, was understood by us to be the voice of God to the church, and that said revelation was presented to said council, as before stated, as coming from Joseph Smith, the prophet of the Lord, and was received by us as other revelations had been. The said Leonard Soby further saith that Elder Austin A. Cowles, a member of the High Council aforesaid, did, subsequently to the 12th day of August, 1843, openly declare against the said revelation on polygamy, and the doctrines therein contained. LEONARD SOBY."

76. Thomas Grover, "Elder Grover's Letter, Farmington, Jan 10, 1885," *DEN*, 2.

77. "Minutes, 1843 February 25–1844 May 11," 14, CHL.

78. Bergera, "'Illicit Intercourse,'" 84–85.

During my administration in the church I saw and heard of many things that was practiced, and taught that I did not believe to be God; but I continued to do and teach such principles as were plainly revealed as the law of the church, for I thought that pure and holy principles only would have a tendency to benefit mankind. Therefore when the doctrine of polygamy was introduced into the church as a principle of exaltation I took a decided stand against it; which stand rendered me quite unpopular, with many of the leading ones of the church.[79]

Although his decision was unpopular, Marks retained his position as stake president and president of the high council, the highest rank in the church under the First Presidency. Prior to Smith's death, polygamy was not the litmus test it later became for the Twelve Apostles. While Marks openly opposed polygamy, he continued to support Smith and his prophetic claims. In fact, Marks was one of Smith's most trusted allies near the end, a fact that was removed from historical records for many decades.[80]

Likewise, Soby also continued to object against plural marriage but remained a member of the high council in good standing until after Joseph Smith's death. He was disfellowshipped by the council on September 7, 1844, over his support for Sidney Rigdon as Smith's successor.[81]

On September 1, 1843, just weeks after learning of the revelation on polygamy, Austin Cowles brought charges against George J. Adams for adultery, for bringing back a new wife and child upon returning from a mission in England, even though he had a wife in Nauvoo. It was clear that Cowles was forcing an issue, as Adams had already been cleared by the First Presidency. Some of Cowles's anger comes through in his ambiguous charges against Adams, including: "putting the stumbling block of his iniquity before his face and raising an image of jealousy and causing people to worship it." Adams pleaded not guilty and "read a document from the First Presidency" settling all charges dated before June 5. Marks, knowing of Smith's teachings and that he had not disciplined Adams, extended "the hand of fellowship" to Adams on behalf of the high council.[82] In protest, Cowles then "resigned his seat in the Council as Councillor to President

---

79. William Marks, "Epistle," ZHBO, 52.

80. For example, on May 4, 1842, Marks received the first anointing in the Quorum of the Anointed. The Willard Richards record, Brigham Young's history, and *The History of the Church* all removed Marks from the list of men receiving the ordinance that day.

81. "Minutes, 1844 September 27," CHL.

82. "Minutes, 1843 February 25–1844 May 11," 16–17, CHL.

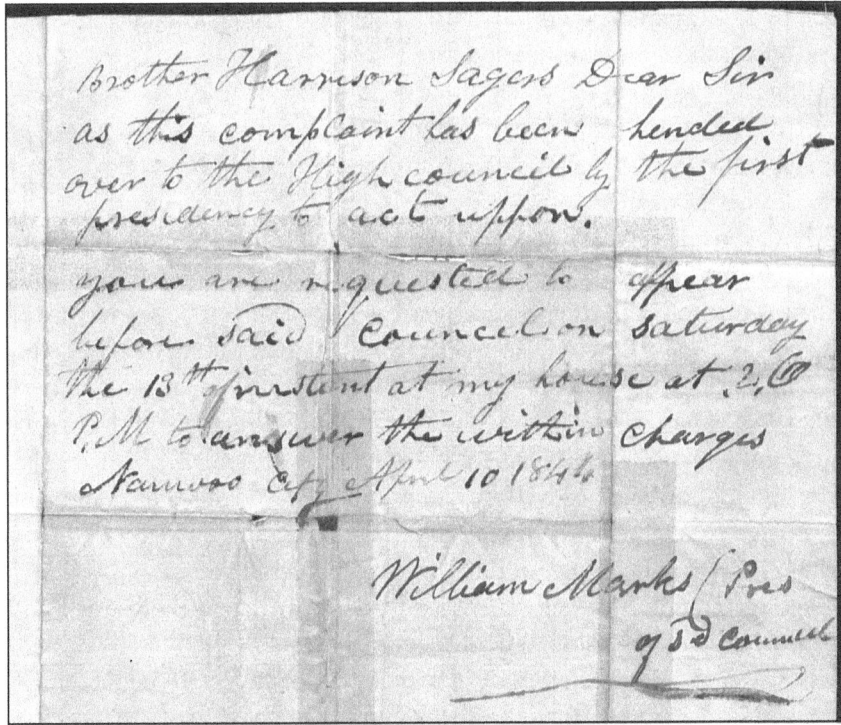

William Marks's written summons for Harrison Sagers to appear before the Nauvoo High Council. Courtesy of LDS Church History Library.

Marks" on September 23.[83] With this action, Cowles "was looked upon as a seceder" and became "far more outspoken and energetic in his opposition to polygamy than almost any other man in Nauvoo."[84] Cowles was "cut of[f] from this church for apostatizing" by the high council on May 18, 1844.[85]

On November 21, 1843, Joseph Smith presented a case before the high council, addressed to Marks by name. Smith charged Harrison Sagers with "trying to seduce a young girl, living at his house by the name of Phebe Madison." Smith said that Sagers used his name "in a blasphemous manner, by saying that I tolerated such things in which thing he is guilty of lying." Marks did not sustain the charge, but he did allow Smith to save

---

83. "Minutes, 1843 February 25–1844 May 11," 17, CHL.

84. Cowles published an affidavit accusing the church of teaching the doctrine of plural marriage in the *Nauvoo Expositor*. "Affidavit of Austin Cowles," *NE*, 2.

85. "Minutes, 1844 May 18–September 10," 3, CHL.

face by finding that Sagers "had taught false doctrine," which Smith was then given the opportunity to correct.[86]

Smith was not tolerant of those who allowed his name to be connected with sexual immorality. Neither did he wish to appear to condone it. According to William Clayton, Smith had helped him procure his first plural wife, Margaret Moon.[87] But when she became pregnant, Smith told Clayton "just keep her at home and brook it and if they raise trouble about it and bring you before me I will give you an awful scourging & probably cut you off from the church and then I will baptise you & set you ahead as good as ever."[88] Clayton was not the only follower willing to take a temporary beating for Joseph. A comparable situation had taken place on May 28, 1842, when Justus Morse was charged with "unchaste and unvirtuous conduct with [Jane] Neyman, the wife of another man."[89] Late in life, Morse spoke of being blessed by the prophet in Missouri "and especially instructed to maintain his [Joseph Smith's] character against all calumnies, which thing I was bound to do . . . because of my oath as a Danite."[90] Perhaps because of his vow, he refused to appear before the council and instead "ordered his name to be struck off the Church Book as he did not wish to stand a trial."[91] Morse was disfellowshipped by the high council, but within a month was back in the church and ordained a high priest. Morse later explained that he had been taught the doctrine of "spiritual wifery" by church leader Amasa Lyman and sealed to that "wife of another man" by John Smith, the prophet's uncle, as a plural wife within a year.[92]

---

86. "Minutes, 1843 February 25–1844 May 11," 21, CHL.

87. "Revelation on celestial marriage, 1874 February 16," 2, CHL. "He had learned that there was a sister back in England to whom I was very much attached. . . . He then said, 'Why don't you send for her? . . . I give you authority to send for her and I will furnish the means,' which he did. this was the first time the Prophet Joseph talked with me on the subject of plural marriage."

88. Smith, ed., *An Intimate Chronicle*, 33.

89. "Minutes, 1842 May 20–1843 February 19," 4, CHL.

90. See Justus Morse's affidavit in Charles A. Shook, *The True Origin of Mormon Polygamy*, 168–71.

91. "Minutes, 1842 May 20–1843 February 19," 4, CHL.

92. Michael S. Riggs, "'His Word Was as Good as His Note': The Impact of Justus Morse's Mormonism(s) on His Families," 54. These incidents have implications for Marks's assertion, later in life, that Joseph Smith regretted polygamy and wanted to stop it right before his death. Perhaps Joseph planned to do a public purge and then bring people in later "through the back door."

Another similar case was that of widower John Bleazard and Mrs. Betsy Pool, who was married to an assumed adulterer. Brigham Young advised Bleazard to leave her alone, but Gustavus Hills thought it was "lawful" for them to marry. Hills said that he consulted Joseph Smith, who directed that the couple should be married. Hills performed a marriage ceremony, but when brought before the high council, Bleazard and Pool were "cut off." Very soon after, the council "decided that they be again admitted to fellowship by baptism."[93] In another case that sounded very much like polygamy, the high council met on January 28, 1843, to consider the case of William Wilsey, who had performed a marriage ceremony for an "adulterous couple." Marks "cautioned against future acts of the kind—that Elders should be cautious & wise in the future." He then suggested that the Wilsey be acquitted, "which was done by vote of the Council."[94]

Marks was a close observer of, and sometimes a participant in, cases where emerging polygamists were publicly chastised for their behavior but almost immediately brought back into full communion with the church.[95] If Joseph Smith was not actively promoting the plural marriage system, he was at the least allowing for very lenient treatment toward offenders.

---

93. "Minutes, 1842 May 20–1843 February 19," 26–28, CHL.
94. "Minutes, 1842 May 20–1843 February 19," 26, CHL.
95. For examples, see D. Michael Quinn, "Evidence for the Sexual Side of Joseph Smith's Polygamy."

CHAPTER 6

A Viper on the Wall

Joseph Smith taught that a temple was necessary to perform many of the new ordinances being revealed to him. Baptism for the dead, for example, was properly a temple ordinance, and its performance could only be allowed outside the temple for a short time.[1] Other ordinances, such as eternal marriage, contained elements that were to be kept confidential, and therefore required a more sacred and private place where they could be administered. Thus, temple building commenced early in the Saints' residence in Nauvoo. On April 6, 1841, William Marks participated in the ceremonial placing of the temple cornerstones.[2] Marks had not been present at the Kirtland Temple cornerstone laying in 1833, nor the Far West Temple cornerstone ceremony in 1838, which were both impressive affairs. But he played an important role in the ceremony at Nauvoo.

The pageantry of the event comprised all Smith, a skilled ritualist, could rally. The date was set for the eleventh anniversary of the church, on April 6. Under the fire of artillery and the discharge of cannon, sixteen companies of the Nauvoo Legion formed a military parade commanded by John C. Bennett, still a respected leader in the church before his subsequent excommunication. The spectacle impressed the ten thousand residents, church leaders, and visiting dignitaries who were gathered, including Thomas Sharp, a journalist from Warsaw, Illinois. Sharp marked the event as the first time he became aware of the frightening potential the Mormons represented for dominating the affairs of the state.[3]

The Nauvoo band and choir performed a series of lusty musical numbers, and Sidney Rigdon provided an energetic dedicatory address about an hour in length,[4] while the crowd paid "breathless attention . . . hanging upon the words that flowed from his lips."[5] He spoke of the multitude being gathered to raise a standard of liberty and law, and stated that the military display honored the power and might of Christ, the chief corner-

---

1. "Revelation, 19 January 1841 [D&C 124]," 5, JSP; "Discourse, 3 October 1841 as Published in *Times and Seasons*," 577, JSP.
2. "Celebration of the An[n]iversary of the Church—Military Parade—Prest. Rigdon's Address—Laying the Corner Stones of the Temple," *TS*, 377.
3. "Growing Conflict in Illinois," *Church History in the Fulness of Times*, 266.
4. "The Mormons' City," *DMR*.
5. "Celebration of the An[n]iversary of the Church," *TS*, 376.

View of Nauvoo. From Holmes & Arnold's "Map of Hancock County, Illinois," 1859. Courtesy of LDS Church History Library.

stone in Zion. Rigdon explained that the laying of the cornerstones of the temple was expressive of the order of the kingdom and a matter of revelation. The southeast cornerstone was laid under the direction of the First Presidency of the church, with Smith pronouncing a blessing as follows:

> This Principal Corner Stone in representation of the First Presidency, is now duly laid in honor of the great God; and may it there remain until the whole fabric is completed; and may the same be accomplished speedily; that the Saints may have a place to worship God, and the son of Man have where to lay his head.

The southwest cornerstone was superintended by officers of the high priesthood and Marks, the northwest cornerstone by the high council, and the northeast stone by the bishops.[6]

As the building of the temple slowly progressed, Marks entered yet another of Smith's societies for gathering his most trusted friends into secret bonds of unity and attachment. On May 4, 1842, after special preparations in the upper story of his store in Nauvoo, Smith organized the Quorum of the Anointed, or the Holy Order of the Priesthood. With his brother Hyrum's help, Smith initiated eight men—Patriarch and Branch President James Adams, First Presidency member William Law, Stake President William Marks, Bishops George Miller and Newel K. Whitney, and Apostles Brigham Young, Heber C. Kimball, and Willard Richards—into what would later be called the "temple endowment."[7] Prominently

---

6. "History, 1838–1856, volume C-1 [2 November 1838–31 July 1842]," 1185, JSP.

7. Later, the official history of the church omits the names of apostates William Law and William Marks as having been in the original group.

excluded were Smith's first counselor, Sidney Rigdon, and Smith's assistant counselor, John C. Bennett. According to Smith's diary, he administered "washings, anointings, endowments and the communication of Keys pertaining to the Aaronic Priesthood, and so on to the highest order of the Melchisedec Priesthood, setting forth the order pertaining to the Ancient of Days." Initiates would be "enabled to secure the fulness of those blessings which have been prepared for the Church of the first born, and come up and abide in the presence of the Eloheim in the Eternal worlds."[8] On May 5, some of the men who had been endowed the day before gave Joseph and Hyrum their endowments. Of this ritual Heber C. Kimball wrote to Parley P. Pratt, "We have received some pressious things through the Prophet on the pr[i]esthood that would cause your Soul to rejoice."[9] Kimball, who had been a Freemason since 1825, recognized the similarity of the endowment ritual and Masonic rites. Speaking of the Mormon temple endowment in 1858, he declared: "We have the true Masonry. The Masonry of today is received from the apostasy which took place in the days of Solomon and David. They have now and then a thing that is correct, but we have the real thing."[10]

During two stressful years of Marks's tenure as stake president, leader of the high council, and alderman on the city council, the meetings with the Anointed Quorum were spiritually uplifting. On June 26, the group held a Sunday prayer circle, dressed in their full ritual temple clothing. This became a cherished tradition.

On May 26 and on May 28, 1843, Hyrum and Joseph Smith and their wives received marriage sealings for eternity.[11] While Marks was not at either meeting, both were important to the history of the church.

---

8. "History, 1838–1856, volume C-1 [2 November 1838–31 July 1842]," 1328, JSP. See also "Journal, December 1841–December 1842," 94, JSP. "Wednesday [May] 4[,1842] In council in the Presidents & General offices with Judge [James] Adams. Hyram Smith Newel K. Whitney. William Marks, Wm Law. George Miller. Brigham Young. Heber C. Kimball & Willard Richards. [blank space] & giving certain instructions concerning the priesthood. [blank space] &c on the Aronic Priesthood to the first [blank space] continueing through the day."

9. Stanley B. Kimball, *Heber C. Kimball: Mormon Patriarch and Pioneer*, 55. "I was aniciated [initiated] into the ancient order was washed and annointed and Sealled and ordained a Preast, and so forth in company with nine others, Viz. Josph Smith, Hiram Smith, Wm. Law, Wm. Marks, Judge [James] Adams, Brigham Young, Willard Richrds, George Miller, N. K. Whitney."

10. Kimball, 85.

11. Devery S. Anderson, "The Anointed Quorum in Nauvoo, 1842–1845," 145.

By May 26, Hyrum accepted the doctrine of polygamy, and by May 28, Emma Smith may have, at least temporarily, done the same. She and Joseph were sealed for time and eternity on that date. Andrew Ehat, a specialist on Mormon polygamy, has suggested that Emma "could not, in good conscience, take upon herself the endowment covenants" if "she was still unwilling to accept the command of the Lord to her husband that he practice plural marriage."[12] In order to receive the sealing ordinance, says Ehat, Emma had to "reconcile herself to the doctrine and practice," because "in the background of Joseph's introduction of the temple ordinances was the principle of plural marriage."[13] Other writers have concurred with this assessment.[14]

However, the sealing of William and Rosannah Marks may provide evidence that the sealing ordinance was not restricted to those who accepted Smith's teachings on marriage. Rosannah was initiated into the Quorum and received her first anointing on October 1, 1843.[15] She and William received the second anointing and were sealed for time and eternity on October 22.[16] Marks later recounted that he was ordained to the office of "prophet, priest, and king . . . under the hands of Joseph Smith."[17] Though they received all the temple ordinances, it is reasonable to believe that neither William nor his wife ever accepted the principle of plural marriage.

It is always possible that, like Emma, the Markses accepted polygamy just long enough to be sealed as a couple.[18] Even after he learned of the doctrine, William Marks continued to meet with the Quorum of the Anointed. On September 3, 1843, just before their sealing, Marks and the Quorum united in prayer for Hyrum's sick child and received "much

---

12. Andrew F. Ehat, "Joseph Smith's Introduction of Temple Ordinances and the 1844 Mormon Succession Question," 60.

13. Anderson, "The Anointed Quorum in Nauvoo," 145; Ehat, "Joseph Smith's Introduction of Temple Ordinances," 44–45.

14. Devery Anderson, Newell and Avery, etc.

15. Devery S. Anderson and Gary James Bergera, *Joseph Smith's Quorum of the Anointed, 1842–1845: A Documentary History*, 27–28.

16. Scott H. Faulring, ed., *An American Prophet's Record: The Diaries and Journals of Joseph Smith*, 423. Smith recorded in his journal, "Wm Marks & <wife> anointed."

17. Samuel James, "For the Messenger and Advocate. Laharp, Ill. January 28th, 1845," *MAR*, 130.

18. Ehat assumed that Rosannah and William Marks's sealing meant they had accepted the principle of plural marriage. Ehat, *Joseph Smith's Introduction of Temple Ordinances*, 44–45.

instruction from the President on future things."[19] This instruction on "future things" might have allowed Marks to accept polygamy as a necessary doctrine to make things right in the hereafter.

On the other hand, troubling remarks by Joseph Smith indicate that opposition and friction continued to exist surrounding the unsettling practice of plurality. In July 1843, Willard Richards recorded a sermon made by Smith, sending his notes to Brigham Young in a letter. Richards wrote that Smith "preached all day. . . . Man[']s foes they of his own house.—the Spirit that crucified christ, same spirit in Nauvoo. Refer[r]ed particularly to—I wont say who." While Smith would not say who, Richards had no problem speculating, "was it Bro. Marks?—did not say."[20] Thus, as early as summer of 1843, there was perceived friction between Marks and Smith.

On December 29, 1843, Smith gave an address to the Nauvoo police in his capacity as mayor of Nauvoo. With Marks and William Law in mind, he stated that his life was in danger from "dough-head" enemies within the city. "I am exposed to far greater danger from traitors among ourselves than from enemies without," Smith said. "[I]f I can escape from the ungrateful treachery of assassins I can live as Caesar might have lived were it not for a right hand Brutus." Switching metaphors, he continued,

> I have had pretended friends betray me. . . . All the hue and cry of the chief Priests and Elders against the Savior could not bring down the wrath of the Jewish nation upon his head and thereby cause the crucifixion of the son of God until Judas said to them "whomsoever I shall kiss, he is the man, hold him fast". Judas was one of the Twelve Apostles even their Treasurer and dipt with their master in the dish and thro<ugh> his treachery, the crucifixion was brought about, and we have a Judas in our midst.[21]

Nauvoo buzzed with speculation as to who the traitors were. At a special session of the city council on January 5, 1844, Marks expressed concern that because of circulating rumors that Smith wanted them "put away," he and Law were in danger. When some men built a fire close to his home, he feared that perhaps it had been kindled by the police under Smith's direction.[22] Not simply their own unwarranted excitement, the

---

19. Faulring, *An American Prophet's Record*, 412.
20. "Willard Richards letter," 2, CHL.
21. "History, 1838–1856, volume E-1 [1 July 1843–30 April 1844]," 1836, JSP.
22. When the incident was written up for the history of the church, commentary was added, likely by George A. Smith in 1855, and presented as if authored by Joseph Smith. See Dan Vogel, ed., *History of Joseph Smith and the Church of Jesus Christ of Latter-day Saints: A Source and Text Critical Edition: Volume 6: 1843–*

effects of the rumors were also testified to by others. Francis M. Higbee stated that although he didn't know of anyone being endangered, Marks, Law, and perhaps others "could not subscribe to all things in the Church, and there were some private matters that might make trouble."[23] Leonard Soby testified that he had asked Warren Smith if he knew who the Brutus was, and Warren "said he believed Wm Law, <was one> & Marks another, they had better not come in my <his> way."[24] Although tensions continued and escalated with Law, it appears by Smith and Marks's later congenial encounters that they resolved their issues satisfactorily.

A final fraternity instituted by Smith was mustered beginning March 10, 1844, one short season before his death. Marks was added to the membership on March 19, of what would soon become approximately fifty loyal members and three supportive non-Mormons, known as the Council of Fifty, or the Kingdom of God. This latter term connoted a political kingdom with theological overtones. Its ceremonial name was the imposing "Kingdom of God and His Law, with the Keys and power thereof, and judgment in the hands of his servants."[25]

Virtually every member of the Council of Fifty was a Freemason, whose members were bound by solemn oaths and obligated to keep each other's secrets.[26] Many members of the Fifty were members of the Nauvoo Legion and felt a sense of obligation to Smith, their file leader and "Major General" of the Legion. Council members who were part of the Anointed

---

1844, 193n392: "he [Marks] then became afraid, & concluded he must either be the Brutus or the Dough Head he laid awake all night thinking they <the police> had built the fire to kill him by— in the morning he called on me <reported the circumstances & expressed his fears> Joseph then scoffed, 'What can be the matter with these men? [I]s it, that the wicked flee when no man pursueth? that hit pigeons always flutter? that drowning men catch at straws? or that <Prests> [William] Law & [William] Marks are absolutely traitors to the Church, that my remarks should produce such an excitement among them <in their minds?>'" "History Draft [1 January–21 June 1844]," 1, JSP.

23. "History, 1838–1856, volume E-1 [1 July 1843–30 April 1844]," 1855, JSP.

24. "Nauvoo City Council Rough Minute Book, November 1842–January 1844," 36–38, JSP.

25. Reading this phrase in context, one can see that the final words which are usually added, "Ahman Christ," are a mode of signature by He who is bestowing the title. "Council of Fifty, Minutes, March 1844–January 1846; Volume 1, 10 March 1844–1 March 1845," 31, JSP.

26. William Morgan, *Illustrations of Masonry by One of the Fraternity Who has Devoted Thirty Years to the Subject*, 73–76.

Quorum had been obligated with key words, signs, and tokens, along with penalties for revealing these secrets.[27] Finally, Council of Fifty members themselves took a Masonic-like oath of secrecy under the penalty of death. After "affirming that they were in fellowship with every other person in the room," they were given a "Charge," a "Name," a "Key word," the "Constitution," and a "Penalty."[28] Marks's inclusion in all four of these allegiance organizations demonstrates his continued deep loyalty to Smith and to the church.

The Council of Fifty was organized by order of age and not the date a man entered the quorum. Voting was done in order of seniority, and the council even sat in order of age. The exception was Smith, who was positioned first, after which the following members were enumerated from sixty-five-year-old Samuel Bent to twenty-five-year-old Lorenzo Wasson. Marks was one of the more seasoned members, being number ten.[29] However, he did not dominate the conversation. The one comment he made that was important enough to be included in the minutes occurred Thursday, April 11, 1844, when "on motion of E[lde]r Wm. Marks it was Resolved, that whenever convenient, our councils shall be opened by prayer, beginning at the oldest and down through the council in order to the youngest."[30] While other members became expressive on the matters of the revolutionary kingdom to which they belonged, Marks desired the council to pray for wisdom, albeit in the order established by the prophet.

The day that Marks spoke in a meeting, April 11, the council upheld Smith as "Prophet, Priest, & King, with a Hosannah Shout."[31] Marks said later that he did not feel "a kingly form of government, in which Joseph

---

27. Brigham Young, quoted in L. John Nuttall, "L. John Nuttall journal, 1876–1877," entry dated February 7, 1877. William Law, Isaac Morley, and Joseph Young were the only living members of the thirty-seven men who belonged to the Anointed Quorum during Smith's lifetime who were not part of the original Council of Fifty.

28. Joseph F. Smith draft journal entry, October 12, 1880, quoted in D. Michael Quinn, "The Council of Fifty and Its Members, 1844–1945," 174. Quinn also cites Franklin D. Richards's journal entry for April 8, 1881, concerning new members of the Council of Fifty and referring to "charge obligation & password."

29. See "List of Members, Council of Fifty, probably between 25 April and 3 May 1844," 1, JSP.

30. "Council of Fifty, Minutes, March 1844–January 1846; Volume 1, 10 March 1844–1 March 1845," 99, JSP.

31. "Council of Fifty, Minutes," 114–15, JSP.

suffered himself to be ordained a king," was in accordance with the laws of the church, but he held his peace.[32]

* * *

On May 20, William Marks, regardless of his status of stake president, was subpoenaed and selected to serve on the grand jury of Hancock County. Described as being "better than a travelling circus," this circuit court was held twice a year, in May and October, for two weeks each time.[33] Grand jurors were selected from throughout the whole county, including both Mormons and their non-Mormon neighbors. Of the eighteen jurors, two Mormons were selected: William Marks and Edward Hunter, as well as Mormon-friendly Daniel H. Wells. Grand jurors who were expecting to hear testimony of crimes such as counterfeiting, larceny, burglary, and assault were surprised to hear testimony regarding the Mormon prophet, Joseph Smith. On May 23, and again on May 24, the grand jury heard statements from William and Wilson Law accusing Smith of adultery and fornication.

By law, the grand jury members were prohibited from making "presentments of their own knowledge, . . . unless the juror giving the information, is previously sworn as a witness."[34] This meant that Marks, a non-polygamist but a polygamy insider in May 1844, was not able to tell the other grand jurors what he knew about Smith's marital or sexual practices. Even so, the jury found "good and sufficient evidence" to indict Smith on three counts.

Smith heard news of at least one indictment from messenger Asahel Lathrop, who precipitously jumped on his horse and rode from Carthage to Nauvoo in two hours and thirty minutes to bring the news. By the time Marks returned to Nauvoo on May 25, Smith was "at home, keeping out of the way of the expected writs from Carthage." Marks and several others informed him that two indictments had been made, one for "false swearing" and "one charging me with polygamy or something else, on the testimony of William Law that I had told him so! [T]he particulars of which I shall learn hereafter." After hearing this, Smith exclaimed, "There

---

32. William Marks, "Epistle," *ZHBO*, 53.

33. Dallin H. Oaks and Marvin S. Hill, *Carthage Conspiracy: The Trial of the Accused Assassins of Joseph Smith*, 1.

34. *The Revised Code of Laws of Illinois: Enacted by the Fifth General Assembly*, 252.

Carthage Courthouse. From Holmes & Arnold's "Map of Hancock County, Illinois," 1859. Courtesy of LDS Church History Library.

was much false swearing before the Grand Jury."[35] Smith, Marks, and several others met to discuss how to deal with these individuals. The group decided that they should not "keep out of their way any longer."[36]

Following this advice, Smith met with Robert D. Foster, who requested a "private interview" away from the mansion house. Smith believed that Foster wanted to lure him away and kill him, and he thus proposed they each select trustworthy men to accompany them. From among the thousands who were loyal to him, Smith chose "Hyrum Smith, Willm. Marks, Lucian Woodworth, and Peter Hawes"[37] Foster declined, and a meeting was never convened.

Nonetheless, the fact that Marks was chosen by Smith in a time when rumors were rampant, church and civic leaders were turning against him, and he was not sure who he could trust, is significant. That Marks, an op-

---

35. "History, 1838–1856, volume F-1 [1 May 1844–8 August 1844]," 53, JSP.
36. "Journal, December 1842–June 1844; Book 4, 1 March–22 June 1844," 132, JSP.
37. "History, 1838–1856, volume F-1 [1 May 1844–8 August 1844]," 79, JSP.

ponent to polygamy, was one of four men named specifically by Smith as loyal to him, demonstrates the confidence in which he was placed.

Others in Smith's close circle, however, were not as dependable.

William Law, a counselor in the First Presidency under Joseph Smith from January 24, 1841, to April 18, 1844, had been building up a head of steam for months. Law had been a staunch defender of Smith against those who accused the church president of polygamy, and it was a cruel blow when he discovered that Smith had been teaching the doctrine all along.[38] Law asked to take a copy of the 1843 plural marriage revelation home to his wife. William and Jane Law struggled mightily to accept this new teaching but could not be convinced. Law "begged of Joseph, and pled with him, as a man might plead for the life of his best friend, to stop all these evils, and save the Church from ruin."[39] Smith would not relent. Law later recalled, "My heart was burning. I wanted to tread upon the viper."[40]

Like Marks, Law was a trusted member of the Nauvoo Legion, the Masonic Lodge, and the Anointed Quorum. His wife was an early member of the Relief Society. But he began to increasingly contend with Smith's teachings and was not invited to participate in the Council of Fifty.

On May 7, 1844, discontents William and Wilson Law, Charles and Robert D. Foster, Chauncey and Francis Higbee, and Charles Ivins set up a print shop on Mulholland Street, near the rising temple. The first and only number of their paper, the *Nauvoo Expositor*, was published on Friday, June 7, 1844—a four-page paper with a print run of one thousand copies. It scathingly denounced Smith's doctrine of a plurality of gods, the secret teaching and practice of plural marriage, and the theocratic nature of Mormonism in Nauvoo.

A prospectus of the *Expositor* detailed subjects it intended to cover, including "the many **gross abuses exercised under the pretended authorities of the Nauvoo City Charter**, by the legislative authorities of said city; and the *insupportable OPPRESSIONS of the MINISTERIAL powers in carrying out the* Unjust, Illegal, and Unconstitutional *Ordinances of the same*."[41]

---

38. According to his diary, Law was first told that Joseph had approved polygamy by his brother Hyrum on January 1, 1844. William Law, "Law Nauvoo Diary, 1 January 1844," 7, 23.

39. "William Law to T. B. H. Stenhouse, November 24, 1871," quoted in Thomas B. Stenhouse, *Rocky Mountain Saints*, 199.

40. William Law, "The Law Interview," *SLDT*.

41. "Prospectus of the *Nauvoo Expositor*," CHL; emphases in original.

With this statement, the *Expositor* not only attacked Smith, but it accused other authorities of impropriety, including Marks.

When the paper appeared, church and city leaders denounced it angrily. The city council took the matter in hand and met the day after the paper's publication on Saturday, June 8, and Monday, June 10 to decide how to respond. Marks was not present at the June 8 meeting, but he did attend on June 10.[42]

The meeting on the tenth discussed many topics, from Robert Foster putting "his hand on a woman's knee," to Joseph H. Jackson being a murderer. Eventually the discussion turned to the *Expositor*. Smith spent much time explaining principles in the plural marriage revelation which he felt had been misrepresented by the tabloid. Smith stated "the Constitution did not authorize the press to publish Libels—and proposed the council make some provision for putting down the Nauvoo Expositor." A sophisticated discussion on the law ensued, with the council referring to James Kent's *Commentaries on America Law*, William Blackstone's *Commentaries on the Laws of England*, the Illinois Constitution, and the United States Constitution. Hyrum Smith suggested they "smash the press all to pieces and pie the type," while Benjamin Warrington suggested they "fine [the paper] 500.00."[43]

Marks was not a leading voice at this council, but he did not object to the decision to destroy the press. The sole dissenter was Warrington, who "did not mean to be und[er]stood to go vs [against the proposition] but [would] not be in haste."[44] By supporting the decision, Marks again demonstrated his allegiance to Smith over the anti-polygamy views of the *Expositor*.

The council then passed its first libel law. Based on that law, Smith, as mayor, directed the destruction of the press, which was carried out by the city marshal and the Nauvoo Legion. They threw and scattered the type outside of the printing office and burned the remaining copies of the paper. The legal issues surrounding the destruction of the *Expositor* have been the subject of much debate, then and now, but there is no debate as to Marks' steadfast loyalty.

After the destruction of the *Nauvoo Expositor*, and as Smith's legal troubles grew, Marks remained the prophet's confidant. Three days after the *Expositor* was destroyed, members of the city council were arrested

---

42. "Records of attendance of city council," 24, CHL.
43. "Nauvoo City Council Rough Minute Book, February 1844–January 1845," 27–28, JSP.
44. "Nauvoo City Council Rough Minute Book," 28, JSP.

on a complaint of Francis Higbee for the "destruction of the Printing establishment of the Nauvoo Expositor."[45] Marks, serving as an associate justice, again showed his support for the destruction of the press when the court held that the city council, "be, jointly and severally, honorably discharged from the accusations and arrest and that they go home without delay."[46] Numerous complaints were made after Smith and the city council were released by the municipal court. To address this, Daniel H. Wells retried Smith on June 17. Smith submitted the following defense at trial:

> Joseph Smith objected to calling in question the doings of the City Council, and referred to the proceedings of Congress to show that all legislative bodies have a right to speak freely on any subject before them, . . . that the execution of such order could not be a riot, but a legal transaction; that the doings of the City Council could only be called in question by the powers above them, and that a magistrate had not that power; that the City Council was not arraigned here for trial, but individuals were arraigned for a riot. If the City Council had transcended their powers, they were amenable to the Supreme Court; and that Judge Thomas had decided that an action could not lie if no riot had been committed.[47]

Judge Wells accepted this defense, which outraged non-Mormons in surrounding areas and throughout the state of Illinois in general. While both sides of this disagreement started to prepare for battle, Governor Thomas Ford went to Carthage to defuse the situation. While there, he demanded that Smith come to Carthage to be tried for the crime again, this time by the circuit court.

This demand came by letter on June 22, 1844. Smith again called some of his trusted friends together: "soon after dark Joseph called A[braham] C. Hodge, Jno. L. Butler, A[lpheus] Cutler, W[ilia]m Marks, and some others into his <upper> room and said 'brethren, here is a letter from the Governor which I wish to have read.'" After reading the demand, Smith suggested that he and Hyrum "cross the river to-night and go away <to the West>."[48]

Ultimately, Smith submitted to the governor's request and went to Carthage to be retried. Marks later recounted that before he left, Smith told him, "Bro. Marks, I have become convinced since I last saw you

---

45. "Nauvoo Mayor's Court docket book, 1841 October–1843 February," 111–12, CHL.
46. "Nauvoo Mayor's Court docket book," 112, CHL.
47. "History, 1838–1856, volume F-1 [1 May 1844–8 August 1844]," 112, JSP.
48. "History, 1838–1856, volume F-1 [1 May 1844–8 August 1844]," 147, JSP.

Hamilton Hotel. From Holmes & Arnold's "Map of Hancock County, Illinois," 1859. Courtesy of LDS Church History Library.

that it is my duty to go to Carthage, and deliver myself up as a lamb to the slaughter."[49] The morning after they arrived in the city, Joseph and Hyrum Smith were arrested for treason. Marks spent part of the day there, supporting his leader as much as he could with his quiet presence.[50] Marks presumably returned home that evening, as Smith sent word back to Nauvoo on June 26 asking Marks to come and testify on his behalf at trial.[51] Before the trial was held, Joseph and Hyrum Smith were murdered on June 27, 1844.

The vigilante murder threw both communities of Nauvoo and Carthage into turmoil. The bodies of Joseph and Hyrum were brought to Hamilton's Hotel and the next morning were tenderly placed in two wagons. In these they traveled home to Nauvoo, accompanied by Artois Hamilton, Williard

---

49. William Marks, "Epistle," *ZHBO*, 53.

50. See "Appendix 3: Willard Richards, Journal Excerpt, 23–27 June 1844," 21–23, JSP. Marks arrived in Carthage at 12:48 p.m.

51. "Historical Department Journal History of the Church, 1844 January–June," 696, under date of June 26, 1844, CHL.

Richards, and Joseph and Hyrum's younger brother Samuel Smith. The trip that had taken messenger Asahel Lathrop two and a half hours now consumed a mournful seven hours in the hot summer sun.

The following day, Marks "washed the bodies from head to foot . . . and laid the bodies out with fine plain drawers and shirts, white neckerchiefs, white cotton stockings and white shrouds."[52] He also helped in keeping the bodies from being desecrated. Both Joseph and Hyrum were placed in coffins that were then placed in a "rough pine box." After an estimated eight to ten thousand people viewed the bodies, the coffins were hidden in a small, locked bedroom in the northeast corner of the mansion house to keep them safe from enemies who had threatened to seize them. The pine boxes were filled with sandbags and nailed shut. These stood in for the real bodies at the funeral, where W. W. Phelps preached a rousing eulogy.[53] The boxes rode in the hearse to the graveyard and were placed in graves in the Nauvoo Cemetery "with the usual ceremonies."[54]

The men who served as Joseph Smith's guard in the Nauvoo Legion and were still faithful and present in Nauvoo served as pall bearers, or "body guards." These included Marks, Alpheus Cutler, John Snyder, Christian Kreymeyer, Thomas Grover, Reynolds Cahoon, John L. Butler, and Samuel Smith. Five others replaced those who had died or apostatized.[55] At this point, Marks was considered a true and loyal friend to Joseph Smith and the church. Marks and several others returned to the mansion house that evening. At midnight, Marks and the other trusted men carried the coffins containing the bodies of Joseph and Hyrum Smith "through the garden, round by the pump, and . . . to the Nauvoo House, which was then built to the first joints of the basement."[56] They hid the corpses of their respected leaders in the rubble of the basement and silently and mournfully departed to their homes.

---

52. "Journal History," 696, CHL.
53. "Funeral Sermon of Joseph and Hyrum Smith," 1–16, CHL.
54. "Historian's Office, Martyrdom Account," 1, JSP.
55. Vinson Knight and Robert B. Thompson had died previously, and William Law and Elias Higbee were apostates. Henry G. Sherwood was not in town. These were replaced by Abraham C. Hodge, Lewis D. Wilson, James Emmett, Shadrach Roundy, and Edward Hunter.
56. "Historian's Office, Martyrdom Account," 1, JSP.

CHAPTER 7

Succession and Shoulder-Rounding

The deaths of Joseph Smith and his brother Hyrum, his most presumed successor,[1] left the Latter Day Saints without a clear plan for who was to lead the church. From the beginning, its structure had been fluid, only gradually evolving into a tiered system.[2] Some members prized charisma and religious experience as leadership qualifications, while others valued placement in the hierarchy. Authorization to govern had been widely distributed, so there were many options.[3] Members of the First Presidency held authority to manage the church in Joseph Smith's absence.[4] Additionally, bodies such as the standing high council, the Quorum of the Twelve, and the First Quorum of Seventy had authority equaling the First Presidency. This system provided an effective balance of power but was not as useful as a succession plan.[5]

Because Joseph Smith had claimed his own authority through ordination by heavenly messengers, the pathway of angelic ordination was

---

1. See D. Michael Quinn, "The Mormon Succession Crisis of 1844," 199–203.

On January 19, 1841, Joseph Smith appointed Hyrum to Oliver Cowdery's former station as associate (assistant) president and ordained successor. Hyrum also held the position of presiding patriarch of the church. On May 27, 1843, Joseph Smith declared, "The patriarchal office is the highest office in the church, and father Smith conferred this office, on Hyrum Smith, on his deathbed." "Minutes, 27 May 1843," 3, JSP.

2. D. Michael Quinn, *The Mormon Hierarchy: Origins of Power*, 7–8.

3. Quinn wrote that the succession crisis following Joseph Smith's death occurred because he "had provided too many precedents and possible authorities for avenues of succession to his office in the event of his death and because he had not published for the benefit of Church members a clearly stated outline of the order and precedence of presidential succession." D. Michael Quinn, "From Sacred Grove to Sacral Power Structure," 12.

4. On April 19, 1834, Smith, Oliver Cowdery, and Zebedee Coltrin "laid hands upon bro[ther] Sidney, and confirmed upon him the blessings of wisdom and knowledge to preside over the church in the abscence of brother Joseph." "Journal, 1832–1834," 79, JSP. See also LDS D&C 90:6.

5. See the system of checks and balances outlined in D&C 107, for instance. "Thus, none [not even the president of the high priesthood] shall be exempted from the justice and the laws of God, that all things may be done in order and in solemnity before him" (LDS D&C 107:84).

another possibility to succession. Finally, heirship could be claimed by Smith's brothers or oldest son, although the prophet's oldest son, Joseph Smith III, was only eleven years old at the death of his father.

William Marks, one of the highest-ranking Latter Day Saint leaders alive at the time, was widely respected and possessed a demeanor that the people of Nauvoo looked to for stability.[6] As early as 1835, Smith had revealed that the high council, equal in authority to both the First Presidency and the Twelve Apostles, was for the "cornerstone of Zion," while the Twelve were a "traveling high council."[7] The standing high council was to succeed Smith "if he should now be taken away."[8] According to published church doctrine, Marks, Nauvoo's stake president and president of the high council, should have presided in Nauvoo, and the apostles only in areas that had not been organized into stakes. Though members of the church would have been aware of this written qualification, Smith had expanded the power and authority of the Twelve in the Nauvoo years, increasing the tension between them and Marks.[9]

Further, Marks's standing in the Quorum of the Anointed was greater than other claimants. Marks was the first non-Smith to receive his second anointing and be ordained as prophet, priest, and king on October 22, 1843, under the hands of Smith.[10] By contrast, Brigham

---

6. Much of this chapter is drawn from John Dinger, "'A mean conspirator' or 'the noblest of men:' William Marks' Expulsion from Nauvoo," 12–38. We are appreciative of Robin S. Jensen's comments and critiques, which helped clarify our understanding of this period in church history.

7. "The Book of the Law of the Lord," 13, JSP (now LDS D&C 124:131); "Instruction on Priesthood, between circa 1 March and circa 4 May 1835," 84, JSP (now LDS D&C 107:33–34).

8. "Minute Book 2," 43–44, JSP. See Quinn, *The Mormon Hierarchy: Origins of Power*, 158n75, quoting Far West Record rephrased in "History of the Church," 2:124. At the end of 1844, the Twelve published a new edition of the Doctrine and Covenants, adding ambiguous wording supporting their authority.

9. Quinn, "From Sacred Grove," 11. Quinn writes that Joseph Smith had given "increasing responsibility and administrative powers to the Quorum of the Twelve Apostles, until by 1844 the Quorum of the Twelve was *de facto* the second most powerful body in the Mormon Church after the First Presidency."

10. Samuel James, "For the Messenger and Advocate. Laharp, Ill. January 28th, 1845," *MAR*, 130. "Mr. Marks then told me he was present when the twelve were ordained, and Brigham Young was ordained under Hyrum Smith, to the office if prophet, priest, and king, and Brigham ordained the rest of the twelve to the same office. And that he (Marks) was ordained to the same office

Young received this ordination from Hyrum Smith on November 22, 1843, and Young then ordained the rest of the Twelve.[11] To make matters more conclusive, Marks outranked all other claimants in the Council of Fifty which, according to William Clayton, used a seniority system. Marks was the tenth most senior member of the Council, outranking both Young and Sidney Rigdon.[12]

In April of 1845, Emma Smith explained her understanding of church succession to James Monroe, her children's schoolteacher:

> The next officer in the Kingdom immediately below the First President would take his Place upon his decease. . . . The next officer is the President of the High Council in Line. . . . Now as the Twelve have no power with regard to the government of the Church in the Stakes of Zion, but the High Council have all power, as it follows that on removal of the first President, the office would devolve upon the President of the High Council in Zion, as the first President always resides there, and that is the proper place for the quorum of which he is the head.

Thus, Emma stated, "there would be no schism or jamming but the Twelve would attend to their duties in the world and not meddle with the government of the church at home." The president of the high council would appoint counselors, form a First Presidency, and preside over "business in Zion," and the high council would choose another president to replace him. Emma specified that "Mr. Rigdon is not the proper successor of Pres[ident] Smith being only his councillor but Elder Marks should be the

---

under the hands of Joseph Smith." See also "George Miller letter, June 26, 1855," in H. W. Mills, "De Tal Palo Tal Astillo," 121. "Many of the Apostles and Elders having returned from England, Joseph washed and anointed as Kings and Priests to God, and over the House of Israel, the following named persons, as he said he was commanded of God, viz: James Adams (of Springfield), William Law, William Marks, Willard Richards, Brigham Young, Heber C. Kimball, Newel K. Whitney, Hyrum Smith, and myself; and conferred on us Patriarchal Priesthood. This took place on the 5th and 6th of May, 1842." See also "Journal, December 1842–June 1844," 142, JSP: "Sunday Oct[ober] 22nd 1843 S[idney] Rigdon preached 1/2 hour on poor rich folks. At home all day. Prayer meeting at Mansion [at] 2 P.M. W[illia]m Marks and <wife anointed> [these two words in shorthand] 24 present."

11. James, "For the Messenger and Advocate. Laharp, Ill. January 28th, 1845," *MAR*, 130.

12. George D. Smith, *An Intimate Chronicle: The Journals of William Clayton*, 129–30. See also Richard Donald Ouellette, *The Mormon Temple Lot Case: Space, Memory, and Identity in a Divided New Religion*, 177–78.

individual as he was not only his councillor at the time of his death but also president of the High Council."[13]

Upon the death of Joseph Smith at the end of June 1844, all the apostles except Willard Richards and John Taylor (who was recovering from wounds received in Carthage Jail) were scattered throughout the United States campaigning for Smith's presidential bid. Rigdon had moved to Pennsylvania to establish residency as Smith's running mate. Throughout the months of June and July, church affairs were superintended by Marks as Nauvoo's stake president and president of the high council. Richards oversaw the office business of the church, and William Clayton directed the workings of the temple. The Twelve began to make their way back to Nauvoo from their missions in the East as quickly as they could.

In the aftermath of the murders, Emma found herself in a complicated financial situation. It was difficult to determine which property and debts belonged to Joseph and which belonged to the church. Clayton stated in his journal:

> The situation looks gloomy. The property is chiefly in the name of the Trustee in Trust while the obligations are considered personal. Woods advised Emma to have all the Deeds recorded at Carthage for he says our Recorders office is not legal. This will cause trouble & much dissatisfaction.[14]

Just as Emma feared, the church owned the assets while she was liable for the debts. Because she was left with a young family and was expecting a child, she looked for ecclesiastical leadership she could trust and who could help her out of her financial mess. Emma was also an ardent opponent of polygamy and wanted the trustee she supported to be an ally. Marks, who rejected the doctrine of plural marriage after hearing it officially taught in high council meeting on August 12, 1843, fit the bill.[15] He was already in Nauvoo and could work on the financial entanglements immediately. Therefore, Emma pushed for Marks's ascension as leader of the church.[16]

For several weeks, a truncated group of the Quorum of the Anointed met to discuss the problem of succession but did not come

---

13. "James M. Monroe journal, 1822–1851," 45–47, CHL.
14. Smith, *An Intimate Chronicle*, 137.
15. John S. Dinger, *The Nauvoo City and High Council Minutes*, 467.
16. "James M. Monroe journal," 45–47, CHL; Smith, *An Intimate Chronicle*, 137.

to an agreement.¹⁷ At a prayer circle meeting at Marks's home on July 4, 1844, Clayton initially recorded that "it seemed manifest" to him, Marks, Alpheus Cutler, and Reynolds Cahoon "that brother Marks['s] place is to be appointed president & Trustee in Trust and this accords with Emma's feelings."¹⁸ However, William W. Phelps and Apostles John Taylor and Willard Richards wanted to wait for more apostles and Council of Fifty members to arrive in Nauvoo before making a decision.¹⁹ At a July 8 meeting, Emma argued that a trustee must be appointed immediately, as her financial situation remained dire. However, she was put off since some present believed that they "could not lawfully do it," and "Dr. Willard Richards and Bishop Newel K. Whitney considered it premature."²⁰

Friday, July 12, 1844, marked an important shift in thought as to who would preside. Marks approached Clayton while he was at the temple and "enquire[d] which was best to do about appointing a Trustee." Working together, they "concluded to call a meeting of the several presidents of Quorums & their council this P.M. at 2 o clock." Before the meeting, Clayton spoke with Bishop Newel K. Whitney, someone who had known and worked with Marks since Kirtland. Whitney was strongly against appointing Marks as trustee. Clayton recorded that Whitney "stated his feelings about Marks being appointed Trustee. He referred me to the fact of Marks being with Law & Emma in opposition to Joseph & the quorum.— And if Marks is appointed Trustee our spiritual blessings will be destroyed inasmuch as he is not favorable to the most important matters."²¹ The

---

17. D. Michael Quinn believes these meetings discussing succession were held by the Anointed Quorum, but Robin Jensen observes that some of them may simply have been comprised of a collection of church leaders or influential residents of Nauvoo.

18. Smith, *An Intimate Chronicle*, 137.

19. These men made a public announcement in the *Times and Seasons* on July 1, 1844, that no decision about new leadership would be made until the arrival of a majority of apostles and "other authorities." W. W. Phelps, W. Richards, and John Taylor, "To the Church of Jesus Christ of Latter Day Saints," *TS*, 568; See also Quinn, *The Mormon Hierarchy: Origins of Power*, 149.

20. Smith, *An Intimate Chronicle*, 138–39; See also "Historical Department Journal History of the Church, 1844 July–December," 39, under date of July 12, 1844, CHL.

21. Smith, *An Intimate Chronicle*, 138.

"spiritual blessings" and "most important matters" spoken of by Whitney referred to the doctrine and practice of polygamy.[22]

After speaking with Whitney, Clayton spoke with Cutler and Cahoon about these concerns. Following some thoughtful discussion, "they both agreed in the same mind with bro[ther] Whitney" that Marks should not be the next leader of the church.[23]

On July 30, 1844, Bishop George Miller and Alexander Badlam asked Apostles John Taylor, George A. Smith, and Willard Richards to organize a meeting of the Fifty. Historian D. Michael Quinn points out the irony "that the Quorum of Anointed, unknown in written revelation or to the Mormon membership, was on the verge of choosing a new president behind closed doors."[24] The apostles replied somewhat pompously that the Council of Fifty, which had been set up to be a political organization, was not an ecclesiastical body, and that "the organization of the church belonged to the Priesthood alone."[25]

The possibility of naming the deceased prophet's thirty-six-year-old brother, Samuel Smith, as successor was quashed by Samuel's death on July 30. The official cause of death was listed as "bilious fever," but another Smith brother, William, whose relationship with the Twelve had increasingly soured, suggested that Samuel had been poisoned "by order of Brigham Young and Willard Richards."[26]

Parley P. Pratt and George A. Smith, who had been electioneering in the Midwest, were the first two members of the Twelve to return to Nauvoo and join Taylor and Richards. They were followed by Rigdon,

---

22. While Whitney considered this a most important matter, he had not yet taken a plural wife. Whitney did so two months later when he married Olive Maria Bishop on September 10, 1844. George D. Smith, *Nauvoo Polygamy*, 631.

23. Smith, *An Intimate Chronicle*, 138. William Clayton was a polygamist at the time, marrying Margaret Moon on April 27, 1843. Reynolds Cahoon became a polygamist in 1842 when he married Lucinda Roberts (Johnson). Alpheus Cutler would not become a polygamist until 1846. Smith, *Nauvoo Polygamy*, 581, 587.

24. Quinn, *The Mormon Hierarchy: Origins of Power*, 150. Unlike the other quorums of the church, the Anointed Quorum did not need a majority to make a decision.

25. "Historical Department Journal History of the Church, 1844 July–December," 95, under date of July 30, 1844, CHL.

26. William Smith, "A Letter from William Smith," *NYDT*, 5. For more information on this incident, see D. Michael Quinn, *The Mormon Hierarchy: Origins of Power*, 152–153. Quinn concludes, "This troubling allegation should not be ignored but cannot be verified."

a surviving member of the First Presidency who returned on August 3, 1844, claiming a revelation had brought him there. Rigdon later admitted that Marks had in fact sent him a letter "soliciting us to repair to Nauvoo. . . . On our arrival he said to us that he had been praying to his God, and that God had revealed to him that we were to lead the church, and that he had made a solemn covenant with God, that if no other person stood by us he would."[27] For Rigdon to make it to Nauvoo only thirty-eight days after the murder of the Smiths, Marks must have sent the letter soon after the prophet's death. It appears that Marks never made a bid for leadership himself. He could have felt uncomfortable with the thought of leading the entire church, and perhaps he saw Rigdon as the proper legal successor.

The day after Rigdon arrived, on Sunday, August 4, he spoke to the Saints on the topic "My Ways Are Not as Your Ways." His speech referred to and challenged the Twelve Apostles, particularly in regard to secret practices like polygamy. In Rigdon's speech, he "related a vision which he said the Lord had shown him concerning the situation of the Church, and said there must be a guardian appointed to build the Church up to Joseph, as he had begun it."[28] Rigdon pushed for a general meeting to vote for a guardian, and Marks announced one for the next Thursday. This action points to Marks's autonomous support of Rigdon's leadership, at least early in the game. Clayton did "not feel satisfied with this move because it is universally understood that the Twelve have been sent for and are expected here every day and it seems a plot laid for the saints to take advantage of their situation."[29] However, Marks was clearly within his rights to call such a meeting. As head of the Nauvoo Stake, subject only to the First Presidency, and as president of the standing high council, his role was to "govern[] members, arbitrate[] disputes, investigate[] misconduct, and over[see] the ecclesiastical and religious life of Mormons within the stake's boundaries."[30] Marks was supported by many people within his jurisdiction. However, for years prior to the martyrdom, the Twelve Apostles had been growing in power, responsibility, and trust, beyond their duty as a

---

27. Sidney Rigdon, "The Purposes of God," *MAR*, 114.

28. "Historical Department Journal History of the Church, 1844 July–December," 109, under date of August 4, 1844, CHL.

29. Smith, *An Intimate Chronicle*, 140.

30. See LDS D&C 102, 107, 124:131; Quinn, *The Mormon Hierarchy: Origins of Power*, 59.

Sidney Rigdon. Courtesy of LDS Church History Library.

"traveling high council." The degree of authority they had in Nauvoo was up for debate and not entirely clear.[31]

On Tuesday, August 6, Phelps met with Rigdon and asked him "why he was so much disposed to hurry matters," pleading with the would-be guardian to "wait until the Twelve returned." Meanwhile, Marks told Alpheus Cutler that "Rigdon was to be president," and he revealed that Rigdon planned to name Marks church "Patriark," successor to Hyrum Smith.[32] That very evening, the highly awaited Apostles Brigham Young, Heber C. Kimball, Lyman Wight, Orson Pratt, and Wilford Woodruff all arrived on the scene.

Concerned with Rigdon's claims, on August 7 the Twelve Apostles and the high council met with Rigdon and asked him to "make a statement to the church concerning his message to the Saints, and the vision & revelation he had received." In a straightforward manner, Rigdon told the assembled men that he had come to Nauvoo to "offer Myself to them as a Guardian." He said that he "had a vision at Pittsburgh, June 27: this was presented to my mind, not as an open vision, but rather a continuation

---

31. For a discussion of the Twelve Apostles' ascension to power, see Quinn, "The Mormon Succession Crisis of 1844," 187–233. See also Quinn, *The Mormon Hierarchy: Origins of Power*, 65–66.

32. Smith, *An Intimate Chronicle*, 140–41; See also "Minutes, 1839 October–1845 October," 8, CHL.

of the vision mentioned in the Book of Doctrine and Covenants. It was shown to me that this church must be built up to Joseph, and that all the blessings we receive must come through him."³³

Rigdon's claim was well crafted, reminding the group of his closeness with Smith and his own revelatory gifts, made manifest in a February 1832 vision of Christ that had been canonized as section 91 of the 1835 Doctrine and Covenants (and later as section 76 beginning with the 1864 Latter-day Saint edition). Ultimately, he concluded,

> I have been consecrated a spokesman to Joseph, and I was commanded to speak for him: the church is not disorganized, though our head is gone. We may have a diversity of feelings on this matter; I have been called to be a spokesman unto Joseph, and I want to build up the church unto him. and if the people want me to sustain this place, I want it upon the principle that every individual shall acknowledge it for himself.³⁴

The meeting on Thursday, August 8, 1844, that Marks had called consisted of a morning and an afternoon session. In the morning, Marks had a platform built for Rigdon so that his voice could carry to the large assembly that was gathered. Rigdon preached a reassuring message that the church still held the authority and priesthood it needed to carry on the kingdom of God in the last days. He wished to maintain the fragile balance among the brethren, with every quorum standing in its current place in the structure that Smith had established. Rigdon, the only surviving member of the First Presidency, would act as "a spokesman for our prophet who has been taken from us."³⁵ Brigham Young next addressed the congregation, saying that he "wanted to sit and weep 30 days" before making a decision, but "in the name of the people," the matter would be settled that afternoon. Young agreed with Rigdon that everyone should retain their places in the priesthood order and that no one could replace Smith. He directed that in the afternoon meeting, the high council, President Marks, the apostles with Rigdon on their right hand, and the

---

33. "Historical Department Journal History of the Church, 1844 July–December," 121, under date of August 7, 1844, CHL.

34. "Historical Department Journal History," CHL; See also Smith, *An Intimate Chronicle,* 141.

35. LaJean Purcell Carruth and Robin Scott Jensen, "Sidney Rigdon's Plea to the Saints: Transcription of Thomas Bullock's Shorthand Notes from the August 8, 1844, Morning Meeting," 129. Rigdon was the only surviving member of the First Presidency, since William Law had been excommunicated in April 1844 and assistant counselor Amasa Lyman had never been formally sustained to replace Law.

lower brethren would all take seats in order of their callings and "we can do the business in 5 minutes."[36]

That afternoon, Young supervised the arrangement of the brethren "in their lot, according to appointment."[37] With this grand visual before them, he asked the assembled Saints, "Do you want a guardian, a prophet, a spokesman, or what do you want? If you want any of these officers, signify it by raising the right hand." None voted for an additional officer to supersede those who were seated in front of them. Young "then gave the saints his views of what the Lord wanted." He pointed out the Twelve, seated highest on the pulpits, and proclaimed them "appointed by the finger of God, who hold the keys of the priesthood, and the authority to set in order and regulate the church in all the world." Next, he motioned to Amasa Lyman (who had been called as a counselor in the First Presidency a year and a half earlier) and Sidney Rigdon: "they were councillors in the first presidency, and they are councillors to the twelve still; if they keep their places; but if either wishes to act as 'spokesman' for the prophet Joseph, he must go behind the veil where Joseph is."[38]

Lyman spoke, agreeing that the Twelve had keys and power that the apostles had anciently. Phelps was called upon to speak for Rigdon, but he instead pointed out that Rigdon had received only a partial endowment and hoped he would submit to receive more. Following these remarks, Rigdon retreated and "refused to have his name voted for as a spokesman or guardian." Marks remained a quiet observer as well. When the question was put, "all in favor of supporting the Twelve in their calling, (every quorum, man and woman,) signify it by the uplifted hand," the vote was nearly unanimous in the affirmative.[39] The congregation did not want to disrupt the priesthood chain of command that Young so visually demonstrated. Many observers later recalled a strong witness that Young spoke with the power and spirit of Joseph Smith.[40]

After this decision was made, Young told the crowd, "The next is President Marks; our feelings are to let him stand as President of the Stake,

---

36. Carruth and Jensen, "Sidney Rigdon's Plea to the Saints," 138–39.
37. "Special Meeting," *TS*, 637.
38. "Special Meeting," *TS*, 638.
39. "Special Meeting," *TS*, 638. See Quinn, *The Mormon Hierarchy: Origins of Power*, 167. Quinn writes that about twenty people voted against the apostles.
40. Compare Jacob Vidrine, "Succession to Brigham Young," 13–35; and Richard S. Van Wagoner, "The Making of a Mormon Myth: The 1844 Transfiguration of Brigham Young," 1–24.

as heretofore."⁴¹ With this statement, Young implied that Marks was serving at the pleasure of the Twelve Apostles, when the vote actually enabled all of the priesthood holders to retain their callings.

In order to stabilize the power advantage held by the Twelve following the meeting, Young quickly began to remove what he perceived as threats to the apostles' authority.⁴² As a result of scampering rumors, Marks found his position precarious. Accused by Clayton of "trying to draw off a party," Marks was summoned to appear before the Twelve Apostles the following day at the temple. Rigdon was also summoned but did not appear, as he "said he was sick and should not attend." The episode set off a chain of events where Marks was mind-numbingly obligated to prove his loyalty again and again.

Young led the meeting and told Marks "that in consequence of rumors & reports of the proceedings of him & E[lde]r Rigdon he had called them together that the thing might be talked over and if possible an union effected." Young then told Marks "what he had heard"—likely the rumors that Rigdon and Marks were planning on forming a church in competition with the Twelve. Marks not only "denied the charges in toto," but he also claimed that "he had been abused by the tongue of slander." That false rumors about Marks were flying through the church at large is illustrated by a letter dated August 16, 1844, and written from Hampton, Illinois, by anti-polygamist Austin Cowles. Cowles had been Marks's counselor in the Nauvoo Stake presidency and was a fellow member of the high council. In the letter he asked Marks and Heman Hyde to come up and see the country with an eye to gathering there with a group of like-minded

---

41. "History, 1838–1856, volume F-1 [1 May 1844–8 August 1844]," 303, JSP.

42. Quinn, *The Mormon Hierarchy: Origins of Power*, 173–74; Quinn, "The Mormon Succession Crisis of 1844," 161, 214–15. For example, in addition to releasing William Marks as Nauvoo stake president, Young "vacated the full First Quorum of Seventy by appointing the sixty-three lesser members of that quorum as presidents over local quorums of seventy, leaving only the first seven presidents of the First Quorum in the original quorum." He removed the majority of men in Nauvoo from the jurisdiction of the high council by making them local Seventies and thus under the authority of the Twelve. He sent high priests abroad as branch presidents in the mission field, placing them under the Twelve as well. He also made retroactive changes in the official *History of the Church* such as an addition to the published minutes of an 1836 meeting of the First Presidency and the Quorum of the Twelve stating, "and where I am not, there is no First Presidency over the Twelve."

people. Cowles wrote that he had been told "Bro[ther] Marks has resigned his office" and shared his opinion: "this is wisdom."[43]

At this point, Marks had no intention of resigning his office or of leaving the church, but he did share concerns he had about the actions of the Twelve Apostles. He "acknowledge[d] that the course the Twelve had pursued was contrary to what he had expected." Marks resented the way the Twelve were asserting their authority since the death of Smith. His challenge cleared the air by putting his uneasiness into words without attempting to grasp power. For the moment, he was able to navigate a difficult situation with integrity, and the meeting was ultimately pronounced "benificial." A repentant Clayton stated that in regards to Marks he "would never listen to reports again."[44]

While Marks had made a temporary peace with the Twelve, Rigdon did not change his course and made plans to lead a church irrespective of the Twelve's wishes.[45] He enlisted others in his cause, including Leonard Soby, a member of the Nauvoo High Council. When this was discovered, Soby was put on trial by the high council on September 7, 1844, for the charge of "saying that Rigdon was president."[46] Again trying to preserve his tenuous position as a loyal member of the church while retaining some sympathy for Rigdon, "E[lde]r Marks proposed that he withdraw. Council member [Thomas] Grover objected untill he had answered certain questions."[47] The record does not preserve what these questions were, but even Marks's fellow council members were holding his feet to the fire, no longer willing to watch him halt between two opinions.

---

43. "Austin Cowles letter Aug. 16, 1844," 3, CHL.

44. Smith, *An Intimate Chronicle*, 146.

45. "Tuesday, September 3 [1844]—Pres Brigham Young had an interview with Brother Sidney Rigdon ^who said that^ ~~He said~~ he had power and authority above the Twelve Apostles and did not consider himself amenable to their counsel. In the evening, the Twelve had an interview with Bro[ther] Rigdon, who was far from feeling and interest with the Twelve. His license was demanded, which he refused to give up, and said 'the church had not been led by the Lord for a long time, and he should come out and expose the secrets of the church." "Historical Department Journal History of the Church, 1844 July–December," 213, under date of September 3, 1844, CHL.

46. "Historical Department Journal History of the Church, 1844 July–December," 235, under date of September 7, 1844, CHL. See also "Minutes, 1844 September 27," CHL.

47. "Minutes, 1844 September 27," CHL.

The following day, Rigdon was cut off by the high council in a public meeting held on a large outdoor meeting ground in Nauvoo. Minutes of the meeting state that "the High Council was organized with Bishop Newel K. Whitney at their head."[48] However, eight members of the Twelve were in attendance, which led to some confusion as to what body cut off Rigdon and the meeting itself being described as "a court of most anomalous character."[49] At the trial, Young acted as both witness and prosecutor.[50] He called upon various apostles to testify, including Orson Hyde, Parley P. Pratt, Amasa Lyman,[51] John Taylor, W. W. Phelps, and Heber C. Kimball, so it looked and sounded to some in attendance like a meeting of the Twelve, but it was the high council that sat in judgment and ruled.

---

48. "Historical Department Journal History of the Church, 1844 July–December," 239, under date of September 8, 1844, CHL; See also "Trial of Elder Rigdon," *TS*, 648. Brigham Young stated, "It is written in the book of Doctrine and Covenants, that the president [of the church] can be tried before a bishop and twelve high priests, or the high council of the church. There are many present this morning who were present at the organization of that quorum in Kirtland. We have here before us this morning, the high council, and bishop Whitney at their head, and we will try Sidney Rigdon before this council and let them take an action on his case this morning; and then we will present it to the church, and let the church also take an action upon it."

49. "The High Council," *VH*, 1.

50. Young used strong rhetoric to situate the Twelve in a position of being Smith's natural successor while making the others seem to be usurpers: "I will now lay before this congregation that it seems there are some for Paul[,] some for Cephas & there are a great many for Christ & I will also say there are some for Bro[ther] Joseph & Hyrum[,] the book of Mormon the book of doctrine & covenants & for the building up of the temple of our God & there are some for Emmet & some for Sidney Rigdon & there will be some for the Twelve[.] therefore I will say that those who are for Brother Joseph & Hyrum & the book of Mormon & doctrine & covenants also the building of the temple are for the Twelve & this will be considered one party & those that are for Sidney Rigdon & the discontinueation of the temple I want them to be just as honest as what they are in their secret meetings & combinations." "Minutes of a special meeting of the Church, 1844 Sep. 8, 10–12," 1, CHL.

51. Lyman became a member of the Quorum of the Twelve on August 20, 1842, replacing Orson Pratt, who had been excommunicated. When Pratt was rebaptized and had resumed his former position, Lyman was dropped from the Quorum. Following the deaths of Joseph and Hyrum Smith and shortly before Rigdon's trial, Brigham Young returned Lyman to the Quorum on August 12, 1844.

While the meeting was conducted under unusual circumstances, Marks made sure it was carried out according to high council rules and was thus a valid excommunication.[52] After watching what had happened to Soby the day before, and hearing all the claims made against Rigdon (especially that he had brought mob violence against the people and would do it again), Marks followed high council protocol by personally offering a defense of Rigdon. "I will take up the opposite side," he said, both because he had "always been a friend to Rigdon"[53] and because, according to revelation, someone from the high council was to "stand up in behalf of the accused" (LDS D&C 102:17).

In doing this, Marks must have known that to defend Rigdon in a public meeting would put him even more at odds with the Twelve than he had been to that point. However, Marks did what he felt was right and offered a defense. He first tried to narrow the issues Rigdon was being accused of by pointing out that although Rigdon had been vaguely accused of many faults and "many great crimes" in the past, none of the charges had been sustained. Therefore the council should only "bring up the charges against him at the present time."[54]

Marks then addressed these particular claims. He told the audience that Rigdon and Smith had reconciled before he went to Pittsburgh: "I have heard Joseph [Smith] say a short time before [Sidney] left to go to Pittsburgh that Sidney was all right & that he had nothing against him." Marks put forth his view of succession in the strongest way he had to date: that "there should always be a first presidency over this people . . . to receive revelations . . . & to lead the Church." He described the Twelve as a "travelling high council to go to all the nations of the earth to build up the kingdom in all the world, & it is my opinion that if this is to be done I think it is enough for twelve men to do." However, Marks maintained his characteristic openness and humility, as he also told the congregation that "If I a[m] wrong I wish to be corrected." Though Marks supported the organization of a new First Presidency, with Rigdon at the head, he was willing to follow the vote of the church. He stated, "I have been a long

---

52. At the July 11, 1840, meeting of the Nauvoo High Council, Joseph Smith set out additional rules for a trial before the high council. He stated that "the Council should try no case without both parties being present or having had an opportunity to be present[.]" "Minutes, 1840 March 8—1842 May 20," 12, CHL.

53. "Minutes of a special meeting of the Church," 10, CHL.

54. "Minutes," 10–11, CHL.

time acquainted with Bro[ther] Sidney . . . but if this congregation feels to sever him from the body I am willing to go by the decision of the church."[55]

Orson Hyde responded that in his opinion, Rigdon wanted "to scatter this people & lead them away instead of gathering them together to build the house of our God."[56] The high council under the direction of Bishop Whitney then moved, seconded, and carried unanimously a motion that Rigdon "be cut off from the church & delivered over to the buffetings of Satan." The congregation as a whole did the same. Even though Marks stated he would go with the majority, he clearly was not trusted, as "[it was] moved & seconded that we get an expression from Bro[ther] Marks if he approves of this day[']s proceedings." Marks calmly "arose and said he was willing to go by the decision of this church."[57]

Because of Marks's actions that day, he ensured that the meeting followed Smith's revelations and that Rigdon was cut off in a valid and correct manner. However, this defense of Rigdon led to an alienation between Marks and many of those who held leading positions in Nauvoo. On September 10, 1844, the high council met to discuss this situation: "The faith, principle and pursuit of Elder Marks was called up—where it was found that he imbibed a notion different from the apostles or council—and was voted that the Council (in future) do business without him at their head." It was further decided that Henry G. Sherwood "acquaint Elder Marks of the proceedings—and obtain from him the papers[,] Book[,] and Pen[,] &c."[58] Seeing how the high council did not have the "papers" or "Book," likely the bound minutes book of the high council, this clearly was not an official meeting. Marks was not present, and he was thus unable to speak in his own behalf. While this was not a disciplinary hearing, the high council did not follow the guidelines set up for them by Smith, who stated on July 11, 1840, to the high council that "the Council should try no case without both parties being present[,] or having had an opportunity to be present."[59] Marks should have had an opportunity to present a defense.

---

55. "Minutes," 10–11, CHL.
56. "Minutes," 14, CHL.
57. "Minutes," 14–15, CHL; See also "Conclusion of Elder Rigdon's Trial," *TS*, 687.
58. "Minutes, 1844 May 18–September 10," 11, under date of September 10, 1844, CHL.
59. "Minutes, 1840 March 8–1842 May 20," 12, CHL.

Although the high council expelled Marks, they did not excommunicate him or even take away his presidency as they did not have the authority to do either.⁶⁰ They simply removed him from the high council, so they could conduct business without him.⁶¹ This was a real blow to a man who was carefully trying to express faithful dissent. There is no precedent in Smith's revelations that would allow a high council to excommunicate or release a stake president. It can also be argued that because Marks received his second anointing, he could not be excommunicated at all.

* * *

Two months after Joseph Smith's death, on August 25, 1844, Emma Smith signed an article of agreement to rent to Marks "the house com[m]only called the Nauvo[o] Mansion," plus the barn and barn lot of the property, for the sum of two hundred dollars per year. Marks agreed to keep the property in good condition and to allow Emma to keep her horse and carriage in the barn.⁶² The mansion was a large structure boasting a total of twenty-two rooms. Since January 1844, Joseph Smith had leased the property to Ebenezer Robinson to manage as a hotel, while reserving three rooms for himself and his family. Marks began the same type of proprietorship in September, and Emma and her children remained in residence.

The mansion served as a source of income for Marks as well as for Emma and her family. One way Marks planned to make this arrangement profitable was to hold a public dance in late 1844. Even though this enterprise was to benefit the Smith family, the Twelve Apostles, in a meeting on September 30, 1844, "concluded to use our influence to prevent the brethren and sisters from attending the ball which William Marks, landlord of the Nauvoo Mansion was making arrangements for."⁶³ With the Twelve Apostles dissuading people from attending the ball, Marks lost much of his remaining credibility in Nauvoo society.

A week later, at the church's October general conference, Marks was again discussed by the leaders of the church. First, "President John Smith moved that William Marks be sustained in his calling as president of this

---

60. For discussion of the second anointing, see David John Buerger, *The Mysteries of Godliness: A History of Mormon Temple Worship*, chapter 3.

61. "Minutes, 1844 May 18–September 10," 11, CHL.

62. Emma Smith and William Marks, signed lease August 25, 1844, CCLA.

63. "Historian's Office History of the Church, 1844 August 9–1845 June 30," 76–77, CHL.

stake." W. W. Phelps objected, citing the high council's expulsion on September 10. Brigham Young opined "that a president of a stake could be dropped without taking his standing from him in the church. But not so with the first presidency or the Twelve. A president of a stake is only called for the time being, if you drop him he will fall back into the High Priests quorum." Young's statement gave the group authority to drop Marks by distinguishing the role of a stake president from that of the First Presidency or Twelve Apostles. With this, Young made the stake president a temporary calling that could be taken away without excommunication. After Young's explanation the "motion was then put, but there was only two votes." The two individuals who wanted Marks to retain his position as stake president remain unknown, but a "contrary vote was put and carried by an overwhelming majority."[64] Marks was no longer the stake president of Nauvoo and had no place in Young's hierarchy after the October conference.

For a time, Marks retained his position as an alderman on the city council and a justice of the municipal court. However, after the death of Smith he rarely attended either body and the Nauvoo police force notified him they would "no more call upon him to act in any matter of Law on Equity: wherein we are conserned as Policemen."[65] An interesting note was included in the record, however, demonstrating the respect that Marks still held in certain circles:

> Alderman William Marks has dealt out Justice towards the police of this city in such a nice mild charitable & christian like manner so strictly according to Law, Equity, and his oath of office & has so abbly defended them against the abuse and insults so frequently heaped upon them while in the discharge of their duty by a lawless set of Ruffians.[66]

After Marks missed the city council meeting on October 12, 1844, at the November 9 meeting "[it was] moved [and] sec[onded] that Ald[erman] [William] Marks be instructed to appear before us" in regards to his management of the city burial ground.[67]

---

64. "Historical Department Journal History of the Church, 1844 July–December," 333, under date of October 7, 1844, CHL.

65. "City Council Proceedings; Petitions, 1844 May–1844 December," 5, under date of July 15, 1844, CHL.

66. "City Council Proceedings," 5, CHL.

67. "Nauvoo City Council Rough Minute Book, February 1844–January 1845," 51, under date of November 9, 1844, JSP.

On November 23, 1844, Marks and his wife were summoned to appear before the high council at the Seventies' Hall.[68] William and Rosannah appeared at the appointed time on Saturday, November 30. When they arrived, they found that not only was the high council present, but also many members of the Quorum of the Twelve, including Orson Hyde, John Taylor, and Heber C. Kimball. The purpose of their summons quickly became apparent when it was "carried unanimously, that the Council proceed to question those individuals who were cited (by vote of the previous meeting), relative to their faith &c."[69]

Before being questioned, Marks "arose and stated that he had never spoken against the Council or Church, but had thought there had been some hasty moves made, but wished to do the thing that was right: [he] did not think of apostatizing, but wished to carry out every righteous principle." Second, he pointed out problems he perceived in the church and actions being taken against him personally. He said, "[There] were things practiced in our midst that were not right, such as stealing and the like which had been a trouble to him, [he] thought some had treated him with coldness and neglect &c." After airing these grievances, he again stated his commitment to the church, claiming he "[w]ished to sustain the Church. As respect[ing] the present organization, he was willing to conform to, and abide by it."[70]

The council then began the questioning by asking Marks to explain his present feelings regarding the church. The former stake president answered honestly that he "did not wish to leave the Church," but that he also did not "wish to crowd himself into the society of those who did not want him with them." He specified how he felt he was not wanted. He stated that he "had heard many threats and hard speeches concerning him," that "there were those who were continually telling foul lies about him," and that there were those who were "stealing every thing ^from him^ they could lay their hands upon."[71]

Marks also told the council that he "had the best of feelings towards those that treated him well," but for the others, he "was willing for the brethren to do with him as they saw fit and he would abide by it." Though he wanted to stay in the church, Marks was still concerned with what had

---

68. "Minutes, 1844 September 21–1845 January 11," 5, under date of November 23, 1844, CHL.
69. "Minutes," 5–6, CHL.
70. "Minutes," 6, CHL.
71. "Minutes," 6, CHL.

happened in August and September. He admitted that "[h]is mind had been in an unsettled state respecting how the church should be organized, but since its present organizatio [he]was, and ever had been[,] satisfied with it."[72]

It appears that the council was satisfied by Marks's explanation. Henry G. Sherwood moved, and David Fulmer seconded, that Marks "have our fellowship, and that we give him our heart and hand for his Spiritual and Temporal welfare." The motion was "carried without a dissenting vote." Alpheus Cutler told Marks that he was "bound to sustain the Twelve, and all the Quorums in the Church with its present organization, for [it was] on [this] that his salvation depended." He asked Marks "if he could take him by the hand as a brother and go with him ^in^ these matters." Marks answered that he could, "Heart and Hand."[73]

This must have been a relief to Marks and his family, as it now seemed that the harassment and theft would end. Marks was able to honestly share his feelings with the council he once presided over, while they told him they sustained him in the church.[74]

However, any relief he might have felt was again temporary. The high council and apostles continued to entertain doubts about Marks's loyalty. Early in December 1844, Council President Samuel Bent presented Marks with a statement, written by the Twelve Apostles, that he was requested to sign. The article "confirm[ed] to them his declarations on last Saturday ^before the Council viz.^ to acknowledge ^and uphold^ the Twelve and all the Quorums of the Church of Jesus Christ [a]s in its present organization, and thereby show to all, his renunciation of Sidney Rigdon and his claims." Marks would not sign the statement. Even when an objectionable clause acknowledging the authority of the Twelve was struck off, Marks "utterly refused to sign it, and said he would sign no paper and did not want his name to go abroad."[75] After months of harassment and being assured the week before that he had the high council's "fellowship" in all things temporal and spiritual, it is no surprise that he refused to sign the document. He had attended every meeting requested

---

72. "Minutes," 6, CHL.

73. "Minutes," 6, 8, CHL.

74. In a 1975 paper, Robert D. Hutchins speculates that since precedents had been set in the past for men who had been removed from their leadership positions to later regain them: "Marks undoubtedly counted on the same sort of policy being extended to him as far as his presidencies were concerned." Robert D. Hutchins, "President William E. Marks . . . A Man Forgotten," 40.

75. "Minutes, 1844 September 21–1845 January 11," 9, CHL.

of him and continually stated his desire to stay with the church. However, it was never enough.

Amasa Lyman, who was present at the meeting, explained that the Twelve "thought it proper to write a manifesto to ~~present to~~ [for] Elder Marks ^to sign^ that he might show or acknowledge that he had been deceived by Sidney Rigdon and that in so doing his name and influence abroad should not be used against this Church." George A. Smith added that "Elder Marks had had more influence abroad than Elder Rigdon."[76] Marks was still a well-known and influential person both in Nauvoo and in areas outside the church. Newspaper articles published far and wide identified Marks and Emma Smith as allies of Rigdon.[77] Rigdon was still using Marks as evidence of his right to lead, and the Twelve wished to transfer that influence to themselves. They "wished his acknowledgements to uphold the Twelve and all the authorities of this Church in its present organization, and his renunciation of S[idney] Rigdon."[78] In a post-Joseph Smith church, the Twelve required abject obedience and unmitigated support to cement their position as successors.

The issue caused "much deliberation," and the council unanimously voted "that Elder Marks be cited for trial . . . for refusing to comply with the Covenant made by him ~~to face~~ [to] said Council on last Saturday, viz to sustain the Twelve and all the Quorums of the Church."[79] On December 9, 1844, Marks appeared for his trial, but it was not held. After more "consultation," he relented, and the Twelve got the signed statement they were looking for:

> After mature and candid deliberation, I am fully ~~factorily~~ and satisfactorily convinced that Mr. Sidney Rigdon's claims to the presidency of the church of Jesus Christ of Latter-Day Saints are not founded in truth. I have been deceived by his specious pretences, and now feel to warn everyone over whom I may have any influence to beware of him and his pretended visions and revelations. The Twelve are the proper ~~authorities~~ persons to lead the church. Nauvoo Dec. 9th 1844. William Marks[80]

---

76. "Minutes," 9, CHL.
77. See, for example, "Mormonism," *WL*, 344.
78. "Minutes, 1844 September 21–1845 January 11," 9, CHL.
79. "Minutes," 10, CHL.
80. "Minutes," 10–11, CHL; See also William Marks, "Notice," *TS*, 742.

The minutes of the high council made sure to note that the "clause acknowledging the authority of the Twelve" was a voluntary addition of Elder Marks.[81]

A concerned onlooker, Samuel James, seeing the statement published in the *Nauvoo Neighbor*, visited Marks to find out "why he had pursued such a course." Marks allegedly explained, "I have got into darkness, and know not who are right. We had a warm time, said he, (referring to being brought before the council) and they declared I should sign that paper or be expelled; I took it home, showed it to my wife, and she said sign it. I did so."[82]

James wrote to Rigdon, providing a secondhand recounting of Marks's reply to the council when asked if he "believed Rigdon should stand at the head of the church." Marks told the men that Rigdon was "ordained to the highest office of any one in the church, of whom I have any knowledge." Apparently the Twelve told Marks that they predicated their authority to lead the church on a statement Smith made at a meeting at the mansion house before his death. Smith told the brethren, "I am tired bearing the burden of the church, you must round up your shoulders, and bear it till I rest." James claimed that Marks, feeling that he had been ordained to the same office of prophet, priest, and king that the Twelve had been, said, "I have no confidence in these fellows (referring to the twelve and others) they are as full of the devil as they can live." Finally, James claimed that he discussed Marks with Erastus Snow, who said, "they had no confidence in him, but had got him where they wanted him, they had destroyed his influence!"[83]

A story reported in *The Warsaw Signal* gave another reason Marks may have signed the statement: "William Marks, who being a man of property, sustained heavy losses by thefts, and on account of the unsettled state of his business could not leave the city.—he, therefore published a note a few weeks since in the Neighbor, renouncing Rigdon—joining the twelve, and exhorted all with whom he had any influence to do likewise."[84] Soon after, the paper reported, his property was returned. Whether it was the request of his wife, pressure from the Twelve, or to regain his stolen goods, Marks signed the document in hopes that the harassment would cease.

The signing of the document seemed to increase Marks' stature for a time. On December 14, Marks attended a city council meeting.[85] The

---

81. "Minutes, 1844 September 21–1845 January 11," 11, CHL.
82. "For the Messenger and Advocate," *MAR*, 129.
83. "For the Messenger and Advocate," *MAR*, 130.
84. "Rich, Decidedly," *WS*.
85. "Records of attendance of city council," CHL.

University of Nauvoo was being discussed, and Marks was one of the original regents appointed in 1841. The mayor, Daniel Spencer, needed to fill the vacancies of the "Trustees & Registrar" and appointed Marks along with John Taylor, Daniel H. Wells, and Newel K. Whitney.[86]

Just as Marks was making way with the hierarchy in Nauvoo, the *Latter Day Saint's Messenger and Advocate*, Rigdon's newspaper, claimed in a statement published on December 16, that Marks was one of its agents in Nauvoo.[87] This claim was repeated in the same paper on January 1, 1845.[88] In the edition published January 15, Marks was no longer listed, but the paper published on January 22 intimated that Marks had perhaps only temporarily reconciled with the Twelve: "It may be all true that Moses Daily[89] has gone back to them [the Twelve], and confessed that he was wrong; but that does not say that he will always be deceived by them—I will say the same of Elder Marks. Time will prove who is right."[90]

---

86. "Nauvoo City Council Rough Minute Book, February 1844–January 1845," 54, JSP. After the death of Joseph Smith, Daniel Spencer was serving as mayor of Nauvoo until the next election could be held. See "Nauvoo City Council Rough Minute Book," 46–47, JSP.

87. "List of Agents," *MAR*, 64.

88. "List of Agents," *MAR*, 80.

89. Sidney Rigdon had attempted to seduce Moses Daley, a member of the church since 1833, into joining his movement by telling Daley that "that he saw him in the great army leading on a battalion." Amasa Lyman, "To the Saints Scattered Abroad," *TS*, 741. Daley rejoined the Twelve and brought his family to the Salt Lake Valley in 1839. He returned and captained a wagon train across the plains in 1853.

90. "To all the Saints Throughout the World," *MAR*, 108. Rigdon claimed that Marks must have come to the belief that "the spiritual wife system is the system that is to prepare the way of the Savior's coming," because Marks had personally told him that "that no person could live at Nauvoo unless he did embrace that system." Rigdon continued to mock Marks by claiming: "How good authority Mr. Marks is we must leave the world to judge, but if he is to be credited, he has gravely told the world that the spiritual wife system is true, and the true order of heaven. To this we have no objection if Mr. Marks wishes to prostitute his wife and daughter and himself also, to prepare the way of the Savior's coming, it is surely his right to do so. But, to do justice to the females of his family, we do believe he never will get them to submit." In Rigdon's attack on Marks, a fact was revealed that was probably unknown to the Twelve Apostles at the time. Rigdon wrote that "he [Marks] wrote letters to us as Pittsburgh soliciting us to repair to Nauvoo, before we had any intention of going, but afterwards went." It is likely the Twelve Apostles learned at this time that it was Marks who alerted and invited

Due to the perceived association with the *Messenger and Advocate* and other incidents, the goodwill engendered from the signing of the document was soon gone. On February 4, Marks was "rejected and dropped" from the Council of Fifty.[91] Thus ended any influence he had with the church hierarchy. Additionally, Marks's safety in Nauvoo was threatened as accusations against him grew more and more heated. He was still running the Mansion House as a business when a man named John C. Elliot came into town and put up there. Hosea Stout, a Nauvoo policeman, claimed that Elliot had been engaged in the murder of Joseph and Hyrum Smith and that Marks not only put the man up in his hotel, but "did all he could to secret him."[92] Stout's claim that Marks was allying himself with the murderers is false and shows extreme bias. Elliot was arrested and tried before the municipal court in Nauvoo, but the testimony showed that rather than being secreted by Marks, he "had been lounging about our city, for a time past, on pretence of legal business pertaining to sheriffality."[93]

A young man named Washington Peck, who was staying with the family, objected to Marks's defamation throughout the city. By so doing, he was "marked as a mean conspirator along with William Marks late president of this stake." Peck was styled as "lurk[ing] about continually in our midst communicating with our enemies & seeking to have the twelve destroyed." One evening, a group of people accosted the young man on his way home "and bedaubed him all over with privy dirt."[94] Marks, who had been holding in his emotions for too long, was furious. Two of the Nauvoo policemen on patrol duty heard a cry down towards the mansion house "as if some one was being killed." They ran to the spot and saw "no one but Wm. Marks who was in a rage because some one had threw some stinking filth and ink upon Washington Peck," whom policeman Allen Stout identified as an "apostate who was boarding at the Mansion."[95]

Rigdon to Nauvoo, and not a revelation as Rigdon previously claimed. Sidney Rigdon, "The Purposes of God," 114.

91. Smith, *An Intimate Chronicle,* 157; See also "Council of Fifty, Minutes, March 1844–January 1846; Volume 1, 10 March 1844–1 March 1845," 305, editorial note, JSP.

92. "Journal volume 1, 1845 May–1846 September," February 12, 1845, CHL.

93. "Examination of John C. Elliott," *NN*, 2.

94. William Clayton, *The Nauvoo Diaries of William Clayton, 1842–1846,* 80. See also Joseph Smith III, "What do I Remember of Nauvoo?" *JH*, 334.

95. "Reminiscences and journal, 1845–1889," 23, CHL. The authors thank John Hajicek for calling this reference to our attention.

In later years, Joseph Smith III recalled guards being set at the Smith and Marks property. He describes two young men who were visiting Marks being attacked by a guard with a knife while the Smiths' large white mastiff entered the fray.[96]

Public opinion became so heated that Marks ultimately found it necessary to move his family out of Nauvoo. To someone who had played such an important part in building and gathering people into what he believed was the kingdom of God on earth, this was a disheartening step. In late February he turned over the running of the mansion house to John Pack, who took possession of it on March 1, 1845.[97] After doing so and recovering his stolen property, he "left town suddenly"[98] and moved to Fulton City, Illinois, a small town 140 miles north of Nauvoo.

The news of Marks's exit from Nauvoo came as good news to the Twelve and their supporters. Zina Huntington Jacobs, plural wife to Brigham Young, wrote, "W[illia]m Marks and family left one day this week, went up the river on the Madison Ferry boat, I expect to unite with others that have gone out from us gone out from us because they ware not of us and love Darkness more than light."[99] Young also seemed relieved that he did not have to result to additional violence or intimidation to remove Marks: "Bro[ther] W[ilia]m. Marks has gone without being w[h]ittled out."[100]

---

96. Joseph Smith III, "What Do I Remember of Nauvoo?" 338–39.

97. John Pack, *John Pack: As Revealed in the Records*, 52–53.

98. "Historian's Office History of the Church, 1844 August 9–1845 June 30," 169, under date of March 12, 1845, CHL.

99. Maureen Ursenbach Beecher, "'All Things Move in Order in the City': The Nauvoo Diary of Zina Diantha Huntington Jacobs," 306.

100. Brigham Young, "History of Brigham Young, Nauvoo, Illinois," 38, CHL. Records from Nauvoo in the months and years following Joseph Smith's death describe various groups of boys, men, deacons, and members of the "old police" who formed "whistling and whittling brigades." To force undesirables to leave town, these brigades would surround the person, whistling discordantly and whittling threateningly with long, fierce knives until he was sufficiently intimidated to leave town. This was termed being "whistled out" or "whittled out." For contemporary accounts, see Thurmon Dean Moody, "Nauvoo's Whistling and Whittling Brigade," 480–90; and Jeffrey David Mahas, "'I Intend to get up a Whistling School:' The Nauvoo Whistling and Whittling Movement, American Vigilante Tradition, and Mormon Theocratic Thought," 37–67.

CHAPTER 8

James J. Strang: Claims and Clashes

William Marks left Nauvoo and arrived in Fulton Township, Illinois, amid the bustle of early Midwestern Manifest Destiny. When white settlers arrived beginning in 1835, there was evidence of relics such as burial mounds, spear heads, brass pots, and knives, as well as primitive works for smelting lead ore. Native populations of the Winnebago, Potawatomi, and Fox tribes remained numerous for a decade, with Natives hunting and trapping at will throughout the Cattail Slough.[1] The Indians were not deemed to be "troublesome" to the settlers, and they mingled freely until forced to leave for reservations further west.

By 1839 the township had a public tavern, and by 1841 a ferry was under construction.[2] In 1845, Fulton resembled Nauvoo when Mormons first started inhabiting the place—a young town experiencing rapid growth. When Marks moved there in 1845, it was "made up of high bluffs, overlooking the river on one side and a wide expanse of country on the other."[3]

Marks moved his family into a house near the banks of the Mississippi River. While he did not live there long, he did like it enough to help convince Emma Smith and her family to join them. Joseph Smith III recalled that due to the threat of Nauvoo's invasion by angry mobs, Marks and Dr. John Bernhisel advised Emma to leave the city, at least temporarily.[4] This move likely occurred in September 1845, and the Smiths lived about a quarter of a mile from the Marks family.[5]

Even after the Quorum of the Twelve took power in Nauvoo, thousands of confused Saints were scattered across the United States and many countries. Had Marks wished to take up the mantle of church leader at this time, many would have supported him, as the Twelve's claim to succession remained precarious. A letter from Hazen Aldrich in Willoughby, Ohio, to Samuel Akers in Erroll, New Hampshire, illustrates the understanding of many of the rank-and-file members of the church concerning the Twelve.

---

1. Charles Bent, *History of Whiteside County, Illinois: From Its First Settlement to the Present Time*, 157–62.
2. Bent, 160.
3. Bent, 156.
4. Joseph Smith III, "What do I Remember of Nauvoo?" 341–42.
5. Joseph III's recollections incorrectly state they moved in September 1846.

They saw the succession move as contrary to written church policy and were horrified by the scattering of the Saints that was happening:

> You will see by the Book of cov[e]nants Sec 3 part 12 that the 12 are a traveling high council & are entirely out of their place in attempting to assume the first presidency & dictate the affairs of the whole church & their folly is now being made manifest for they have almost broken up the church. Indeed they have broken it to peices.[6]

With Marks's reticence to step forward, Sidney Rigdon's offer to be a guardian for the church put down, and the Twelve's proposition to lead the church as a body without selecting a prophet to replace Smith, members of the original church were indeed "broken to pieces." Into the maelstrom stepped a contender for succession who claimed both earthly and heavenly sanction to occupy the prophetic office: James J. Strang.

It was in Fulton that Marks first became associated with this new contender. Strang was a convert of four months when Joseph Smith died, and was therefore relatively unknown in the church. Nevertheless, he claimed succession both by a letter of appointment he said was written to him by Smith dated June 18, 1844, and by angelic ordination at the moment Smith died on June 27.[7] Strang's letter of appointment directed him and his followers to gather in a city that would be called "Voree," meaning Garden of Peace. "If they gather to my city, Voree," the letter stated, "there will I keep them under the shadow of my wings . . . and my people shall again be restored to their possessions."[8] Members of the church, including many prominent Latter Day Saints and respected priesthood leaders, began to move to Voree by late 1845. At this early date, however, Strang seemed cognizant of the threat a rapid gathering could pose to outsiders. A correspondent from the *Ottawa Constitutionalist* reported, "It is not his design to gather all the church into one place," but rather to assemble a few thousand at a time, "so as to secure a full enjoyment of the peculiar rites and ceremonies of his church" while "avoiding those jealousies which the assembling of the whole church at one place naturally engenders."[9]

Joseph Smith III wrote that while their family was living in Fulton, "Elder William Marks received a visit from James J. Strang of Beaver

---

6. "Samuel Akers correspondence, 1843–1846," 2, CHL. Hazen Aldrich supported the claims of James Strang as successor.

7. John J. Hajicek, ed., *Chronicles of Voree, 1844–1849*, 1–6.

8. Joseph Smith, attributed, "Letter of Appointment."

9. "Voree and the Prophet," *VH*, 4.

Shabbona, a chief of the Bodéwadmi (Potawatomi). Courtesy of Chicago History Museum.

Island celebrity."[10] Smith saw him at the home of Marks where there was to be an "evening meeting," likely a time for Strang to put forth his claims and try to convert both the Marks and Smith family. Smith did not record what happened at the meeting as he could not attend due to a "violent attack of earache."[11]

Shortly thereafter, both families left Fulton Township. The Smith family moved back to Nauvoo, and the Marks family moved to Shabbona Grove, Illinois, in DeKalb County. Shabbona (or Shabbona's) Grove is seventy miles east of Fulton Township, right between Fulton and Chicago. Named after an old Potawatomi chief, the grove consisted of fifteen hundred acres of "one of the finest bodies of timber in the State . . . well covered with heavy white, burr and black oaks, and black walnut." One county history described it as an "embryo town. Nestling on the southern edge of the timber, it at once afforded suggestions of many cozy homes safely sheltered from the wintry blasts which swept down from across the bleak prairie."[12]

This area of the United States had recently been embroiled in tensions with Native American residents. Shabbona, a lieutenant under Shawnee chieftain Tecumseh, had in his later years come to accept the inevitability

---

10. This later remembrance has Strang "of Beaver Island celebrity," but Strang and his followers did not begin moving to Beaver Island until 1847.
11. Smith, "What Do I Remember of Nauvoo?" 343–44.
12. Lewis M. Gross, *Past and Present of DeKalb County, Illinois*, 122.

of the wave of westward-moving white colonists. He was instrumental in convincing the Potawatomi not to participate in the 1832 Black Hawk War, in which Black Hawk's band was massacred. In 1835, under the United States' policy of "Indian removal," the Potawatomi were forced to march to Council Bluffs, Iowa, along the "Trail of Death." Somehow, in 1836, Shabbona's community was also compelled to join this westward emigration, though their reserve of 1,280 acres was protected under the 1829 treaty of Prairie du Chien. Shabbona sold some of the land, but he and other members of the band continued to maintain ties to their treaty-reserved homeland until his death in 1859.[13] Upon the removal of the Potawatomi, DeKalb County and northwest Illinois became prominent in eastern newspaper reports, where they were described as rich and fertile farmlands that prospective settlers might easily obtain. Soon, colonizers began to occupy the area.

Among the earlier settlers were the Markses, who in 1845 were one of the first families to settle there, along with others who constituted "an honest and law-abiding population, and struggled courageously with the poverty and many hardships which were common to all the inhabitants at this early day."[14]

On December 28, 1845, Aaron Smith, a missionary for Strang en route to Nauvoo, wrote: "From St. Charles we started toward Shabbona's Grove intending to visit Pres. William Marks, late president of the Stake at Nauvoo."[15] Smith was one of the witnesses of Strang's discovery of the "Voree plates," six small brass sheets of "an alphabetical and pictorial record" that Strang said were an account of an ancient people. By translating this record, Strang gained additional notoriety as a prophet, seer, and revelator in the same tradition as Joseph Smith. More and more of the Mormons accepted Strang, several traveling to established branches of Joseph's church with a proselyting message, urging Latter Day Saints to gather with this new prophet. Joseph Smith's brother, William, wrote an endorsement in the first volume of Strang's newspaper, *Zion's Reveille*: "As to the claims of Brother James J. Strang, as the President of the Church of

---

13. See "Tribal History," Official Website of the Prairie Band Potawatomi Nation. "Since an act of Congress or a subsequent treaty is necessary to extinguish the Tribe's rights to the reservation and it wasn't included in the cession treaties," the Potawatomi consider that "it continues legally to belong to the Prairie Band." See also "Chief Shabbona public profile," Geni.

14. Henry L. Boies, *History of DeKalb County, Illinois*, 527.

15. Hajicek, *Chronicles of Voree*, 51.

Jesus Christ of Latter Day Saints, Prophet, Seer, and Revelator, I entertain no doubt whatever." William urged, "Come up, brethren, to Voree, the great gathering place appointed of God, here the people will have peace, and Heavenly Father will here give us great prosperity."[16]

At the time that missionaries were trying to convince him of the validity of Strang's leadership, Marks was becoming a leading figure in Shabbona Grove. Upon moving to the town, Marks purchased a farm and opened a tavern.[17] He became the first postmaster and managed the Chicago & Galena stagecoach line, whose "passengers consisted mainly of miners and those connected with the lead mines of Galena, which were in a flourishing condition." His son William Jr. drove the stagecoach. To these business interests, Marks added "a small stock of general goods" in a store he owned with S. B. Warren.[18]

In the spring of 1846, precinct elections were held in Marks's home, and he was elected Justice of the Peace, a position he had some familiarity with since aldermen in Nauvoo were also Justices of the Peace.[19] One month after being elected a judge of men, he would also be appointed to be a judge in Israel by Strang. Rejected by Brigham Young and the Twelve, Marks was courted and recruited by Strang, who recognized his talents and leadership—and the prestige he carried under his former priesthood position. Marks personally attended the April 6, 1846, Voree General Conference, and there he was "appointed and ordained Bishop of the Church."[20]

In this new capacity, Marks was given the charge to visit Nauvoo and make arrangements to bring Mother Lucy Smith to Voree where she would be supported "at the expense of the Church."[21] Marks made it clear at this conference that he had accepted the claims of his benefactor. Records of the conference state: "On motion of Elder William Marks it was unani-

---

16. William Smith, "To the Church of Jesus Christ of Latter Day Saints," *ZR*, 3.

17. Charles B. Thompson, "April 18th, 1852," *ZHBO*, 30.

18. Gross, *Past and Present of DeKalb County*, 122; [Chapman Brothers], *Portrait and Biographical Album of de Kalb*, 835, 884. As postmaster, Marks earned $42.75 in 1850 and $61.71 in 1851, which in 2022 dollars would be $1,554.98 and $2,273.78 respectively.

19. [Chapman Brothers], *Portrait and Biographical Album of de Kalb*, 836; Boies, *History of DeKalb County*, 400.

20. "Conference at Voree," *VH*, 17.

21. Hajicek, *Chronicles of Voree*, 69. There is no evidence that Marks ever attempted to fulfill this charge. Lucy Mack Smith remained in Nauvoo and died there in 1856.

mously Resolved that the Church receive, acknowledge, and uphold James J. Strang as President of this Church, Prophet, Seer, Revelator, and Translator, with our faith and prayers."[22] Marks was an important figure at this conference, for "whenever President Strang left the chair William Marks, president *pro.tem.* of the high priests, assumed it as the next in order."[23] As second-in-command at this conference, Marks was very involved in the business of the new church. Besides making a motion to uphold Strang as prophet, seer, and revelator, he made several other motions before the body of the church. He motioned that the body "sustain and uphold Aaron Smith as Counsellor to the first President," "that the case of Elder Rigdon be laid over till the October Conference for final action and in the meantime a delegation be sent to visit Elder Rigdon personally,"[24] and that the various presidents of the Seventies at Nauvoo who followed Brigham Young "be required to appear at the October Conference to answer to charges for official misconduct."[25]

While this last motion gave a hint of his feelings on the church led by Young, the events of the following day, April 7, 1846, put them into action. That day, he participated in the excommunication of Young and many of the Twelve Apostles, as one of the voting members of the newly formed high council. The trial started, as they did in Nauvoo, with the presentation of charges against the accused. The accused in this case were "Brigham Young, Heber C. Kimball, Orson Hyde, Parley P. Pratt, John Taylor, Willard Richards and George A Smith, all members of the quorum of the Twelve." In all, twenty-two specific charges in five categories were made against the men.

---

22. "On the 6th day of April," *VH*, 27.
23. "AntiMormonism," *ZR*, 3.
24. Strang believed that although Rigdon "had a perfect right to officiate in his place [as a member of the First Presidency] he had no right to place himself at the head of the Church. His office as an associate or member of the first Presidency does not constitute him a regular successor to Joseph Smith." James Strang, "An Epistle," *VH*, 2. By September 1846, when Strang and George Adams visited Philadelphia, they said "the Rigdonite organization there may be considered at an end." "Philadelphia," *VH*, 3. At the general conference on October 19, 1946, John C. Bennett moved "that President Strang enquire of the Lord in relation to the final disposition of President Rigdon's case." "Conference Minutes," *VH*, 1. George J. Adams was subsequently appointed to replace Rigdon as a member of the First Presidency.
25. Hajicek, *Chronicles of Voree*, 62–65.

First, the Voree High Council accused the Twelve of "conspira[c]y to overthrow the order of the Church." Specifically, they claimed these men taught the church was "to have no successor" and that they would not allow any discussion or "arguments on that question." They felt this group was wrong in "assuming that the Twelve as Apostles, have power to dictate all the affairs of the Church in all the world without a presidency to direct them." They also objected to the Twelve Apostles excommunicating and driving from Nauvoo those whom they disagreed with.[26]

Second, they accused the Twelve of "Usurpation," or "exercising authority that belongs to the First Presidency, the High Council, and lesser priesthood quorums." They were also accused of "Selling and offering to sell church property without authority," "Commanding the church, in the name of God to go into the wilderness" (thereby styling the move west as scattering rather than gathering), and "Giving a pretended endowment without authority and altogether out of order."[27]

Third, they charged the Twelve with "Tyrannous Administration"—specifically, of excommunicating members who had committed no crime, the unlawful collection of tithing, "abolishing the liberty of speech and the press by command and violence," and using church funds for themselves.[28]

Fourth was an accusation of "teaching false doctrines." The doctrines that the Strang High Council objected to were, "that polygamy fornication adultery and concubinage are lawful and commendable," "that murder theft and rebellion are justifiable and necessary in building up Gods Kingdom," and "that lying, to build up the Church of God, is justifiable."[29]

Finally, the Twelve were accused of "blasphemy." Their blasphemous actions principally consisted of cursing Strang.[30]

The high council then heard testimony from many witnesses, including John E. Page, Jehiel Savage, Collins Pemberton, Isaac Cleveland, Charles B. Thompson, Philip H. Buzzard, Moses Smith, John Gaylord, James M. Adams, Samuel Shaw, Increase Van Dusen, Joseph Younger, and Reuben Miller. The testimony was not recorded in the records of Strang's church or their newspapers, but whatever was said, the high council, along with Marks, all agreed "that the charges had been proven." The council then declared:

---

26. Hajicek, 72–73.
27. Hajicek, 72–76.
28. Hajicek, 73–74.
29. Hajicek, 74.
30. Hajicek, 74.

It is adjudged that Brigham Young, Heber C. Kimball, Orson Hyde, Parley P. Pratt, John Taylor, Willard Richards and George A. Smith, be excommunicated from the Church of Jesus Christ of Latterday Saints: their Priesthood be taken away; and they delivered over to the buffetings of Satan in the flesh.[31]

With his participation in this trial, Marks made clear that he did not believe in or support the Brigham Young–led church and had found a new religious home with the followers of Strang.

However, soon after this conference, Marks's participation with the Strang group was disrupted. Marks never explained this, but the historical record shows his 1846 alienation directly corresponds to the time John C. Bennett joined Strang. From this time until 1851, Marks careened in and out of favor with Strang and his organization, showing his hesitancy to fully commit.

Marks's long history with Bennett, when, as president of the high council in Nauvoo, he investigated Bennett's unauthorized polygamy, soured him on the man. He had also presided, as stake president, over the excommunications of many of Bennett's followers.[32] Marks described Bennett as "a vile and wicked adulterous man, who pays no regard to the principles of truth or righteousness, and is unworthy the confidence of a just community." He also added, "I know many of his statements to be false, and that I believe them all to be the offspring of a base and corrupt heart."[33] Other followers of Strang were equally wary of Bennett. Regardless, Strang accepted Bennett who joined the movement and on July 5, 1846, was "ordained to the office of a High Priest."[34]

Two weeks after Bennett joined with the new church, another conference was held at Voree on July 20, 1846. Marks was not in attendance, and apparently in a burst of protest he resigned all his positions at this time. The *Chronicles of Voree* recorded that "Pres. Strang stated that the President of the Stake had resigned his office and the resignation was accepted."[35] While it does not name the "President of the Stake," it is likely Marks for two reasons: 1) he is referred to as "Pres. of the Stake

---

31. Hajicek, 75–76.

32. Gary Bergera, "'Illicit Intercourse,' Plural Marriage, and the Nauvoo Stake High Council, 1840–1844," 59–90; See also John S. Dinger, ed., *The Nauvoo City and High Council Minutes*, 414–19.

33. "Certificates of William and Henry Marks," *TS*, 875.

34. Hajicek, *Chronicles of Voree*, 84.

35. Hajicek, 95.

at Nauvoo" in the *Chronicles of Voree*,³⁶ and 2) in the November *Zion's Reveille*, Marks is not listed as the bishop or in any other capacity in the church.³⁷ Marks also failed to attend conferences at Voree on September 1, 1846, and October 6, 1846. Bennett was present at both meetings and had an active participatory role.

From the beginning of his association with Strang, Bennett was influential in shaping theology and doctrine of the movement in an esoteric direction. He developed a ritual named the "Halcyon Order of Illuminati" based on Masonic components and imperial nomenclature.³⁸ If Marks withdrew because of Bennett's inclusion, he was not the only one who was horrified by the direction Strang's movement was taking. Jacob Bump and three others wrote a letter to Strang objecting to the "secret Society," the "Oaths, Signs and grips," and "the many damnable heresys and doctrines that the devil J.C. Bennett" and others had introduced. They explained that they had been teaching many "honest good men" from the east who had been investigating Strang's claims and were well disposed toward them,

> but my-god how can we present the head & horns of Such a damnabel beast that we (and when I say we I mean all the Saints or those that are fit to be called Saints in Kirtland) have to present when we are inquired of how they are getting along at Voree when if we tell the truth the whole truth and which is at presant <is> the uppermost in our minds that the Devils thare [there] impos[e] fals[e] prophets whose mungers and all the hosts of hell have taken up there aboud [abode] in that Expected beautiful Citty of Saints Called Voree.³⁹

In October 1846, while Strang was out of town, Aaron Smith, as "Junior President of the Church of Jesus Christ of Latter Day Saints," called an independent meeting of the Voree High Council.⁴⁰ This group tried Bennett "for Teaching False Doctrine such as Polygamy & Concubinage

---

36. For example, see Hajicek, 69.
37. James M. Adams, et al., "To the Church of Jesus Christ of Latter Day Saints," *ZR*, 1–2.
38. For more on Bennett's influence on Strang's ritual, see Cheryl L. Bruno, "Strangite Masonry and the Order of Illuminati," 1–21.
39. Jacob Bump, Leonard Rich, Amos Babcock, and S. B. Stoddard, letter to James J. Strang, October 16, 1846.
40. The following men were organized as "a Quoram of High Council": 1) Allen Waite, 2) Dorias Race, 3) John Gaylord, 4) Benjamin Andrews, 5) Jared Carter, 6) J. B. Wheelan, 7) Isaac Scott, 8) Hazen Aldrich, 9) Eleazer Davis, 10) Duty Griffith, 11) A. B. Fuller, 12) John Allen. "Minutes of the High Council at Voree," October 4, 1846.

and attempting to carry them into practice" as well as for "threat[e]ning Life, and ridiculing sacred things."[41] Many individuals testified at the hearing and accused Bennett of the same kinds of teachings that got him in trouble in Nauvoo. Moses Smith testified that Bennett taught "that it was no harm for married men to have intercourse with other woman." A Brother Scott testified that a certain girl "told my sister that Bennett had tried to seduce her & then was two other girls that he tried to seduce."[42]

Strang later published an article in *Zion's Reveille* calling those responsible for this action "Brainless Pseudoes" and clarifying that the excommunication was not authorized.[43] In response to the high council action behind his back, Strang took steps to remove Aaron Smith from leadership. With no indication of any sort of rift between himself and Marks over his earlier resignation of his positions, Strang delivered a revelation on November 6, 1846, which read, "And because my servant William Marks loveth me with full purpose of heart and seeketh unto me, to serve me; therefore shall he be counselor unto thee instead of my servant Aaron and shall assist thee by his counsels and by his wisdom which I have given unto him." Marks was promised that if he served faithfully, the Lord would "sustain him and lift him up, and by his hands the poor shall prosper." This revelation also appointed Joseph Smith III, who was only fourteen years old, "as one of the First Presidents of my Church." Marks was then told that he was to assist Joseph III and "uphold him, and be in all things a Coadjutor unto him in the First Presidency of my Church." Marks was further told to "give unto him wise counsel, and build him up in righteousness, and hold up his hands, and admonish him of every evil."[44]

Marks's assigned mission to assist Joseph III was not a secret. Only two days after the revelation was received, Reuben Miller wrote Brigham Young a letter regarding the Strang group, stating:

> Mr Strang will not be able to keep his head above watter long. They are nearly equally divided, Many have come out desidely opposed to him as their Leader from his counciler was removed to any by revelation, and Marks is to take his place[.] Joseph the Son of Joseph is called to be one of the presi-

---

41. Robin Scott Jensen, "Gleaning the Harvest: Strangite Missionary Work, 1846–1850," 86.
42. "Minutes of the High Council at Voree," October 4, 1846.
43. "Brainless Pseudoes," *ZR*, 2.
44. "Revelation given to James Strang, November 6, 1846," in Hajicek, *Chronicles of Voree*, 119.

dency There, and Mr. Marks is to teach and bring him all in the fear nu[r]ture and admonition of the Lord.⁴⁵

Although Marks was given this task, there is no suggestion that he attempted to fulfill the revelation, nor is there any historical evidence that he even attempted to contact Joseph III at this time.

By April 1847, Marks had re-engaged with Strang, though Bennett still had Strang's ear. At the annual general conference, Marks was appointed to a committee on church property and became a member of a group overseeing the standing of Strang's Quorum of Twelve. There, he opened the conference's second day with prayer. This was later followed by a speech in which Strang described his hierarchical organization: "In the Presidency I am assisted by George J. Adams and William Marks, who stands as coadjutor to Joseph Smith, and a counsellor in the presidency. William Smith is Patriarch, and, with John C. Bennett, is a member of the council in the sittings of the First Presidency."⁴⁶ Marks was back in favor, but he would not have to work with Bennett for long. Two months later, on June 7, 1847, Strang announced:

> JOHN C. BENNETT has been removed from all official standing in the church, for the following reasons: — 1st. Suppressing letters addressed to Pres. Strang. 2d. Giving instructions to the Saints, purporting to be by the authority of the First Presidency, which were entirely unauthorized, and directly contrary to their known instructions and settled policy. 3d. Teaching unsound doctrine. JAMES J. STRANG.
>
> Voree, June 7th, 1847.⁴⁷

Though Marks was now attending conferences, he remained at arm's length and did not relocate to Voree, Wisconsin. However, various members of Strang's organization would stop and visit Marks when passing through Shabbona Grove, Illinois. William Smith reported to the *Zion's Reveille*: "We called on President Marks, and found him strong in the faith of the gospel—tarried with him all night."⁴⁸ Marks also kept in contact with Strang, writing to him in May 1847 and reporting his activities:

> I have made up my mind to day to start tomorrow morning for the State of Vermont and shall be gon[e] probably three ^four^ or five weeks[.] I was makeing my calculations to be at Voree this week but have changed my mind

---

45. "Reuben Miller letter," 1, CHL.
46. James Strang, "Message to the Conference," *ZR*, 52.
47. James Strang, "John C. Bennett," *ZR*, 68.
48. William Smith, "It being a little stormy to-day, I gladly sit down to commune," *ZR*, 58.

on account of some business in the East that requarers amidiate attention[.] I am sor[r]y it has so hap[p]ened for I antisapated spendin[g] some time with you this somer [summer.] I shall endeavour to indicate the Cause and advocate your Claims in all places where it shall be propper[.] I do[n]'t feel at all discouraged about the work all the it seems rather a dark time at present[.] I shall endeavour to ^be^ at your place as soon as I can make it convien[i]e[n]t after my return[.][49]

In 1847, Strang began to resettle his followers on a sparsely populated island near the northern end of Lake Michigan. A message reprinted in the church's *Gospel Herald* urged, "dear brethren and sisters, be of good cheer, and begin from the receipt of this to set your affairs in order to gather here or to Beaver Island as soon as possible."[50] One of Strang's trusted followers, James Madison Adams, was placed in charge of emigration to Beaver Island, where the congregation would establish a town named Saint James. Ten years previously, in 1837, Adams had been an elder in Kirtland, Ohio, and doubtless knew Marks, who was his stake president there. At some point during Adams's association with Strang, he and Marks developed a close friendship and began exchanging letters expressing their deepest religious hopes and fears and support for each other on their spiritual journeys.

Adams had served a mission with Book of Mormon witness Hiram Page in 1841, and another in Ohio the next year. Following the death of Joseph Smith and after Strang announced his appointment as prophet, Adams was one of the first to advocate for Strang in Nauvoo. He moved to Voree and served on the Voree High Council in 1846. At the April 1846 general conference, he was ordained one of Strang's quorum of twelve apostles,[51] and a year later he was appointed to a committee overseeing the standing of the First Presidency in the April 1847 conference. Here he stood and testified he knew by revelation that Strang was the Lord's anointed.[52]

Shortly thereafter, however, Adams and Strang had a falling out over "the spiritual wife doctrine," which Strang accused Adams of supporting.[53] It wasn't long before Adams made an exit from Strang's organization.

---

49. William Marks, letter to James Strang, May 23, 1847.
50. "To the Saints in All the World," *GH*, 181.
51. Hajicek, *Chronicles of Voree*, 68.
52. Hajicek, 136.
53. James Strang, "Extract of a Letter," *GH*, 120. Adams wrote a letter to Strang on August 13, 1847. In it, he expressed his faith in Joseph Smith, the first prophet of the Restoration. Then, in a postscript, he wrote of his discovery that

Marks attended the October 1847 general conference in Voree. This conference was notable for a show of pageantry and the dedication of a lot for the building of a temple. John E. Page, president of the Twelve, acted as master of ceremonies and "arranged the congregation in the order of rank and priesthood, beginning with the First Presidency at the principal gate of the Temple." The congregation sang "How Firm a Foundation," after which "Presidents Strang and Marks proceeded to the centre of the Temple lot." There, Strang offered the dedicatory prayer, "which was responded to by the Conference by a hearty amen." The two men "returned to their former position and broke ground for the Temple, followed by the several quorums in the order in which they were placed."[54] Marks spoke to those in attendance and "exhorted the saints to be united and use their exertions to build the Temple according to the commandment of God."[55] The next day, he and Strang also spoke on temple-building, followed by a unanimous resolve to appoint them both to a "committee of two" with the responsibility "to take charge of the work upon the temple."[56]

This October 1847 conference also removed the problem of John C. Bennett for good. On October 6, many individuals were excommunicated, among them William Smith, James Adams, and Bennett (this time

---

Strang had "been circulating the report that . . . I was a believer in the spiritual wife doctrine." Adams boldly insisted "that the man nor woman does not exist that ever heard me say that I had any faith in that system." Strang reprinted portions of the letter in the *Gospel Herald* and replied bitingly to the charges, insinuating that Adams had something to hide. "By the way," Strang wrote, "will Mr. Adams tell all the world 'how he believes the spiritual system.' It would not make him quite as popular as telling how wicked Prophets are. We don't wish to tell on him, but it ain't pretty." Here Strang was likely accusing Adams of belief in plural marriage while denying that he believed in the "spiritual wife doctrine." Beginning in 1840s Nauvoo, members of the church maintained plausible deniability by making a distinction between spiritual wifery (as practiced by John C. Bennett) and plural marriage (as taught by Joseph Smith). That this distinction was being made in Voree is evidenced by the high council trial of John W. Crane on October 2, 1847. Crane was charged with publicly declaring that he believed in the spiritual wife system. He "pled that he did not and does not beli[e]ve in the spiritual wife system but did beli[e]ve in the plurallity of wives and so declared." Hajicek, *Chronicles of Voree*, 150.

54. "Conference of the Church of Jesus Christ of Latter Day Saints, at Voree," *GH*, 122.

55. "Conference of the Church," *GH*, 122.

56. "Conference of the Church," *GH*, 122.

legitimately). Smith was "Charged with adultery and Apostacy." Though Smith did not appear at his trial, Marks, a Sister Ellsworth, and Ebenezer Page all provided testimony to support the charges. Smith was "found guilty and excommunicated from the Church and delevered over to the buffitings of Satan untill he repent and make satisfaction."[57] Adams was "excommunicated for apostacy and believing the spiritual wife system."[58] Bennett was excommunicated "for apostacy, conspiracy to establish a stake by falsehood, deception, &c., and various immoralities." He was "delivered over to the buffetings of Satan till the day of the coming of the Lord, and sealed up against all gospel privileges on earth. The whole congregation lifted their hands against him."[59]

In 1848, Marks had to focus on his temporal situation, rather than his spiritual one.[60] That year the citizens of Shabbona Township learned

---

57. "Conference of the Church," *GH*, 122; See also Hajicek, *Chronicles of Voree*, 152. Dale Broadhurst notes, "It is probably significant that the Strangite Conference did not deliver William Smith 'over to the buffetings of Satan till the day of the coming of the Lord, and sealed up against all gospel privileges on earth.' Rather, a chance was left open for him to 'repent and make satisfaction.' Strang knew that by cutting William off, he was effectively losing the adherence of Mother Smith and any other of William's close relatives, previously allied with the Strangite cause. Probably Strang held open the slender hope that William would one day return to full fellowship at Voree. He did not." "Newspapers of James J. Strang: 1846–1847 Articles," Uncle Dale's Readings in Mormon History.

58. "Conference of the Church," *GH*, 122; Hajicek, *Chronicles of Voree*, 153. Adams did not appear at his trial. Two letters to President Strang were introduced as testimony, and John W. Crane, Daniel Avery, Samuel Wright, and William Savage testified against him.

59. "Conference of the Church," *GH*, 122; Hajicek, *Chronicles of Voree*, 151. High councilors in this case were: 1) M. M. Aldrich, 2) John Porter, 3) Ben. G. Wright, 4) Francis Fox, 5) Alden Hale, 6) John W. Archer, 7) U. C. H. Nickerson, 8) William Savage, 9) James Blakeslee, 10) Finley Page, 11) Daniel Avery, 12) Ebenezer Page.

60. "William Marks letter," CHL. "In closing up the business for Brother Joseph with Esq Russel in Kirtland for the purchase of his Farm I had to becum obligated to Esq Russel to defray the expences of foreclosing a mortgage that he had upon the farm to Ensure or Make good the title as he said there was Judgments standing against Br joseph at that time and was fearful that a Deed from him would not make the title good[.] some 2 or 3 three years after I left Kirtland Russel Closed the Mortgage to perfect the title which ^the expense^ stood Against me which amounted to Eighty three Dollars[.] I speak to Brother Joseph about it and he said he would sitle it as soon as he could I told him I had some property there and they

that the land they had purchased and built a town on was not valid. The United States government ruled that Chief Shabbona had no right to sell the lands that he had been granted in the 1829 treaty. Since the lands referred to were "no longer occupied by the persons for whose use they were reserved," the commissioner of the General Land Office assumed authority "to dispose of the same as other public lands of the United States." Thus, on August 12, 1848, the lands were "ordered into market."[61] The citizens of Shabbona Grove were forced to purchase their lands again, this time at market price, rates which at auction might reach forty times the government entry price, and which they could not afford to pay. The men "met in council, [and] selected William Marks and Reuben Allen, two of their most respected fellow townsmen, to bid in the land at the minimum rate of $1.25 an acre." To make sure Marks and Allen could obtain the land at the minimum price, the people "arm[ed] themselves with clubs and pistols . . . fully resolved to prevent (by force if necessary) all others from bidding upon the lands." Though there were others who assembled at the auction at Dixon, the Shabbona Grove citizens threatened to drown any bidders in Rock River, and Marks and Allen successfully purchased their lands at the lower rate.[62]

Marks's withdrawal from church interests prompted Isaac Scott to write to William E. McLellin on April 4, 1848, announcing, "William Marks has left Strangism. But still Strang seems determined to make some capital out of his ism before it is numbered with the things that

---

would sarifise it probably to cancel the demand he told me I had better Deed it to Brother Johns as he considered him a verry honest man[.] I accordingly did so and Deeded him the house and lot known as the Rigdon house and lot with an express agree=ment for him ^Johnson to Redeed^ is back to me again when the matter was arranged with Esq Russel[.] when I left Nauvoo it was not settled but that summer I paid the Eight three Dollars and canseled the demand and caldon Br Johnson to quit Claim back to me the place but he refused to do soe and has actuly sold the place as I understand[.] William Marks."

This constitutes an example of what Joseph Smith was accustomed to doing with property in Kirtland. When Smith was legally in arrears he would deed his property (e.g., the Kirtland Temple and the printing office) to another person so it could not be seized to settle his debt. In this example, Smith advises William Marks to follow the same procedure.

61. John Gilmore, Receipt #12744, 160 Acres, section 34, range 1. See also James Dowd, *Built Like A Bear*, 151.

62. Boies, *History of DeKalb County*, 526; See also Gross, *Past and Present of DeKalb County*, 18.

were."⁶³ Days later at the April conference, Marks was not present. He was discussed, and it was reported, "Pres. William Marks was appointed one of the building committee of the Temple, but had not acted in that capacity."⁶⁴ Marks was replaced. Marks also failed to appear at the October conference, though he did donate a wagon valued at $75 to the endeavor of building the temple.⁶⁵

In early 1849, James Strang delivered a revelation rebuking Marks and calling him to repentance:

> Behold, my servant William Marks has gone far astray in departing from me, yet I give unto him a little space that he may return and receive my word, and stand in his place; for I remember his work that he has done in the time that is past. If he will return and abide faithful, I will make him great, and his possessions shall be great, and he shall possess a city, and his children shall dwell therein; a nation shall call him blessed.⁶⁶

There were rumors that Marks would abide the revelation and appear at the April conference as the conference minutes recorded that "he was expected before the close of Conference."⁶⁷ When he did not appear, a resolution was unanimously passed, stating "that if Bro. Wm. Marks will magnify his office according to the requirements of the revelation of Jan. 7th, that we will receive, uphold and sustain him by our faith, confidence and prayers, as one of the First Presidency."⁶⁸

A resolution was also passed at this conference making it an "imperative duty" of the saints to "come up to the places of gathering," and to "rejoice in the establishment and prosperity of the Order of Enoch,"⁶⁹ which was a system of consecration whereby the saints would donate their

---

63. "Isaac F. Scott to William E. McLellin, April 4, 1848," 138.

64. "Minutes of the Annual Conference of the Church of Jesus Christ of Latter Day Saints, held at Voree April 6th, 7th, 8th and 9th, 1848," *GH*, 16.

65. "Minutes of the Annual Conference of the Church of Jesus Christ of Latter Day Saints, held at Voree on the Sixth, Seventh and Eighth of October, 1848," *GH*, 147.

66. James Strang, "Revelation, Given Jan. Seventh, 1849," *GH*, 234; See also Hajicek, *Chronicles of Voree*, 185.

67. "Minutes of the Annual Conference of the Church of Jesus Christ of Latter Day Saints, held in Voree on the Sixth, Seventh, and Eighth of April, 1849," *GH*, 16.

68. "Minutes of the Annual Conference of the Church of Jesus Christ of Latter Day Saints, held in Voree on the Sixth, Seventh, and Eighth of April, 1849, concluded," *GH*, 17; See also Hajicek, *Chronicles of Voree*, 192.

69. "Minutes, concluded," *GH*, 16.

earnings to the church. It is not evident that Marks made any effort to gather with the saints or to participate in the order of Enoch. He was comfortable and prosperous in Shabbona Grove.

However, Marks did visit Voree in August 1849. With only nine days' notice, a conference was held on August 25 and 26, and it was well attended. Strang was sustained as president of the church with counselors George J. Adams and William Marks "as associate Presidents and Presidents in his absence." Here Marks humbly asked the assembled church for forgiveness:

> Pres. Marks arose and said that he felt that he ought to make a confession to the saints for not acting in his calling, and also to ask their forgiveness. He gave a brief history of the course he pursued after the martyrdom of the prophet Joseph. Testified that he ever had the fullest confidence in the great work of the last days, and knew it was of God, and was now determined by the help of God to go forth in the discharge of his duty, and act in the place unto which he was called by revelation of God through his servant James.[70]

Those present "rejoiced with joy unspeakable to see an old saint coming back," and a resolution was passed "that we will forgive Bro. Marks, and sustain him in his calling by our faith, confidence and prayers." James Strang then put a little pressure on Marks, reminding him that he had been "appointed by revelation [as the] spiritual guardian of Joseph Smith, the son of the prophet Joseph."[71]

In the afternoon session of August 26, Marks was "ordained, consecrated and set apart an Apostle of the Lord Jesus Christ, a Counselor to the prophet, one of the First Presidency, and a prophet of the most high God under the hands of President St[r]ang and Adams." Additionally, Marks and Adams were anointed, ordained, and set apart to administer baptism for the dead, and the entire company dismissed to meet at the water's edge "for the purpose of attending to baptisms both for the living and the dead."[72] This highlight of the conference reintroduced one of Joseph Smith's Nauvoo innovations that Marks helped direct in the 1840s. In Nauvoo, Marks oversaw and called a special conference to "appoint . . . [r]ecorders for the baptism of the dead."[73] Marks had

---

70. "Minutes of a Conference of the Church of Jesus Christ of Latter Day Saints, held in Voree August 25th and 26th, 1849," *GH*, 106; See also Hajicek, *Chronicles of Voree*, 200–1.

71. "Minutes," *GH*, 106.

72. Hajicek, *Chronicles of Voree*, 204–5.

73. "Journal, December 1842–June 1844; Book 3, 15 July 1843–29 February 1844," 24, JSP.

personally performed proxy baptisms for at least two of his kindred in Nauvoo—his deceased cousin, Ira Goodrich, in 1841, and his son Ephraim, who died in 1842 at the age of twenty-four.[74] However, it appears he never followed through with Strang's assignment, and this was the last of his conferences Marks attended.

Even though Marks stopped participating, Strang continued to use the former Nauvoo Stake President's influence for a time, just as Isaac Scott had predicted. At a June 1850 conference, Strang laid before the people "A Testimony to the Nation," a document "written in the form of a memorial to the President and Representatives of the United States." The document continued Joseph Smith Jr.'s petition to the United States government for redress for the persecution and losses the early Saints suffered in 1838 Missouri. It added the losses incurred from being expelled from Nauvoo and asked the United States President and Congress "to pass a law giving the consent of the nation that the saints may settle upon and forever occupy all the uninhabited lands of the islands in lake Michigan."[75] Marks was listed as a joint author of the document, but he was not present, nor is there any evidence that he helped in its creation.

Prior to this conference, and unknown to Marks at the time, Strang had entered into polygamy when he married a second wife in secret on July 13, 1849. Startlingly, Elvira Field had been accompanying Strang as he traveled on church business, disguised as his male assistant, and going by the name of Charles Douglass. By the summer of 1850, "news of Strang's second marriage was common knowledge to Saints living at Voree."[76] James Blakeslee, one of Strang's most ardent followers and missionaries, wrote him an impassioned letter saying that "Brig[g]s of Voree, Adams of Orrora [Aurora], and Spinning of this place have all Been Busily engaged in making and spreading lies about the Saints of the Island. . . . [T]he report curant about here that you have two women. . . . [P]leas[e] write on receipt of this."[77]

Documents associated with Strang's movement do not explain specifically why Marks left their ranks. However, he left at a time when Strang's polygamy was being discussed and condemned. As members of Strang's

---

74. Susan Easton Black and Harvey Bischoff Black, *Annotated Records of Baptisms for the Dead, 1840–1845, Nauvoo, Hancock County, Illinois,* 4:2308.

75. James J. Strang, George J. Adams, and William Marks, "A Testimony to the Nation," *GH,* 95.

76. John Quist, "Polygamy among James Strang and His Followers," 34, 37–38.

77. James Blakeslee, "Blakeslee to Strang."

church learned of his second marriage and his attempts to hide it, many acted. Blakeslee withdrew from the church, citing "the works of the flesh manifested."[78] Strang's Philadelphia branch "apostatized," and the New York City branch "withdrew fellowship" from their leader.[79] It is likely that Marks also departed for these same reasons.

This same year, Marks was elected to represent Shabbona on the DeKalb County Board of Supervisors. He was thus not present when a royal procession of two hundred and thirty-five of Strang's still loyal followers gathered at the Beaver Island tabernacle on June 8, 1850, to crown Strang the "King of the Kingdom of God on Earth,"[80] a culmination of Joseph Smith's theocratic ideas.

In the nineteenth-century publication *The Latter Day Precept*, it was claimed that "our church records show that he [Marks] was excommunicated and his priesthood taken from him in 1851, after being condemned by the mouth of three witnesses."[81] Whether this is true or what these three witness said is unknown, but it is clear that Marks ended his association with the followers of James Strang by 1851.

Strang had come to represent many of the things that Marks objected to in Mormonism. "When the doctrine of polygamy was introduced into the [Nauvoo] church as a principle of exaltation, I took a decided stand against it," Marks insisted. Strang, on the other hand, eventually taught that all church elders must marry at least two wives, although no more than twenty men in his movement were known to have married plurally. Strang married a third wife in 1852, and a fourth and fifth in 1855, eventually fathering twelve children.

Marks also expressed discomfort with Joseph Smith's theocratic aspirations, and surely frowned upon the same in Strang. Marks wrote that in Nauvoo he was "witness of the introduction (secretly,) of a kingly form of government, in which Joseph suffered himself to be ordained a king, to reign over the house of Israel forever." Marks thought that he "could not conceive [this] to be in accordance with the law of the church," but he thought it was none of his business to oppose it at the time.[82]

---

78. James Blakeslee, "Communications," *ZHBO*, 21.

79. Quist, "Polygamy among James Strang," 35–36. Strang's polygamist wife dressed like a man, acted as his secretary, and went by the alias Charles J. Douglass to hide the marriage.

80. "Record of the Organization of the Kingdom," SP.

81. John Flanders, "Do You Know that Wm. Marks," 42.

82. William Marks, "Epistle," *ZHBO*, 53.

After the exit of Marks and many of his followers who had held important positions in the early church, Strang and his people overwhelmed Beaver Island, causing the displacement of both Native Americans and resident fishermen. Strang's men assumed all political offices and Strang himself was elected to the Michigan State legislature. Tensions with both locals and ex-affiliates grew until their culmination in Strang's murder by a group of four conspirators armed with pistols in 1856. By then, William Marks had long since departed to pursue his spiritual quest elsewhere.

CHAPTER 9

Charles B. Thompson's Gathering Committee

At the time that William Marks left the James Strang movement, he was deeply involved in community affairs in the growing township of Shabbona Grove. Besides having the confidence of his neighbors, Marks had prospered financially after fleeing Nauvoo. His well-appointed farm, worth $4,000, comfortably housed him, his wife, and his three adult children: Goodrich, William Jr., and Llewellyn. His daughter Sophia lived next door with her husband, George Shaw, and baby Ellee.[1] Daughter Lucy lived not far away, in Paw Paw Township, with her husband, Henry McHenry, and three sons. Also living in Paw Paw was Marks's son Fayette, his wife, and their three children.[2] One might think that William Marks had everything he needed for success and happiness. But he was still a seeker. The principles of the gospel founded by Joseph Smith had been imprinted upon his heart; he couldn't stop looking for a worthy successor to put the fragmented church together again. It was during this time—spring of 1852—that Marks began to investigate the claims of Charles B. Thompson.

Charles Thompson joined the Latter Day Saints in Kirtland, Ohio, in 1835, a year before his marriage at the tender age of twenty-two. He organized a branch of the church at Sandusky, Ohio, soon after, in 1837. The next year found Thompson and his young family in the midst of the persecutions in Missouri, and they were forced to leave the state under Governor Boggs's extermination order. Being faithful and vigorous, Thompson was called to New York, where he was successful in bringing many converts into Mormonism and where he organized the Genessee Conference of the church. But while he was on this mission, his wife died of the exposure she had suffered when expelled from Missouri, leaving behind a five-month-old daughter.[3]

In 1840 Thompson wrote *Evidences in Proof of the Book of Mormon*, one of the first apologetic treatments of LDS scripture. This book included a poem with an intricate acrostic spelling out "CHARLES-THOMPSON-AN-ELDER-OF-THE-CHURCH-OF-JESUS-CHRIST-OF-LATTER-

---

1. 1850 U.S. census, DeKalb County, Illinois, p. 351.
2. 1850 U.S. census, DeKalb County, Illinois, p. 351.
3. C. R. Marks, "Monona County, Iowa, Mormons," 89–90.

DAY-SAINTS" and calling for friends and family to depart from the wickedness of the world to come into the restored church[4]—a theme that would be repeated throughout his ministry.

Thompson remained in Nauvoo after Joseph Smith's death, at first supporting the Twelve. There, he was ordained a high priest and he joined the Masonic Lodge,[5] an act that would have profound influence on his later religious workings. He received the Nauvoo temple endowment on Christmas Eve, 1845.[6] Although he remarried and was sealed to both this second wife and his tragically deceased first wife,[7] Thompson emphatically opposed polygamy, and broke with Brigham Young over this principle.

In 1846 Thompson, like William Marks, affiliated with James J. Strang, but by 1848 he rejected Strang's claims of authority.[8] Thompson left the group months before Strang manifested any public interest in polygamy,[9] so it's likely he had not yet discovered that his new prophet would take up the practice which he so despised. Instead, Thompson criticized Strang for his ordination by an angel, his inability to translate without heavenly assistance, and for moving his headquarters to Beaver Island.[10] Furthermore, Thompson said that he had received his own revelation that the original church had been rejected by God upon the death of the prophet Joseph. Thus, it had no power to reorganize "until after the redemption of Zion," but those already holding priesthood could continue to exercise it.[11]

After breaking with Strang, Thompson moved to St. Louis, Missouri, with his wife Catherine and his children. There, he formed the Congregation of Jehovah's Presbytery of Zion (or "Conjeprizites"). In 1848 he issued his first "Proclamation,"[12] in which the Latter Day Saint doctrine on gather-

---

4. Charles B. Thompson, *Evidences in Proof of the Book of Mormon*, 238–40.

5. Mervin B. Hogan, *The Official Minutes of Nauvoo Lodge U.D.*, 68. Charles B. Thompson was raised a Master Mason in Nauvoo Lodge on November 8, 1844.

6. Lisle G. Brown, *Nauvoo Sealings, Adoptions, and Anointings: A Comprehensive Register of Persons Receiving LDS Temple Ordinances, 1841–1846*, 311.

7. Brown, *Nauvoo Sealings, Adoptions, and Anointings*, 311.

8. Junia Braby, "Charles B. Thompson: Harbinger of Zion or Master of Humbuggary?" 149–64.

9. David Rich Lewis, "'For life, the resurrection, and the life everlasting': James J. Strang and Strangite Mormon Polygamy, 1849–1856," 278. Strang began to show interest in polygamy sometime after the church conference at Voree in April 1848.

10. Charles B. Thompson, "For the Gospel Herald," *ZHBO*, 22–24.

11. Heman C. Smith and F. Henry Edwards, *History of the Reorganized Church of Jesus Christ of Latter Day Saints*, 3:53–61.

12. Charles B. Thompson, "A Proclamation," *ZHBO*, 1.

ing was elegantly presented. By proclamation, the nations of the earth were informed that the Lord had given the land of Jerusalem to the Jews, who were currently returning. The land of America had been given to the descendants of the Book of Mormon Nephites—"the present race of Indians." Though the natives had dwindled in unbelief, a group of chosen Gentiles had been raised up to bring forth their record and establish the Church of Christ. The leaders of this restored church (Joseph and Hyrum Smith) were rejected and killed, and their followers had failed to accomplish the command to build the temple before their death, so the fullness of the gospel was again taken from the earth. The only alternative remaining was to support a law that had been given in its place. The agent of this law was Charles Thompson, who would direct the Saints to build a temple and "establish schools for the instruction of the remnant of Joseph."[13]

Like Strang and Young, Thompson advertised his views in several monthly publications. *Zion's Harbinger and Baneemy's Organ*, running from 1849 to 1854, kept alive an enigmatic otherworldly character named "Baneemy." Joseph Smith had used this Hebrew transliteration of "my sons" to replace the words "mine elders" in the 1844 edition of the Doctrine and Covenants. Since other Hebrew code words were used in the Doctrine and Covenants to refer to specific individuals, a controversy sprang up over who Baneemy was.[14] In the style of the ancient writers of pseudepigrapha, Thompson claimed to be commissioned by Baneemy as his duly authorized agent on the earth, and he bolstered his theological

---

13. Thompson, "A Proclamation," *ZHBO*, 2.
14. Charles B. Thompson, "Who is Baneemy?" *ZHBO*, 14. "Professor Orson Pratt, who was in this city a short time since, teaching that the practice of Polygamy was a saving principle—necessary to salvation; says, that Baneemy is Sidney Rigdon; and that Baneemy is a fictitious name given to him, in Kirtland, Ohio, by the Lord through Joseph to enable him (Rigdon) to cheat his creditors out of their just dues. Elder Orson Hyde, late Editor of the Fronteer Guardian, says that Hyrum Smith was Baneemy, and that it is so written in the sacred records of the church; Almon W. Babbitt, Esq., late Congressman from the state (no state) of deseret, says that Baneemy is Thomas B. Marsh; formerly President of the Twelve Apostles of the church, but Apostatized in the fall of 1838. Ebenezer Robinson, Esq., formerly Editor of the Times & Seasons at Nauvoo, Ills., and more recently Editor of the Messenger and Advocate of the church of Christ, (so called) at Greencastle, Pa., under the Presidency of Sidney Rigdon, says that Baneemy is nobody but Charles B. Thompson himself. And we have recently received a letter from one of Strang's Apostles, who says that Baneemy is Lymon Wight, who is now in Texas presiding over a small church of his own, in which (we are informed) the plurality wife system is practiced."

views by placing them in the mouth of this prophetic figure. Thompson's creativity further expressed itself in the poems and hymns he composed and included in his publications. These conveyed his unique mystical ability and reflected doctrinal innovations found in his short-lived group.[15] Altogether, Thompson's publications were theologically dense compared to those of the other Mormon succession groups. They reflected on the doctrines and policies of the different Mormon factions and responded to letters of correspondents and subscribers, and they attracted many individuals who would later play a role in the Reorganized Church, such as James Adams, James Blakeslee, and Josiah Ells.[16]

Not intended to take the place of a church, Thompson's group was an extra-ecclesiastic body of the priesthood. Thompson envisioned Masonically-inspired Schools of Faith and Schools of Works, each encompassing several degrees. The full name of the group, "The Free and Accepted Order of Baneemy, and Fraternity of the Sons of Zion," also demonstrates Masonic influence, patterned as it was after the "Free and Accepted Order of Masons." As the system developed, it would include a catechism for instruction, a covenant or oath that members agreed to, with an allegorical new name—all features found in contemporaneous Freemasonry.[17]

In 1849, Thompson claimed that he had received the "Grand Key" by which he organized classes and acted as "Chief Teacher."[18] In order to progress through the degrees, followers studied, performed tasks, and entered long, formal covenants, all in a quest to become worthy to receive

---

15. See Cheryl L. Bruno, "The Melodious Sounds of Baneemy's Organ," 152–76.

16. In addition to *Zion's Harbinger and Baneemy's Organ*, a weekly family newspaper called *Preparation News and Ephraim's Messenger* was established about 1855. In 1857, another weekly periodical was published at Preparation—the *Western Nucleus and Democratic Echo*. This was "devoted to politics, science, arts, literature, and general intelligence." RLDS *History of the Church*, 3:53–54.

17. Charles B. Thompson, "The Word of the God of Abraham, of Isaac and of Jacob to his servants of the seed of the Church of Jesus Christ of Latter-day Saints, Having the testimony of Jesus Christ, Concerning their Organization, in preparation for the Endowments of the Priesthood, and their Regeneration in the Family of Israel," *ZHBO*, 2; Charles B. Thompson, "Covenant, to be taken upon entering the Congregation of Jehovah's Presbytery of Zion," *ZHBO*, 9. The covenant to be taken upon entering the first department of the School of Faith began, "I do now most solemnly and sincerely subscribe, with my hand unto Jehovah, and surname myself Israel, that I may be called after the name of Jacob, in Jehovah's Presbytery of Zion."

18. C. R. Marks, "Monona County," 91.

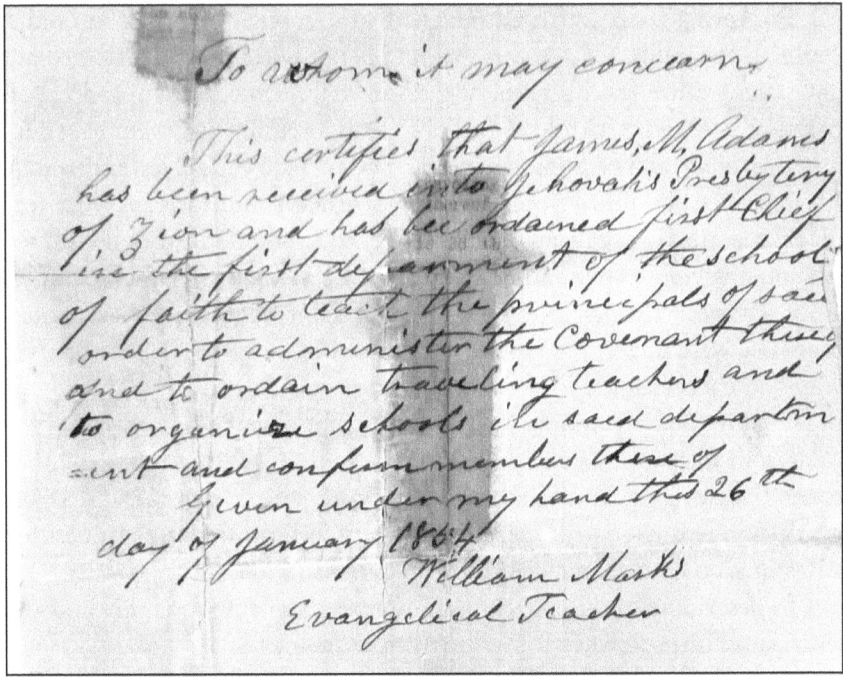

James Adams ordination certificate in Jehovah's Presbytery of Zion. Courtesy of Community of Christ Library and Archives.

the Key Words of the Holy Priesthood themselves. Additional officers and teachers were elected to guide others in these steps. One of the degrees in the Schools of Faith was a traveling department from which came missionaries, divided into quorums of fifteen, and assigned areas in the country in which to proselytize.[19] Thompson kept a close eye on developments in the Latter Day Saint diaspora, often commenting on them in the pages of his paper. In communications in 1850, Thompson condemned Strang, James Colin Brewster, and William Smith for contradicting Joseph Smith's revelations on gathering. This "cannot be of God," he pronounced.[20]

---

19. C. R. Marks, "Monona County," 96; Junia Braby, "Charles B. Thompson: Harbinger of Zion or Master of Humbuggery?" 153. "Each 'School' had a pattern of requirements that evolved over time, becoming increasingly difficult to fulfill. These requirements were closely related to the needs of the community as determined by Thompson and in relation to the response of the group to his demands and revelations. He equated the fulfilling of these 'requirements' as a measure of faithfulness and devotion of members."

20. Charles B. Thompson, "For the Gospel Herald," *ZHBO*, 23; Charles B. Thompson, "An Address," *ZHBO*, 6, 8.

By April 15, 1852, Thompson had won enough followers to hold a "Solemn Assembly." While this meeting had biblical roots, its immediate antecedent came from a revelation given to Joseph Smith in 1833. The Saints at Kirtland were told to "call a solemn assembly" to "assemble yourselves together, and organize yourselves, and prepare yourselves, and sanctify yourselves; yea, purify your hearts, and cleanse your hands and your feet before me, that I may make you clean."[21] Thompson decided to hold three triannual assemblies to be convened on April 15, August 29, and December 27 of each year. His first solemn assembly was not well attended—he noted that "few were present."[22] However, one of these few was William Marks, who had cautiously decided to join the new movement. Just a week after the solemn assembly, Marks wrote to friend and fellow searcher, James M. Adams, in what was to be the beginning of an intimate correspondence between the two men. In a group of letters written between 1852 and 1856, Marks and Adams shared their opinions and feelings about their quest for a Restoration church to succeed Joseph Smith's.

In describing his attendance at Thompson's solemn assembly and the conversion he experienced, Marks wrote to Adams:

> I arrived there on that day with but little understanding of the work and about as much faith, for I have been so often disappointed that I had become fearful and unbelieving, and with a determination to be very inquisitive, for I have learned from experience that it is a very easy thing to be deceived.[23]

Besides himself, there were five brethren in attendance, including Thompson, the "chief teacher." These, wrote Marks, "constituted about the same number that was present at the organizing of the church."[24]

Marks was nearly swept away with Thompson's enthusiasm in greeting his former associate in the Mormonism of both Joseph Smith and James Strang, and Thompson immediately invited Marks to support his efforts. Thompson believed that Joseph Smith had given a "last charge" to the Nauvoo High Council, the church's "highest tribunal: its chief Judicial Court: and the exponent of its laws." Smith's description of that July 3, 1834 charge was quoted as follows:

---

21. "History, 1838–1856, volume A-1 [23 December 1805–30 August 1834]," 250, JSP.
22. Charles B. Thompson, "April 18th, 1852," *ZHBO*, 30.
23. William Marks, letter to James M. Adams, April 23, 1852, CCLA.
24. Marks, letter to James M. Adams, April 23, 1852, CCLA.

I gave the Council such instructions; in relation to their high calling as would enable them to proceed to minister in their office, agreeable to the pattern heretofore given; read the revelation upon the subject, and told them that if I should be now taken away, I had accomplished the great work the Lord had laid before me, and that which I had desired of the Lord—and that I had done my duty in organizing the high Council, through which council, the will of the Lord might be known upon all important occasions, in the building up of Zion, and establishing truth in the earth.' . . . if the church had continued its allegiance to heaven; the responsibility of its continued truthful guidance, devolved upon the high council.[25]

Since the church had not, in Thompson's eyes, remained faithful, authority devolved upon the appointment of Baneemy on June 22, 1834.[26] This belief highlights the importance of having made a convert of William Marks, president of the Nauvoo High Council upon Joseph's death.

At that first Thompsonite Solemn Assembly in 1852, Marks was "chosen & ordained, and endowed" to be a traveling teacher of the School of Faith. (This language came from the Kirtland temple endowment of 1836, where missionaries received a spiritual "endowment" before being sent out to preach. The parlance would have seemed familiar and comfortable to Marks.) He was also made leader of the School of Faith quorum and Thompson's first "Chief of the Traveling Teachers."[27] In addition, Marks was chosen to be a member of "a Committee to locate a present place of gathering for the Schools of Jehovah's Presbytery of Zion." Thus, Marks, along with Richard Stevens and Harry Childs, "having been appointed by revelation," were to "search out a proper location on the frontier, which may serve as a gate of entrance into the land of Ephraim," and to report to Thompson when they had located a suitable site for the group to gather.[28]

Marks had lived through unpleasant experiences with gathering both in Kirtland and Missouri, so he had been hesitant in 1839 when the decision was being made whether to gather at Nauvoo. While Joseph Smith

---

25. From a letter by Josiah Ells to James J. Strang that Thompson published "for the vindication of the truth." Josiah Ells, "Bro. Ells' Rejoinder," *ZHBO*, 75.

26. See D&C 102:8, 1844 edition, now LDS D&C 105:27, with the word "Baneemy" changed to "mine elders."

27. "Acts of the Solemn Assembly," *ZHBO*, 31.

28. "Acts of the Solemn Assembly," *ZHBO*, 31–32; "The Dark and Cloudy Day," RLDS *History of the Church*. "On April 9,1853, a revelation appointing Richard Stevens, William Marks, and Harvey Childs a locating committee, "to search out a proper location on the frontier, which may serve as a gate of entrance into the land of Ephraim," etc., was presented by Elder Thompson."

was still incarcerated in Missouri, Marks spoke up at a meeting of church leaders, where he expressed his willingness to make a purchase of land where the Saints could gather, but because of their past "circumstances of being driven from the other places, he wished to be confident that it was the will of the Lord that the Saints should gather at that time."[29] After Smith's insistence on congregating his followers during the scant four years in Nauvoo, the gathering of the Saints again ended in disaster. Perhaps because of this, Marks appeared altogether unwilling to gather with Strang's followers at Voree or Beaver Island. However, Thompson's approach to gathering at this stage was measured and reasonable and would have appealed to Marks's deliberate, restrained personality. Thompson cautioned the assembly: "Let all remember the commandments concerning the gathering, which says, 'let not your gathering be in haste, neither go by flight; but observe to have all things prepared before you.'" Further, he instructed, "And to this end, let men be sent before you to provide you a place, who are wise and judicious, and let there be no confusion in your gathering."[30] Under Thompson, Marks demonstrated confidence in the principle, at least for a time, and led the committee in an effort to find a location for a gathering.

Days after the solemn assembly at which Marks was ordained to positions of leadership, Thompson wrote to his church, singling out the importance of Marks as one of his adherents:

> Wm. Marks is a man of experience as well as of character and influence. He was appointed President of Nauvoo Stake when it was first organized on the 5th of October, 1839, and continued in that office until after Joseph's death. On the 7th of October, 1844, he was superseded in his office, by John Smith, because he boldly protested against the usurpation and corruptions of the Twelve. Br. Marks maintained that they had no right to usurp the authority of the first Presidency.[31]

While Marks was certainly welcomed because of his talents and ability, he was also being used to lend legitimacy to Thompson's group, just as Strang had used him. The fact that Marks joined this group, accepted a position of Chief of the Quorum of Traveling Teachers, and was preparing a place of gathering for the community raised Thompson's credibility with other non-polygamist Saints.

---

29. "Far West Committee minutes," CHL.

30. Charles B. Thompson, "April 18th, 1852," *ZHBO*, 31; Charles B. Thompson, "St. Louis, Mo., October 1st, 1852," *ZHBO*, 79.

31. Thompson, "April 18th, 1852," *ZHBO*, 30.

Traveling teachers were expected to report their work to their leaders on a regular basis. Marks did this in a letter to Thompson on June 1, 1852. He confessed, a little shamefacedly: "I have been so busy in preparing for the discharge of the duties of the committee, that I have not spent any time to instruct others."[32] Nevertheless, though sixty years old, Marks seemed to place himself into the work with dedication.

Marks, Stevens, and Childs had been communicating by letter and had decided to start their search at the end of June. Marks began a 450-mile journey on horseback, looking for land in the area of St. Joseph, Missouri. He wrote to Thompson that the trip was not going well, as "the surrounding country here, we think it will be very, difficult to obtain a suitable location for the Saints to gather, too near this place, on account of the high price of land." Marks noted they would look 130 miles further north into Kanesville, Pottawatamie County, Iowa (now known as Council Bluffs).[33]

Thompson held a second, larger solemn assembly at his home in St. Louis on August 29, 1852. The traveling teachers had organized schools and churches in many states, and the circulation of *Zion's Harbinger* had grown.[34] By September 1, Marks and Childs selected a location for gathering. They had discovered that the land around Kanesville, temporarily settled by Brigham Young's people, had been vacated as they migrated west. Now many of the land claims in the area were open for settlement.[35] Thompson agreed with the choice and thought it was "exceedingly proper" that Jehovah's Presbytery of Zion should take the place where the old organization of Mormons "went to pieces."[36] Marks wrote again to Thompson to tell him they had purchased a house for him and his family, and they left the house in charge of Gladden Bishop until Thompson could move to Kanesville and take possession of it.[37]

Following the solemn assembly, Thompson promptly wrote an explanatory article in the *Harbinger* titled "The Gathering," propounding

---

32. William Marks, "Movements of the Committee of Location," *ZHBO*, 55.

33. William Marks, "News from the Committee of Location," *ZHBO*, 71–72; C. R. Marks, "Monona County," 93.

34. C. R. Marks, 93.

35. C. R. Marks, 93–94.

36. C. R. Marks, 94.

37. Charles B. Thompson, "The Gathering," *ZHBO*, 16. Gladden Bishop was, at the time, the leader of a Restoration sect of his own. Though he never joined Jehovah's Presbytery of Zion, he seems to have had a close connection with William Marks.

its doctrinal purpose in terms of Kirtland-era theology. The gathering provided a place for the remnant of Israel to "be organized according to the pattern of the Holy Priesthood of the sons of God" and to "receive that endowment necessary to qualify them to bear the kingdom to Israel." With nineteenth-century Manifest Destiny rhetoric, Thompson exhorted:

> Let us haste therefore and gather together unto the place selected and be qualified to go forth unto this remnant of Jacob [Native Americans] with the keys of deliverance and retribution, and also that we may go forth, for the last time among the Gentiles, with the law of Justification, to bind it up, and to seal up our testimony unto the Gentiles, that they may be left without excuse, if they refuse to assist us in our labor of love, in changing their savage enemy to a humane friend.[38]

He told the Saints to bring all their wealth with them to Kanesville, and not hold some back like the New Testament Ananias and Sapphira.[39] "Let none suppose that it will benefit them to belong to the covenant of Israel," Thompson wrote, "unless they progress unto perfection; and receive the key words of power."[40]

Thompson's movement had grown enough to catch the attention of Orson Pratt, who wrote his observations to Brigham Young in late 1852:

> Charles B. Thompson is publishing a monthly paper in which many revelations are printed, purporting to be revealed by an unknown personage, calling himself "Baneemy" which you will at once recognize as one of the fictitious names, which Joseph substituted for the real names in certain revelations in the Book of Covenants. Thomson is sending out his teachers, & they have already introduced many scores, in different parts, into their organization. Their committee, consisting of Wm Marks & others, have, I understand, located their place of gathering near Kanesville.[41]

William Marks did his part to introduce the newly-founded sect to these "many scores" of people who were dissatisfied with Young, Strang, and the several other contenders for Mormon succession. This was a change for Marks. In his Kirtland days, he had been given a calling as the

---

38. Thompson, "The Gathering," 15–16.
39. See Acts 5. Ananias and Sapphira were wealthy members of the early Christian community in Jerusalem. They sold a piece of property and brought the proceeds to the apostles, but they secretly kept back some of the money for themselves while pretending to donate the full amount. The Lord punished them for their deceit by striking them dead.
40. Thompson, "The Gathering," 16.
41. "Orson Pratt Letter, November 20, 1852," CHL.

Kirtland stake president that occasioned him to stay in one place and not to participate in traveling missionary work. He was in the same position in Nauvoo as stake president and president of the high council. When many of his contemporaries were traveling through the Eastern States, Great Britain, and all around the world to preach the gospel, Marks was caring for the temporal needs of the Saints at home. It does not appear that he did traveling missionary work under Strang, either, when he was building his home and businesses in Shabbona Grove; traveling back and forth to Voree to attend conferences seemed almost as much as he could manage.

In a February 17, 1853, letter to Thompson, Marks had "some good news to communicate." In his travels around Illinois, he encountered "a good many of the former members of the church scattered around in this section of country." He did describe a sort of fatigue he found among those he was attempting to convert—just as he had, "they have been through so many isms, it is very difficult to make them believe the truth." He also found it "very unpleasant travelling over these bleak prairies in the winter." Yet he soon saw his efforts succeed. With companion John Gould, he "administered the covenants to three persons" in Kendall, Illinois, and there left Gould to "organize a class." He then traveled thirty miles to Batavia, Illinois, spent Sunday with fellow Strang disaffiliates James Blakeslee and Jehiel Savage, who he also convinced to follow Thompson, and "administered the covenant to four in that place." Before leaving, he organized a quorum in Batavia with Blakeslee as chief and Savage as teacher.[42]

On April 1, Marks wrote again to Thompson, sharing his intent to "go up to the Bluffs" at Kanesville, where the new gathering place, a city named "Preparation," was to be established. This name signaled the community's intention to prepare for the coming of the Lord "Shiloh."[43] A horsepower sawmill Marks was building in Shabbona Grove was to be finished by then, and he had arranged "for two or three men to go with me, that are used to the business of sawing lumber, to put the mill in

---

42. "Bro. Marks has visited us at my residence, and has administered the covenant to three more in this place, two 'old members of the church,' and one who has never been a member." James Blakeslee, "Having entered into the covenant of the Fathers myself," *ZHBO*, 22.

43. Shiloh is a Hebrew name in Genesis 49:10 that Thompson, along with other Christian sects, interpreted to denote the Messiah. See, for example, "Origin, Promises, Present Condition, and Future Destiny of the Jews," *ZHBO*, 27–30.

operation at Kanesville, or in that vicinity" in preparation for the coming assembly of the Saints.[44]

Privately, in a letter to James Adams, Marks admitted to some reservation about gathering, especially if it were to happen too quickly. "The country is very new and we will have to undergo a great many privations," he observed. The buildings abandoned by Brigham Young's people were "very poor," having been intended as temporary. Marks wrote, "We have seen so much misery and distress by gathering in haste, I think we had better follow a different course with the present work." He shared with Adams his plan to go to the Bluffs on the first of April and said that he would bring his newly purchased horsepower sawmill along with a man to tend it. This would address the lack of lumber currently available for building. Marks further thought that to "save great inconvenience," small groups of families should choose one person to go to the gathering place in the spring, secure locations, and prepare before the rest arrived.[45] This type of sensible observation demonstrates why Marks's talents were so useful to Joseph Smith, James Strang, and Charles Thompson. His thoughts about the practicalities of gathering had developed over several years of thoughtful leadership.

At a solemn assembly held in St. Louis in April 1853, Marks was given additional responsibility. Not only was he sustained as First Chief of the First Quorum of Traveling Teachers (with his friend J. M. Adams as his Second Chief), but Thompson also moved "that a Quorum of Evangelical Teachers, be appointed and ordained; and that Wm. Marks, be the Chief of the Quorum." Now there were three quorums of Traveling Teachers, with a quorum of Evangelical Teachers placed over them, making almost fifty ordained missionaries, when two years previous "there was but one."[46] Marks, however, was absent from the meeting. He had intended to stop by the assembly on his way to Kanesville,[47] but he wrote to Thompson saying he would be delayed "on account of the sickness of his wife." Thus, his ordination was "postponed for the present." Marks promised that as soon as he could leave home, he would "be at the place of gathering according to previous arrangements."[48]

---

44. William Marks, "Communications," *ZHBO*, 20.
45. William Marks, letter to James Adams, January 25, 1853, CCLA.
46. "The first Tri-annual Solemn Assembly," *ZHBO*, 32.
47. Marks, "Communications," *ZHBO*, 20.
48. "The first Tri-annual Solemn Assembly," *ZHBO*, 32. See also "The Gathering," *ZHBO*, 46.

During this time, an unusual proposal was made by one of Thompson's followers, Josiah Ells, regarding the location of the gathering place: "to the effect that the committee appointed by revelation, to select the location, be recommended to reconsider their report in reference to the central point upon which to gather." Ells suggested "another and more suitable location somewhere in the vicinity of Kanesville." In order to "expedite this business," a subcommittee under the direction of Marks and Childs was selected. It is not known what was objectionable about the proposed center place, nor why a second committee was appointed, but Thompson urged that this action "not retard the exertions of any to move up to the vicinity of Kanesville."[49] Shortly after the assembly, the town of Preparation was established at a new location in Monona County, fifty miles north of Kanesville.

Though Marks missed the April assembly, he made it to Kanesville with his mill by June 12. He left one of his partners there to run the mill until it could be moved to a more permanent location at the place of gathering. Later that week, he was back in St. Louis with Thompson.

On June 15, 1853, in his role as "Chief Evangelical Teacher in the School of Faith," Marks wrote a letter to the church that would become his most-often quoted writing. The formally-styled "Epistle" began with Marks stating it was his duty "to say something by way of encouragement and also by way of instruction to those who are placed under my care, and supervision." He then told of his history in the church and described trouble creeping into the church in Nauvoo. Though he personally doubted that some of the practices he encountered during those days were aligned with God's will, he remained committed to upholding and imparting principles that were clearly disclosed as part of the church's doctrine. His rationale was that embracing solely pure and virtuous principles would ultimately contribute to the betterment of humanity.[50]

Marks specified and spoke of polygamy, as well as a "kingly form of government, in which Joseph suffered himself to be ordained a king." However, he claimed that Smith repented and changed his views on polygamy:

> Joseph, however, became convinced before his death that he had done wrong; for about three weeks before his death, I met him one morning in the street, and he said to me, Brother Marks, I have something to communicate to you, we retired to a by-place, and set down together, when he said: "We are a ruined people." I asked, how so? he said: "This doctrine of polygamy,

---

49. "The first Tri-annual Solemn Assembly," *ZHBO*, 31–32.
50. William Marks, "Epistle," *ZHBO*, 53.

or Spiritual-wife system, that has been taught and practiced among us, will prove our destruction and overthrow. I have been deceived," said he, "in reference to its practice; it is wrong; it is a curse to mankind, and we shall have to leave the United States soon, unless it can be put down. and its practice stopped in the church."[51]

William Marks's opinion about Smith's polygamy has been difficult to analyze. First and foremost, the testimony establishes that Marks was aware that the doctrine "was introduced into the church as a principle of exaltation" while Smith was still living.[52] But, perhaps because he is speaking to a group of those who reject polygamy, he holds back from naming Smith as its instigator. He also describes Smith as passively "suffering himself" to be ordained as king, seemingly placing the onus of this presumptive action upon others. The epistle can thus be read as though Smith had been deceived by others who had championed the cause of polygamy. In this scenario, he tells Marks that he has decided to set things right, and enlists Marks's help to end the practice.

A different view of Marks's narrative might be that Smith was concerned over the negative effects his polygamy doctrine was having upon the church and saw that it might lead to their destruction. He therefore concocted a plan with Marks whereby he would publicly repudiate the principle: "Brother Marks, you have not received this doctrine, and how glad I am." Because Marks had not been a participant, Smith could now instruct him to "go into the high council, and I will have charges preferred against all who practice this doctrine, and . . . I will go into the stand, and preach against it, with all my might, and in this way we may rid the church of this damnable heresy."[53] Thereby, those who had not kept their plurality a secret could be publicly chastened and perhaps the church would not encounter so much opposition. This seems to have been an approach that Smith utilized in other situations,[54] and it would be used by the branch of Mormonism led by Brigham Young in the future. For example, the 1890

---

51. Marks, 53.

52. Marks, 53.

53. The words "this damnable heresy" perhaps represented Marks's view of polygamy rather than Joseph's.

54. One example of this is recounted in William Clayton's journal of October 19, 1843: Joseph advised Clayton to allow his plural wife to live in his home even though people might talk. "Says he [Joseph] just keep her at home and brook it and if they raise trouble about it and bring you before me I will give you an awful scourging & probably cut you off from the church and then I will baptise you &

manifesto against polygamy in Utah was such an action: the church publicly renounced plural marriage while secretly continuing to sanction it.[55]

After Smith's death, Marks could plainly see that the Nauvoo Twelve were determined to continue the esoteric practices of polygamy and temple work. Explaining his feelings at this juncture, he wrote: "When I found that there was no chance to rid the church of that abominable sin, as I viewed it, I made my arrangements to leave Nauvoo, and I did so firmly believing that the plans and designs of the great Jehovah, in inspiring Joseph to bring forth the book of Mormon, would yet be carried out in his own time." Marks's activity with Thompson was a further rejection of the Nauvoo developments of the church as well as Strang's polygamy.

In this epistle to the Congregation of Jehovah's Presbytery of Zion, Marks was as fervently passionate as any of his writings or extant descriptions portray him. "Well brethren," he wrote:

> I have lived to sce [sic] the foundation, and the platform laid, the principles, revealed, and the order given, whereby the great work of the Father, can, and will be accomplished. There is no doubt resting on my mind in reference to this work of Baneemy being the work of God . . . spoken of in the book of Mormon, to prepare the way for the restoration of his covenants to the house of Israel.[56]

Marks stated his intention "from this time henceforth to labor in the cause, and give my influence, and substance to speed the work," and exhorted his fellow believers to "move forward and take a decided stand to labor for Jehovah and the benefit of mankind." He asked them to get ready to gather themselves and "the remnant seed of the church" to the place that would be announced. "All should be prepared," he said, "to send up an offering of sufficient magnitude to entitle them to receive a large blessing." Financial offerings were necessary to replenish the movement's treasury, to obtain a printing press, and to help move Thompson and his family to the place of gathering.[57]

In the same issue of *Zion's Harbinger*, Thompson reiterated Marks's call for donations. He asked his followers to bring their oblations to the next solemn assembly, to be held on August 29, 1853, and instructed them to send their money by mail if they could not come to the assembly

---

set you ahead as good as ever." James B. Allen, *Trials of Discipleship: The Story of William Clayton, a Mormon*, 194–95.

55. See D. Michael Quinn, "LDS Church Authority and New Plural Marriages, 1890–1904," 9–105.

56. Marks, "Epistle," 53.

57. Marks, 53–54.

in person. In doing so, Thompson requested that "none fail to send an accurate statement of their worldly possessions, in the following form: 1st, the value of your real estate, 2nd, value of your personal property, 3rd, cash on hand."[58] This was necessary, Thompson warned, in order to advance in the School of Works and to receive blessings.

Marks's plans were to attend the August solemn assembly, to go from there to the gathering place, where he would remain through the winter. Thompson also announced his intention to move to Preparation after the assembly, provided that the people had furnished the necessary means to move him and his family by that time.[59]

Marks, however, would not make it to Preparation until the following year, as for the rest of the summer and early fall of 1853 he was struck with ill health that kept him at home. Unable to attend the assembly, he did send money to St. Louis as instructed and helped contract for a printing press.[60]

The August 1853 issue of *Zion's Harbinger and Baneemy's Organ* was the last to be printed in St. Louis. The September issue was printed in Preparation, and in the letterhead Thompson gave his address as "Preparation, Iowa, Magnolia Post Office, Harrison County."[61] This issue contained several pages of Enoch pseudepigrapha, which Thompson had been publishing for many months, as well as a list of remittances received for a newspaper subscription. The name William Marks, of Shabbona Grove, was at the top of the list. James M. Adams of Vienna, Wisconsin, was also prominent among the subscribers.[62]

By the end of 1853, many of the fifty or sixty families who made up the "Baneemies" (as they were locally called) had gathered to Monona County. On December 27, 28, and 29, 1853, a solemn assembly was held in the "Lord's House" at Preparation, attended by more than one hundred persons. These renewed their covenant to, among other things, "renounce all connexion, fellowship and faith, in any and all church orga-

---

58. Charles B. Thompson, "The Gathering and the August Assembly," *ZHBO*, 55.
59. Thompson, *ZHBO*, 55.
60. Inez Smith Davis, *The Story of the Church*, 312.
61. Since the nearest post office in Magnolia was twenty miles away, the settlers established a "temporary Post Office," with Thompson as postmaster, "until the heads of the Department at Washington City can be notified of our condition, and petitioned to establish a Post office here, and a mail route to this place." "Preamble and Resolutions," *ZHBO*, 72.
62. "List of Letters," *ZHBO*, 69.

nizations, now upon the earth."⁶³ Oblations were offered, tithing records were entered, the entire company partook of a ceremonial feast, and all advanced to the second department of the Schools of Faith and Works by signing additional covenants attached thereto. Priesthood quorums were also formed, and leaders were confirmed by the laying on of hands. Though Marks was not present at this assembly, he was recognized as a Chief Evangelical Teacher, with Rowland Cobb. Under these two brethren were five Quorums of Traveling Teachers, James Adams being First Chief of the First Quorum.

On March 2, 1854, Adams wrote to Marks to ask his advice on moving to the new settlement. In reply, Marks suggested, "I would say in regard to the first request on Moveing this spring or summer would be right according to my judgment." The first business in such an undertaking, Marks wrote, was breaking prairie, and "such work was verry high [expensive] when I was there. Cook stoves was dear but there was a plenty of them at Kanesville." Mechanical items were also limited when he was last there, so he suggested that Adams "take such articles as you would most kneed it will save a good deal of time in procuring them when you get there." Marks also gave Adams advice on travel arrangements, suggesting that he cross the Mississippi at Albany, then take the direct route to Iowa City, and from there go to Fort Des Moines. He noted, "I discovered in the last paper, if a man would pay his tithing he could have one acre of land in the Town and as much land ajasent [adjacent] as he wished to work."⁶⁴ But, cautioned Marks, that would not be the way he would like to farm: "I should rather live on my farm but what will be the order of the day I [k]no[w] not but we can learn when we get there." Marks mused darkly: "Money seams to be quite an object at present but [it's] possible it is all right[—]that has been the cry ever since we first hear[d] of Mormonism."⁶⁵

In April 1854, Thompson mentioned twenty permanent families who had moved to the settlement, with "fifteen to twenty families more on their way." That month's solemn assembly was held in what was termed "the House of the Lord," with one hundred twenty in attendance and a customary accompanying "Feast of the Covenant."⁶⁶ There, Thompson

---

63. "Covenant, to be taken on entering the Congregation of Jehovah's Presbytery of Zion," *ZHBO*, 9.
64. See Charles B. Thompson, "The School of Works," *ZHBO*, 28.
65. William Marks, letter to James Adams, March 18, 1854, CCLA.
66. Charles B. Thompson, "The Progress of the Work of the Father," *ZHBO*, 61.

came down hard on the participants with regards to compliance with the law of tithing, which he followed up with a lengthy article in that month's *Zion's Harbinger*. Newcomers were to turn over ten percent of all their worldly goods and property and would receive an "inheritance" of one acre of land, with ten percent of whatever was produced upon it due to the Lord's Steward every year "forever."[67] Ten percent of everything they possessed at the beginning of the year was tithed, ten percent of the family's time and labor, and ten percent of their "increase" at the end of the year. If they wanted to repudiate the bond, they must give back the land, withdraw from the School, and "their names will be blotted out of the Book of Remembrance."[68]

A few days after the solemn assembly on April 15, 1854, Marks arrived in Preparation and began to make arrangements "to build all the necessary buildings for the use of his family."[69] However, his stay would not be long. In May's issue of *Zion's Harbinger*, the reader is given a clue as to what happened next, to sour William Marks on the Presbytery of Zion. Charles Thompson received a revelation referencing the committee to which Marks had been assigned to select the place of gathering.[70] The Lord told Thompson that the committee "hearkened not to my voice" and had done only part of what they were asked to do: "I rejected their work, saith the Lord . . . [for they] have not hearkened to my voice, and have kept part, or all of their Tything back."[71] The Law of Sacrifice was then unveiled, asking for a "voluntary" agreement to "give up all earthly possessions to the Lord to enrich his treasury." This sacrifice was embodied in the third degree of the Department of Works, and in two years it would cease to be voluntary and would become mandatory.[72] After ten or twelve days in Preparation, and apparently in reaction to this stricter interpretation of the principle of tithing, Marks headed back to Shabbona Grove.

---

67. Thompson was the "Agent" appointed by the Lord to receive and manage tithing, and it was not permitted to ask the Lord's agent for an accounting of how it was managed. Charles B. Thompson, "The Law of Tything again," *ZHBO*, 56–57.

68. Thompson, *ZHBO*, 57.

69. "The Progress of the Work of the Father," *ZHBO*, 62.

70. The revelation is labeled as follows: "The word of the Lord, by the voice of Baneemy, came unto Charles B. Thompson, Chief Steward of the Lord's House, in June, 1854." This was printed in the May 1854 issue of *Zion's Harbinger*, which was issued late.

71. Charles B. Thompson, "Revelation," *ZHBO*, 69.

72. Charles B. Thompson, "The Law of Sacrifice," *ZHBO*, 70–74.

Months passed, and Thompson's temporal arrangements became more and more unpopular. At the end of August, Thompson reached out to Marks with a "small note sent in an envelope stating that many had turned away, but urging [Marks] to make all possible speed" back to Preparation. "There was still a chance," he wrote, "for those who was willing to make the sacrifice of all they possess of this world's goods."[73] Marks did not take the bait.

In a private letter to James Adams at the beginning of September, Marks disclosed his disillusionment with Thompson. He told Adams that when he'd visited Preparation in the spring he found "that there was a great many that was quite dissatisfied, principally with the time tithing." Marks himself had gone to the gathering place with the intention of moving there, but instead he "came to the conclusion that there was the greatest oppression that I ever saw imposed upon a community." By the time he left, he "thought I would wait a short time and see what would be the result of things, for I was satisfied that many would leave."[74]

Indeed they had. Thompson later estimated that about fifty percent of the congregation pulled out.[75] James Adams, too, had decided not to settle at Preparation. In his letter, Marks asked Adams to "write me, and give me your views of all the proceedings as you understand them," as well as give him the names of some of the others who had left.

By the end of the next year, *Zion's Harbinger and Baneemy's Organ* would publish its last issue under the date of December 1855. Conjeprizites had become disillusioned with the hardscrabble aspects of their communal lifestyle. Eventually, thanks to escalating demands and poor decisions on Thompson's part, his disgruntled followers booted him out quite dramatically, signaling the collapse of the settlement in October 1858.

William Marks likewise lost the enthusiasm he initially felt for Thompson's message. His choice not to relinquish the proceeds of his hard labor and his family's security into the common treasury had made him an outcast once again. Marks later avowed that "while under the influence of Baneemyism I lost all of my strength and former vigor. I never went on a mission without returning home, sick and finally reduced so low as to despair of ever being able to do anything more."[76]

---

73. William Marks, letter to James Adams, September 3, 1854, in Heman C. Smith, "William Marks," *JH*, 25.

74. Marks, letter to James Adams, September 3, 1854, 25.

75. Charles B. Thompson, "Close of the First Year," *ZHBO*, 24.

76. William Marks, letter to James Adams, July 26, 1855, 27, CCLA.

CHAPTER 10

The Weary Wanderer

William Marks's quest for a spiritual home in a rapidly changing religious landscape set the stage for a compelling exploration of his own capabilities as a leader. He feared becoming a perpetual seeker—"always searching, and never able to come to the knowledge of the truth" (2 Tim. 3:7). This made him feel, as he wrote to his friend James Adams, as if "it would be policy for me to stand still for a short time."[1] So many succession movements had unsuccessfully tried to gather the Saints that Marks became discouraged at the very thought. His sister and brother-in-law had followed Brigham Young and were building up family kingdoms in the West.[2] But for Marks, conflicts with Young had made that impossible. By 1854, he had rejected the claims of James Strang and Charles Thompson, and their groups would peter out by 1856 and 1858. Sidney Rigdon's group had largely disintegrated.[3] Lyman Wight led a small Restoration group far away in Texas, but they practiced polygamy, which Marks detested. So did William Smith, Joseph Smith's brother, who also led a small group but was considered rather a loose cannon. David Whitmer would not form a viable Restoration group until 1876.

This left Alpheus Cutler, then living in Manti, Iowa, some sixty miles southeast of Kanesville. Cutler had served alongside Marks on the Nauvoo High Council, as well as in Joseph Smith's Anointed Quorum and Council of Fifty. Like Thompson, Cutler believed that the Nauvoo church had been rejected by God due to their failure to complete the temple there and thus ceased to exist after the martyrdom. He also believed that he had the priesthood authority to restore the church. While Marks agreed that the Lord had rejected the church for "depart[ing] from its foundation," he still felt that it had not yet warranted a "funeral-sermon."[4] Thus, though he must have been aware of Cutler's community, Marks did not consider Cutler's claims to be a feasible option. To Adams, he lamented, "I can see

---

1. William Marks, letter to James M. Adams, November 15, 1854, CCLA.
2. Prudence Marks Miles and her husband Samuel Miles moved to the Salt Lake Valley by 1849.
3. This group was later revitalized under William Bickerton and legally organized in 1865.
4. William Marks, letter to James Adams, June 11, 1855, CCLA.

no more that can have any favorable claims to come out and claim to be a prophet."[5]

Perhaps Marks, having reached his sixties, lacked the vigor to investigate another claimant. He nevertheless still yearned to gather with others: "I have had it in my mind to try and form a settlement of brethren and try to live according to the law of God. . . . I should like to live where I could enjoy the society of friends and brethren."[6] However, in this stage in his life, he had lost confidence in gathering under any church organization. In May 1855, he wrote to his friend James Adams:

> I know of nothing better than the pure principles of the gospel. I have recently come to the conclusion to teach repentance and faith on the Lord Jesus Christ and baptism for the remission of sins and the laying on of hands for the gift of the Holy Spirit. . . . Teach the pure principles of the gospel, and every man stand or fall.[7]

Marks told Adams that he believed "all men that worketh righteousness in all nations shall be accepted of God."[8] The rejection of traditional church structures in favor of pure gospel principles mirrored the broader societal shifts that challenged the established norms.

Adams was a sympathetic ear to Marks, as his journey followed much the same path. Adams joined with the early Saints in Kirtland in 1837, served as branch president in Ashtabula, Ohio, and moved to Nauvoo in 1845. That same year he was ordained a high priest by Marks's successor, John Smith. He also affiliated with James Strang for a time as one of his apostles, as well as First Chief of the First Quorum of Traveling Teachers with Charles Thompson's group. But by 1854, he, much like Marks, had once again become a seeker.

The same year, Marks was visited by his brother-in-law, George Robinson, who was looking to invest a few thousand dollars in government lands. The 1850s were marked by financial opportunities and land speculation, and Robinson told Marks of land warrants becoming available in New York City in August and September of 1855. Robinson said they would be available at a reduced price under a new Act, and he offered to give Marks a share and pay him for locating investment property. Marks, who seemed throughout his life to be aware of financial opportunities, was interested and began to research property that might be available in New

---

5. William Marks letter to James Adams, May 20, 1855, CCLA.
6. Marks, November 15, 1854, CCLA.
7. Marks, May 20, 1855, CCLA.
8. Marks, May 20, 1855, CCLA.

York City as well as elsewhere. In particular, he reached out to Adams to see if he knew of land investment ventures in his home state of Iowa. "My faith as to spiritual things and temporal things are so connected," Marks told Adams.[9] The convergence of economic prospects and spiritual musings highlights Marks's multifaceted approach to the challenges of the time.

During the years following his departure from Charles Thompson's Baneemyism, Marks retained the prestige he had as president of the high council at Nauvoo under Joseph Smith. Although he no longer belonged to any church organization, he soon found that many former Saints looked up to him and shared his views on preserving the simple principles of the gospel. A group of eight to ten Saints from Aurora, Illinois, contacted him, wanting him to come and baptize them and wishing to gather together "a band of brethren."[10] At this point, however, Marks was hesitant to affiliate himself with anyone. As he wrote to Adams,

> [W]e are living in a day when the Devil has great power and it appears from what we see and hear and read that he will, if possible, deceive the whole world. Therefore it is highly necessary that we are watchful and prayerful that we may not be deceived. Try the spirits faithfully by the written word. I well remember what Oliver Cowdery told me when on his way to Council Bluffs. He said the work was of God, and the end would be accomplished "let men do or act as they pleased!"[11]

Former Apostle John Edward Page was another who had become disillusioned with joining a particular church organization. He had been called as an apostle by Joseph Smith following the heartbreaking experience of his wife and two daughters being murdered by mobs in Missouri. After Smith's assassination, Page broke with the Quorum of the Twelve and soon affiliated with Strang, where he was ordained an apostle. His stay with Strang did not last long, and after a brief association with James C. Brewster, Page's belief in the necessity of prophet-leaders began to wane. Instead, he came to believe that "true religion was found in the Book of Mormon and in the heart of the believer, rather than within a church."[12] Page's journey, from apostleship in Strang's movement to a belief in individual spirituality, mirrored the broader questioning of institutional authority in the 1850s United States, as well as Marks's own views.

---

9. Lisle G. Brown, *Nauvoo Sealings, Adoptions, and Anointings*, 311

10. Marks, May 20, 1855, CCLA.

11. Marks, June 11, 1855, CCLA.

12. John Quist, "John E. Page: An Apostle of Uncertainty," 53.

After he left Strang's Voree, Page lived near Marks in DeKalb County with his second wife and children. His youngest son described him as always preaching to an audience, "generally in village stores and shops, where groups would gather to hear him, some times in discussion with other Ministers and much in private conversation."[13]

In 1855 and 1856, Marks and Page began to meet occasionally for religious services with a small group of like-minded Saints, including John Gaylord, John Landers, Russell Huntley, William W. Blair, and others. Gaylord was an early church member who had been excommunicated at the time of the Kirtland Bank failure. He was rebaptized in 1839, received his endowments in the Nauvoo Temple, and then chose to follow Strang, where he was president of the Voree Stake from 1846 to 1847. After breaking with Strang, Gaylord would eventually become a leader in the Reorganized Church of Jesus Christ of Latter Day Saints. Landers was also a member of the early church who subsequently followed Strang. He was ordained a high priest by Strang in 1846 and lived on Beaver Island until 1854. Blair was an 1851 convert of William Smith who soon after aligned with Charles B. Thompson. Blair remembered this as a time when "my meditations and convictions were of such range and force as to finally lead me to resolve that, whatever others might do, it was my duty to seek to live in harmony with the light I had received of [God]."[14]

Adams, now located in Wisconsin, did not live close enough to meet with these brethren, but he continued to have religious reflections and experiences to share with his friend William Marks. Although his letters are not extant, we can sometimes divine his writings from Marks's replies. In a June 1855 letter, Adams related preaching discourses on the first principles of the gospel and the law of adoption as led by the Spirit.[15]

---

13. Quist, 65n52.

14. Frederick B. Blair, comp., *The Memoirs of President W. W. Blair*, 6.

15. Adams could have been preaching adoption in the Christian sense, referring to theological concept of believers being adopted into the family of God through faith in Jesus Christ. However, with his Mormon background, it is possible Adams was teaching the doctrine known as the Law of Adoption, a concept some believe originated with Joseph Smith, whereby a man holding the priesthood could symbolically seal other adults to himself, extending his family beyond the bounds of biology to create a larger, interconnected family kingdom that would endure beyond death. Several restoration groups that succeeded Joseph Smith practiced the Law of Adoption for the first few decades after his death. The practice continues in a few fundamentalist sects in the current day.

Marks responded by telling Adams that if his thoughts were truly of the right spirit, they had "incalculable meaning." "O how it would rejoice my heart," Marks rhapsodized, "to see the true light break forth again, that we might know of a surety, for I have long been wandering in darkness, and following false prophets until I had become tiresome and weary."[16]

Marks maintained his correspondence with Adams as he tried to work out his feelings. He told Adams that his "mind has never been at rest since the breaking up of the church (or the death of Bro. Joseph)" and that "false prophets have arisen." With false prophets around, he stated that the only way to find the truth was by "asking our heavenly Father to direct us, and claim the promise, If any man lack wisdom let him [ask] God."[17] Lacking wisdom and asking God was clearly an allusion to Joseph Smith's experiences as a young man that led to the First Vision.

Marks's thoughts continued to dwell on the principle of gathering which had been responsible for his many moves and travels throughout his associations with the church. Missing his fellowship with other saints, he contemplated looking for "a good location somewhere in the West" with a "large tract of land" where he might (if enough of his friends would agree) "invite all of the honest in heart and as many as was disposed to gather around where we could enjoy some society, for it is like living alone in the world as many of us do."[18]

To Marks's pleasure, many "seemed very much pleased with [his] views," and he seemed eager to move on his plan as "I am somewhat advanced in age, near 64 years, but my health was never better than at present, although I can't endure so much hardship." Regardless of a gathering or not, Marks was dedicated "to observe the law and keep the commandments of God that we shall know for a surety all that will be necessary for us to know."[19]

By this time, Marks's subscription to Thompson's paper had expired, and he had no interest in renewing. He asked Adams to write and tell him the news of what was happening there and "what you mentioned that was taught at Preparation, of probation and regeneration."[20] As much as Marks and his friends professed that they wanted to stick to gospel

---

16. Marks, June 11, 1855, CCLA.
17. William Marks, letter to James Adams, July 26, 1855, CCLA.
18. Marks, July 26, 1855, CCLA.
19. Marks, July 26, 1855, CCLA.
20. Marks, July 26, 1855, CCLA.

basics, they remained curious about esoteric doctrines circulating among the Restoration branches.

In turn, Marks told Adams what some of their mutual friends had been doing. "Bro. George," he said, "had made complete shipwreck of his faith." It appeared to Marks that this Brother George's only object was "to get gain," and he wanted no connection with him. Gaylord and Page were of a like mind with Marks about wanting to gather. However, they suggested the place of gathering be "on the Colorado." Marks ventured that he agreed with Adams's opinion that "the prospect in Shelby County [Ohio] for entering land [was] quite good."[21]

A few months later, in September, Marks again wrote to Adams, still thinking about gathering but agonizing over whether this was according to the will of God. Contemplating the daunting task of starting a new church after the collapse of so many others, Marks acknowledged the gravity of the path ahead. "It looks like a long journey for me to undertake," he penned, "and I have had some fears rise in my mind of late that possibly it might prove a failure."[22] If the effort fell flat, Marks said that he would be mortified. His lack of confidence provides insight into why he hadn't pressed a case for his own leadership after Joseph Smith's death. He had been a solid leader when appointed and supported by a superior, but he lacked the self-assurance to take up the reins on his own. Opting to defer any decisions until spring, Marks planned to utilize the winter months to better understand the perspectives of his brethren, having had limited opportunities for interaction thus far.

Feeling a deep need for divine guidance, Marks expressed a profound desire for faith and prayers from Adams and others, seeking the intervention of the spirit of truth: "[I]f I ask in a right frame of mind he will instruct me." Finally, in a cautionary tone, he described a letter he had just received from William Smith, who was then preaching in Kirtland. Smith taught basic principles, but "would not trouble about church matters, as there were so many, lo here and lo there!"[23]

Indeed, there was a profound development in religious perspectives throughout middle America, influenced by the broader context of the

---

21. Marks, July 26, 1855, CCLA. In this letter to Adams, Marks also mentioned "McHenry and family," asking Adams to tell them the Markses were all in good health and that they should write soon. It is possible that this refers to Marks's daughter and his son-in-law, Henry McHenry.

22. William Marks, letter to James M. Adams, September 23, 1855, CCLA.

23. Marks, September 23, 1855, CCLA.

Restoration Movement, the Spiritualist Movement, and the Adventist Movement. These movements collectively contributed to a diverse and evolving spiritual landscape, challenging established norms and paving the way for a more individualized and experiential approach to faith. Though many of Marks's expressed sentiments had their roots in early Mormonism, they can also be viewed as a microcosm of these larger religious and cultural shifts occurring in 1850s America.

Marks's longing for a settlement of brethren and a commitment to living by the law of God echoes the ideals of the Restoration Movement. This movement, championed by figures like Alexander Campbell and Barton Stone, sought to restore Christianity to its original form based solely on the teachings of the Bible. It was influential in the rise of Mormonism in the 1830s, but it lost momentum as the church became more institutionalized. Marks's loss of confidence in organized church structures and his emphasis on teaching pure gospel principles reflect a desire to return to the roots of Christian faith, free from the complexities introduced by institutionalization.

Furthermore, Marks's expressed wish to form a settlement where he could enjoy the society of friends and brethren resonates with the communal and spiritual aspects of the Spiritualist Movement. This movement, gaining prominence in the mid-nineteenth century, emphasized personal spiritual experiences and direct communication with spirits and the divine. Similarity with the Adventist Movement is evident in Marks's beliefs regarding the laying on of hands for the gift of the Holy Spirit and his conviction that righteous individuals in all nations would be accepted by God. His emphasis on repentance, faith, and the acceptance of righteous individuals aligns with certain Adventist beliefs, particularly the Millerite movement of the 1840s that anticipated the imminent return of Christ and fostered a climate of moral and spiritual fervor.

Simultaneously, the nation teetered on the brink of Civil War. The contentious issues of slavery and westward expansion painted a picture of a nation in turmoil. Marks could not remain oblivious to the political and social rifts that echoed the struggles within the Mormon community. His personal journey mirrored the broader national struggle for identity and unity. The impending Civil War became a metaphor for the battles within his soul.

As much as institutionalization was unpopular, some organization was necessary if the scattered Saints were to come together in fellowship. In 1856, Marks started meeting more formally with Blair, Page, and

Gaylord.[24] These men "agreed to call a conference . . . and organize." The point of meeting together was to "discuss the subject" of assembling a group and "try to get a starting point." Marks again expressed his desire to take things slow, to concentrate their mutual faith and strength, and to "try to come into union." They would spend the summer traveling and giving notice to interested parties with the goal to then "call a conference in the fall, disseminating our views and preaching."[25]

Marks's plan to call a conference came from a renewed interest in the Book of Mormon. He wrote to Adams:

> It has been manifested to me in a few days past to organize as the Nephites did, with a high priest to preside over the whole church, with elders, priests, and teachers; the high priest to be elected by the voice of the people. This requires a man of God and of great faith. This I should wish to defer until we could get a more general expression of the brethren. . . . The Book of Mormon is of great worth to us in our day. I read it with more interest than, I ever did before.[26]

It is unclear if Marks was to be this "man of God and of great faith," as he was the presiding high priest in Nauvoo in the 1840s. While his intentions were unknown, there is no evidence of Marks attempting to be selected by the people to lead this group of like-minded believers.

Marks and his new associates continued to meet, and many joined their ranks—including Edmund Briggs, Israel Rogers, and James Blakeslee, all of whom would later became leaders in the Reorganized Church.[27] A conference was held on April 10–12, 1856, but it did not generate enough enthusiasm to propel the scattered seekers into gathering. It is impossible to say why Marks was unable to knit together these like-minded Saints. Perhaps the absence of a strong leader was a hindrance, as many seemed ready to follow Marks if he had had the confidence to take up the cross of leadership. This lack of a clear and confident leader is perhaps what Blair referred to when he later discounted this period of time with Marks and the others as lacking "the needed favor of God through the Holy Spirit."

Marks's hesitancy to affiliate with any particular group and his candid acknowledgment of fears regarding potential failures in leadership offer valuable insights into the complex dynamics that unfolded in the after-

---

24. Ruth Wildermuth, "William Marks after Nauvoo," 5–6.
25. William Marks, letter to James M. Adams, March 16, 1856, CCLA.
26. Marks, March 16, 1856, CCLA.
27. Mark Albert Scherer, *The Journey of a People: The Era of Reorganization, 1844 to 1946*, 69.

math of Joseph Smith's death. The absence of a charismatic figure like Smith and the deficits of others who stepped into the leadership vacuum prompted individuals like Marks to grapple with the daunting responsibility of guiding a religious movement. Marks, who had flourished during his time in Nauvoo under Smith's support, now deferred the challenge of stepping into a leadership role independently. His reluctance to press a case for his own leadership highlights the profound impact that a charismatic figurehead can have on the cohesion and direction of a religious community. Navigating the intricate landscape of post-succession Mormonism was challenging. Followers sought virtuous spiritual guidance while leaders, like Marks, contended with the weighty task of succeeding an authoritative and magnetic Joseph Smith.

While Marks and his associates equivocated, other unaffiliated Saints contended with similar issues. The 1850s continued much as they had begun, with groups of Saints traveling to gather with Brigham Young and his polygamy supporters on one side of the Rocky Mountains, and scattered families, tiny branches, and unstable tribes remaining steadfastly on the other.

CHAPTER 11

Reorganizing Zion

Just north of where William Marks and his compatriots were meeting and musing over whether there would ever be a successful succession movement, Jason W. Briggs—once leader of the Beloit, Wisconsin, branch of the church—experienced his own frustrating search. Separating from Brigham Young's faction in 1848, Briggs affiliated with James Strang until 1850, when he left due to Strang's acceptance of polygamy. He briefly joined William Smith, the prophet's brother, but was distressed to discover that William was teaching polygamy as well.[1]

Briggs prayed for revelation regarding the church and received what he considered to be the word of the Lord on November 18, 1851. He prepared a document that was distributed to individuals and the few branches of the church that had not joined with any would-be successors to Joseph Smith. The purpose of the revelation was four-fold:

> to denounce other claimants to prophetic authority; to enjoin the elders to preach against false doctrines that had overtaken the church; to instruct the elders to teach the original gospel law as found in the Bible, the Book of Mormon, and the Doctrine and Covenants; and to promise that from the lineage of Joseph Smith, Jr., would come the proper leader of the church.[2]

Several motivated and capable Saints in the Midwest—including Zenos H. Gurley Sr., who led a branch of the church in Wisconsin—coalesced around the idea that the original church could be continued.[3] A conference of church elders met as early as June 12–13, 1852, to endorse Briggs's revelation. By October, a pamphlet had been prepared to inform the public of the new movement, and two thousand copies were drawn up, including the revelation plus three pages denouncing polygamy. At

---

1. "J. W. Briggs Letters," *TR*, 3. In October 1851, Briggs was initiated into William Smith's inner circle. "But in less than one year he exhibited the cloven foot and boomed polygamy afresh in the name of God and his brother Joseph."

2. Richard P. Howard, "Reorganized Church of Jesus Christ of Latter Day Saints (RLDS Church)," 1212.

3. The June 1852 conference resolved "that we believe that the Church of J̶e̶s̶u̶s̶ ^Christ^ organized on the 6th of April A. D. 1830 exists as on that day wherever six or more Saints are Organized according to the Pattern in the Book of Doct & Covenants." "Minutes of a Conference, June 12, 1852," *Early Minutes of the Restoration*, 3–4.

a three-day conference beginning on April 6, 1853, a committee chose seven new apostles to preside over the movement, after which the original church was considered "reorganized."[4] The Zarahemla Stake was created in Wisconsin, led by a bishop and two counselors. Several men were also ordained as Seventies.

On October 6–8, 1853, another conference was held in which missionaries were appointed, Briggs was authorized to print a proselyting pamphlet, and Samuel Blair was assigned to select hymns and publish a hymnal.[5] During the months following this conference, difficulties began to arise of a sort not entirely unsurprising in an organization without strong central leadership. Occasionally in public meetings, those who felt they were moved by the spirit would make loud accusations of others, pointing them out by name and striking them physically. One such speaker demanded that the accused "get upon their knees to them, while another one was by the spirit moved to bark like a wolf."[6] In January 1854, a splinter group who believed that "the expected son of Joseph had neglected to comply with the will of God, and had forfeited the right" to lead the church proposed that a new first presidency be ordained and that rebaptism be required to join the church. This disagreement resulted in two apostles being removed from office and the schismatics being disfellowshipped at the conference of October 1854. The next year, at the October 1855 conference, a resolution was adopted that reaffirmed "that the successor of Joseph Smith must come from his seed."[7] The movement as a whole had not given up faith that one of Smith's sons would succeed him, though the Smith boys had not shown interest in church leadership of any variety.

In true Latter Day Saint fashion, the elders of the Reorganization traveled about, preaching of their movement that aspired to be a continuation of the early church minus the bane of plural marriage. They particularly searched out those who had been followers of Joseph Smith, Jr. but had rejected the principle of polygamy. Many of their converts had likewise been disillusioned by James Strang and other succession groups.

---

4. Heman C. Smith and F. Henry Edwards, *History of the Reorganized Church of Jesus Christ of Latter Day Saints*, 3:218–24.

5. "Minutes of a Conference, Oct. 6, 1852," *Early Minutes of the Restoration*, 7.

6. Smith and Edwards, *History of the Reorganized Church*, 3:227.

7. Smith and Edwards, 3:232; "Minutes of a Conference, Oct. 6, 1855," *Early Minutes of the Restoration*, 4.

Somewhat typical of conversion to this movement is that of William W. Blair. At the end of November 1856, Edmund C. Briggs and Samuel H. Gurley (brother and son of Jason Briggs and Zenos Gurley) visited Blair, representing themselves as "sent forth of God by prophecy from Zarahemla, Wisconsin, to visit the Latter Day Saints and tell them that the Lord was reviving his work" and "had begun the reorganization of the church in that region." The elders told Blair that "the time was near at hand when the Lord would call Joseph, the son of Joseph Smith the Seer, to take the lead of the church." Blair invited them to his home, where they engaged "in a spirited discussion" until three in the morning.[8]

The next day they continued the discussion along with a powerful prophecy by Briggs, stating that Blair "would soon be released from [his] temporal affairs, would be called to the ministry, would be made 'an apostle of the Lamb of God,' be called to preach the gospel and 'thresh the Gentiles by the power of God's Spirit.'" He further declared that "the Lord would soon call Joseph, the son of Joseph the Seer, to be president of the church, and that the standard then erected would never fall." Blair felt that he had been given "abundant evidence through the Holy Spirit" that these elders were the Lord's servants.[9]

Briggs and Gurley were among the first missionaries of the new movement and had been "commissioned by the branch at Zarahemla, Wisconsin, to deliver the 'Word of the Lord' to young Joseph [Smith III]."[10] After meeting with Blair, they continued their journey to Nauvoo, arriving on Friday, December 5, 1856. There, they first spoke with Major Lewis Bidamon, the second husband of Emma Smith and the stepfather of Joseph III. He directed them to a farm where the newly married Joseph III was living. There followed an emotional meeting during which the elders handed Joseph a letter from "The Church of Zarahemla, Wisconsin, to Joseph Smith," signed by "J. W. Briggs, Representative President of the Church and the Priesthood in Zarahemla." The letter exhorted the twenty-four-year-old Smith not to be "unmindful or indifferent" to his "right and Heaven-appointed duty" to succeed his father as "lineal descendant of the chosen seed to whom the promise was made."[11]

Smith handed the letter back and vigorously forbade the elders to speak one word about religion in his home. A short time before, he informed

---

8. Frederick B. Blair, comp., *The Memoirs of President W. W. Blair*, 7–8.
9. Blair, 8–10.
10. Edmund C. Briggs, *Early History of the Reorganization*, n.p.
11. Briggs, n.p.

them, Elders George A. Smith and Erastus Snow had visited him imploring him to move to Utah and unite himself with Brigham Young's contingent of the church. Young Joseph made it clear that he had no intention of going to Utah, and that he was firmly opposed to the doctrine of polygamy, but neither was he inclined to listen to Elders Briggs and Gurley.

While in Nauvoo, the two elders spent time conversing with Emma, and they asked her opinion of some of the key figures in the Restoration movement. She had no confidence in Young, but she praised Marks, saying that her husband had trusted him.[12]

After their visit to Nauvoo, Gurley became discouraged and traveled back to his home in Wisconsin. Edmund Briggs, however, considered it his duty to remain in the mission field until Joseph Smith III could be convinced to affiliate with the Reorganization movement.

Following tradition in the original church, annual and semiannual conferences of the Reorganized Church were held in April and October, along with district and special conferences from time to time. At the April 1857 annual conference in Zarahemla, Jason W. Briggs was sustained as president of the Twelve and "representative of the legal heir."[13] In this way, Saints of the Reorganization could retain their hope that young Joseph would eventually join them, while putting in place a leading authority to stabilize the church. In April 1858, there was reference to Edmund Briggs's mission to Joseph III, to which he had been appointed to continue until Joseph III accepted his call as his father's lineal descendant who would preside over the Restoration. Members of the conference solemnly promised that they would "uphold him by our Prayers & Faith untill the final fulfillment of his mission."[14] In October 1858, W. W. Blair, who had been converted by Briggs at the beginning of this mission, was ordained an apostle.

The annual conference of April 1859 was held near Beaverton, Illinois, instead of in Zarahemla. This was attended by William Aldrich and J. C. Gaylord, associates of Marks. Aldrich and Gaylord became interested in the work of the Reorganization and were received by the conference in full fellowship.[15] They requested that Briggs and Blair stay in the area and do missionary work among the group of people who had once followed Strang. Though many had become disillusioned with the Latter Day Saint

---

12. Briggs, n.p..
13. Smith and Edwards, *History of the Reorganized Church*, 3:217.
14. "Minutes of a Conference, Apr. 6, 1858," *Early Minutes of the Restoration*, 42.
15. "The Annual Conference, Apr. 6, 1859," *Early Minutes of the Restoration*, 49.

movement as a whole after their experiences with Strang, others joyfully accepted the message of Reorganization.

Aldrich and Gaylord urged their friend William Marks to attend a June 1859 meeting at a schoolhouse in Amboy, Illinois, less than thirty miles from his home in Shabbona Grove. Marks was reluctant to make the effort, but upon their urgent insistence, he finally acquiesced. There, he was received just as he was whenever he attended a Latter Day Saint sect: those in attendance were excited to see him. Elder Zenos Gurley invited Marks to sit on the stand with him, and the meeting—devoted to prayer, testimony, and partaking of the sacrament—was later remembered by some in attendance as "one of the most spiritual seasons enjoyed in those days by the faithful Saints." According to Blair, Marks was presented with "convincing and satisfactory evidence" that the Reorganization had the approbation of the Lord.[16] Spiritual gifts were manifested, as when the twelve-year-old daughter of C. G. Lanphear arose and spoke in tongues. Another sister, the young, newlywed Helen Pomeroy, was prompted to rise up from her seat and walk up the aisle to where Marks was seated in front of the congregation. She lifted up her hands and said,

> Thus saith the Lord; O thou man of God! In times past thou hast sat with my servant Joseph the Seer; and in times near to come thou shalt sit in council with his son. When I called my servant Joseph he was as a lone tree; but when I shall call his son he shall be as one of a forest.[17]

This greatly affected Marks, who also stood, weeping. His words were later remembered as follows:

> This manifestation I know is by the Spirit of God. It is the same Spirit the faithful Saints ever enjoyed when I first received the gospel in the state of New York, and which we also enjoyed in Kirtland, Missouri, and at Nauvoo, when we lived uprightly before the Lord. I know by the evidences I see and feel her[e] to-day that God loves and owns this people and the work they have in hand.[18]

Gurley introduced Marks to the congregation and explained his former position in the early church. After this, the Saints voted to accept Marks into fellowship under his former priesthood. The next day, Marks

---

16. Blair, *Memoirs*, 15.
17. Blair, 16.
18. Blair, 16.

was received as a high priest and appointed part of a committee of three to work on the publication of a new hymnbook.[19]

Some sources claim that Marks was rebaptized on June 11, 1859, which would have been at the time of this conference.[20] It is true that several baptisms took place in connection with the conference. The baptisms of six people, all named, were recorded on Sunday, June 12, 1859, with the ordinance performed by Blair. While Marks was one of those who participated in the confirmations, no contemporary record of a rebaptism of Marks at this conference exists. Indeed, the Reorganized church had clarified at the April 1854 annual conference that members should be accepted on the strength of their former baptisms into the pre-martyrdom church—"where the evidence of a legal baptism once having been received, and in the absence of evidence of expulsion or apostasy, it was not admissible to require a rebaptism, to be identified with the Reorganization; but that in such cases it was optional with the persons themselves—a matter of conscience with them alone."[21]

For these reasons, it seems unlikely that Marks was baptized at the time of his affiliation with the Reorganization, because both his former baptism and priesthood ordination were honored. At this time, he probably became a member of the Amboy Branch of the church, where this conference was held, although the next year's conference would mention a branch at Sandwich, which was a few miles closer to his home in Shabbona Grove.

While Marks was respected and favored as a valuable member of the Reorganization, the Utah Saints painted him as a villain. Brigham Young started this ball rolling early after Marks left Nauvoo, when in March 1845, Young publicly vilified him as a "most low, dishonest mean" person. Then at general conference a month later, William Clayton labeled him an "apostate."[22] On April 12, 1845, a comedy musical number was produced by the Nauvoo old police, who invited the Twelve and their families to a party and "comfortable repast" at the Masonic Hall. During the evening,

---

19. "Conference, Jun. 10, 1859," *Early Minutes of the Reorganization*, 50–51.
20. "Marks, William," JSP.
21. Smith and Edwards, *History of the Reorganized Church*, 3:229.
22. "Historical Department Journal History of the Church, 1845," March 16, 1845, and April 7, 1845, CHL.

the police performed a disparaging piece entitled "Father Marks' Return to Mormonism."[23]

Despite this, the following November Marks continued to show his cordiality by quitclaiming the Kirtland Temple back to the Twelve Apostles for the "consideration of One Dollar and the 'love and goodwill' he bore to the Church."[24] But the brethren were untouched. On December 21, 1845, Heber C. Kimball addressed a meeting and spoke about the founding of the Quorum of the Anointed. He stated, "About 4 years ago next May nine persons were admitted into the Holy order 5 are now living. B. Young W. Richards George Miller N. K. Whitney and H. C. Kimball two are dead, and two are worse than dead."[25] The two he called "worse than dead" were William Marks and William Law.

This ill-will toward Marks continued in Utah, where in 1855, George A. Smith addressed Saints attending the Salt Lake City Tabernacle:

> While he [Joseph Smith] was thus preaching [about sealing] he turned to the men sitting in the stand, and who were the men who should have backed him up, for instance, to our good old President Marks, William and Wilson Law, and father Cowles, and a number of other individuals about Nauvoo, for this occurred when the Twelve were in the Eastern portions of the United States, and said, "If I were to reveal the things that God has revealed to me, if I were to reveal to this people the doctrines that I know are for their exaltation, these men would spill my blood."

Four years later, Heber C. Kimball would reiterate his negative feelings about Marks: "If William Law, William Marks and hundreds of others had known that Joseph was a Prophet, they would not have betrayed him, nor tried to take away his life."[26] Not only did Kimball come to consider Marks an apostate who did not believe in the prophetic mission of Joseph Smith, but he also accused Marks of being involved in Smith's murder.

The Saints of the Reorganization, on the other hand, respected the aging leader. Many of them were acquainted with Marks's activities in the early church, and they looked to him for leadership and counsel during these formative days. At the semiannual conference held October 6–10, 1859, in Israel Rogers's grain barn, Marks participated along with the rest

---

23. *History of the Church*, 7:395; "Historical Department Journal History of the Church, 1845," April 12, 1845, CHL.

24. Kim L. Loving, "Ownership of the Kirtland Temple: Legends, Lies, and Misunderstandings," 13.

25. George D. Smith, *An Intimate Chronicle: The Journals of William Clayton*, 222.

26. Heber C. Kimball, "Discourse," August 28, 1859, 399, CHL.

of the elders in the report on mission work, though he had only affiliated with the Restoration since June. (At the April 1857 conference, it had been "resolved that it shall be the duty of all who are connected with us holding Priesthood to report themselves personally or by Letter once in six months showing their Faith & Labor in this work.")[27] In his report, Marks allowed that he had not done much in the way of preaching in those months. The conference resolved that he be assigned to "travel to & through the Western part of Iowa, organizing Branches, & doing such other church business as will best promote the interests of said church."[28] Marks's talents, however, were for organizing and managing, not proselyting to strangers. He had rarely participated in traveling mission work, and there is no evidence that he did so during his final years with the Reorganized Church. At the same conference, a resolution was passed to publish a monthly church paper. Elders Z. H. Gurley, Senior, Marks, and William W. Blair were appointed a committee to supervise the publication. Marks was also assigned in a committee to solicit subscriptions and donations to sustain it.[29] Thus, the *True Latter Day Saints' Herald* issued its first publication in January 1860 out of Cincinnati, Ohio, with Isaac Sheen as editor.

The first issue of the *Herald* stated that it was published by "the New Organization of the Church of Jesus Christ of Latter Day Saints." It began with a short introduction by the publishing committee of Gurley, Marks, and Blair, followed by a six-page article titled "Polygamy Contrary to the Revelations of God." The following articles, "Fruits of Transgression" and "Lineal Priesthood," established the necessity of a successor to Joseph Smith and the movement's belief that Smith would be succeeded by his posterity. Conference minutes of the October 1859 conference were given, followed by a history and testimony of the Reorganization by Zenos Gurley. Next, a testimony by Marks appeared. This testimony was an expansion of the article Marks had published in June 1853 in Charles Thompson's *Zion's Harbinger and Baneemy's Organ* which recounted Joseph Smith's final instructions to Marks regarding polygamy.

In the *Herald* article, Marks described, for the first time, feelings that he said he'd had since 1844 that the church would be put out of order and would require reorganization:

---

27. "Minutes of a Conference, Apr. 6, 1857," *Early Minutes of the Reorganization*, 36.

28. "Conference Minutes of the Church, Oct. 6, 1859," *Early Minutes of the Reorganization*, 57.

29. "Conference Minutes, Oct. 6, 1859," *TH*, 20.

About the first of June, 1844 . . . my convictions at that time were, that the Church in a great measure had departed from the pure principles and doctrines of Jesus Christ. I felt much troubled in mind about the condition of the Church. I prayed earnestly to my Heavenly Father to show me something in regard to it, when I was wrapt in vision, and it was shown me by the Spirit, that the top or branches had overcome the root, in sin and wickedness, and the only way to cleanse and purify it was, to disorganize it, and in due time, the Lord would reorganize it again.[30]

Evidence suggests that Marks was at least partially reinterpreting his past experiences in light of his new beliefs. For a short time back in Nauvoo, he attempted to keep the church together with the Twelve Apostles as succeeding Joseph.[31] Strang's group did not consider that the church had ever been disorganized, but that Strang had become the new leader by prophetic administration and divine ordination. Charles Thompson considered the church disorganized, but he did not believe it could be reorganized in anything resembling its initial form. All indications show that Marks believed the teachings of these leaders at the time he associated with them. He did admit in this same article that events of the past had become hazy, stating, "There were many things suggested to my mind, but the lapse of time has erased them from my memory."[32]

During this time, Joseph Smith III had been thinking deeply about the invitation extended to him by Edmund Briggs and Samuel Gurley. In the fall of 1859, a watershed moment took place when Smith decided it was his duty to continue the work his father had begun. After much thought, he received spiritual assurance that the Saints reorganizing at Zarahemla were the only ones accepted of the Lord. As winter settled in, Smith, then twenty-seven years old, wrote a letter announcing his intentions to Marks, who was still residing at Shabbona Grove:

NAUVOO, March 5, 1860.

Mr. William Marks; Sir.-I am soon going to take my father's place at the head of the Mormon Church, and I wish that you, and some others, those you may consider the most trustworthy, the nearest to you, to come and see me; that is, if you can and will. I am somewhat undecided as to the best course for me to pursue, and if your views are, upon a comparison, in unison

---

30. William Marks, letter to Isaac Sheen, October 23, 1859, in Charles A. Shook, *The True Origin of Mormon Polygamy*, 157.

31. John S. Dinger, "'A Mean Conspirator' or 'The Noblest of Men:' William Marks's Expulsion from Nauvoo," 12–38.

32. Shook, *True Origin*, 157.

Joseph Smith III, daguerreotype. Courtesy of LDS Church History Library.

with mine, and we can agree as to the best course, I would be pleased to have your coöperation. I would rather you would come previous to your conference in April at Amboy. I do not wish to attend the conference, but would like to know if they, as a body, would indorse my opinions. You will say nothing of this to any but those who you may wish to accompany you here.

With great regard, I subscribe myself,
Yours most respectfully,
Joseph Smith.[33]

Smith explained that he reached out to Marks first "because Elder Marks was the president of the stake at Nauvoo, and also of the High Council, at the time of my father's death. He had retained his faith in Mormonism, as taught by Joseph and Hyrum, and his counsel would now be valuable."[34] Marks wasted no time in getting to Nauvoo, taking Israel Rogers and William W. Blair with him. The group traveled to Burlington on Monday, March 19, and reached Nauvoo by steamboat on Tuesday afternoon. They were greeted by Joseph III and Emma Smith, who put them up for the night. The interview could not have lasted long, as Marks, Rogers, and Blair departed by 10:00 a.m. the next morning with all in agreement that Joseph III should lead the Reorganization movement. During the meeting, Marks is reported to have sensibly and pointedly observed, "We have had enough of man-made prophets, and we don't want any more of that sort.

---

33. Smith and Edwards, *History of the Reorganized Church*, 3:265.
34. Smith and Edwards, 3:263–65.

If God has called you, we want to know it. If he has, the church is ready to sustain you; if not, we want nothing to do with you."³⁵

Joseph III and Emma arranged to attend the 1860 annual conference in Amboy in April. Joseph wrote that the trip took place "in the face of one of the fiercest tempests that had blown that spring," and Emma remarked "that thus it had been all through her life; that whenever she set out to do anything for the gospel's sake, the old boy seemed to be in the elements trying to prevent." After traveling by boat and rail, they arrived in Amboy "wet with spray, but strong in purpose." When Joseph joined the Saints for prayer on the evening of April 5, he learned for the first time that

> it had been prophesied among them that I should come to the Amboy conference of 1860. Whether these sayings had been known to Brethren Marks, Rogers, and Blair at the time of their visit to me, I do not know; but if so, they had not so stated to me; though there was a general expectancy that I would be there. A strange thrill pervaded the air, and when Elder Z. H. Gurley, Sen., in one of his impulsive, impassioned exhortations, referred to the fulfillment of the "word of the Lord to them," by the fact of my being there, the whole people sobbed aloud in their joy and gratefulness.³⁶

The next morning, on the auspicious date of April 6, 1860, Zenos H. Gurley was chosen president of the conference and William Marks, assistant. Sermons were given by Gurley, Samuel Powers, and Edmund C. Briggs, each calling attention to the difference in the Reorganized movement and the sect led by Brigham Young. After a short adjournment, the conference met again in the afternoon. As was the custom, those who wished to unite with the church were invited to make their desires known, and they were then received and welcomed by the members.

At last, the moment that had been long anticipated by Jason W. Briggs and many others had arrived. "Joseph Smith, son of Joseph Smith, the prophet, seer & revelator, & lineal heir to said office & station, according to the law & order of the holy priesthood was then introduced to the Conference" by Zenos Gurley, and he "delivered an address explanatory of his views, principles, doctrine & faith."³⁷ Isaac Sheen motioned, and the conference of about three hundred attendees resolved that Smith be chosen prophet, seer, and revelator of the Church of Jesus Christ and the

---

35. Smith and Edwards, 3:264.
36. Smith and Edwards, 3:263–65.
37. "Minutes of the Annual Conference, April 6, 1860," *Early Minutes of the Reorganization*, 59–60. Joseph Smith III's full speech is available at "The Mormon Conference," *TH*, 101–5.

successor to his father.³⁸ He was ordained president of the high priesthood by Zenos H. Gurley and William Marks. The significance of Marks performing the ordination was not lost on the congregation. The Reorganized church considered that "President Marks, at the time of the death of Joseph the Seer, held the highest local presiding authority of any person in the church, being the president of the High Council over the whole church, and also the president of the Nauvoo stake of Zion."³⁹ Thus he was arguably the appropriate priesthood holder to ordain a new First Presidency when the old one was dissolved upon the death of Joseph Smith.⁴⁰

Twelve men were sustained as high councilors, and Marks participated in ordaining them as well. Along with Blair, Marks ordained Isaac Sheen to the presidency of the high priests' quorum. He further participated in the ordination of the seven presidents of the Seventies, the president of the elders' quorum, and the president of the quorum of Seventies.⁴¹

At this time Emma Smith Bidamon was also received into fellowship by a unanimous vote. Those who had been assigned on the committee to work on the new hymnbook were discharged and replaced by her.

Six months later, Marks attended the semiannual conference on October 6–9, 1860, and was chosen as one of three persons to select the men to fill remaining seats in the Quorum of the Twelve Apostles.⁴² Marks was not mentioned at any of the following four general conferences: April 1861; October 1861 at Sandwich, Illinois; April 1862 at Mission, LaSalle, Illinois; and October 1862 at Galland's Grove, Iowa. In those years, it was recommended that all elders labor in the ministry, and it was customary

---

38. Smith and Edwards, *History of the Reorganized Church*, 3:250–51.

39. W. W. Blair, "The Successor of Joseph the Seer," *TS*, 3.

40. Jason W. Briggs explained: "On 'the question of *authority*,' we have ever courted, and still do, investigation in the rigid character of the facts in the first organization. Here they are: Joseph Smith and Oliver Cowdery were ordained to the lesser priesthood by an angel; then by this authority and a commandment, they on the 6th day of April ordained each other Elders, and this Eldership ordained High Priests and Apostles, and this high priesthood ordained, by commandment, the president of the high priesthood, the highest office in the church; so that the alleged lesser, ordained the greater, is common to both the first organization and the Reorganization alike." In addition to this technical authority, Briggs taught the ordination was directed by the Holy Spirit. "History of the Reorganization of the Church of Jesus Christ of Latter Day Saints," *MRLDS*, 27.

41. "Minutes of the Annual Conference, April 6, 1860," 60–61.

42. "Minutes of the Semi-Annual Conference, Oct. 6th to 9th, 1860," *TH*, 236.

that they report their missionary labors at each conference. If he was in attendance, Marks neither reported, spoke, nor performed ordinances.

In 1862, a Masonic lodge was organized in Shabbona Grove, and a handsome Masonic Hall was built the same year. Marks joined this lodge as a charter member along with his two sons, William Jr., who served as the lodge's first Senior Deacon, and Llewellyn, who served as Junior Warden.[43] When elections were held at the end of the year, Marks was made secretary of the lodge, and he served in this position until his death in 1872.[44] Like Joseph Smith and other early Mormon Masons, Marks did not consider affiliation with Freemasonry to be at odds with membership in the church. In fact, his actions were similar to those of Sidney Rigdon, who joined his three Mormon sons-in-law to petition for a Lodge in Friendship, New York, in the spring of 1851. All four of these men had been raised Master Masons in the Nauvoo Lodge and deemed it important to continue to affiliate with Freemasonry.[45] Rigdon was a "very devoted Mason and was a regular attendent [sic] at the Masonic Lodge" and was "frequently called upon to speak on public occasions of the order," and when he died, he was buried with Masonic honors.[46]

At a general conference in Amboy, Illinois, on April 6, 1863, the principle of gathering was considered. Many of those joining the Reorganized church, like Marks, had been concerned about this principle ever since

---

43. William Marks joined the Shabbona Grove Lodge upon the strength of his raising as a Master Mason in the Nauvoo Lodge on April 22, 1842. It is very interesting that his sons were charter officers of the Shabbona Grove Lodge. Both were too young to have joined the lodge in Nauvoo. This means that they must have become Masons at some point before 1862 and after 1851 for William Jr. and after 1853 for Llewellyn.

44. See Henry L. Boies, *History of DeKalb County*, 528; [Chapman Brothers], *Portrait and Biographical Album of DeKalb County*, 838.

45. *History of Friendship: sesquicentennial, 150 years of Friendship, 1815–1965*, 31; John Stearns Minard and Georgia Drew Merrill, eds., *Allegany County and its People: A Centennial Memorial History of Allegany County, New York*, 717; *Proceedings of the Grand Lodge of Free and Accepted Masons of the State of New York, One Hundred and Twenty-Ninth Annual Communication*, 185. Among the charter members of Allegany Lodge #225 were Sidney Rigdon, George W. Robinson, Jeremiah Hatch, and Edward B. Wingate. The lodge received a dispensation on April 25, 1851, with Robinson as Worshipful Master and Hatch as Junior Warden.

46. John W. Rigdon, "Life Story of Sidney Rigdon," 186–87, CHL; E. J. Cannon, "Masonic," *FR*.

the death of the first Mormon prophet. It was resolved at this time that "in the opinion of this Conference, there is no Stake to which the Saints on this Continent, are commanded to gather at the present time." Saints outside of the United States were advised to come to this land "preparatory to the re-establishment of the Church in Zion," and all were assured that the promises of God regarding inheritances in Jackson County, Missouri, would be fulfilled in the future. The Saints should "turn their hearts and their faces towards Zion, and supplicate the Lord God for such deliverance."[47] It is not known how involved Marks was in making this decision, but it certainly sounds like one that would have set well with him. While he believed strongly in the principle of gathering in theory, it had always been difficult for the practical, reasonable Marks to make the literal move away from a secure home he had worked hard to establish for himself and his family.

On the final day of the April 1863 annual conference, J. W. Briggs brought up a point of order regarding Marks. In June 1859, at the first meeting of the Reorganization that Marks had attended, a woman had prophesied that one day he would become a counselor to the president of the church. This had not happened by March 1863, and a further revelation was given wherein the Lord reiterated his will to the conference that "you ordain and set apart my servant William Marks, to be a counselor unto my servant Joseph, even the President of my Church, that the first presidency of my Church may be more perfectly filled."[48] Accordingly, Marks was then ordained a counselor in the First Presidency under President Joseph Smith III and sustained by the congregation. Reflecting on this ordination, Smith later wrote of the status Marks's new position offered to the developing movement:

> Having felt the call of the spirit of the Reorganization he [Marks] had given credence to and united with it, which gave a prestige to the church of no small importance, and I counted it fortunate for me that the Lord recognized his worth and ordered his ordination to the co-ordinate position in the First Presidency.[49]

As Marks passed his seventieth birthday, he experienced a "lite shock of the palsy" and his handwriting became unsteady, but he still remained

---

47. "Minutes of the Annual Conference, April 6th, 1863," *TH*, 196.

48. "Minutes of the Annual Conference, April 6th, 1863," *TH*, 197; Scherer, *Journey of a People*, 163.

49. Ruth Wildermuth, "William Marks After Nauvoo," 6.

a thoughtful servant of the Restoration.[50] His experience was broad and rich, and he constituted a link for the Saints between the original church founded by Joseph Smith Jr. and the Reorganization. His role as a counselor to the still young and inexperienced Joseph III gave them a sense of continuity and security.[51]

Marks was not mentioned at the October conferences of 1863, 1864, and 1865. It had become customary to hold these semiannual conferences in Iowa, where a large contingent of Saints was affiliating with the Reorganization. In his early seventies, and before rail service, it would have been difficult for Marks to travel the almost four hundred miles. He did attend the annual conference in April 1864, which was held in Amboy. At that conference, he assisted in leading the meeting with Joseph Smith III. Marks did not report any mission work, but he participated in an ordination for a bishop of the Nauvoo Conference. At a special conference held in Amboy on July 15, 1864, Marks, "one of the presidents of the church," acknowledged his failure to report his mission labors for the past several conferences: "Bro. Marks spoke by the way of confession for his neglect of duty, but he knew that he had a duty to do and he was now determined to work as he did in days that are past."[52]

Marks also associated with Smith in presiding at the April 1865 conference in Amboy. At this time, Marks and the rest of the publishing committee were released from their office, and Isaac Sheen was given a vote of thanks for his "unceasing efforts" as editor. The *Herald* had been publishing at Plano for two years, and Smith now planned to "take charge of the publishing and editorial department of the *Herald* and of all our publications."[53]

After Smith became editor of the *Herald*, he began to provide more instruction to the Saints within its pages. In the June issue of 1865, he included extracts from the minutes of a council meeting of the First Presidency and Quorum of the Twelve held the first week of May. Marks was present at this important meeting, where it was clarified that "the doctrine of sealing, as relating to marriage for eternity, is a heresy."[54] The Reorganization had been preaching against polygamy since its found-

---

50. William Marks, letter to Hiram Faulk and Josiah Butterfield, Oct. 1, 1865, 3, CCLA.
51. Wildermuth, "William Marks After Nauvoo," 6.
52. "Special Conference, June 25 and 26, '64," *TH*, 20–21.
53. "Annual Conference, April 6, 1865," *TH*, 126.
54. "Council," *TH*, 163.

ing, and this was likely a reaction to the eternal marriage doctrine of the Latter-day Saints in Utah, which included plural marriage.

The unedited minutes of this council meeting show that Marks was esteemed for the additional context he could add to the discussion from his experience in the early church. At one point, "the Question arose as to whether Joseph the Martyr taught the doctrine of polygamy." Marks responded by telling of an encounter with Hyrum Smith, who said "he did not believe in it and he was going to see Joseph about it and if he had a revelation on the subject he would believe it." After this, Marks said, "Hyrum read a revelation on it in the High Council." Marks "felt that it was not true but he saw the High Council received it."[55] This statement by Marks provides strong corroboration that the "polygamy revelation" (later LDS D&C 132) was introduced to the Nauvoo High Council by Hyrum. While the event seemed to have changed Hyrum's mind about plural marriage, it did not have the same effect on Marks. Neither did it change the council's opinion on warning the Midwest Saints against the eternal marriage doctrine.

An additional resolution brought forth at this meeting may have also been responding to the Utah Saints' policies excluding Black people from the priesthood and temple ordinances. It may have also been prompted by the events of the American Civil War, which had come to an end a month earlier:

> *Resolved,* That the gospel makes provision for the ordination of men of the Negro race, who are received into the Church by obedience to its ordinances.

Smith, Marks, and the seven apostles who were present discussed this principle at length and decided that they should fast and pray for the Lord's will to be revealed upon the matter. The next day, Smith presented to the group a revelation for the church indicating that the gospel should go forth to all nations and that there were some of the "Negro race . . . who are chosen instruments to be ministers to their own race."[56]

One of the other discussion topics at this 1865 meeting was baptism for the dead, a practice that was introduced in Nauvoo in August 1840. For about a year, early members of the church were enthusiastic about providing the essential ordinance of baptism on behalf of those who had died and no longer had physical bodies. At a general conference on October 2, 1841, Joseph Smith Jr. instructed that the baptisms for the

---

55. "Council of Twelve Minutes, Book A," 11, CCLA.
56. "Council," *TH*, 163–64.

dead then being performed in the Mississippi River should stop "until the ordinance can be attended to in the font of the Lord's House. . . . For thus saith the Lord!"[57] Remembering this sermon through the haze of twenty-four years, Marks told the brethren "when Joseph stopped the Baptism for the dead He stated that He did not believe it would be practised any more until there was a fountain built in Zion or Jerusalem."[58] Without wanting to jettison the principle entirely, the council resolved "that it is proper to teach the doctrine of Baptism for the dead, when it is necessary to do ^so^ in order to show the completeness of the plan of salvation." However, they cautioned, "wisdom dictates that the way should be prepared by the preaching of the First principles." Thus began a long history of ambivalence regarding baptism for the dead in the Reorganization tradition.[59]

The next year, Smith and Marks presided at the April 1866 conference held in Plano. There, a strong interest was manifested in the inspired revision of certain chapters of the Bible done by Joseph Smith in the early days of the church. It was resolved that the time had come to publish this "New Translation" and that the church should take steps to do this "as speedily as possible." To this end, Marks, Israel Rogers, and William Blair were appointed to a committee to approach Emma Smith Bidamon "respecting the relinquishment of the manuscripts of the New Translation of the Scriptures, for the purpose of publishing the same to the church and to the world," and to enter into and fulfill a publishing contract. In order to ensure the preservation of the manuscript, it was to be copied before being given to the printer. Furthermore, the committee was to make sure they did not employ any person to work on the manuscript who was not a believer in the Restoration or did not favor the coming forth of the New Translation. To fund the project, presidents of missions, districts, and

---

57. "Discourse, 3 October 1841 as Published in *Times and Seasson*," 577, JSP.

58. "Council of Twelve Minutes, Book A," 13. Baptisms for the dead were resumed in Nauvoo in the unfinished temple when the baptismal font was completed, beginning November 21, 1841, and continuing through 1846. With some few exceptions, these baptisms stopped among the Brighamite church for twenty-six years, until it was reinstituted in the Salt Lake City Endowment House in June 1867. Followers of James Strang and Lyman Wight practiced baptism for the dead for a short time but this was discontinued upon the deaths of their leaders. Thus, at the time William Marks was meeting with the RLDS Council of Twelve, baptisms for the dead were not generally being done by the Mormon sects.

59. See Roger D. Launius, "An Ambivalent Rejection: Baptism for the Dead and the Reorganized Church Experience," 61–84; Stassi Cramm, "The 150-Year Journey of Rejection of Baptism for the Dead," 87.

branches solicited donations from the members. Everyone who donated was promised one of the books at cost.[60]

On May 2 following the conference, Marks and the others traveled to Nauvoo to meet with Bidamon. To their satisfaction, she willingly provided the manuscript and refused any payment other than to receive a copy of the book when it was published. Marks, Blair, and Rogers then worked diligently to ensure that a perfect copy was made for publication, with Blair later insisting that the manuscript had remained under their close supervision and that the committee was "careful in copying to follow the MSS as they found it, as near as chaptering, versifying, punctuation, &c., would permit."[61] The first copies of what became the "Inspired Translation of the Holy Scriptures" were printed by the end of 1867.[62]

During the decade of 1860 to 1870, the aged Marks served as a figurehead in the growing movement. These years saw the Reorganized Church of Jesus Christ of Latter Day Saints grow from a tiny group of believers to a full-fledged sect on several continents. Marks brought some of his family members along with him into the Reorganization, but others of his children "became so disgusted at the doings in Nauvoo" that he feared "they had lost all of their faith in the work."[63]

Marks also sorrowed at the passing of some of his nuclear family. His youngest daughter, Sophia Shaw, who was living with her husband George and daughter Ella close to William's home in Shabbona Grove, died in 1861; his wife, Rosanna, passed away on October 18, 1862; and a year later his son Ira Goodrich Marks also died. Their daughter Lucy Ann and her husband, Henry McHenry, lived in Paw Paw, DeKalb County, until they moved to Bigler's Grove, Harrison County, Iowa, around 1856. Henry died in 1860, and Lucy and her youngest son were enumerated in the Morning Star Branch of the RLDS church in 1863. Lucy died in August 1866 and is buried in Bigler's Grove Cemetery.

Given his involvement with temple ordinances in Nauvoo, it is hard to imagine that Marks did not have at least some slight angst over his eternal state of plurality when the seventy-three year old remarried a forty-four-year-old widow on September 5, 1866. Marks had known Julia Ann Durfee for a long time. In 1842 the Durfee family lived in the Fourth

---

60. "Annual Conference, April 6–13, 1866," *TH*, 125.
61. "Letter from Bro. W. W. Blair," *TH*, 76.
62. Inez Smith Davis, *The Story of the Church*, 437.
63. William Marks, letter to Hyrum Faulk and Josiah Butterfield, October 1, 1865, 4, CCLA.

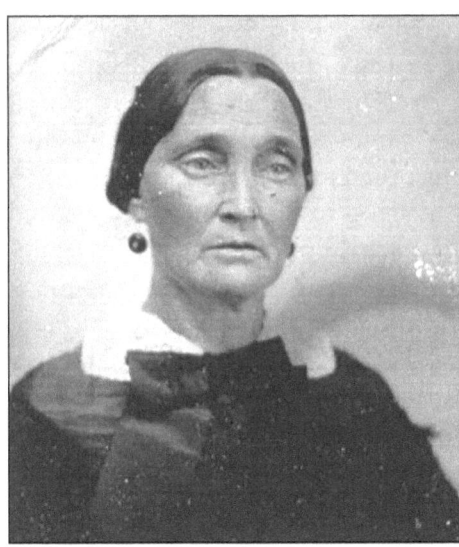

Julia Ann Durfee Anderson Muir Marks. Courtesy of Find a Grave.

Ward in Nauvoo, the same as Joseph Smith and the William Marks family.[64] Julia's father, Jabez Durfee, a widower, was married to Elizabeth Davis Durfee, who had become Smith's plural wife and was said to have facilitated some of his other plural marriages. Julia was one of two daughters from Jabez's first marriage who were brought into Smith's home in the fall of 1842. Julia, twenty years old at the time, worked as a seamstress and teacher to the Smith children. Joseph III remembered his earliest educational experience as being at her hand.[65] Savilla, seventeen, had general maid duties.[66] One can hardly refrain from comparing them with other sets of sisters who lived in Joseph Smith's home about the same time and were sealed to him polygamously. Emily and Eliza Partridge allegedly married Smith in early 1843 at ages nineteen and twenty-two; and Sarah and Maria Lawrence in mid-1843 at ages seventeen and nineteen.

After Smith's death, Julia married Blakley B. Anderson and was endowed in the Nauvoo Temple on January 22, 1846. The two of them associated with the Alpheus Cutler group. They had two daughters, Eliza and Mary, and lived in St. Joseph, Missouri. After Anderson's death in 1849, Julia was married in 1851 to James Muir. They moved to Shenandoah,

---

64. Book of Assessment, Fourth Ward, 1842, 9.
65. Mary Audentia Smith Anderson, ed., "The Memoirs of President Joseph Smith (1832–1914)," *SH*, 1480.
66. Linda King Newell and Valeen Tippetts Avery, *Mormon Enigma: Emma Hale Smith, Prophet's Wife, "Elect Lady," Polygamy's Foe, 1804–1879*, 85.

Iowa, and had four children before James died on May 3, 1862, making Julia a widow for the second time. In 1864, she joined the Reorganized Church at Nauvoo and was confirmed by her former student, Joseph Smith III.[67] Through her experiences in different Restoration groups, Julia could probably relate to Marks's long search for a spiritual home.

Though Marks had been very attached to his business dealings and his residence in Shabbona, he finally made the move that he had been unwilling to undergo as a member of James Strang's or Charles Thompson's groups. In October 1865, Marks wrote some thoughts about his keen interest in the gathering of the Jews. He had been subscribed to a paper edited by a Jewish convert to Christianity out of New York City, and this kept him abreast on the gathering of the Jews from all parts to Jerusalem, "and the Citty is fast building up." This turned his thoughts toward the gathering of the Latter Day Saints:

> I apprehend that the time is not far distant when we shall be permitted to go back to Mosora [Missouri] the land has been literal[l]y redeemed by blood[.] One of our neighbors was a Captian of a Company was chaising ould Price through Jackson County and other Counties a[d]joining he said he traveled forty miles didn't see but one family[.] The country was laid waste.

Marks wrote that he had sold all his land except one house and lot, and "I am ready to gether with the Saints."[68]

Joseph Smith III had made Plano, Illinois, his home and base of operations by 1866, and this is where Marks relocated when he finally made the decision to gather. On June 2, 1867, Marks was voted a member of the Plano Branch and his wife Julia Ann Marks was received upon the presentation of a letter from her former branch, the Olive Branch at Nauvoo. The family was enumerated there in the 1870 census.[69] Plano Branch records indicate Marks's activity in the work of the local congregation. For example, at the branch meeting on July 18, 1871, Marks weighed in on a local controversy of whether the pastor should have counselors (Marks did not consider counselors necessary). Marks also housed ten out-of-town conference attendees at his home.[70]

---

67. "Obituary of Julia Marks," *SH*, 320.

68. William Marks, letter to Hiram Faulk and Josiah Butterfield, October 1, 1865, 2, CCLA.

69. 1870 census, Little Rock Township (in which Plano is the largest city).

70. Wildermuth, "William Marks After Nauvoo," 6. Marks moved between January 1869, when his address in the January 15, 1867 *Herald* is listed as Shabbona, and June 1869, when he was voted into the Plano branch.

Marks was still serving as Joseph Smith III's first and only counselor, still highly esteemed in the Reorganized church and still being respectfully sustained at local and church-wide conferences until his death on May 22, 1872, at age 79. He was buried next to his first wife, Rosannah, at the Shabbona Grove Cemetery. Having been baptized in 1834 at age 41, Marks had been a servant of the Restoration for nearly half his life.

CONCLUSION

Quiet Cornerstone

Gathering was a major theme in the life of William Marks, though Zion seemed to elude him at every step. He joined the Latter Day Saints in 1834 and did not have the opportunity to march to Missouri with Zion's Camp. Marks moved to Kirtland during troubled times, set out for Missouri with his family, and arrived almost to the day of the expulsion of the Mormons at Far West. In the next few years, he established a home in Nauvoo, and for a brief period experienced fellowship and the esteem that came with his several positions of leadership within the community. Unbeknownst to many, troubles began to simmer, as polygamy was being practiced in secret by Joseph Smith and others in Nauvoo. With bitter hindsight, William Law wrote of Marks: "There was now and then, a good man in Mormondom, for instance William Marks. He was a very good man and knew as little of the secret crimes of the leaders as I knew myself. . . . Marks, Yves [Charles Ivins], I, and some others had, for a long time, no idea of the depravity that was going on."[1]

Marks's position within the inner circle ended with the death of Joseph Smith, prophet and protagonist of the latter-day gathering. Cast out by one group of Smith's successors, Marks investigated, followed, and then parted ways with two other succession groups in rapid succession.

The final station in Marks's journey placed him into close proximity with Joseph Smith III, but there were differences in the churches of the first Restoration prophet and his son. In the Reorganization, for example, there was no temple endowment, which Marks had received under the direction of Joseph Smith as a member of the Anointed Quorum.

Nevertheless, the Reorganized church was a place where Marks could gather with like-minded restorationists in his final years. There, he participated in the development of an ecclesiastical organization that emphasized peace, valued moral convention, and prioritized social responsibility. Among the Reorganized Latter Day Saints, he was once again accepted and respected. In Marks's obituary, Joseph III wrote: "Br. Marks was one of the noblest of men. He has lived a life of most singular usefulness to his

---

1. W. Wyl, "Interview with William Law, March 30, 1887," *SLDT*; See also Heman C. Smith, *The History of the Reorganized Church of Jesus Christ of Latter Day Saints*, 3:250–51.

fellow men. Kind and upright in thought, it was known of him that his acts were founded in consciousness of right; and what was wrong to him he would not do." Looking back to the 1840s, Smith wrote:

> As the President of the Stake at Nauvoo, Br. Marks was one of the most faithful and steadfast men the church had. He was an example of clearheaded wisdom, a man who ruled his own spirit, and consequently one who controlled others. He was a wise counselor and a wise administrator; and became one of the most valued and trusted friends of the Martyr Joseph. His integrity was incorruptible.[2]

After Marks's death, his history and influence was debated, edited, used, and rejected at times by the major Restoration churches, especially the Latter-day Saints who had moved west to the Great Basin under the leadership of Brigham Young. In 1909, the Latter-day Saints' Northern States Mission, headquartered in Chicago, Illinois, published a tract called *Corner Stones of "Reorganization."*[3] This tract is an unflattering look at RLDS history, including Marks. Prior to the printing of this tract, Marks seemed to have been largely written out of LDS history except as a turncoat and defector. He was featured in this publication largely because he "ordained the Son of the Prophet to succeed his father as President of the Church." The tract unfairly, and without context, looked at a few incidents in the life of Marks, using them to show he was an "apostate."[4]

Corner Stones first discusses Marks in Nauvoo. It notes that he was the president of the Nauvoo Stake on June 27, 1844, gives the date of the martyrdom, and then claims that Joseph Smith publicly condemned Marks. This tract quoted from a work described as the "prophet's journal," ostensibly written in the voice of Smith: "Whatever can be the matter with these men (Law and Marks)? Is it that wicked flee when no man pursueth? . . . or that Presidents Law and Marks are absolutely traitors to the Church, that my remarks should produce such excitement in their minds?"[5] However, this alleged quotation does not come from Smith's journal, nor was it written near the time of the martyrdom. Instead, the statement is from the highly edited *Manuscript History of the Church* for the date of January 5, 1844, which was purportedly drawn from meeting notes of a special session of the city council. Still, the above-quoted "jour-

---

2. "Obituary of Elder Wm. Marks," *TH*, 336.
3. *Corner Stones of "Reorganization": A Few Facts Concerning Its Founders . . . Compiled From Early Church History.*
4. *Corner Stones*, 1.
5. *Corner Stones*, 2.

nal" entry does not appear in the original minutes. Historian Dan Vogel, in his source and text critical edition of the *Manuscript History*, reasons that these words were likely written by George A. Smith in 1855,[6] when it was common for him and other scribes to alter, remove, or create narratives to fit their own perspectives and beliefs about Restoration history.

The tract continues by claiming that Marks was "dropped from his position as president of Nauvoo Stake" and adds the unsubstantiated claim that he was excommunicated, for which there is no evidence.[7] It then moves to Marks's involvement with James Strang, highlighting his leading part in the movement's formation, including his appointment as a bishop and later as an apostle. Continuing the tract's effort to negatively portray Marks, it quotes Strang's revelation in 1849 calling Marks to repentance. Following this, the tract discusses his time in Thompson's organization and criticizes Marks for his involvement and his attempts to find a gathering place for the group. The tract does not consider the letter Marks wrote in 1853 discussing Smith's renunciation of polygamy.[8]

Corner Stones ends with criticizing Marks for joining with John E. Page and the Reorganization. The tract calls him an "apostate" and asks, "Why did the 'Reorganization' receive the Apostate Marks on his ORIGINAL baptism and ORIGINAL ordination after he had joined 'The Strang faction,' 'The Thompson faction,' 'The Page faction,' and 'became divested of all authority?'"[9] This view of Marks as a defector reflects the way Latter-day Saints in the Brigham Young tradition had viewed Marks through much of the twentieth century.

The RLDS Church responded to *Corner Stones of the "Reorganization"* with a pamphlet of their own, published in 1911. Written by Heman C. Smith and titled *Duplicity Exposed*, this tract immediately questioned the authenticity of the statement, "Whatever can be the matter with these men (Law and Marks)?"[10] The responding tract challenged the Northern States Mission to produce "any *early* church history containing this quotation." Smith clearly believed it to be a later fabrication, and he countered this supposed statement with one of his own. Quoting from a March 1854 issue of the *Millennial Star*, which the Latter-day Saints in Utah

---

6. Dan Vogel, ed., *History of Joseph Smith and the Church of Jesus Christ of Latter-day Saints: A Source and Text Critical Edition*, 6:193n392.
7. *Corner Stones*, 2–3.
8. *Corner Stones*, 3–7.
9. *Corner Stones*, 8.
10. Heman C. Smith, *Duplicity Exposed*.

continued ownership of, Smith's response recounted a vision Joseph Smith had of Marks where the Lord reached out his hand to Marks and said, "Thou art my son, come here." This statement of acceptance by the Savior was from a time when Marks was "pursued by an innumerable concourse of enemies," presumed to be those who deposed him in Nauvoo.[11]

In discussing the removal of Marks as stake president, *Duplicity Exposed* notes, "We need only say that this was after the death of Joseph Smith and after Brigham Young and supporters had assumed control, and had adopted the policy of removing from office everyone who was not subservient to their dictation." Thus, Marks's removal was not a disgrace but rather "a credit to William Marks."[12] In regard to the many sects Marks joined, the tract stated that Marks had never "sacrificed his honor or was false to his faith." Instead, it concludes that this shows that he was "seeking the right," and when he learned a sect was not of God, he left it, "thereby manifesting a courage rarely exercised in those days of blind obedience to priestly authority."[13]

It is not likely that either of these tracts convinced anyone to change their views on William Marks. However, they did set the tone for how historians from each church would view him over the years. The Reorganized church claimed he was a man of God, loyal to Joseph Smith and opposed to the practice of polygamy. The Saints in Utah, on the other hand, argued that Marks was an apostate. B. H. Roberts's *The Rise and Fall of Nauvoo*, as well as his book on succession in the church, paint Marks as a traitor to Joseph Smith and the church without recognizing his contributions as stake president, president of the high council, or alderman. Quoting the disputed Joseph Smith journal entry, Roberts writes:

> This Wm. Marks afterwards was prominent among those who induced the Prophet to come back and deliver himself up to his enemies after the Prophet had started west. After the Prophet's death he joined the apostate James J. Strang in his attempt to lead The Church, and still later was a principal factor in bringing into existence the "Josephite" or "Reorganized Church."[14]

---

11. Smith, 2–3. See also "History of Joseph Smith," *MS*, 131.
12. Smith, *Duplicity Exposed*, 4.
13. Smith, 5.
14. B. H. Roberts, *The Rise and Fall of Nauvoo*, 281. See also B. H. Roberts, *Succession in the Presidency of the Church of Jesus Christ of Latter-day Saints*, 76, 98. In 2002, LDS historian Glen Leonard continued in this vein in his comprehensive history of Nauvoo, the first in decades. Leonard puts Marks in the category of "Mormon dissenters," writing "William Law, the Prophet's second counselor,

Subsequent Latter-day Saint historians over the years have largely followed Roberts by reducing Marks to a one-dimensional character: an apostate. In these histories Marks is selectively used and generally only discussed in relation to polygamy.[15]

From the Reorganized tradition's point of view, historian Robert Flanders wrote *Nauvoo: Kingdom on the Mississippi* in 1965. His volume similarly does not discuss Marks's contributions at great length, but he does cite Marks's 1853 letter to Charles B. Thompson:

> "During my administration [as stake president]," said Marks, "I saw and heard of many things that were practiced and taught that I did not believe to be of God; But I continued to do and teach such principles as were plainly revealed as the law of the Church. . . . Therefore, when the doctrine of polygamy was introduced into the Church I took a decided stand against it; which stand rendered me quite unpopular with many of the leading ones of the Church."[16]

However, Flanders ends the quotation here and omits the subsequent paragraph in which Marks claims that "Joseph . . . became convinced before his death that he had done wrong" and that the prophet confessed to him, "This doctrine of polygamy, or Spiritual-wife system, that has been

---

had believed Bennett's exaggerated claims of immoral behavior and was already a staunch opponent of anything resembling the teaching about spiritual wives. Siding with him were William Marks, the fifty-one-year-old Nauvoo stake president, and high council members Austin A. Cowles and Leonard Soby." Glen M. Leonard, *Nauvoo: A Place of Peace, a People of Promise*, 357, 611, 354.

15. For example, Richard Bushman, in his seminal biography of Joseph Smith, *Rough Stone Rolling*, says nothing of Marks's participation in the building of the church except as he relates to polygamy. He notes that Marks opposed the practice and was worried about the Nauvoo police force, and he discusses the 1853 letter, but discounts it by saying it "runs contrary to everything else Joseph said in this period." Even Benjamin Park's award-winning *Kingdom of Nauvoo*, the most recent comprehensive work on the subject—though it treats Marks more fairly than other works and avoids the caricature of Marks as an apostate— focuses on his involvement, or lack thereof, with polygamy. Marks's contributions to the formation of Nauvoo are not discussed. Richard Lyman Bushman, *Joseph Smith: Rough Stone Rolling, A Cultural Biography of Mormonism's Founder*, 528–30, 662n44; Benjamin E. Park, *Kingdom of Nauvoo: The Rise and Fall of a Religious Empire on the American Frontier*, 150, 177, 181, 245, 259, 272.

16. Robert B. Flanders, *Nauvoo: Kingdom on the Mississippi*, 274n94; ellipses and bracketed text belong to Flanders.

taught and practiced among us, will prove our destruction and overthrow. I have been deceived."[17]

Flanders's work highlights a problem created by RLDS historians and their church's use of Marks, specifically his 1853 letter. However, he was not the first to selectively edit Marks's statements to discredit polygamy while removing Joseph Smith's involvement. In 1860, the RLDS *True Latter-day Saints Herald* published an 1859 letter from Marks to Isaac Sheen, titling it "Opposition to Polygamy by the Prophet Joseph":

> I met with Brother Joseph. He said that he wanted to converse with me on the affairs of the Church, and we retired by ourselves. I will give his words verbatim, for they are indelibly stamped upon my mind. He said he had desired for a long time to have a talk with me on the subject of polygamy. He said it eventually would prove the overthrow of the Church, and we should soon be obliged to leave the United States, unless it could be speedily put down. He was satisfied that it was a cursed doctrine, and that there must be every exertion made to put it down.... There was much more said, but this was the substance.[18]

Here the letter had obviously been edited, as it did not contain the spelling or grammatical errors common in Marks's other writings. More importantly, Marks suspiciously omits his repeated claim of Joseph's purported confession that he had been "deceived." For example, in an 1865 letter to Hyrum Faulk and Josiah Butterfield, Marks described his meeting with Smith prior to the martyrdom:

> Brother Joseph came to me about two weeks before he was kil[l]ed and sais Brother Marks I want to talk with you we went by our selves and sais this Poligamy business in the Church must be stopt or the Church is ruend and we cant stay in the United States I have been dec[e]ive[d] in this thing and it must be put down I thought it would be an advantage to Mankind but I find it proved a curse.[19]

Mark Forscutt also recounted a private conversation in which Marks told him: "Near two weeks before Joseph was killed he told me [Marks] that I was the only one of the authorities of the Church not in polygamy; that polygamy was an evil, and that in it he [Joseph] had been deceived." When

---

17. William Marks, "Epistle," *ZHBO*, 53.
18. William Marks, "Opposition to Polygamy by the Prophet Joseph," *TH*, 26.
19. William Marks, letter to Hyrum Faulk and Josiah Butterfield, October 1, 1865, CCLA.

Forscutt asked Marks directly "if Joseph was in polygamy," he replied, "Yes he and Dr. Bennett were the first that went into it."[20]

Despite having access to all these similar accounts, in 1897 the RLDS church simply reprinted *The True Latter-day Saints Herald*'s "Opposition to Polygamy by the Prophet Joseph" for its *History of the Church.* This became the official account throughout the nineteenth and twentieth centuries.[21] Likewise, in 1901, RLDS Apostle Edmund Briggs reported a previous meeting he had with Marks:

> Brother Marks was all alive to the interest of the gospel and latter-day work, and as proof that he had great confidence in the Prophet Joseph, and knew that he was a man of God, said, "Just before his death I had quite a long talk with him. I had been feeling badly about the rumors that were being circulated about polygamy, and those old stories started by John C. Bennett concerning spiritual wives, and I was fearful that Joseph was mixed up with them in some way. But in his conversation he denounced all those things in the strongest language possible, and I became satisfied that Joseph was not abetting the crime of polygamy in any sense or form. In fact, he told me be would go on the stand the very next Sunday and denounce it publicly, and also advised me to look up the matter in the most thorough manner, and if I found anyone in the church who was teaching spiritual wives or any form of polygamy to bring charges against them, and he would help me to prosecute them until the church was cleansed of all such characters."

Briggs went so far as to say that Marks claimed to have "never saw any such thing . . . nor did I ever hear of it during Joseph's life" of the revelation on polygamy—that it "was evidently gotten up by Brigham Young and some of the Twelve after Joseph's death."[22] This, of course, contradicts

---

20. Mark Hill Forscutt, Journal.

21. Heman Smith, *The History of the Reorganized Church of Jesus Christ of Latter Day Saints*, 2:733–34.

22. Edmund C. Briggs, "Autobiographic Sketch and Incidents in the Early History of the Reorganization.—No. 10," 185. See also Briggs, "No. 22," 363–64. "And it is evident from Elder Marks' letter in this same HERALD that Joseph never had any affiliation with it; and proposed immediately to make a thorough investigation and find out who were in any way favoring it, and cut them off from the church. Bro. Marks said this to me personally, referring to his talk with President Smith upon this conversation set out in this HERALD. He has not given it in full as he did to me. I said to him, 'Did you, when you had that conversation with Bro. Joseph, think he had been in any way mixed up in polygamy, or had favored it?' He replied, 'No. I had more confidence in him at that time than I ever had in all my life before, and was satisfied that he was pure

Marks's own 1853 statement that "when the doctrine of polygamy was introduced into the church as a principle of exaltation I took a decided stand against it."[23]

William Marks provides a rich and important insight into polygamy. He epitomizes the conundrum of those who believe in the prophetic claims of Joseph Smith but cannot accept the principle he was secretly teaching and practicing. During Smith's life, few of his followers knew and practiced polygamy, and it was not expected of a priesthood holder as it was later under Brigham Young and the Twelve. There is little contemporary evidence that Smith regarded Marks as an enemy or an apostate for his position on the issue. And Marks is the lone source who suggests that perhaps Smith was contemplating renouncing plural marriage near the end of his life.

But Marks should be remembered for more than just his stance on polygamy. The historical record shows a different picture of Marks than has been preserved by any of the written histories thus far. He was a loyal and

---

from that gross crime. I had been troubled over the condition of the church for some time, and been fearful that Joseph did not bring the pressure against some men in the church that he should have done. You see from John C. Bennett's time there had been so many rumors going the rounds, I was fearful that there might be something in the stories afloat that might implicate Joseph. But Joseph was so free and positive in his denunciation of polygamy in every form, that I took courage; and I could see Joseph was in earnest and felt just as I did about it. But before the Sunday following our conversation, Joseph was having his suit, and he was killed before he had a chance to commence his investigation against those whom he had suspicioned of teaching it privily. But I thought he had been deceived in some of the men and elders of the church, and had too much confidence in some of them. But I guess it was to be so to fulfill the Scriptures in relation to the latter-day apostasy.' I then said, 'Bro. Marks, did you ever see the revelation on polygamy before it was published in 1852 by Mr. Pratt?' Marks emphatically replied, 'No, never.' 'You were president of the stake at Nauvoo, and if Joseph had such a revelation, would you not have been privileged, according to custom, to have seen it, or heard of it?' He replied, 'Yes, without a doubt. There was no such revelation in existence during Joseph's life. Brigham Young and his clique got that up after Joseph's death; for if there had been any such revelation in existence when I lived in Nauvoo, just after Joseph's death, Brigham Young would have showed it to me when I opposed his measures. But he never pretended to any such thing to me, that there was such a revelation on the subject from Joseph.'"

23. Marks, "Epistle," *ZHBO*, 52.

respected member from his first months in the church in New York and his arrival in Kirtland. He was present when the church's stance on gathering was debated and when policies were developed around the principle. Marks became one of the most influential and esteemed men in Nauvoo during the years of 1839 to 1844. He was entrusted with positions and labor requiring considerable practical know-how and great generosity of spirit. He served faithfully as the Nauvoo stake president, keeping a watchful eye over the large influx of people coming into the city from all over the United States, Europe, and other worldwide locations. As president of the high council, he played a key role in forming a city from the ground up, involved in daily affairs as well as ecclesiastical decisions. In this position, he saw firsthand how polygamy, both authorized and unauthorized, affected the church. As a member of the Nauvoo City Council, Marks served on the municipal court and was involved in many important legal cases, including those involving Joseph Smith. Marks not only passed laws and served as a judge regarding extradition attempts by Missouri, but he also testified numerous times on Smith's behalf, especially against charges made by John C. Bennett.

Marks was a staunch ally of Smith and a member of some of the most exclusive groups the prophet built to engender bonds of loyalty and support. These included the Masonic Lodge, the Quorum of the Anointed, the Council of Fifty, and even the military arm of the city, the Nauvoo Legion. A study of Marks in Nauvoo gives a glimpse into almost every major ecclesiastical and civil organization. It also gives real insight into the pain and confusion caused by the succession crisis after Smith's death. In this challenging moment, Marks shone as he, at great expense to his own membership, stood by his principles and ensured the high council followed rules established by Smith when it excommunicated Sidney Rigdon. The church's official account of Rigdon's excommunication in the *Times and Seasons* quotes Marks saying, "When I have set with the High Council, I have always tried to divest myself of prejudice."[24] Nonetheless, through a wrenching turn of events, Marks was disassociated, step by step, from his position of leadership and good fellowship among the Saints who followed the Quorum of the Twelve Apostles. Part of this was due to the problem he presented to Smith's inner circle with his opposition to polygamy, but he also posed a threat to their efforts to unify the body of the church under the authority of the Twelve.

---

24. "Continuation of Elder Rigdon's Trial," *TS*, 666.

Marks made significant contributions to three succession movements. To those of James J. Strang and Charles B. Thompson, he added a legitimacy that strengthened their claims. In Thompson's group, Marks devoted considerable effort to locating a gathering place where followers could commune and from which Thompson could publish his teachings. Marks was invaluable to the Reorganization, both in helping Joseph Smith III decide to lead the movement and in ordaining him to his position. As he had done for the church under Joseph Smith Jr., Marks provided a stabilizing influence for the Reorganized Church of Jesus Christ of Latter Day Saints and a solid connection back to the original organization.

Many figures in Mormon history are remembered for their loyalty to the Prophet Joseph Smith; for example, Hyrum Smith, Brigham Young, and Orrin Porter Rockwell are specifically spoken of as steadfastly standing by his side. Marks, though not as ostentatious as these, should be remembered in a similar fashion. Only weeks before his death, Smith named Marks one of his trusted friends. Marks proved this by serving his friend until the end of his life, acting as a member of the honor guard at Smith's funeral and helping bury and rebury his body.

Marks may not have had the humility of Hyrum Smith, but he had his heroism. He didn't meekly and willingly accept teachings on polygamy, but he stuck to his principles even when his own membership was at stake.

Marks may not have had the leadership abilities of Brigham Young, but he was loyal to his fellow Saints. He didn't coordinate the migration of thousands of people across uncharted territory, but he continued to help those who remained behind build a community of faith.

Marks may not have had the power of Porter Rockwell, but he had his persistence. He wasn't known for physically striking down the enemies of the church, but he persisted in finding a restoration group that followed Smith's teachings and the principles of religion he believed in.

William Marks may not have had the charismatic gifts of Joseph Smith, but he had a staunch commitment to the restoration Joseph ushered in, and Marks still stands today as a quiet but steadfast cornerstone in Zion.

Shabbonas Grove May 23th 1847

Brother James J Strang Dear Sir

I have made up my mind to day to start tomorrow morning for the State of Vermont and shall be gon probably four or five weeks I was makeing my calculations to be at Voree this week but have changed my mind on account of some business in the East that requares amediat attention I am sorry it has so hapened for I antisapated spendin some time with you this somer I shall endeavour to vindicate the Cause and advocate your Claims in all places where it shall be propper I do'nt feel at all discouraged about the work all tho it seems a other a dark time at presgrent I shall endeavour to be at your place as soone as I can make it convenet after my return

Yours with true respect
William Marks

William Marks, letter to James J. Strang, May 23, 1847. Courtesy of Beinecke Rare Book and Manuscript Library, Yale University.

APPENDIX A

William Marks—Letters

A letter from William Marks to James Strang is located in the James Jesse Strang Collection, WA MSS 447, at Yale University's Beinecke Library. Strang's son, Charles Jesse Strang, compiled most of the material in this collection, which after his death in 1916 passed to his brother Clement James Strang, who then gave the material to Milo Milton Quaife, author of Kingdom of St. James. *Quaife sold the material, probably between 1948 and 1951, to the bookseller Edward Eberstadt & Sons, which hired Dale L. Morgan to describe it in an item-level catalog, "The Strang Manuscripts," in 1951. The bookseller then sold the material to William Robertson Coe, who gave it to Yale University in 1951. Charles Eberstadt from the firm then gave the remaining material in this collection as a gift in 1956.*

William Marks, letter to James J. Strang, May 23, 1847, James Jesse Strang Collection, WA MSS 447, James Jesse Strang Collection, Beinecke Rare Book and Manuscript Library, Yale University. Typescript by the authors of this book.

        Shabbonas Grove May 23th 1847
        Brother James J Strang Dear Sir
    I have made up my mind to day to start tomorrow morning for the State of Vermont and shall be gon probably ~~three~~ ^four^ or five weeks I was making my calculations to be at Voree this week but have changed my mind on account of some business in the East that requarers amidiate attention I am sory it has so hapened for I antisapated spendin some time with you this somer I shall endeavour to indicate the Cause and advocate your Claims in all places where it shall be propper I do't feel at all discouraged about the work all tho it seems rather a dark time at presentt I shall endeavour to ^be^ at your place as soone as I can make it convienet after my return
                      Yours with all respect
                      William Marks

In 1907, Apostle Heman C. Smith of the Reorganized Church of Jesus Christ of Latter Day Saints wrote that "a series of letters written by Elder Marks during a part of these years of uncertainty, which throw some light upon, his movements" had recently "come into our hands" "through the kindness of S[iste]r. Byron Adams, of Logan, Iowa."[1] Smith's daughter Inez Smith Davis did transcriptions of the following letters from William Marks to James Adams, then in the possession of her father, in his private collection. These transcriptions by Davis are reproduced below. The spelling and punctuation has apparently been edited and corrected. The authors have been unable to locate the handwritten letters; they may have been lost in the 1907 Herald House fire, which destroyed many of the original records then held by the RLDS church.

William Marks letters to James M. Adams, typescripts in Inez Smith Davis Papers, P23 F61, Community of Christ Library and Archives, Independence, MO.

    1852, April 23
    1852, September 17
    1853, January 23
    1853, June 25
    1853, November 12
    1854, November 15
    1855, May 20
    1855, June 11
    1855, July 26
    1855, September 23
    1856, March 16

---

1. Heman C. Smith, Frederick M. Smith, D. F. Lambert, eds., *Journal of History, January, 1908* (Lamoni, Iowa: Board of Publication of the Reorganized Church of Jesus Christ of Latter Day Saints, 1908) 1:24. Byron Chauncey Adams (1835–1907) was the son of James Marvin Adams (1806–1873), to whom the letters were addressed.

Inez Smith Davis Typescript, addressed to Vienna, Wisconsin.

Shabbona Grove April 23/52

Br Adams Dear Sir

    On my return from St. Louis I found a letter from you, dated April 6th for which you requested an answer. I will endeavor to give you a statement of a few things that may be the most interesting to you. I went there to meet in the solemn assembly which convened on the 15th day of April. I arrived there on that day with but little understanding of the work and about as much faith, for I had been disappointed so often that I had become fearful and unbelieving and with a determination to be very inquisative, for I have learned from experience that it is a very easy thing to be deceived. I found when I arrived five brethren and my self made six and Brother Thompson, our chief teacher. which constituted about the same number that was present at the organizing of the church. After organizing a school in the second department with one Chief and two councilors, Br. Thompson commenced to teach us the principles of the great work in the last days of restoring the covenants to the house of Israel and the rejection of the church, and its becoming the second beast as prophecied by John, which beast must be the apostasy of the true church together with the teachings and the spirit and power that accompanied the Word. It removed all doubts and fears from my mind that the gospel dispensation has closed with the Gentiles and every preparation is making to carry it to Ephraim, as he is the first-born. The return of the gift of the pure language is a great blessing. Brother Thompson has the alphabet written out and can read and write it with ease and says a good scholar can learn it in one week. The alphabet consists of twelve letters or characters. It is so far explained. It appears to be a very easy matter to learn it. There seems to be a great inquiry about who Baneema is, but I think if you should meet in the solemn assembly you would be satisfied on that subject. There appears to be great wisdom used on this subject. <u>The draft of the temple to be built in Jackson County is a curiosity which is in the hands of Br. Thompson.</u>

    There are many things I might mention to you, but you cannot get the idea as well as you can to see and hear for yourself, which you will have an opportunity. There was a committy appointed by Revelation given on the 9th day of March if I recollect right for which I was one of the committy to look out a location on or near the frontiers of the Lamanites. I am now expecting to start on that mission sometime in the month of May. You mentioned in your letter you wished to go to St. Louis with me. The probability is that I shall not go to St. Louis till the 15th day of August. There is to be another solemn assembly to commence on that day. If you take the papers you will get all the information necessary to keep you on the trace. You aught to be in the field laboring for the time is short that we have allotted to gather up the remnant of the church or those who have kept the testimony of Jesus.

  I will defer writing any more in this letter.
  And subscribe myself your friend and brother
    William Marks

Inez Smith Davis Typescript.

Shabbona Grove, September 17, 52

Bro. Adams Dear Sir:

On my return I learned you and your wife had been here. I was sorry I was not at home, but I was detained longer than I expected to be. It was a long journey. I traveled about eleven hundred miles on horseback. I called on Bro Stevens at St. Joseph, as he was appointed one of the committee. Found him quite sick, so that he was not able to travel with me. We had anticipated of finding a location in that region of country, but land was too high there and we thought it best to look further. Myself and Brother Childs started up the river as far as Kanesville 150 miles. There was found a location that is very well calculated for a large settlement. The land is not in the market and is settled by making claims. The Mormons left there, about three thousand the last of June and there was any quantity of farms to be bought, very low, too, or the claims and a great chance for making knew claims. The country north for one hundred miles was good and but few inhabitants. The soil was the best I ever saw. We made no purchase except a house and lot in Kanesville. We thought the chance would be as good to buy next spring as now. Br Thompson will move there this fall, we expect. We wrote to him what we had done and to Br Stevens also.

Now Br. Adams we are engaged in a work that fills my heart with joy and satisfaction, it brings that peace and consolation that I never before experienced when we see the work of the father commenced to gather Israel and to build up a kingdom that he will administer to himself and that we have the privilege to come into it, which no Gentiles have had before. This is the Kingdom representing the glory of Sun. The gospel to the Gentiles is the kingdom representing the glory of the moon and is administered by the Saviour, and the great mass of mankind go into the glory of the Stars and then differ in glory as one star differs from another.

I would write more, but my pen has failed, but I would say: Make the necessary arrangements to gather when it is advisable and I think that will be next spring to be more fully taught in the principles that will prepare us for the celestial glory.

Yours in the bonds of the covenant. William Marks

Inez Smith Davis Typescript.

Shabbona, DeKalb County, Ill Jan 23/53

Br J. M. Adams Dear Sir:

I received yours the 8th of January and was pleased to hear from you and learn you had received the Covenant. As to giving you any new construction relative to the work, I am not able to do so for I have not heard from Br Thompson for a long time. You expressed a desire that you wished me to call on you if it was convenient to do so. I should be very happy to make you a visit this winter if it were consistent for me to leave home, but I am alone and no one to assist me and it occupies all of my time to see to my domestic affairs. I can hardly get time to answer all the letters I receive. There are quite a number writing for information about the location at the Bluffs and the most prudent course to pursue. I would say to you, Br. Adams, that the country is very new, and we will have to under go a great many privations. What buildings there are in the surrounding country are very poor. They were only put up for the present. I think it would be policy if a few families were going from a neighborhood to have someone go and make some preparation. It will save great inconvenience. I think this spring will be a good time to secure locations. I am expecting to start about the first of April. I have purchased a horse power sawmill and man an arrangement with a man to go with me and tend it. I found when I was there there was a great lack of lumber.

Br. Gold was here a few weeks ago. I mentioned to him to go up to your place. He said he would go and try to enlist Br. Savage. I understand he lives near Batvaia on Fox River, and they would go to Wisconsin. Bro. Gold is quite broken on account of the shock of the palsy he had last spring. We have seen so much misery and distress by gathering in haste I think we had better follow a different course with the present work.

I don't think of anything of importance at present to write. All well at present. Yours in the bonds of peace. William Marks

Inez Smith Davis Typescript.

Shabbona Grove, June 25, 1853
DeKalb Co, Ill.

Brother James M. Adams Dear Sir:

    I started from home last Thursday to go to your place, but feeling quite unwell after I started, and learning that Br. Paden had been there, I returned home and thought I would drop you a line and turn my course another way. There are so many calls for teaching and information, that I hardly know which way to go first, but I am now going West. I have chosen you to fill my place as First Chief in the First quorum and my main object was to ordain you to that appointment, but I thought it might be deferred till the August Assembly which will be very necessary you should be there. I have just returned from St. Louis and am satisfied the time has come for us to labor with our might or we shall be rejected and others appointed in our place. It is of vast importance that we purchase a printing press and it appears there is none that has much means to spare and if you can assist us some in this undertaking, it will be thankfully received and we want you to be there in St. Louis without fail. You will see in the July number in an epistle that I wrote in St. Louis what is the reason of the attendance. Bro. Adams, the work is verily true and we need not fear to go ahead.

    Yours truly,
        William Marks

Inez Smith Davis Typescript.

Shabbona Grove, DeKalb Co, Ill Nov 12/53

Brother J. M. Adams
    Dear Sir:

    I received yours of November 4 and was glad to hear from you. I wrote you sometime in August, I think. I have not heard from you since and came to the conclusion it did not reach you. I returned from St Louis the last of June and was taken sick immediately after I got home, and was confined to the house most of the time for months. My intentions were to visit your place immediately on my return for it is necessary that you should be ordained chief in my place in the first department in the School of Faith, but since I recovered my health, I have found no time to leave. My wife has been sick very sick for the last eight months past and has just recovered her health in a measure and my boys have all left for themselves and it is very difficult for me to leave home at all at present. I am trying to sell my farm and think I shall succeed in doing so in the spring when I hope to be more at liberty. I sent some money to Br. Thompson about the time you sent yours and requested him to answer it as he had been negliegent in doing so formerly, and he wrote me immediately after the solemn assembly, acknowledging the receipt of it and stating that the brethren had come forward manfully and contributed sufficient to purchase a printing press and he had a contact for it and should be able to start for the Bluffs in a few days, and I have not heard anything from him since, nor anything from the brethren there. I have been waiting to hear from Bro. Thompson, supposed he would write me on his arrival there.

    I would be glad to have you come here, as soon as your health will admit. I see nothing but I shall be confined at home the most part of the winter, although I don't feel satisfied when I reflect on the importance of the great and glorious work that we have engaged in and the importance of teaching our fellow man.

    I can't give you much information how the work progresses at present for I have not heard much from the brethren of late, but I fear there are some who have excuses to make, some like myself in doing their duty, but I don't feel as though I were entirely excusable, but one thing I have desired to be at home for the purpose of meeting with a chance to sell as there are many from the East this fall to buy farms.

    I shall look for you till you come. We are in usual health. Our best respects to yours and family.
                  William Marks

Inez Smith Davis Typescript.

SHABBONA Grove, DeKalb Co, Ill November 15/54

Brother James M. Adams Dear Sir:

I would offer an apology for not answering your letter before this time. It is in consequence of a multitude of business. I have been engaged in building a house for the last eight weeks. I have had five men to work on it the most of the time. We have just finished it all but plastering, but the weather is so it will be very uncertain whether we shall plaster this fall.

So much for temporal things and as to spiritual things, I hardly know what to say for I hear but little about it here. I received the June number from Preparation the other day and I made up my mind that all intelligence had departed from that source or at any rate there was not much in that number.

I feel that it would be policy for me to stand still for a short time I have had it in my mind to try and form a settlement of brethren and try to live according to the law of God but there has been so many attempts made to gather that I am almost discouraged to make any such attempt, although I should like to live where I could enjoy the society of friends and brethren, but I think we had better try to live and try to do as near right as we know how, and the time will come when we will be rewarded for our works. I have several letters to write today and so will close and write again soon. Write on the receipt of this. Yours truly

William Marks

There has been a great excitement in money matters here for the last two or three weeks, but it has rather subsided. Almost all the banks in northern Illinois have been closed, but it is stated that most of them will resume business this week. It has reduced the price of produce and pork. Pork is worth only $3.50 per hundred, Wheat 80 cents, has been $1.05 a bushel. It is supposed there will be a change in times. Money is quite hard to get now. I have made the deed out for my farm and the man has taken possession.

William Marks

Inez Smith Davis Typescript, addressed to Magnolia, Iowa.

Shabbona, May 20th, 1855 DeKalb, Illinois
Brother James M. Adams Dear Sir:

It has been a long time since I have heard from you by letter. I heard by the Mrs. McHenry a few weeks ago news that greatly rejoiced my heart, that you had been healed by the power of God, of the great malady that was preying upon your system, that must from all appearances soon have terminated your existence. Mrs. McHenry said we should soon hear from you by letter she thought I have deferred writing for some two weeks looking and expecting to hear from you, but could not wait any longer. I must express some of my views that have lately occurred to my mind, as regards my faith. I can see no more than can have any favorable claims to come out and claim to be a prophet. I think our minds can be at rest and we can have a little peace on that subject I think we have followed the requirements of St. Paul to prove all things and hold fast to that which is good and I know of nothing better yhan [sic] the pure principles of the gospel. I have recently come to the conclusion to teach repentance and faith on the Lord Jesus Christ and baptism for the remission of sins and the laying on of hands for the gift of the Holy Spirit. Don't believe in any church organization. Teach the pure principles of the gospel and every man stand or fall be his own Master. We read that all men that worketh righteousness in all nations shall be accepted of God. I received a letter a few days ago from a man living in Aurora, saying he wished me to come there? There were eight or ten wished to be baptized and were gathering a band of brethren. I do not know how this came, for I have said nothing of my views recently on the subject, except to my wife. I have written to them today my views. If they want me to come, I shall probably go and baptize them.

So much as regards my faith as to spiritual things and temporal things are so connected I must write something on temporal. Br. George Robinson was here a few days ago and said he wished to invest a few thousand dollars in government lands. I told him I thought it might be found in your region of the country. I would write to you in the subject. If I could learn from you whether there was much of a chance for entering lands in that part of the country, I would write to him and let him know.

I feel some considerable interest on the subject for he said he thought he could buy land warrents in the latter part of August and September in the city of New York at a reduced price, as the government would commence to issue them the first of August under the new Act and would let me have a share of them and pay me for locating his. I wish you and Mr McHenry would ascertain what you can about vacant land and the locations and inform me on the subject as early as convenient.

We are all well. Haven't got done building yet, to work on a barn. Produce is high. Wheat is $1.50, corn 60 cents, oats forty cents at this date. Great time for selling goods. Money quite plenty.

Yours with due respect
William Marks

Inez Smith Davis Typescript, addressed to Magnolia, Iowa.

Shabbona Grove, DeKalb Co, Ill
June 11th, 1855

Brother James M. Adams Dear Sir:

    Your letter of the 14th of May has been received and I have read it over and over again. Its contents awere known, or some of them, and some are of vast importance. It rejoiced my heart to learn that you were healed of so great a malady, that from all earthly appearances was so soon to terminate your usefulness and existence here on earth. It seems from the tenor of your letter that there has been two spirits manifest, the one asking you if you would deny Christ if you could be healed, I should think was to tempt you or try your faith, the other has led you to preach some very interesting discourses such as the first principles of the gospel and the law of adoption and that the Lord has not rejected this Nation. That I never did believe all that Brigham Young claimed it to be As to the church departing from the foundation that I think could be clearly shown, but the funeral sermon of the church was a thing quite foreign to my thoughts. If this is from the right spirit it has incalcuable meaning. It seems to have put an end to so much false pretention and false prophets and foolery that has been going on for ten or twelve years. O how it would rejoice my heart to see the true light break forth again, that we might know for a surety, for I have long been wandering in darkness and following false prophets until I had become tiresome and weary. I came to the conclusion in the forepart of last winter to reject all organizations and teach the first principles of the gospel and baptism for the remission of sins and the laying on of hands for the gift of the Holy Spirit. I find recently there is quite a number in this region of country have come to the same conclusion. John E. Page is one and some 8 or ten at Aurora. They want me to baptize them, and I want you to advise on the subject.

    Brother Adams we are living in a day when the Devil has great power and it appears from what we see and hear that he will if possible deceive the whole world, therefore it is highly necessary that we are watchful and prayerful; that we may not be deceived by the spirits faithfully to the written word. I well remember what Oliver Cowdery told me here when on his way to Council Bluffs. He said the work was of God and the end would be accomplished let men do or act as they pleased. I would like to see you. I could better communicate my thoughts to you than I can write them. Probably I may. I wrote one letter to you about the date of your last to me, and one since to McHenry to ascertain something about government land. Br George Robinson was here some three weeks ago and wanted I should locate some land for him as soon as he could obtain some certificates. The government are now issuing them. If I come to your section of country, I shall probably start in August.

Please write soon I want to be posted up on every thing that is interesting

We are all well. The season has been rather dry and cold. The prices of grain is high, wheat $1.50 a bushel, corn 70 cents.

  I remain as ever yours
   William Marks

N.B. Tell McHenry to write often. We want to hear from you all.

Inez Smith Davis Typescript, addressed to Magnolia, Iowa.

Shabbona Grove, DeKalb Co. Ill.
July 26/55

Brother James M. Adams, Dear Sir.

Your letter of the 9th of July has just been received. I had waited with intens anxiety to hear from you and I have perused it untill I fully understand its contents as it respects our views in relation to the course to pursue in preaching the Gospel of the Kingdom of Christ I fell well satisfied with and have been blesed and enjoyed great peace of mind since I came to that conclusion.

My mind has never been at rest since the brakeing up of the Church (or the death of Br Joseph) I have always had fears that all was not right but I am satisfied now that all the fals Prophets have arisen that can with any degree of plausibility and if there can be any sustem adopted that will be calculated to mitigate the condition of the faithful Saints that are scatered about on the face of the land it will rejoice my hart.

I would state my views and then I should like to get the views of my Brethren on the subject asking our hevenly Father to direct us and claim the promis if any Man lack wisdom let him (ask) God.

I had it in cntemplation when I wrote you the last letter to look out a good location some where in the west and enter a large trac of land if it was thought advisable by my friends and bretheren and invite all of the honest in hart and as many as was desposed to gather around where we could enjoy secure society for it is like living alone in the wood as may of us do I have mentioned my views to several of the Bretheren since I wrote to you and they seamed very much pleased with my views and hoped that I would do it by all means for they would gladly fall in with the ide.

And now Br Adams, I want your advise on the best course to pursue asking our hevenly Fath to direct you in this matter and want your answer on this subject as soon as posible for if I should conclude to make a location this fall it would be necessary to make a move before a great while and your opinion about where to make the location if it should meet your views.

I am sum what advanced in age, near 64 years, but my health was never better than at presant all tho I cant endure so much hard ship my strnth has been hreatly encreased since I have cum to the present conclusion while under the s½orot of Benemaism I lost all of my strenth, and former vigour. I never went on a mission without returning hom sick, and finaly reduced, so low as to despair of ever being able to do anything more.

Tell McHenry and family that we are all in good health and should like to hear from them by letter soon. I wanted no connection with Br Gorge in entering land for it appeared from his conversation whil here that he had made compleat shiprack of his faith; it appeared that all his object was to get gain.

I saw Br Little John Galard at Chicago two days since. He said he had been writing a large pamphlet on the futur result of Busha [Russia] and the Eastern powers he said he had been to J.E.Pages about three weeks, a coppying the work; he said his views and Br. Pages was much like mine accept the gathering; they thought must be on the Colrado.

I think if we are faithful to observe the law and keep the commandments of God that we shall no for a surety all that will be necessary for us to no.

In your next letter I wish you would give anxplination of your views of what you mentioned that was taught at Prepperation of the different states of probation and regeneration and all the prepporation news as far as you have it. The papers have stopt and I dont feel interest enough to subscribe for any more. The prospect in Shelby County for entering land is quite good I think according to your discription.

I dont think of any more to write on this subject at presant. Our crops are all good as far as they have cum to maturity and the balance did fare. it is very shoury [showery], rain every day and verry warm I feer the crops will be ingored [injured] for we are right in the midst of cutting our grain.

       Yours as ever with due respect,
          William Marks

Inez Smith Davis Typescript, addressed to Magnolia, Iowa.

>Shabbona Grove, DeKalb Co, Ill sept 23 1855
>Brother James M. Adams Dear Sir:

I have delayed some time to answer letter, hardly knowing what to write but have come to the conclusion that I shant come into your section of the country this fall. It was so late in the season before I could leave, I thought it would not be prudent to start, for fear that I might be out too late in bad weather. It looks like a long journey to me to undertake, and I have had some fears arise in my mind of late that possibly it might prove a failure and if so it would be very mortifying to me, as there have been so many failures. I thought that I would defer it until spring; learn more of the feelings of the brethren on the subject this winter as I have had but little opportunity to see but a few as yet. I have felt very much of late to claim the promise if any lack wisdom let him ask of the Lord and I feel if I ask in a right frame of mind he will instruct me.

I want your faith and prayers that we may be instructed by the Spirit of Truth that we may not make any move that will not be pleasing in the sight of our Heavenly Father. I have no particular news to write. We are all well. Business is very brisk. Wheat $1.00 to $1.10. Cattle and horses very high. Money quite plenty. I received a letter from Wm Smith this morning from Kirtland. It was on business. Said he was preaching there but would not trouble about church matters as there was so many, lo here and there.

>Yours truly
>William Marks

Say to McHenry's family we will answer their letter soon.

Inez Smith Davis Typescript, addressed to Magnolia, Iowa.

Shabbona Grove, March 16th, 1856

BROTHER James M. Adams Dear Sir:

It is a long time since I have written to you. I have been waiting to hear from you. I received a letter from McHenry last night, stating that you were well, which I was glad to hear. I had deferred writing because I had not much of importance to say, but through faith and prayer and the gift of the Holy Spirit, I believe I have partially come to an understanding. I consulted with some of the brethren here, stating my views in part and we agreed to call a conference to be held on the tenth day of April, which comes on Thursday to meet at 2 O.C.P.M. and organize on that day and continue till Saturday evening, preaching on Sunday. We meet at East Pawpaw. We have engaged the seminary. It was granted us with all freedom by the trustees and a great anxiety manifested to hear and that seems to be a general feeling in our section of the country. We had but about a months notice before our conference, so we have had to notify mostly by letter. I should have written you before but there was not time for you to attend, if you should have been disposed. Our object is to meet and discuss the subject and try to get a starting point, and not complete an organization then but try to come into union and to concentrate our faith and strength and travel this summer and give a general notice and call a conference in the fall, disseminating our views and preaching. My views are to organize according to the Book of Mormon These are the views of some of the brethren, but I have not seen but a few to converse with.

It has been manifested to me in a few days past to organize as the Nephites dis [sic] with a High Priest to preside over the whole church with elders, priests, and teachers, the High Priest to be elected by the voice of the peple. This requires a man of God and of great faith. This I should wish to defer until I could get a more general expression of the brethren.

It is very evident to me that the sayings of Nephi have literally been fulfilled when the work of the Father should commence in preparing the way for the fulfilling of his covenants, which he hath made to his people who are of the house of Israel. I am satisfied that this organization will be the one to go to the Lamanites, and this was the organization, in part, with the Jews, only the preaching of the gospel. But I think this will be the order that will go to them. The Book of Mormon is of great worth to us in our day. I read it with more interest than I ever did before. I can't give you but a short sketch of my views in this letter, but I think I shall visit your section of country this summer We shall endeavor to have all the travel and preaching that we can. I want you to write immediately upon receipt of this and give me your views on the subject. I will write you again immediately after the conference.

I will send a few lines in this to McHenry, as I have nothing of importance to write. The place at Kanesville you may do as you think best. I think you had better rent it. It may come into play sometime. There may be a gathering of the saints in that region someday. Deacon Pritchard died about three weeks ago and Mister Madison is very low. No great change in times. Land is rising. There has been a falling of prices in produce. Money is very scarce. We are all well.

              William Marks

One handwritten letter from William Marks to James Adams, dated March 18, 1854, was located in the Miscellaneous Letters and Papers P13, F96 file at RLDS Library/Archives on August 19, 1991. It is now in the Community of Christ Library and Archives. It was not part of the collection of letters transcribed by Inez Smith Davis. The Archives has no additional information on the provenance of this letter.

William Marks, letter to James M. Adams, March 18, 1854. Original letter in Miscellaneous Letters and Papers, P13, F96, Community of Christ Library and Archives, Independence, MO. Typescript by the authors.

     Shabbonas Grove DeKalb Co Ill March 18/54
Br. James, M, Adams Dear Sir
 Yours of March 2d is duly received and I was glad to hear from you in your letter you wished me to give you all the advise and counsil I could I don't feel my self verry well qualified for such an undertakeing I would say in regard to the first request on moveing this spring or summer would be right according to my judgment, brakeing Prarie will be all most the first business and such work was verry high when I was there Cook stoves was dear but there was a plenty of them at Kanesvill all kinds of mecanical work was dear when I was there but how much change there has been since I am not able to say but I should think on the hole it would be best to take such articles as you would most kneed it will save a good deel of time in procureing them when you get there and will cost a nough more to pay transpotation, as it regards crossing the Missippy I can hardly tel you, ^where^ where, we cross at Albeny when we go from here you want to get on the direct rout to Iowa City that is a point you will have to make, from there to Fort Desamoin [Des Moines]. in regard to a location I discovered in the last paper stateing if a man would pay his titheing he could have one acrer of land in the Town and as much land ajasent as he wished to work but that is not the way I should like to farm it I should rather live on my farm but what will be the order of the day when I no not but we can learn when we get there Money seams to be quite an object at present but possible it is all right that has been the cry ever since we first heard of Mormonism Br Joseph Younger wrote that he had a Preemption with some improvements on it that he wanted to sell as his preemption run out the first of July and he was not able to enter it he said it was 40 Miles from North of Kanesvill and wished it I would find some one to buy him out, I am expecting to start in a bout ten days I expect to go by

Shabbonas Grove DeKalb Co Ill March 18 /54
Br. James M. Adams Dear Sir
Yours of March 2 is duly received and I was glad to hear from you in your letter you wished me to give you all the advise and counsel I could I dont feel my self verry well qualified for such an undertakeing I would say in regard to the first request on moveing this spring or summer would be right according to my judgment, brakeing Prarie will be all most the first business and such work was verry high when I was there Cook Stoves was dear but there was a plenty of them at Kanesville all kinds of Mecanical work was dear when I was there but how much change there has been since I am not able to say but I should think on the hole it would be best to take such articles as you would most kneed it will save a good deal of time in procureing them when you get there and will cost a nough more to pay transportation, as it regards crossing the Misippy I can hardly tel you where we cross at Albery when we go from here you want to get on the direct rout to Iowa City that is a point you will have to make, from there to Fort Desamoin. in regard to a location I discovered in the last paper stateing if a man would pay his tithering he could have one Acer of land in the Town and as much land a Jasent as he wished to work but that is not the way I should like to farm it I should rather live on my farm

William Marks letter to James Adams. Courtesy of Community of Christ Library and Archives.

but what will be the order of the day when I no not but we can learn when we get there Money seams to be quite an object at present but possible it is all right that has been the cry ever since we first heard of Mormonism Mr Joseph Younger wrote that he had a Preemption with some improvement to on it that he wanted to sell as his preemption run out the first of July and he was not able to enter it he said it was 40 Miles from North of Kanesville and wished I would find some one to buy him out, I am expecting to start in a bout ten days I expect to go by water in company with one of our neighbors he is a going to move to the Bluffs Mr Savage was to start some few days ago there was five waggons to go in company with him I want to be there at the next assembly which will commence on the 15 day of April
I think of nothing more to write at present
Yours with due respect —
William Marks

William Marks letter to James Adams. Courtesy of Community of Christ Library and Archives.

water in company with one of our neighbors he is a going to move to the Bluffs Br Savage was to start some five days ago there was five waggons to go in company with him I want to be there at the next assembly which will commence on the 15 day of April

    I think of nothing more to write at presant
        Yours with due respect
            William Marks

An incomplete part of a letter from William Marks to James Adams dated September 3, 1854 is quoted in Heman C. Smith's Journal of History, January 1908, *pp. 25–26. This letter was not part of the collection of letters transcribed by Inez Smith Davis; however, it was likely included with the series of letters donated to the RLDS church by Sister Byron Adams. The authors have been unable to find any other trace of this letter.*

William Marks, portion of a letter to James M. Adams, September 3, 1854, in Heman C. Smith, Frederick M. Smith, D. F. Lambert, eds., *Journal of History*, January, 1908. Lamoni, Iowa: Board of Publication of the Reorganized Church of Jesus Christ of Latter Day Saints, 1908.

"I just received a paper from Bro. Thompson and a small note sent in an envelope stating that many had turned away, but urging me to make all possible speed to get there for there was still a chance for those who was willing to make the sacrifice of all they possess of this world's goods. I discovered when I was there last spring that there was a great many that was quite dissatisfied, principally with the time tithing. I was there some ten or twelve days. I came to the conclusion that there was the greatest oppression that I ever saw imposed upon a community, but I had heard nothing from there since and don't know what has been the cause of their leaving. I suppose by your not settling at Preparation that you discovered something that you was not satisfied with. On the receipt of this I wish you would write me, and give me your views of all the proceedings as you understand them.

I had always felt an assurance that the work was of God. I went there last spring with the view of making preparation to move there, but when I left there I thought I would wait a short time and see what would be the result of things, for I was satisfied that many would leave. In your letter I wish you would mention the names of some that has left. I have heard that Bro. Savage and Bro. Messenger and many others also."

1848
Shabbona Grove De Kalb Co Illinois March 1st
A Statement of facts as they exist between my self and
brother Aaron Johnson.

In closing up the business for brother Joseph with Esq Russel
in Kirtland for the purchase of his farm I had to become
obligated to Esq Russel to defray the expences of foreclosing
a Mortgage that he had upon the farm to Ensure or Make
good the title as he said there was judgments standing
against Br Joseph at that time and was fearful that
a Deed from him would not make the title good
some 2 or 3 three years after I left Kirtland Russel
Closed the Mortgage to perfect the title which stood the expence
against me which amounted to eighty three Dollars
I spoke to brother Joseph about it and he said he would
sittel it as soone as he could I told him I had some
property there and they would sacrifice it probably to
cancel the demand he told me I had better Deed
it to brother Johns as he considered him a verry honest man
I accordingly did so and Deeded him the house and lot
known as the Rigdon house and lot with an express agree
=ment for him Johnson to Kellogg it back to me again when the matter
was arranged with Esq Russel when I left Nauvoo it was not
settled but that summer I paid the Eighty three Dollars
and canceled the demand and called on Br Johnson to quit
Claime back to me the place but he refused to do so and
has lately sold the place as I understand William Marks

N.B. This I have stated by request of brother B. Young
Wm M

William Marks, letter to Brigham Young, March 1, 1848, Brigham Young Incoming Correspondence, 1839–1877, CR 1234 1, box 21, fd. 13, Church History Library, https://catalog.churchofjesuschrist.org/assets/bc8f1245-261e-41f1-a42c-d9d38eb8b411/0/0. Typescript by the authors.

    Shabbonas Grove De Kalb Co Illinois March 1st 1848
    A statement of facts as they exist between my self and Brother Aaron Johnson.

In closing up the business for Brother Joseph with Esq Russel in Kirtland for the purchase of his Farm I had to becum obligated to Esq Russel to defray the expences of foreclosing a Mortgage that he had upon the farm to Ensure or Make good the title as he said there was Judgments standing against Br Joseph at that time and was fearful that a Deed from him would not make the title good some 2 or 3 three years after I left Kirtland Russel Closed the Mortgage to perfect the title which ^the expense^ stood against me which amounted to Eighty three Dollars

I speak to Brother Joseph about it and he said he would sitle it as soone as he could I told him I had some propperty there and they would sarifise it probablily to cancel the demand he told me I had better Deed it to Brother Johns as he considered him a verry honest man

I accordingly did so and Deeded him the house and lot known as the Rigdon house and lot with an express agreement for him ^Johnson to Redeed^ it back to me again when the matter was arranged with Esq Russel when I left Nauvoo it was not setled but that summer I paid the Eighty three Dollars and canseled the demand and caldon Br Johnson to quit Clame back to me the place but he refused to do soe and has lately sold the place as I under stand William Marks

    N.B. This I have [?uted] by request of Brother [T Young?]
    Wm M

One handwritten letter dated October 1, 1865 from William Marks to Hyrum Faulk and Josiah Butterfield is located in the Community of Christ Library and Archives. It was acquired in January 1922 by Paul Hanson from C. L. Butterfield, son of Josiah Butterfield. C. L. wrote that Josiah possessed several letters written to him by William Marks, but these letters were destroyed soon after Josiah's death.

William Marks to Hyrum Faulk and Josiah Butterfield, October 1, 1865, P12-1, F13, Inez Smith Davis Papers, Community of Christ Library and Archives, Independence, MO. Typescript by the authors.

Shabbonas Grove DeKalb County Illinois
October 1st 1865

Dear Bretheren I received your kind letter Sept the 26th it did my soul good to hear from my ould friends, I left you at Nauvoo not expecting to see you again, but the prospects are flattering that we may meet together again.

I must give you a short history of my experiance at Nauvoo before I left in a prair metting sum six months before there was any appearan^ce^ of Poligamy we was warned buy the spirit that the Lord ^was^ agone to endow the Church with the gretest endowment that was ever bestowed on Man and the Devel was much displeased with it and determined to prevent it and would pour out the spirit of audultry ~~which~~ upon the hol Church which was the easiest sprit to take there wase ^was^ in ^the^ world and ~~verry near~~ he woul verry near succeed in over thouwing the Church but shoul ^not^ quite succeed and giving direction how we might no when it begun, and ended with a long exertation to the saints to be ware of that spirit this warning sunk deep into my mind and ^did^ kept me on the lookout and another thing decided the thing in my mind Brother Joseph came to me abut two weeks before he was kiled and sais

Brother Marks I want to talk with you we went by ourselves and ^he^ sais this Poligamiy business in the Church must be stopt or the Church is ruend and we cant stay in the United States I have been deceive in this thing and it must be put down I thoght it would be an advantage to Mankind but I find it proves a curs I asked him how it coul be dun

he said I must go into the high Council and ^he^ would prefur charges agaist. those in adultry and imust cut them off and he would go on the stand and preach against it and thought buy so doing we might putit it down but the mob son commenced gethering and there was nothing dun.

I told sum of my friends what Broth Joseph had told me O Brother Marks has apostized it is only sum of his lies I thought if that was all they cared about it they might take thre own course and I woul take mine These are all soll^em^ truthes tho there was much other conversation at thim that I not writen.

I will give you a short sceth [sketch] of the rice [rise] of the of the reorganization of the Church there was sum of the ould members of the Church living near to gether and they commenced holding a prair metings and soon they goot the spit of prophisy and they was told that young Joseph was the rightful are to the presidency they soon gave notice for a Confrence to the few scatered saints and so we begun to gether to confrence and we held a number and frequntly was directed how to proced and finaly we was commanded to organize on the six of April 1860 and Broth Joseph would be ther to take his place

him and his Mother ware both ther it was dun at Amboy about 25 miles from my place it was the hapyest day I think that I ever experancd in my life I am living abut 25 miles from Plano where our paper is printed Brother Joseph is expecte to Move ther with his family in a few days he has the charge of th Printin press

it appears the Lord is asending out his hunters to hunt them ^up^ we have hunted up a goodly number

I apprehend the time is not far distant when we shall be permeted to go back to Mosora [Missouri] the land has been litteraly ~~been~~ redeamed by blood one of our neighbours was a Captian of a Company was chaising ould Price through Jac^kson County and other Counties a joining he said he traveled forty miles didint see but one family the cuntry was

laid waste we have past through the war have not suferd but verry little in this section of contry accept in high taxes. I am living on the same ground that I landed after leveing Nauvoo I lost my Wife about three years ago. I have hired a house keeper and am keeping house. I have sold all my land accept a house & lot

I am ready to gether with the Saints.

My age is something of a hindrence to my geting about my lims are sum affected. I had a lite shock of the polsy a fiew years ago and it trobbles me much a bout wrighting my hand is qute unstedy my age is Sevnty thre 73 years.

I am verry much interested in the gathering of the Juse [Jews] I take a paper printed in New York Citty by a Converted Ju he gets news from

Shabbona Grove DeKalb County Illinois
October 1st 1865

Dear Brotheren I recived your kind letter Sept the 26th
it did my soul good to hear from my ould friends, I left you
at Nauvoo not expecting to see you again, but the prospects are flattering
that we may meet together again.
I must give you a short history of my experiance at Nauvoo before
I left ine a praimetting sum six months before there was any appreciation
of Poligamy we was warned by the Spirit that the Lord a gone to
endow the Church with the gretest endowment that was ever
bestowed on Man and the Devel was much displeased with it
and determind to prevent it and would pour out the spirit of
adultry upon the hol Church which was the nearest spot to
take there so as in the world and we would very near
succeed in our throwing the Church but would not quite sicceed
and giving direction how we might no when it begun &c
with a long exortation to the saints to be ware of that spirit
this warning sunk deep into my mind and kept me on the lookout
and another thing decided the thing in my mind. Brother Joseph
came to me about two weeks before he was killed and said
Brother Marks I want to talk with you we went by our
selves and said this Poligamy business in the Church must
be stopt or the Church is ruined and we cant stay in the United
States I have been decieved in this thing and it must be put
down I thought it would be an advantage to Mankind but I
find it proves a curse I asked him how it could be dun
he said I must go into the high council and I would profer
charges agaist those in adultry and I must cut them off and
he would go into the stand and preach against it and
thought by so doing we might put it down but the mob
son commenced gethering and there was nothing dun.
I told sum of my friends what Broth Joseph had told me
& Brother Marks has apostizyed it is only sum of his lies I thought
if that was all they cared about it I would take there own
course and I want take nine wives nor all sols either
their there was much other conversation at then that I do not write

William Marks letter to Hyrum Faulk and Josiah Butterfield. Courtesy of Community of Christ Library and Archives.

I will give you a short scetch of the rise of the
of the reorganization of the Church there was sum
of the ould members of the Church living near
together and they commenced holding prair meetings
and soon they goot the spirit of prophesy and they
was told that young Joseph was the rightful are
to the presidency they soon gave notice for a Confrence
to the few scatered saints and so we begun together
to Confrence and we held a number and frequntly
was directed how to proceed and finaly we was commanded to organize on the Six of April 1860
and Broth Joseph would be ther to take his place
him and his Mother ware both ther it was dun
at Amboy about 25 miles from my place
it was the happyest day I think that I ever experenced
in my life I am liveing about 25 miles from
Plano where our paper is printed Brother Joseph
is expecte to Move there with his family in a few
days he has the charge of the Printing press
it seames our mission is to hunt up the ould saints
it appears the Lord is asending out his hunters to
hunt them up we have hunted up a goodly number
I apprehend the time is not far distant when we shall
be permited to go back to Mesora the land has been
litteraly been redeamed by blood one of our
nighbours was a Captian of a company was chaising
ould Price through Jackson County and other
Counties a joining he said he traveled forty
miles didnt see but one family the cuntry was
laid waste we have past through the war have not
sufered but verry little in this section of contry
exept in high taxes. I am living on the same ground
that I landed after leaving Nauvoo I lost my Wife about
three years ago I have hired a house keepir and am a
keepinghouse I have sold all my land acept a house & lot
I am ready to gather with the saints

William Marks letter to Hyrum Faulk and Josiah Butterfield. Courtesy of Community of Christ Library and Archives.

My age is something of a hindrence to my geting about my lims are sum affected I had a lite shock of the polsy a few years ago and it troubles me much about wrighting my hand is quite unstedy my age is seventy three 73 years. I am verry much interested in the getherin of the Jews I take a paper printed in New York City by a converted Jew he gets news from Jerusalem about every month said they are getherin from all parts and the City is fast building up
If I could see you all I could tell you much more then I can write

It was shone in the commencement that we must turn to the law given in the Book of Covenents and obzerve it and teach it to the saints and the revalations and be strict to observe them it was quite neglected formily
We have had a great deal of prejidice to overcum the name of Salt lak Marmons was a disgrace but we have satifyed the community in a mesure that we have no fellow ship for such doctrin as tought by Brigham
Our government sent a party of men through there this summer and they called on Brigham and have long talk on polygamy Brigham told them they had a Revilation to quit it. Mr Colfax told him he guest he would have a revalation to go out of it.
Brother Joseph is a verry discreat man not at all like his father rather slow to acte but very apt to teach and his teachings are good the Church is in a verry good situation in section of country we have some able ministers in the corum of the twelve Brother Buterfuld it rejois me much to learn that you and your wife have joined the reorganization I wish to be remembered to your wife and all of the brethren A man by the name of Capt Heman Hide I would like to hear from he was a naighbor to me in York State there was a good many oulde friends in Lawrence that I have allways remembered that I would like to hear from

William Marks letter to Hyrum Faulk and Josiah Butterfield. Courtesy of Community of Christ Library and Archives.

my address is Shabbona P. O. DeKalb County Ill

My family became so disgusted at the doings at
Nauvoo I fear they have lost all of their faith the
work all the sum of them have joined the Church
Goodrich and Sophiah are dead Goodrich
went to California, was at Saltlake died in
California

Brother Falk you did say that you had joined
the Church but I feared that you had by what
you said about the Sectarian Priest

Give my love to all the Bretheren tell them
we have got a Church established on pure principles
Hiram Falk and Josiah Butterfield
                                William Marks
NB, I have a son by the name of William nearly the same letters
that I have not on I would like to keep up a correspondence
                                Wm. Marks

William Marks letter to Hyrum Faulk and Josiah Butterfield. Courtesy of Community of Christ Library and Archives.

Jerusalem about evry month sais they are getherin from all parts and the Citty is fast building up

If I could see you all I could tell you much more than I can write

we was shone in the commencement that we must turn to the law given in the Book of Covents and obzerv it and teach it to the saints and the revalations and be strict to observe them it was quite neglected formily

We have had a great deal of prejidice to over cum the name of Satlak [Salt Lake] Mormons was a disgrace but we have satified the communty in a mesure that we have no fellow ship for has ^such^ doctrin as tought by Brigham

Ourr Government sent a party of ^men^ through there this summar and they called on Brigham and ^had a^ long talk on poligamy Brigham told then they had a Revilation to go in to it Mr. Colfax told him he guest he woul have a revalation to go out of it

Brother Joseph is a verry discreat man not at all like his father rather slow to acte but verry apt to teach and his teachings are good the Church is in a verry good situation in section of country we have some able ministers in the Corum of the twelve Brother Buterfield it rejoses me much to learn that you and your wife have joined the Reorganization I wish to be remembered to your wife and all of the Bretheren

A man by the name of Capt Heman Hide I woul like to hear from he was a naighbor to me in York State there was a good many ould frinds in Nauvoo that I have allways remembered that I would like to hear from

my address is Shabbony P.O. De Kalb County Ill

My family became so disgusted at the doings at Nauvoo I fear they have lost all of their faith in the in work all tho sum of them hav joined the Church

Goodrich and Sophiah are dead Goodrich went to Californy was at Saltlak died in Calliforny

Brother Falk you did say that you had joind the Church but i[n]fer[r]ed that you had by what you said about the Sectarin Priest

Give my love to all the Bretheren tell them we have got a Church established on pure principals

Hiram Falk and Josiah Butterfield

William Marks Sen

NB, I have a Son by the name of William near by he opens all letters that have ^not^ Sen on I woul like to keep up a corrspodace

Wm Marks

APPENDIX B

William Marks—Publications

William Marks and the High Council, "The High Council of the Church of Jesus Christ, to the Saints of Nauvoo, Greeting," *Times and Seasons* 3, no. 8 (February 15, 1842): 699–700.

THE HIGH COUNCIL OF THE CHURCH OF JESUS CHRIST TO THE SAINTS OF NAUVOO, GREETING:—

DEAR BRETHREN,—As watchmen upon the walls of Zion, we feel it our duty to stir up your minds, by way of remembrance, of things which we conceive to be of the utmost importance to the saints. While we rejoice at the health and prosperity of the saints, and the good feeling which seems to prevail among us generally, and the willingness to aid in the building of the "House of the Lord," we are grieved at the conduct of some, who seem to have forgotten the purpose for which they have gathered. Instead of promoting union, appear to be engaged in sowing strifes and animosities among their brethren, spreading evil reports; brother going to law with brother, for trivial causes, which we consider a great evil, and altogether unjustifiable, except in extreme cases, and then not before the world.—

We feel to advise taking the word of God for our guide, and exhort you not to forget you have come up as Saviors upon Mount Zion, consequently to seek each other's good,—to become one: inasmuch as the Lord has said, "except ye become one ye are none of mine." Let us always remember the admonitions of the Apostle:—"Dare any of you having a matter, to to law before the unjust and not before the saints? Do ye not know the saints shall judge the world? And if the world shall be judged by you, are ye unworthy to judge the smallest matter?— Know ye not that we shall judge Angels? How much more things that pertain to this life? If, then, ye have judgment of things pertaining to this life, set them to judge who are least esteemed in the church. I speak to your shame. Is it so, that there is not a wise man among you? no, not one that shall be able to judge between his brethren. But brother goeth to law with brother, and that before the unbelievers. Now therefore there is utterly a fault among you, because ye go to law one with another. Why do ye not rather take wrong? why do ye not rather suffer yourselves to be defrauded? Nay, ye do wrong, and defraud, and that your brother. Know ye not that the unrighteous shall not inherit the kingdom of God? Be not deceived; neither fornicators, nor adulterers, nor effeminate, nor abusers of themselves with mankind. Nor theives, nor covetous, nor drunkards, nor revilers, nor extortioners, shall inherit the kingdom of God. 1 Cor. 6:1-11. Who, observing these things, would go to law, distressing his brother; thereby giving rise to hardness, evil speaking, strifes and animosities amongst those who have covenanted to keep the commandments of God—who have taken upon them the name of saints, and if saints are to judge angels, and also to judge the world—why then are they not competent to judge in temporal matters, especially in trivial cases, taking the law of the Lord for their guide, brotherly kindness, charity, &c, as well as the law of the land. Brethren, these are evils which ought not to exist among us. We hope the time will speedily arrive when these things will be done away, and every one stand in the office of his calling, as a faithful servant of God—building each other up—bearing each other's infirmities, and so fulfill the law of Christ.

SAML. BENT,
LEWIS D. WILSON,
DAVID FULMER,
THOMAS GROVER,
NEWELL KNIGHT,
LEONARD SOBY,
JAMES ALLRED,
ELIAS HIGBEE,
GEORGE W. HARRIS,
AARON JOHNSON,
WM. HUNTINGTON, Sr.,
DANIEL CARRIER.
WILLIAM MARKS, President.
AUSTIN COWLES   }
CHARLES C. RICH   }Councellors.
Attest—HOSEA STOUT, Clerk.

William Marks and the High Council, "An Epistle," *Times and Seasons* 3, no. 15 (June 1, 1842): 809-810.

AN EPISTLE

Of the High Council of the Church of Jesus Christ of Latter Day Saints, in Nauvoo, to the saints scattered abroad, greeting:

Dear Brethren: inasmuch as the Lord hath spoken; and the commandment hath gone forth for the gathering together of his people from Babylon, that they may partake not of her sins, and receive not of her plagues;" it seemeth "good unto us, and also to the Holy Ghost" to write somewhat for your instruction, in obeying that commandment. That you have no need that we exhort you to the observance of this commandment, is evident; for yourselves know that this is that which was spoken by the Lord in the parable of the Tares of the field, who promised that in the harvest he would say to the servant, "gather the wheat into my barn;" the signs of the times proclaim this; the end of the world; and thus admonish us to the performance of this duty. "Yet notwithstanding the spirit testifieth of these things, and you desire with great anxiety to gather with the saints; yet are many of you hindered even to this day:" so that to will to obey the commandment is present; but how to perform, you find not." Feeling therefore, the responsibility binding on you to observe the statutes and commandments of the Lord, and living in the midst of a generation that are ignorant what the mind of the Lord is concerning his people, and of the things that belong to their peace: we are well aware of the embarrassments under which many of you labor in endeavoring to obey the laws pertaining to your salvation. It is then no marvel that in this day when darkdess [*sic*] covers the earth, and gross darkness the people," that this generation "who know not the day of their visitation, nor the dispensation of the fulness of the times in which they live, should mock at the gathering together of the saints for salvation, as did the antidiluvians at the mighty work of righteous Noah in building an ark in the midst of the land, for the salvation of his cause by water, seeing then that such blindness hath happened to the gentile world which to them is an evident token of perdition, but to you of salvation." and that of God, think it not strange that you should have to pass through the like afflictions which all your brethren the saints in all ages have done before you; to be reviled, persecuted, and hated of all men, for the name of Christ and the gospel's sake, is the portion of which all saints have had to partake who have gone before you. You then can expect no better things than that there be men of corrupt minds, reprobate concerning the truth, who will evil entreat you, and unjustly despoil you of your property and embarrass you in pecuniary matters, and render it the more difficult to obey the command to gather with the saints pretending to do God service, "whose judgment now lingereth not, and their damnation slumbereth not."

But brethren with all these considerations before you in relation to your afflictions, we think it expedient to admonish you, that you bear and forbear, as becometh saints, and having done all that is lawful and right to obtain justice of those that injure you wherein you come short of obtaining it, commit the residue to the just judgment of God, and shake off the dust off your feet as a testimony of having so done.

Finally, brethren, as it is reported unto us that there be some who have not done that which is lawful and right, but have designedly done injury to their neighbor, or creditor by fraud, or otherwise thinking to find protection with us in such iniquity: let all such be warned, and certified, that with them we have no fellowship when known to be such, until all reasonable measures are taken to make just restitution to thos unjustly injured.

Now therefore let this epistle be read in all the branches of the church, as testimony, that as representatives thereof, we have taken righteousness for the girdle of our loins, and faithfulness for the girdle of our reins," and that for Zion's sake we will not rest; and for Jerusalem's sake we will not hold our peace, until the righteousness thereof go forth as brightness and the salvation thereof as a lamp that burneth."

Your brethren and servants in the kingdom and patience of Jesus.

WILLIAM MARKS }
AUSTIN COWLES }Presidents
CHARLES C. RICH }
JAMES ALLRED
ELIAS HIGBEE
GEORGE W. HARRIS
AARON JOHNSON
WM. HUNTINGDON, SEN.
HENRY G. SHERWOOD
SAMUEL BENT
LEWIS D. WILSON,
DAVID FULMER,
THOMAS GROVER,
NEWELL KNIGHT,
LEONARD SOBY,
Attest, HOSEA STOUT, Clerk.
May 22, 1842

William Marks and the City Council, "Affidavit of the City Council," *Times and Seasons* 3, no. 19 (August 1, 1842): 869–70.

AFFIDAVIT OF THE CITY COUNCIL

We the undersigned members of the city council of the City of Nauvoo, testify that John C. Bennett was not under duress at the time that he testified before the city council May 19 th 1842 concerning Joseph Smith's innocence, virtue, and pure teaching—his statements that he has lately made concerning this matter are false,—there was no excitement at the time, nor was he in anywise threatened menaced or intimidated, his appearance at the city council was voluntary, he asked the privilege of speaking, which was granted, after speaking for some time on the city affairs, Joseph Smith asked him if he knew any thing bad concerning his public, or private character; he then delivered those statements contained in the testimony voluntarily, and of his own free will, and went of his own accord as free as any member of the council.

We further testify that there is no such thing as a Danite Society in this city nor any combination, other than the Masonic Lodge, of which we have any knowledge.

WILSON LAW,   GEO. A. SMITH,
JOHN TAYLOR,   GEO. W. HARRIS,
W. WOODRUFF,   N. K. WHITNEY,
VINSON KNIGHT,   BRIGHAM, YOUNG,
H. C. KIMBALL,   CHARLES C, RICH,
JOHN P. GREEN,   ORSON SPENCER,
WILLIAM MARKS,

Subscribed, and sworn to, by the persons whose names appear to the foregoing affidavit, this 20th day of July, A. D. 1842; except N. K. Whitney, who subscribed and affirmed to the foregoing this day, before me,

DANIEL H. WELLS,
Justice of the Peace, within and for Hancock County, Illinois.

William Marks, "Certificates of William and Henry Marks," *Times and Seasons* 3, no. 19 (August 1, 1842): 875.

CERTIFICATES OF WILLIAM AND HENRY MARKS

Inasmuch as John C. Bennett has called upon me through the Sangamo Journal to come out and confirm the statements which he has made concerning Joseph Smith and others, I take this opportunity of saying to the public, that I know many of his statements to be false, and that I believe them all to be the offspring of a base and corrupt heart, and without the least shadow of truth, and further that he has used my name without my permission. I believe him to be a vile and wicked adulterous man, who pays no regard to the principles of truth or righteousness, and is unworrhy [unworthy of] the confidence of a just community. I would further state that I know of no Order in the Church which admits of a plurality of wives, and do not believe that Joseph Smith ever taught such a doctrine, and further, that my faith in the doctrines of the Church of Jesus Christ of Latter Day Saints, and in Joseph Smith, is unshaken.

WILLIAM MARKS

Nauvoo, July 26, 1842.

Inasmuch as the Sangamo Journal has called upon me to come out and make an expose against Joseph Smith; this is to certify that I know nothing derogatory to the character of Joseph Smith, neither in a religious or a moral point of view; and that Doctor Bennett and the Journal used my name without my knowledge or consent; and further that I believe Doctor Bennett to be a bad man and unworthy of public confidence.

HENRY MARKS

Nauvoo, July 28, 1842.

William Marks, "To Whom it may Concern," *Times and Seasons* 4, no. 19 (August 15, 1843): 303.

Nauvoo, September 2d, 1843.
TO WHOM IT MAY CONCERN.
This is to certify that Elder George J. Adams has been honorably acquitted by the High Council in Nauvoo, from all charges heretofore preferred against him from any and all sources; and is hereby recommended as a faithful laborer in the Church of Jesus Christ of Latter Day Saints, and a servant of the Lord that is entitled to the gratitude, confidence, liberality and clemency of the Saints and honorable men in all the world.
WM. MARKS, President.
HOSEA STOUT, Clerk.

William Marks, "Notice," *Times and Seasons* 5, no. 23 (December 15, 1844): 742.

NOTICE!!
After mature and candid deliberation, I am fully and satisfactorily convinced that Mr. Sidney Rigdon's claims to the presidency of the church of Jesus Christ of Latter-day Saints, are not founded in truth. I have been deceived by his specious pretences, and now feel to warn every on over whom I may have any influence to beware of him, and his pretended visions and revelations. The Twelve are the proper persons to lead the church.
WILLIAM MARKS.
Nauvoo, Dec. 9, 1844.

Marks wrote three letters to Charles B. Thompson that were transcribed and published in Zion's Harbinger and Baneemy's Organ shortly after having been written:

William Marks, letter to Charles B. Thompson, June 1, 1852, Published in *Zion's Harbinger and Baneemy's Organ* 2 no. 7 (July 1852): 55.

MOVEMENTS OF THE COMMITTEE OF LOCATION
Brother Marks writes as follows:—
        SHABBANA, June 1st, 1852

Br. C. B. Thompson.
    Dear Sir—Yours of May 19th was received some two days since, but on account of a multitude of business I neglected to answer it immediately. I was extremely glad to hear from you, and shall always be happy to receive instruction on the great, and impor tant work that lies before us.
    I wrote you in my former letter that Bro. Childs had not made up his mind to accept the appointment as one of the Committee: but he came here some four days since, and said he had made up his mind to go with us, and we agreed to start the 13th day of June.
    * * * I received a letter from Bro. Stephens a few days ago: he states that he shall start for the upper country about the first of June, and will be ready to meet the balance of the Committee about the 25th of June, and I have made calculations accordingly.
    I have no news at present in relation to the work in this section of the country. I have been so busy in preparing for the discharge of the duties of the committee, that I have not spent any time to instruct others.
Yours in the bonds of the new covenant,
        WILLIAM MARKS.

William Marks, letter to Charles B. Thompson, February 17, 1853, published in *Zion's Harbinger and Baneemy's Organ* 3 no. 3 (March 1853): 20.

COMMUNICATIONS. SHABBONA GROVE, De Kalb co., Ills., Feb. 17. '53

Bro. C. B. THOMPSON:

Dear Sir:— I have some good news to communicate. I started from home on the 10th inst., called on Bro. Jno. Gould about 20 miles from my place, found him very feeble, but he started with me, and after travelling nine miles we stopped and administered the covenant to three persons; this was in the town of Fox, Kendall co., Ills. Here I left Bro. Gould to organize a class. I then travelled 30 miles to Batavia, Kane co., Ills., found Bro. Blakeslee and Bro. Savage, stopped with them over Sunday, and administered the covenant to four in that place. I find a good many of the former members of the church scattered around in this section of country, but they have been through so many isms, it is very difficult to make them believe the truth, many of them are disposed to abuse all who attempt to present anything that alludes to the latter-day work; nevertheless I should like to spend more time in trying to teach them, but my circumstances will not admit of it at present, besides it is very unpleasant travelling over these bleak prairies in the winter. I am making every preparation to leave here the 1st of April to go up to the Bluffs; my mill (a horse power sawmill) is to be finished then, and I have made arrangement for two or three men to go with me, that are used to the business of sawing lumber, to put the mill in operation at Kanesville, or in that vicinity. I organized a quorum at Batavia—James Blakeslee was chosen Chief and Jehial Savage Teacher. I ordained them to their offices, and they said they had a satisfactory evidence that the work is of God. I feel as though I was well paid. Bless and praise the Lord. I shall stop at the Assembly on my way to Kanesvile. No more at present. Yours in the bonds of the covenant, WM. MARKS.

William Marks, "Epistle," *Zion's Harbinger and Baneemy's Organ* 3, no. 7 (July 1853): 52–54.

EPISTLE.

of Wm. Marks, Chief Evangelical Teacher in the School of Faith, to all the Traveling Teachers, Quorums and Classes of said School, is Jehovah's Presbytery of Zion, Greeting;

BELOVED BRETHREN:

Having been chosen and ordained chief Evangelical Teacher of the Schools of Faith in Jehovah's Presbytery of Zion, it becomes my duty, to say something by way of encouragement. and also by way of instruction to those who are placed under my care, and supervision. and first, by way of encouragement let me state what I know in reference to the work in which we are engaged, in order to do this I must of necessity refer to my experience in the church. I was a member of the Church, some ten years before the death of Joseph and Hyrum Smith. I was appointed President of the Stake in Kirtland, Ohio. in 1837, and continued in that office at Kirtland until the fall of 1838, when I was called by Revelation to Far-West, Mo.: but before I arrived there. the Saints were ordered to leave the State: and when the Stake was organized at Nauvoo in the fall of 1839, I was appointed President thereof and continued in that office up to the death of Joseph the prophet. I always believed the work was of Divine origin, and that Joseph Smith was called of God to establish the church among the Gentiles.

During my administration in the church I saw and heard of many things that was practiced, and taught that I did not believe to be God; but I continued to do and teach such principles as were plainly revealed, as the law of the church, for I thought that pure and holy principles only would have a tendency to benefit mankind. Therefore when the doctrine of polygamy was introduced into the church as a principle of exaltation, I took a decided stand against it; which stand rendered me quite unpopular, with many of the leading ones of the church. I was also witness of the introduction (secretly,) of a kingly form of government, in which Joseph suffered himself to be ordained a king, to reign over the house of Israel forever; which I could not conceive to be in accordance with the law of the church, but I did not oppose this move, thinking it none of my business.

Joseph, however, became convinced before his death that he had done wrong; for about three weeks before his death, I met him one morning in the street, and he said to me, Brother Marks, I have something to communicate to you, we retired to a by-place, and set down together, when he said: "We are a ruined people." I asked, how so? he said: "This doctrine of polygamy, or Spiritual-wife system, that has been taught and practiced among us, will prove our destruction and overthrow. I have been deceived," said he, "in reference to its practice; it is wrong; it is a curse to mankind, and we shall have to leave the United States soon, unless it can be put down. and its practice stopped in the church. Now," said he. "Brother Marks; you have not received this doctrine, and how glad I am. I want you to go into the high council, and I will have charges preferred against all who practice this doctrine, and I want you to try them by laws of the church, and cut them off, if they will not repent, and cease the practice of this doctrine; and" said he, "I will go into the stand, and preach against it, with all my might, and in this way we may rid the church of this damnable heresy."

But before this plan could be put into execution, the mob began to gather, and our attention, necessarily, was directed to them.

I again met Joseph when he was about to start for Carthage. He said to me, "Bro. Marks, I have become convinced since I last saw you, that it is my duty to go to Carthage, and deliver myself up as a lamb to the slaughter."

I mentioned the circumstances of these conversations with Joseph. to many of the brethren, immediately after his death; but the only effect it had was to raise a report that Brother Marks, was about to apostatize: and my statement of the conversation in reference to the practice of polygamy, was pronounced false by the Twelve, and disbelieved; but I now testify that the above statements are verily true, and correct.

When I found that there was no chance to rid the church of that abominable sin, as I viewed it, I made my arrangements to leave Nauvoo, and I did so firmly believing that the plans and designs of the great Jehovah, in inspiring Joseph to bring forth the book of Mormon, would yet be carried out in his own time, and in his own way. Well brethren I have lived to see. the foundation, and the platform laid, the principles, revealed, and the order given, whereby the great work of the Father, can, and will be accomplished. There is no doubt resting on my mind in reference to this work of Baneemy being the work of God, for I am fully convinced that it is the work it purports to be, the work of the Father, spoken of in the book of Mormon, to prepare the way for the restoration of his covenants to the house of Israel. Now all who are convinced of this fact, ought to move forward and take a decided stand to labor for Jehovah and the benefit of mankind.

I intend from this time henceforth to labor in the cause, and give my influence, and substance to speed the work. Now, I call upon you my brethren, one and all, who have been ordained, and set apart to teach, and gather up the remnant seed of the church, to use all diligence and perseverance, to gather them up to the place of preparation, (which place will be made known through the Harbinger and Organ, in the sub-committee's report,) that we may be prepared, and receive the necessary instructions, to bear the kingdom to Israel.

It is necessary that all should bear in mind that the school of works in its first department will be opened at the next Solemn Assembly; and all should be prepared to send up an offering of sufficient magnitude to entitle them to receive a large blessing. The present impoverished condition of the Lord's treasury and the urgent necessity of obtaining a printing Press, and the removing of the Chief Teacher, to the place of gathering, and other contingent expenses, appeal forcibly to us, to bring a large offering to the next Solemn Assembly to meet the present requirements of the work. A printing Press, we must have, and Brother Thompson must be removed, which will require means to accomplish, and all should have the privilege of contributing their gift oblations, for the accomplishment of so desirable an object.

The gathering should be taught, and all who have means to remove and to sustain themselves through the winter should be to the place of gathering this fall, so as to get the necessary instructions, for the work hereafter to be assigned to them. I epect to be at the Solemn Assembly in August, and to go from thence to the place of gathering, there to remain during the winter, and I want the Chiefs of the different Quorums of Traveling Teachers to report to me as often as once in a month, that I may know of their whereabouts, and what they are doing, that I may communicate to them such information, as they need in reference to their mission, and that of their Quorums.

Signed, WM. MARKS.
St Louis, June 15, 1853.

William Marks, "For the Herald. Opposition to Polygamy, by the Prophet Joseph," *The True Latter Day Saints' Herald* 1, no. 1 (January 1860): 22–23.

For the Herald.

OPPOSITION TO POLYGAMY,
BY THE PROPHET JOSEPH.

BROTHER SHEEN.—I feel desirous to communicate through your periodical, a few guggesions [sic] made manifest to me by the Spirit of God, in relation to the Church of Jesus Christ of Latter-Day Saints. About the first of June, 1844, (situated as I was at that time, being the Presiding Elder of the Stake at Nauvoo, and by appointment the Presiding Officer of the High Council) I had a very good opportunity to know the affairs of the Church, and my convictions at that time were, that the Church in a great measure had departed from the pure principles and doctrines of Jesus Christ. I felt much troubled in mind about the condition of the Church. I prayed earnestly to my Heavenly Father to show me something in regard to it, when I was wrapt in vision, and it was shown me by the Spirit, that the top or branches had overcome the root, in sin and wickedness, and the only way to cleanse and purify it was, to disorganize it, and in due time, the Lord would reorganize it again. There were many other things suggested to my mind, but the lapse of time has erased them from my memory. A few days after this occurrence, I met with Brother Joseph. He said that he wanted to converse with me on the affairs of the Church, and we retired by ourselves. I will give his words verbatim, for they are indelibly stamped upon my mind. He said he had desired for a long time to have a talk with me on the subject of polygamy. He said it eventually would prove the overthrow of the Church, and we should soon be obliged to leave the United States, unless it could be speedily put down. He was satisfied that it was a cursed doctrine, and that there must be every exertion made to put it down. He said that he would go before the congregation and proclaim against it, and I must go into the High Council, and he would prefer charges against those in transgression, and I must sever them from the Church, unless they made ample satisfaction. There was much more said, but this was the substance. The mob commenced to gather about Carthage in a few days after, therefore there was nothing done concerning it. After the Prophet's death, I made mention of this conversation to several, hoping and believing that it would have a good effect, but to my great disappointment, it was soon rumored about that Brother Marks was about to apostatize, and that all that he said about the conversation with the Prophet was a tissue of lies. From that time I was satisfied that the Church would be disorganized, and the death of the Prophet and Patriarch, tended to confirm me in that opinion. From that time I was looking for a reorganization of the Church and Kingdom of God. I feel thankful that I have lived to again hehold [*sic*] the day, when the basis of the Church is the revelations of Jesus Christ, which is the only sure foundation to build upon. I feel to invite all my brethren to become identified with us, for the Lord is truly in our midst. WILLIAM MARKS *Shabbonas, De Kalb Co., Ill., Oct. 23, 1859.*

Bibliography

Abbreviations Used in Footnotes

CCLA — Community of Christ Library and Archives
CHL — LDS Church History Library
DEN — *Deseret Evening News*
DMR — *Daily Missouri Republican*
DN — *Deseret News*
DT — *The Daily Tribune*
EJ — *Elder's Journal*
EMS — *The Evening and the Morning Star*
FR — *Friendship Register*
GH — *Gospel Herald*
HHL — Henry E. Huntington Library
JD — *Journal of Discourses*
JH — *Journal of History*
JSP — *The Joseph Smith Papers*
LDP — *The Latter Day Precept*
MA — *Latter Day Saints' Messenger and Advocate*
MAR — *Latter Day Saints' Messenger and Advocate* [Rigdon]
MRLDS — *The Messenger of the Reorganized Church of Jesus Christ of Latter Day Saints*
NE — *Nauvoo Expositor*
NN — *Nauvoo Neighbor*
NYDT — *New York Daily Tribune*
PLDT — *Public Ledger and Daily Transcript*
PR — *Painesville Republican*
SJ — *Sangamo Journal*
SLDT — *Salt Lake Daily Tribune*
SP — James Jesse Strang Papers
TH — *The True Latter Day Saints' Herald*
TR — *The Return*
TS — *Times and Seasons*
VH — *Voree Herald*
WE — *Women's Exponent*
WL — *Western Luminary*
WS — *Warsaw Signal*
WWP — Wilford Woodruff Papers
ZHBO — *Zion's Harbinger and Baneemy's Organ*
ZR — *Zion's Reveille*

Works Cited

1850 U.S. census, DeKalb County, Illinois, schedule I, Shabbona Township, p. 351. Ancestry. www.ancestry.com.
"A Great Moral Victory." *Times and Seasons* 2, no. 8 (February 15, 1841): 320–21.
"Account of Hearing, 4 January 1843 [Extradition of JS for Accessory to Assault]." The Joseph Smith Papers. https://www.josephsmithpapers.org/paper-summary/account-of-hearing-4-january-1843-extradition-of-js-for-accessory-to-assault/1.
"Acts of the Solemn Assembly." *Zion's Harbinger and Baneemy's Organ* 2, no. 4 (April 1852): 31–32.
Adams, James M., et al. "To the Church of Jesus Christ of Latter Day Saints." *Zion's Reveille* 1, no. 11 (November 1846): 1–2.
"Affidavit, 1839 May 15." MS 892. LDS Church History Library, Salt Lake City, UT. https://catalog.churchofjesuschrist.org/assets/ac19f6b7-dd3a-45db-8bf9-8a5a72dc1f1b/0/.
"Affidavit from Daniel Avery, 28 December 1843." The Joseph Smith Papers. https://www.josephsmithpapers.org/paper-summary/affidavit-from-daniel-avery-28-december-1843/1.
"Affidavit of Austin Cowles." *Nauvoo Expositor* 1, no. 1 (June 7, 1844): 2.
"Affidavit of Leonard Soby." In *Doctrines and Dogmas of Mormonism Examined and Refuted* by Davis H. Bays, 378–79. St. Louis: Christian Publishing Company, 1897. https://archive.org/details/doctrinesdogmas00bays/page/378/mode/2up.
"Affidavit of the City Council." *Times and Seasons* 3, no. 19 (1 August 1842): 869–70.
"Affidavit of William Law." *Nauvoo Expositor* 1, no. 1 (June 7, 1844): 2.
"Alanson Ripley Statements, circa 1845 January." CR 100 396. LDS Church History Library, Salt Lake City, UT. https://catalog.churchofjesuschrist.org/assets/512f3b47-15d3-4d7e-ad74-7c2993f73564/0/0.
Allen, James B. *Trials of Discipleship: The Story of William Clayton, a Mormon*. Urbana: University of Illinois Press, 1987.
Anderson, Devery S. "The Anointed Quorum in Nauvoo, 1842–1845." *Journal of Mormon History* 29 no. 2, (2003): 137–57.
Anderson, Devery S., and Gary James Bergera. *Joseph Smith's Quorum of the Anointed, 1842–1845: A Documentary History*. Salt Lake City: Signature Books, 2005.
"The Annual Conference, Apr. 6, 1859." *Early Minutes of the Reorganization*, typescript. https://latterdaytruth.org/pdf/101027.pdf.
"Annual Conference, April 6, 1865." *The True Latter Day Saints' Herald* 7, no. 8 (April 15, 1865): 124–27. https://latterdaytruth.org/pdf/100913.pdf.
"Annual Conference, April 6–13, 1866." *The True Latter Day Saints' Herald* 9, no. 8 (April 15, 1866): 122–26. https://latterdaytruth.org/pdf/100933.pdf.
"AntiMormonism." *Zion's Reveille* 1, no. 11 (November 1846): 3.
"Articles of Agreement for the Kirtland Safety Society Anti-Banking Company, 2 January 1837." The Joseph Smith Papers. https://www.josephsmithpapers.org/paper-summary/articles-of-agreement-for-the-kirtland-safety-society-anti-banking-company-2-january-1837/3.

"Assignment of Judgment, 1 March 1838 [Rounds qui tam v. JS]." The Joseph Smith Papers. https://www.josephsmithpapers.org/paper-summary/assignment-of-judgment-1-march-1838-rounisaac ds-qui-tam-v-js/1.

"Austin Cowles letter Aug. 16, 1844." Brigham Young office files, 1832–1878, CR 1234 1. LDS Church History Library, Salt Lake City, UT. https://catalog.churchofjesuschrist.org/assets/a5524518-ef7b-4f5a-9fdf-ef615dd6a925/0/0.

"Authorization for Hyrum Smith and Isaac Galland, 15 February 1841–B." The Joseph Smith Papers. https://www.josephsmithpapers.org/paper-summary/authorization-for-hyrum-smith-and-isaac-galland-15february-1841-b/1.

"Authorization for Oliver Granger, 13 May 1839." The Joseph Smith Papers. https://www.josephsmithpapers.org/paper-summary/authorization-for-oliver-granger-13-may-1839/1.

"Autobiography, 30 March, 1881." MS 744. LDS Church History Library, Salt Lake City, UT. https://catalog.churchofjesuschrist.org/assets/2c0cb6bb-493b-417a-8bd5-dce48180827f/1/0.

Backman, Milton Vaughn, Jr., Keith Perkins, and Susan Easton Black. *A Profile of Latter-day Saints of Kirtland, Ohio and Members of Zion's Camp, 1830–1839: Vital Statistics and Sources*. Provo: Brigham Young University Department of Church History and Doctrine, 1983.

Beecher, Maureen Ursenbach, ed. "'All Things Move in Order in the City': The Nauvoo Diary of Zina Diantha Huntington Jacobs." *BYU Studies Quarterly* 19 (Spring 1979): 285–320.

Bennett, John C. "6th Letter From Gen. Bennett." *Sangamo Journal* 10, no. 52 (August 19, 1842): 2.

———. "Further Mormon Developments!! 2d Letter From Gen. Bennett." *Sangamo Journal* 10, no. 47 (July 15, 1842): 2.

———. "Gen. Bennett's third Letter." *Sangamo Journal* 10, no. 47 (July 15, 1842): 2.

Bennett, Richard E., and Rachel Cope. "'A City on a Hill'–Chartering the City of Nauvoo." *The John Whitmer Historical Association Journal* 21, Nauvoo Conference Special Edition (2002): 17–40. https://www.jstor.org/stable/i40125420.

Bent, Charles. *History of Whiteside County, Illinois: From Its First Settlement to the Present Time*. Clinton, IA: L. P. Allen, 1877.

Bergera, Gary James. "'Illicit Intercourse,' Plural Marriage, and the Nauvoo Stake High Council, 1840–1844." *The John Whitmer Historical Association Journal* 23 (2003): 59–90. http://www.jstor.org/stable/43200169.

———. "Identifying the Earliest Mormon Polygamists, 1841–44." *Dialogue: A Journal of Mormon Thought* 38, no. 3 (2005): 1–74.

Bishop, M. Guy, et al. "Death at Mormon Nauvoo, 1843–1845." *Western Illinois Regional Studies* 9, no. 2 (Fall 1986): 70–83.

Black, Susan Easton. *Early Members of the Reorganized Church of Jesus Christ of Latter Day Saints*. Provo: Brigham Young University Religious Studies Center, 1993.

———. *Membership of the Church of Jesus Christ of Latter-day Saints, 1830–1848*. 50 vols. Provo: Brigham Young University Religious Studies Center, 1984–1988.

Black, Susan E., Harvey B. Black, and Sarah Allen. "The University of the City of Nauvoo, 1841–1845." Wilmington, DE: World Vital Records, Inc., 2008.

Blair, Frederick B., comp. *The Memoirs of President W. W. Blair*. Lamoni, IA: Herald Publishing House, 1908.

Blair, W. W. "Letter from Bro. W. W. Blair." *The True Latter Day Saints' Herald* 18, no. 5 (March 1, 1868): 74–77. https://latterdaytruth.org/pdf/100180.pdf.

———. "The Successor of Joseph the Seer." *The Saints' Herald* 38, no. 1 (January 3, 1891): 1–4.

Blakeslee, James. "Having entered into the covenant of the Fathers myself." *Zion's Harbinger and Baneemy's Organ* 3, no. 3 (March 1853): 20–22.

"Blakeslee to Strang." Strang Manuscripts, Document 244. James Jesse Strang Collection. Yale University Beinecke Rare Book and Manuscript Library, New Haven, CT.

Boies, Henry L. *History of DeKalb County, Illinois*. Chicago: O. P. Bassett, 1868.

"Book of Assessment, Fourth Ward, 1842." MS 16800. LDS Church History Library, Salt Lake City, UT. https://catalog.churchofjesuschrist.org/assets/fd98b7e7-b8d4-4461-9c82-4decf0d987de/0/8.

"Book of Commandments, 1833." The Joseph Smith Papers. https://www.josephsmithpapers.org/paper-summary/book-of-commandments-1833/.

"The Book of the Law of the Lord." The Joseph Smith Papers. https://www.josephsmithpapers.org/paper-summary/the-book-of-the-law-of-the-lord/.

Braby, Junia. "Charles B. Thompson: Harbinger of Zion or Master of Humbuggary?" *John Whitmer Association Journal* 23 (2003): 149–64.

"Brainless Pseudoes." *Zion's Reveille* 1, no. 12 (December 1846): 2.

Briggs, Edmund C. "Autobiographic Sketch and Incidents in the Early History of the Reorganization.—No. 10." *The Saints' Herald* 48, no. 10 (March 6, 1901): 184–87.

———. "Autobiographic Sketch and Incidents in the Early History of the Reorganization.—No. 22." *The Saints' Herald* 50, no. 16 (April 22, 1903): 360–65.

———. *Early History of the Reorganization*. Centerplace. http://centerplace.org/library/books/EarlyHistoryoftheReorganization.htm.

Briggs, J. W. "J. W. Briggs Letters." *The Return* 4, no. 21 (December 1, 1895): 2–3.

Brodie, Fawn McKay. *No Man Knows My History: The Life of Joseph Smith, the Mormon Prophet*. New York: Vintage, 1995.

Brooks, Juanita, ed. *On the Mormon Frontier: The Diary of Hosea Stout, 1844–1861*. 2 vols. Salt Lake City: University of Utah Press, 1964.

Brown, Lisle G. *Nauvoo Sealings, Adoptions, and Anointings: A Comprehensive Register of Persons Receiving LDS Temple Ordinances, 1841–1846*. Salt Lake City: The Smith-Pettit Foundation, 2006.

Brown, Samuel Morris. *In Heaven as it is on Earth: Joseph Smith and the Early Mormon Conquest of Death*. Oxford: Oxford University Press, 2012.

Bruno, Cheryl L. "Keeping a Secret: Freemasonry, Polygamy, and the Nauvoo Relief Society, 1842–44." *Journal of Mormon History* 39, no. 4 (Fall 2013): 158–81.

———. "The Melodious Sounds of Baneemy's Organ." *John Whitmer Historical Association Journal* 34, no. 1 (May 2014): 151–76.

———. "Strangite Masonry and the Order of Illuminati." *Journal of Mormon History* 47, no. 3 (July 2021): 1–21.

Bruno, Cheryl L., Joe Steve Swick III, and Nicholas S. Literski. *Method Infinite: Freemasonry and the Mormon Restoration*. Salt Lake City: Greg Kofford Books, 2022.

Buerger, David John. *The Mysteries of Godliness: A History of Mormon Temple Worship*. San Francisco: Smith Research Associates, 1994.

Bump, Jacob, Leonard Rich, Amos Babcock, and S. B. Stoddard. Letter to James J. Strang, October 16, 1846. James Jesse Strang Papers, P11-9, F1, Community of Christ Library and Archives, Independence, MO.

Burdick, Thomas. "List containing the names of Ministers of the Gospel." *Latter Day Saints' Messenger and Advocate* 2, no. 9 (June 1836): 335–36.

Bushman, Richard Lyman. *Joseph Smith: Rough Stone Rolling, A Cultural Biography of Mormonism's Founder*. New York: Vintage, 2007.

Bushman, Richard Lyman, Ronald K. Esplin, Dean C. Jessee, eds. *The Joseph Smith Papers, Journals, Volume 1: 1832–1839*. Salt Lake City: Church Historian's Press, 2008.

Butler, John. "Autobiography of John Butler." Typescript. L. Tom Perry Special Collections, Harold B. Lee Library, Brigham Young University, Provo, UT.

Cannon, E. J. "Masonic." *Friendship Register* (July 18, 1876). Typescript at Uncle Dale's Readings in Early Mormon History. http://www.sidneyrigdon.com/dbroadhu/Y/miscNYS5.htm.

Carruth, LaJean Purcell, and Robin Scott Jensen. "Sidney Rigdon's Plea to the Saints: Transcription of Thomas Bullock's Shorthand Notes from the August 8, 1844, Morning Meeting." *BYU Studies Quarterly* 53, no. 2 (2014), 121–39.

"Celebration of the An[n]iversary of the Church—Military Parade—Prest. Rigdon's Address—Laying the Corner Stones of the Temple." *Times and Seasons* 2, no. 12 (April 15, 1841): 376.

"Cemetery record and store ledger, 1839–1845, 1861–1866." MS 22047. LDS Church History Library, Salt Lake City, UT. https://catalog.churchofjesuschrist.org/assets/1919c258-9ca1-40de-954c-4f4eb07e667f/0/0.

"Certificates of William and Henry Marks." *Times and Seasons* 3, no. 19 (August 1, 1842): 875.

"Chandler Rogers statement, 1845 September." CR 100 396. LDS Church History Library, Salt Lake City, UT. https://catalog.churchofjesuschrist.org/assets?id=88c01eb3-8d75-4fcb-9eba-de7159fbb75e&crate=0&index=0.

[Chapman Brothers]. *Portrait and Biographical Album of de Kalb*. Chicago: Chapman Brothers, 1885.

"Charles B. Hancock autobiography, circa 1882." MS 5285. LDS Church History Library, Salt Lake City, UT.

"Chauncy L. Higbee." *Nauvoo Neighbor* 2, no. 7 (May 29, 1844): 3.

"Chief Shabbona public profile." Geni. https://www.geni.com/people/Chief-Shabbona-aka-Shabonne/6000000040562563200.

"The City Charter: Laws, Ordinances, and Acts of the City Council of the City of Nauvoo. And also, the Ordinances of the Nauvoo Legion: from the commencement of the city to this date." LDS Church History Library, Salt Lake City, UT. https://catalog.churchofjesuschrist.org/assets?id=6eb08ee6-38af-4194-8136-ddc9ef91518f&crate=0&index=0.

"City Council Proceedings; Petitions, 1844 May–1844 December." MS 16800. LDS Church History Library, Salt Lake City, UT. https://catalog.churchofjesuschrist.org/assets?id=de1d32f5-3e42-4ad2-a5e0-05636671111a&crate=0&index=4.

Clark, John A. *Gleanings By the Way*. Philadelphia: W. J. and J. K. Simon, 1842. http://solomonspalding.com/docs1/1842ClkB.htm.

Clayton, William. *The Nauvoo Diaries of William Clayton, 1842–1846*. Salt Lake City: n.p., 2010.

"Complaint, 30 November 1842 [City of Nauvoo v. Davis for Slander of JS–C]." The Joseph Smith Papers. https://www.josephsmithpapers.org/paper-summary/complaint-30-november-1842-city-of-nauvoo-v-davis-for-slander-of-js-c/1.

"Conclusion of Elder Rigdon's Trial." *Times and Seasons* 5, no. 19 (October 15, 1844): 687.

"Conference at Voree." *Voree Herald* 1, no. 4 (February 1846): 17.

"Conference, Jun. 10, 1859." *Early Minutes of the Reorganization*, typescript. http://latterdaytruth.org/pdf/101028.pdf.

"Conference Minutes of the Church, Oct. 6, 1859." *Early Minutes of the Reorganization*, typescript. https://latterdaytruth.org/pdf/101029.pdf.

"Conference Minutes, Oct. 6, 1859." *The True Latter Day Saints' Herald* 1, no. 1 (January 1860): 20–21.

"Conference of the Church of Jesus Christ of Latter Day Saints, at Voree." *Gospel Herald* 2, no. 30 (October 14, 1847): 122–23.

"Continuation of Elder Rigdon's Trial." *Times and Seasons* 5, no. 18 (October 1, 1844): 666.

Cook, Lyndon. "Isaac Galland—Mormon Benefactor." *BYU Studies Quarterly* 19, no. 3 (Spring 1979): 261–84.

Corner Stones of "Reorganization": A Few Facts Concerning Its Founders . . . Compiled From Early Church History. Chicago: Northern States Mission, 1909.

Cornwall, Edward E. *William Cornwall and His Descendants: A Genealogical History of the Family of William Cornwall, One of the Puritan Founders of New England, Who Came to America in or before the Year 1633, and Died Middletown, Connecticut, in the Year 1678*. New Haven, CT: The Tuttle, Morehouse & Taylor Company, 1901.

Corrill, John. "From Missouri." *The Evening and the Morning Star* 2, no. 16 (January 1834): 124–26.

"Council." *The True Latter Day Saints' Herald* 7, no. 11 (June 1865): 163–64.

"Council of Fifty, Minutes, March 1844–January 1846; Volume 1, 10 March 1844–1 March 1845." Editorial note. The Joseph Smith Papers. https://www.

josephsmithpapers.org/paper-summary/council-of-fifty-minutes-march-1844-january-1846-volume-1-10-march-1844-1-march-1845/305.
"Council of Twelve Minutes, Book A." Community of Christ Library and Archives, Independence, MO.
"Covenant, to be taken on entering the Congregation of Jehovah's Presbytery of Zion." *Zion's Harbinger and Baneemy's Organ* 4, no. 1 (January 1854): 9.
Cowdery, Oliver. Letter to Joseph Smith, January 21, 1838. In Oliver Cowdery Letterbook, 1833–1838. Henry E. Huntington Library, San Marino, CA.
———. Letter to Warren A. Cowdery, January 21, 1838. In Oliver Cowdery Letterbook, 1833–1838. Henry E. Huntington Library, San Marino, CA.
Cowdery, Warren. "The Change of Times." *Latter Day Saints' Messenger and Advocate* 3, no. 9 (June 1837): 520–22.
———. "Freedom, April 3, 1835." *Latter Day Saints' Messenger and Advocate* 1, no. 7 (April 1835): 101.
Crary, Christopher B. *Pioneer and Personal Reminiscences*. Marshalltown, IA: Marshalltown Printing Co., 1898.
Davis, Inez Smith. *The Story of the Church*. Independence, MO: Herald Publishing House, 1938.
"Deed to William Marks, 5 November 1841." The Joseph Smith Papers. https://www.josephsmithpapers.org/paper-summary/deed-to-william-marks-5-november-1841/1.
"Deed, William and Rosannah Robinson Marks to Mead, Stafford & Co., 11 July 1837." The Joseph Smith Papers. https://www.josephsmithpapers.org/paper-summary/deed-william-and-rosannah-robinson-marks-to-mead-stafford-co-11-july-1837/2.
Deming, Arthur B. "James Thompson's Statement." *Naked Truths about Mormonism* 1, no. 2 (April 1888): 3.
Dinger, John S. "Joseph Smith and the Development of Habeas Corpus in Nauvoo, 1841–44." *Journal of Mormon History* 36, no. 3 (Summer 2010): 135–71.
———. "'A mean conspirator' or 'the noblest of men:' William Marks' Expulsion from Nauvoo." *The John Whitmer Historical Association Journal* 34, no. 2 (Fall/Winter 2014): 12–38.
———. *The Nauvoo City and High Council Minutes*. Salt Lake City: Signature Books, 2011.
———. "Sexual Slander and Polygamy in Nauvoo." *Journal of Mormon History* 44, no. 3 (July 2018): 1–22.
"Discourse, 3 October 1841 as Published in *Times and Seasons*." The Joseph Smith Papers. https://www.josephsmithpapers.org/paper-summary/discourse-3-october-1841-as-published-in-times-and-seasons/1.
"Discourse, 5 January 1841, as Reported by William Clayton." The Joseph Smith Papers. https://www.josephsmithpapers.org/paper-summary/discourse-5-january-1841-as-reported-by-william-clayton/.
"Discourse, 6 April 1837." The Joseph Smith Papers. https://www.josephsmithpapers.org/paper-summary/discourse-6-april-1837/.

"Discourse, 9 April 1842, as Reported by Wilford Woodruff." The Joseph Smith Papers. https://www.josephsmithpapers.org/paper-summary/discourse-9-april-1842-as-reported-by-wilford-woodruff/.

"Docket book of Ebenezer Robinson." In Chicago Historical Society collection of Mormon materials, 1836–1886. MS 8136. LDS Church History Library, Salt Lake City, UT.

"Docket Entry, between 30 November and circa 3 December 1842 [City of Nauvoo v. Davis for Slander of JS–C]." The Joseph Smith Papers. https://www.josephsmithpapers.org/paper-summary/docket-entry-between-30-november-and-circa-3-december-1842-city-of-nauvoo-v-davis-for-slander-of-js-c/1.

"Docket Entry, Costs, circa 5 June 1837 [Patterson and Patterson v. Cahoon, Carter & Co. and Rigdon, Smith & Cowdery]." The Joseph Smith Papers. https://www.josephsmithpapers.org/paper-summary/docket-entry-costs-circa-5-june-1837-patterson-and-patterson-v-cahoon-carter-co-and-rigdon-smith-cowdery/.

"Doctrine and Covenants, 1835." The Joseph Smith Papers. https://www.josephsmithpapers.org/paper-summary/doctrine-and-covenants-1835/.

Document Containing the Correspondence, Orders, &c, in Relation to the Disturbances with the Mormons; and the Evidence Given Before the Hon. Austin A. King. Fayette, MO: Boon's Lick Democrat, 1841. https://archive.org/details/documentcontaini00miss/page/97/mode/1up?view=theater.

Dowd, James. *Built Like A Bear.* Washington: Ye Galleon Press, 1979.

Ehat, Andrew F. "Joseph Smith's Introduction of Temple Ordinances and the 1844 Mormon Succession Question." Master's thesis, Brigham Young University, 1982. MSS 6154. L. Tom Perry Special Collections, Harold B. Lee Library, Brigham Young University, Provo, UT.

Ellis, Franklin, ed. *History of Cattaraugus: Illustrations And Biographical Sketches Of Some Of Its Prominent Men And Pioneers.* Philadelphia: L. H. Everts, 1879.

Ells, Josiah. "Bro. Ells' Rejoinder." *Zion's Harbinger and Baneemy's Organ* 3, no. 10 (October 1853): 73–80.

Encyclopaedia Britannica. https://www.britannica.com.

"Erastus Snow Journal, 1838 January–1841 June." MS 1329. LDS Church History Library, Salt Lake City, UT. https://catalog.churchofjesuschrist.org/assets/e6cc997c-1739-4acf-a9db-9185e6991036/0/104.

"Examination of John C. Elliott." *Nauvoo Neighbor* 2, no. 42 (February 19, 1845): 2.

"Far West Committee minutes." MS 2564. LDS Church History Library, Salt Lake City, UT. https://catalog.churchofjesuschrist.org/assets?id=b4a7fd1f-54f4-42be-a64c-0e16535d72f1&crate=0&index=6.

"Far West, Missouri, 1839 April 26." Historian's Office general Church minutes, 1839–1877. CR 100 318. LDS Church History Library, Salt Lake City, UT. https://catalog.churchofjesuschrist.org/assets?id=3f9eb33a-4b0a-4393-ad3e-9037384b9b8f&crate=0&index=0.

Faulring, Scott H., ed. *An American Prophet's Record: The Diaries and Journals of Joseph Smith.* Salt Lake City: Signature Books, 1989.

Flanders, John. "Do You Know that Wm. Marks." *The Latter Day Precept* 1, no. 6 (January 1920): 42.
Flanders, Robert B. *Nauvoo: Kingdom on the Mississippi*. Urbana: University of Illinois Press, 1975.
"For the Messenger and Advocate." *Latter Day Saints' Messenger and Advocate* [Rigdon] 1, no. 9 (March 1, 1845): 129.
Forscutt, Mark Hill. Journal. Mark Hill Forscutt Collection 1855–1900. MSS 811, Box 1, Folder 9. L. Tom Perry Special Collections, Harold B. Lee Library, Brigham Young University, Provo, UT.
"Funeral Sermon of Joseph and Hyrum Smith." MS 5878. LDS Church History Library, Salt Lake City, UT. https://catalog.churchofjesuschrist.org/assets/ab9cc5cb-e328-4c4c-be6b-b12382d08970/0/0.
Geauga County Deed Records. Book 23.
Geauga County Deed Records. Book 24.
"George W. Russell letter to A. M. Musser." Historian's Office history of persecutions, 1879–1880. CR 100 96. LDS Church History Library, Salt Lake City, UT. https://catalog.churchofjesuschrist.org/assets?id=48221650-0fd0-4e00-ba9e-09af2ba74959&crate=0&index=0.
Gilmore, John. Receipt #12744, 160 Acres, section 34, range 1. Illinois State Archives. RG 952.342. Register of Receipts June 1841–September 1844.
Gross, Lewis M. *Past and Present of DeKalb County, Illinois*. Chicago: Pioneer Publishing Company, 1907.
Grover, Thomas. "Elder Grover's Letter, Farmington, Jan 10, 1885." *Deseret Evening News* 19, no. 41 (January 11, 1886): 2.
"Growing Conflict in Illinois." In *Church History in the Fulness of Times* Student Manual, 263–71. Salt Lake City: The Church of Jesus Christ of Latter-day Saints, 2003.
Hajicek, John J., ed. *Chronicles of Voree, 1844–1849*. J. J. Hajicek, 1992.
Hales, Brian C. *Joseph Smith's Polygamy, Volume 1: History*. Salt Lake City: Greg Kofford Books, 2013.
"Hancock County justice of the peace docket." MS 8136. LDS Church History Library, Salt Lake City, UT. https://catalog.churchofjesuschrist.org/assets/fe5414e2-87cc-4727-8194-a5dd2cc2477f/0/0.
Heman C. Smith. "William Marks." *Journal of History* 1, no. 1(January 1908): 25.
"The High Council." *Voree Herald* 1, no. 2 (February 1846): 1–2.
"The High Council of the Church of Jesus Christ, to the Saints of Nauvoo, Greeting." *Times and Seasons* 3, no. 8 (February 15, 1842): 700.
Hill, Gordon Orville. "A History of Kirtland Camp: Its Initial Purpose and Notable Accomplishments." Master's thesis, Brigham Young University, 1975. https://scholarsarchive.byu.edu/cgi/viewcontent.cgi?article=5789&context=etd.
"Historian's Office History of the Church, 1844 August 9–1845 June 30." CR 100 102. LDS Church History Library, Salt Lake City, UT.
"Historian's Office, Martyrdom Account." The Joseph Smith Papers. https://www.josephsmithpapers.org/paper-summary/historians-office-martyrdom-account/86.

"Historical Department Journal History of the Church, 1838." CR 100 137. LDS Church History Library, Salt Lake City, UT. https://catalog.churchofjesuschrist.org/record/3ffad93a-5200-4a7e-9d68-2f4e42a13188/aa97d6d9-2160-4bcf-b2ce-8d30b5ce5843.

"Historical Department Journal History of the Church, 1844 January–June." CR 100 137. LDS Church History Library, Salt Lake City, UT. https://catalog.churchofjesuschrist.org/assets/defa0fde-6c02-4355-a87b-2aca53bb6344/0/0.

"Historical Department Journal History of the Church, 1844 July–December." CR 100 137. LDS Church History Library, Salt Lake City, UT. https://catalog.churchofjesuschrist.org/assets/35b0f8c1-9c1c-435a-890b-131709100e97/0/.

"Historical Department Journal History of the Church, 1845." CR 100 137. LDS Church History Library, Salt Lake City, UT. https://catalog.churchofjesuschrist.org/assets?id=2987565f-96fb-470c-88c0-08c3ec43e3fe&crate=0&index=63.

"History, 1834–1836." The Joseph Smith Papers. https://www.josephsmithpapers.org/paper-summary/history-1834-1836/.

"History, 1838–1856, volume A-1 [23 December 1805–30 August 1834]." The Joseph Smith Papers. https://www.josephsmithpapers.org/paper-summary/history-1838-1856-volume-a-1-23-december-1805-30-august-1834/.

"History, 1838–1856, volume B-1 [1 September 1834–2 November 1838]." The Joseph Smith Papers. https://www.josephsmithpapers.org/paper-summary/history-1838-1856-volume-b-1-1-september-1834-2-november-1838/.

"History, 1838–1856, volume C-1 [2 November 1838–31 July 1842]." The Joseph Smith Papers. https://www.josephsmithpapers.org/paper-summary/history-1838-1856-volume-c-1-2-november-1838-31-july-1842/.

"History, 1838–1856, volume C-1 Addenda." The Joseph Smith Papers. https://www.josephsmithpapers.org/paper-summary/history-1838-1856-volume-c-1-addenda/.

"History, 1838–1856, volume D-1 [1 August 1842–1 July 1843]." The Joseph Smith Papers. https://www.josephsmithpapers.org/paper-summary/history-1838-1856-volume-d-1-1-august-1842-1-july-1843/.

"History, 1838–1856, volume E-1 [1 July 1843–30 April 1844]." The Joseph Smith Papers. https://www.josephsmithpapers.org/paper-summary/history-1838-1856-volume-e-1-1-july-1843-30-april-1844/.

"History, 1838–1856, volume F-1 [1 May 1844–8 August 1844]." The Joseph Smith Papers. https://www.josephsmithpapers.org/paper-summary/history-1838-1856-volume-f-1-1-may-1844-8-august-1844/.

"History Draft [1 January–31 December 1840]." The Joseph Smith Papers. https://www.josephsmithpapers.org/paper-summary/history-draft-1-january-31-december-1840/.

"History Draft [1 January–30 June 1842]." The Joseph Smith Papers. https://www.josephsmithpapers.org/paper-summary/history-draft-1-january-30-june-1842/.

"History Draft [1 January–3 March 1843]." The Joseph Smith Papers. https://www.josephsmithpapers.org/paper-summary/history-draft-1-january-3-march-1843/.

"History Draft [1 January–21 June 1844]." The Joseph Smith Papers. https://www.josephsmithpapers.org/paper-summary/history-draft-1-january-21-june-1844/.

"History of Brigham Young, Nauvoo, Illinois." CR 100 102. LDS Church History Library, Salt Lake City, UT. https://catalog.churchofjesuschrist.org/assets/9d8bd63b-1a81-4f06-983e-34c343f844c2/0/173.

History of Friendship: sesquicentennial, 150 years of Friendship, 1815–1965. New York: Friendship Sesquicentennial Corporation, 1965.

"History of the Reorganization of the Church of Jesus Christ of Latter Day Saints." *The Messenger of the Reorganized Church of Jesus Christ of Latter Day Saints* 2, no. 7 (May 1876): 26–27.

Hogan, Mervin B. *The Official Minutes of Nauvoo Lodge U.D.* Des Moines, IA: Research Lodge No. 2, n.d.

Hollister, Hiel. *Pawlet for One Hundred Years.* Albany, NY: J. Munsell, 1867.

"Hotchkiss Purchase, Commerce, Illinois." The Joseph Smith Papers. https://www.josephsmithpapers.org/place/hotchkiss-purchase-commerce-illinois.

Howard, Richard P. "Reorganized Church of Jesus Christ of Latter Day Saints (RLDS Church)." In *Encyclopedia of Mormonism*, 4 vols., 3:1211–16. New York: Macmillan, 1992.

Howe, E. D. *Mormonism Unvailed.* Painesville: E. D. Howe, 1834.

Hutchins, Robert D. "President William E. Marks . . . A Man Forgotten." Unpublished paper, December 3, 1975.

"Illinois vs. Joseph Smith and O. P. Rockwell, on habeas corpus, 1842 August 8." In "Nauvoo (Ill.) records, 1841–1845, Judicial Proceedings, Municipal Court." LDS Church History Library, Salt Lake City, UT. https://catalog.churchofjesuschrist.org/assets/ed212139-d217-4525-a0f2-52ac7204ec8e/0/0.

"Indictment, circa 10 April 1839 [State of Missouri v. Gates et al. for Arson]." The Joseph Smith Papers. https://www.josephsmithpapers.org/paper-summary/indictment-circa-10-april-1839-state-of-missouri-v-gates-et-al-for-arson/.

"Instruction on Priesthood, between circa 1 March and circa 4 May 1835." The Joseph Smith Papers. https://www.josephsmithpapers.org/paper-summary/instruction-on-priesthood-between-circa-1-march-and-circa-4-may-1835-dc-107/.

"Introduction to Boosinger v. JS et al. and Boosinger v. O. Cowdery et al." The Joseph Smith Papers. https://beta.josephsmithpapers.org/paper-summary/introduction-to-boosinger-v-js-et-al-and-boosinger-v-o-cowdery-et-al/1.

"Isaac F. Scott to William E. McLellin, April 4, 1848." In *Papers from a Conflicted Family: Letters, Journals, and Histories of the Jacob and Sarah Warnock Scott Family 1839–1892*, compiled by Robert M. Call. Richmond, MO: Civicus, 2012.

Jackson, Joseph H. *A Narrative of the Adventures and Experience of Joseph H. Jackson in Nauvoo*. Warsaw, IL: 1844.

"James M. Monroe journal, 1822–1851." MS 7061. LDS Church History Library, Salt Lake City, UT. https://catalog.churchofjesuschrist.org/assets?id=66d24b60-0c34-4f70-a63f-63e4394944cb&crate=0&index=24.

James, Samuel. "For the Messenger and Advocate. Laharp, Ill. January 28th, 1845." *Latter Day Saint's Messenger and Advocate* [Rigdon] 1, no. 9 (March 1, 1845): 129–31.

Jensen, Robin Scott. "Gleaning the Harvest: Strangite Missionary Work, 1846–1850." Master's thesis, Brigham Young University, 2005.

"Jesse N. Smith autobiography and journal, 1855 October–1906 June." MS 1489. LDS Church History Library, Salt Lake City, UT. https://catalog.churchofjesuschrist.org/assets/c79a1a09-80ff-4509-9cbe-fd810a7d5fea/0/0.

Jessee, Dean C., and David J. Whittaker. "The Last Months of Mormonism in Missouri: The Albert Perry Rockwood Journal." *BYU Studies* 28 (Winter 1988): 5–41.

———. *Personal Writings of Joseph Smith*. Salt Lake City: Deseret Book, 2002.

"John Pulsipher Journal Vol. 1 (March 1835–October 1874)." MSS 1839. L. Tom Perry Special Collections, Harold B. Lee Library, Brigham Young University, Provo, UT.

"John Smith letter, Kirtland, OH, Jan. 1, 1838." MS 1322. LDS Church History Library, Salt Lake City, UT. https://catalog.churchofjesuschrist.org/assets/db0dc949-0eec-424e-92ec-282d8d8f2ea8/0/10.

"John Smith letter, Kirtland, OH, Jan. 15, 1838." MS 1322. LDS Church History Library, Salt Lake City, UT. https://catalog.churchofjesuschrist.org/assets/db0dc949-0eec-424e-92ec-282d8d8f2ea8/0/15.

"Jonathan H. Hale reminiscences and journals, 1837–1840." MS 1704. LDS Church History Library, Salt Lake City, UT.

Journal of Discourses. 26 vols. London and Liverpool: LDS Booksellers Depot, 1854–86.

"Journal, 1832–1834." The Joseph Smith Papers. https://www.josephsmithpapers.org/paper-summary/journal-1832-1834/.

"Journal, 1835–1836." The Joseph Smith Papers. https://www.josephsmithpapers.org/paper-summary/journal-1835-1836/.

"Journal, 1839." The Joseph Smith Papers. https://www.josephsmithpapers.org/paper-summary/journal-1839/.

"Journal, December 1841–December 1842." The Joseph Smith Papers. https://www.josephsmithpapers.org/paper-summary/journal-december-1841-december-1842/.

"Journal, December 1842–June 1844; Book 1, 21 December 1842–10 March 1843." The Joseph Smith Papers. https://www.josephsmithpapers.org/paper-summary/journal-december-1842-june-1844-book-1-21-december-1842-10-march-1843/.

"Journal, December 1842–June 1844; Book 3, 15 July 1843–29 February 1844." The Joseph Smith Papers. https://www.josephsmithpapers.org/paper-summary/journal-december-1842-june-1844-book-3-15-july-1843-29-february-1844/.

"Journal, December 1842–June 1844; Book 4, 1 March–22 June 1844." The Joseph Smith Papers. https://www.josephsmithpapers.org/paper-summary/journal-december-1842-june-1844-book-4-1-march-22-june-1844/.

"Journal, March–September 1838." The Joseph Smith Papers. https://www.josephsmithpapers.org/paper-summary/journal-march-september-1838/.

"Journal volume 1, 1845 May–1846 September." MS 8332. LDS Church History Library, Salt Lake City, UT. https://catalog.churchofjesuschrist.org/record/6e2c3cec-3d74-406b-9ff6-2ce427bd8b65/2efb3e0d-c41f-4f50-a590-47da6ef789ef

"Justice of the peace docket, 1837–1841." MS 29489. LDS Church History Library, Salt Lake City, UT. https://catalog.churchofjesuschrist.org/assets/9a77f750-7c5d-46c7-a252-2238ada5f8e0/0/0.

Kelley, Edmund L., and Clark Braden. *Public Discussion of the Issues between the RLDS Church and the Church of Christ (Disciples) Held in Kirtland, Ohio, Beginning February 12, and Closing March 8, 1884 between E. L. Kelley, of the Reorganized Church of Jesus Christ of Latter Day Saints and Clark Braden, of the Church of Christ.* Lamoni, IA: Herald Publishing House, 1913.

Kimball, Heber C. "Discourse." In "Historical Department Journal History of the Church," 339–41, under date of August 28, 1859. LDS Church History Library, Salt Lake City, UT.

———. "Epistle." *Times and Seasons* 6, no. 6 (April 1, 1845): 859–63.

Kimball, James L., Jr. "The Nauvoo Charter: A Reinterpretation." In *Kingdom on the Mississippi Revisited: Nauvoo in Mormon History*, edited by Roger D. Launius and John E. Hallwas, 39–45. Chicago: University of Illinois Press, 1996.

Kimball, Stanley B. *Heber C. Kimball: Mormon Patriarch and Pioneer*. Chicago: University of Illinois Press, 1981.

"Kirtland, Sept. 9th, 1837." *Latter Day Saints' Messenger and Advocate* 3, no. 12 (September 1837): 574.

"Kirtland elders' certificates, 1836–1838." CR 100 401. LDS Church History Library, Salt Lake City, UT.

"Kirtland Elders Quorum Record 1836–1841." Community of Christ Library and Archives, Independence, MO.

"Kirtland High Council minutebook, Conference A, 1832–1837." MS 3432. LDS Church History Library, Salt Lake City, UT.

Launius, Roger D. "An Ambivalent Rejection: Baptism for the Dead and the Reorganized Church Experience." *Dialogue: A Journal of Mormon Thought* 23, no. 2 (1990): 61–84.

Law, William. "The Law Interview." *The Daily Tribune*. July 31, 1887. Transcript at Mormon Research Ministry. https:// www.mrm.org/law-interview.

———. "Law Nauvoo Diary, 1 January 1844." In *William Law: Biographical Essay, Nauvoo Diary, Correspondence, Interview*, compiled by Lyndon W. Cook. Orem, UT: Grandin Book, 1994.

Leonard, Glen M. *Nauvoo: A Place of Peace, a People of Promise*. Salt Lake City: Deseret Book, 2002.

"Letter from William Perkins, 29 October 1838." The Joseph Smith Papers. https://www.josephsmithpapers.org/paper-summary/letter-from-william-perkins-29-october-1838/.

"Letter to Edward Partridge and the Church, circa 22 March 1839." The Joseph Smith Papers. https://www.josephsmithpapers.org/paper-summary/letter-to-edward-partridge-and-the-church-circa-22-march-1839/.

"Letter to Horace Hotchkiss, 25 August 1841, Copy." The Joseph Smith Papers. https://www.josephsmithpapers.org/paper-summary/letter-to-horace-hotchkiss-25-august-1841-copy/2.

"Letter to Isaac Galland, 22 March 1839." The Joseph Smith Papers. https://www.josephsmithpapers.org/paper-summary/letter-to-isaac-galland-22-march-1839/.

"Letter to the Church and Edward Partridge, 20 March 1839." The Joseph Smith Papers. https://www.josephsmithpapers.org/paper-summary/letter-to-the-church-and-edward-partridge-20-march-1839/.

"Letter to the Saints Abroad, 24 May 1841." The Joseph Smith Papers. https://www.josephsmithpapers.org/paper-summary/letter-to-the-saints-abroad-24may-1841/1.

"Letter to William Marks and Newel K. Whitney, 8 July 1838." The Joseph Smith Papers. https://www.josephsmithpapers.org/paper-summary/letter-to-william-marks-and-newel-k-whitney-8-july-1838/1.

"Letter, Vinalhaven, Maine, to Wilford Woodruff, Castline, Maine, March 1, 1838." MS 19509. LDS Church History Library, Salt Lake City, UT. https://catalog.churchofjesuschrist.org/assets/dde2b192-608e-4720-a9e1-e7bf6e4b8050/0/1.

"Letterbook 2." The Joseph Smith Papers. https://www.josephsmithpapers.org/paper-summary/letterbook-2/.

"Letters from John C. Bennett and James Sloan, 17 May 1842." The Joseph Smith Papers. https://www.josephsmithpapers.org/paper-summary/letters-from-john-c-bennett-and-james-sloan-17-may-1842/1.

Lewis, Ann Laemmlen. "Death of Mary Clift Turley, wife of Theodore, 30 March 1850, Salt Lake City." Ann's Stories, March 30, 2017. https://annlaemmlenlewis1.wordpress.com/2017/03/30/death-of-mary-clift-turley-wife-of-theodore-30-march-1850-salt-lake-city/.

Lewis, David Rich. "'For life, the resurrection, and the life everlasting': James J. Strang and Strangite Mormon Polygamy, 1849–1856." *Wisconsin Magazine of History* 66, no. 4 (Summer 1983): 274–91.

"Life Story of Sidney Rigdon." MS 3451. LDS Church History Library, Salt Lake City, UT. https://catalog.churchofjesuschrist.org/assets/a4629ae5-a0a6-445f-bdf4-dda30a7e743a/0/1.

"List of Agents." *Latter Day Saint's Messenger and Advocate* [Rigdon] 1, no. 4 (December 16, 1845): 64; 1, no. 5 (January 1, 1846): 80.

"List of Letters." *Zion's Harbinger and Baneemy's Organ* 3, no. 9 (September 1854): 69.

"List of Members, Council of Fifty, probably between 25 April and 3 May 1844." The Joseph Smith Papers. https://www.josephsmithpapers.org/paper-summary/list-of-members-council-of-fifty-probably-between-25-april-and-3-may-1844/1.

Loving, Kim L. "Ownership of the Kirtland Temple: Legends, Lies, and Misunderstandings." *Journal of Mormon History* 30, no. 2 (2004): 1–80.

Mace, Wandle. "Journal of Wandle Mace." Typescript. Harold B. Lee Library, Brigham Young University, Provo, UT. http://www.boap.org/LDS/Early-Saints/WMace.html.

Mahas, Jeffrey David. "'I Intend to get up a Whistling School:' The Nauvoo Whistling and Whittling Movement, American Vigilante Tradition, and Mormon Theocratic Thought." *Journal of Mormon History* 43, no. 4 (October 2017): 37–67.

Maki, Elizabeth. "'Go to the Ohio.'" In *Revelations in Context*, edited by Matthew McBride and James Goldberg, 70–73. Salt Lake City: The Church of Jesus Christ of Latter-day Saints, 2016.

Malmene, Waldemar. *The Freemason's Hymnal: A Collection of Original and Selected Hymns, Odes, and Songs for the use of Lodges, Chapters, and Commanderies*. St. Louis: Southwestern Book and Publishing Company, 1875.

Marks, C. R. "Monona County, Iowa, Mormons." In *Proceedings of the Academy of Science and Letters of Sioux City, 1903–4*. Vol. 1. Sioux City, IA: Academy of Science and Letters of Sioux City, 1904–1906.

"Marks, William." The Joseph Smith Papers. https://www.josephsmithpapers.org/person/william-marks.

Marks, William. "Communications." *Zion's Harbinger and Baneemy's Organ* 3, no. 3 (March 1853): 20.

———. "Epistle." *Zion's Harbinger and Baneemy's Organ* 3 no. 7 (July 1853): 52–54.

———. Letter to Hyrum Faulk and Josiah Butterfield, October 1, 1865. Typescript in Inez Smith Davis Papers, P12-1, f13. Community of Christ Library and Archives, Independence, MO.

———. Letter to James M. Adams, April 23, 1852. Typescript in Inez Smith Davis Papers, P23, f61. Community of Christ Library and Archives, Independence, MO.

———. Letter to James M. Adams, July 26, 1855. Typescript in Inez Smith Davis Papers, P23, f61. Community of Christ Library and Archives, Independence, MO.

———. Letter to James M. Adams, June 11, 1855. Typescript in Inez Smith Davis Papers, P23, f61. Community of Christ Library and Archives, Independence, MO.

———. Letter to James M. Adams, March 16, 1856. Typescript in Inez Smith Davis Papers, P23, f61. Community of Christ Library and Archives, Independence, MO.

———. Letter to James M. Adams, March 18, 1854. Original letter in Miscellaneous Letters and Papers, P13, f96. Community of Christ Library and Archives, Independence, MO.

———. Letter to James M. Adams, May 20, 1855. Typescript in Inez Smith Davis Papers, P23, f61. Community of Christ Library and Archives, Independence, MO.

———. Letter to James M. Adams, November 15, 1854. Typescript in Inez Smith Davis Papers, P23, f61. Community of Christ Library and Archives, Independence, MO.

———. Letter to James M. Adams, September 23, 1855. Typescript in Inez Smith Davis Papers, P23, f61. Community of Christ Library and Archives, Independence, MO.

———. Letter to James Strang, May 23, 1847. James Jesse Strang Collection, Beinecke Library, Yale University, New Haven, CT.

———. "Movements of the Committee of Location." *Zion's Harbinger and Baneemy's Organ* 2, no. 7 (July 1852): 55.

———. "News from the Committee of Location." *Zion's Harbinger and Baneemy's Organ* 2, no. 9 (September 1852): 71–72.

———. "Notice." *Times and Seasons* 5, no. 23 (December 15, 1844): 740–42.

———. "Opposition to Polygamy by the Prophet Joseph." *The True Latter-day Saints Herald* 1, no. 1 (January 1860): 25–26.

Marsh, Thomas B. "Dear Brother, We Lament that Such Foul and False Reports Should Be Circulated." *Elder's Journal* (July 1838): 45–46.

"Mary Fielding Smith letters to Hyrum Smith, 1839, 1842." MS 2779. LDS Church History Library, Salt Lake City, UT. https://catalog.churchofjesuschrist.org/assets/cf9f4a90-ef84-488d-8040-e411c4dea4f7/0/4.

Mead, Stith, ed. *A General Selection of the Newest and Most Admired Hymns and Spiritual Songs Now in Use.* 2nd ed. Lynchburg, VA.: Jacob Haas, 1811.

Miller, George. "George Miller letter, June 26, 1855." In "De Tal Palo Tal Astillo," compiled by H. W. Mills. *Annual Publication of the Historical Society of Southern California* 10, no. 3 (1917): 86–172.

Minard, John Stearns, and Georgia Drew Merrill, eds. *Allegany County and its People: A Centennial Memorial History of Allegany County, New York.* Alfred, NY: W. A. Fergusson & Co., 1896.

"Minute Book 1." The Joseph Smith Papers. https://www.josephsmithpapers.org/paper-summary/minute-book-1/241.

"Minute Book 2." The Joseph Smith Papers. https://www.josephsmithpapers.org/paper-summary/minute-book-2/.

"Minutes, 15 February 1841, Draft." The Joseph Smith Papers. https://www.josephsmithpapers.org/paper-summary/minutes-15-february-1841-draft/.

"Minutes, 17 September 1837–B." The Joseph Smith Papers. https://www.josephsmithpapers.org/paper-summary/minutes-17-september-1837-b/1.

"Minutes, 1839 October 20–1840 May 2." LR 3102 22. LDS Church History Library, Salt Lake City, UT. https://catalog.churchofjesuschrist.org/assets/51afec20-84fe-4da4-b423-7b8de8fb5422/0/0.

"Minutes, 1840 March 8–1842 May 20." LR 3102 22. LDS Church History Library, Salt Lake City, UT. https://catalog.churchofjesuschrist.org/assets/75eb5e4f-7d07-4136-807c-e16a3b03c11b/0/.

"Minutes, 1842 May 20–1843 February 19." LR 3102 22. LDS Church History Library, Salt Lake City, UT. https://catalog.churchofjesuschrist.org/assets/1a3b9e33-bf31-4e57-afb7-9aa73039034c/0/0.

"Minutes, 1843 February 25–1844 May 11." LR 3102 22. LDS Church History Library, Salt Lake City, UT. https://catalog.churchofjesuschrist.org/assets/e7896b07-224e-4dd8-8790-b7f995838c46/0/13.

"Minutes, 1844 May 18–September 10." LR 3102 22. LDS Church History Library, Salt Lake City, UT. https://catalog.churchofjesuschrist.org/assets?id=03907391-af2e-48d2-a438-eaeb7f58cb8f&crate=0&index=2.

"Minutes, 1844 September 21–1845 January 11." LR 3102 22. LDS Church History Library, Salt Lake City, UT. https://catalog.churchofjesuschrist.org/assets/bfbd5238-6eb5-4fc5-8e0e-5b8af7946efd/0/0.

"Minutes, 1844 September 27." LR 3102 28. LDS Church History Library, Salt Lake City, UT. https://catalog.churchofjesuschrist.org/record/e1e728e4-7486-4f84-afac-31603df86d43/0?view=summary&lang=eng.

"Minutes, 19 May 1842." The Joseph Smith Papers. https://www.josephsmithpapers.org/paper-summary/minutes-19-may-1842/1.

"Minutes, 27 May 1843." The Joseph Smith Papers. https://www.josephsmithpapers.org/paper-summary/minutes-27-may-1843/.

"Minutes, 3 September 1837." The Joseph Smith Papers. https://www.josephsmithpapers.org/paper-summary/minutes-3-september-1837/3.

"Minutes, 30 January 1843." The Joseph Smith Papers. https://www.josephsmithpapers.org/paper-summary/minutes-30-january-1843/.

"Minutes, 7–11 April 1841." The Joseph Smith Papers. https://www.josephsmithpapers.org/paper-summary/minutes-7-11april-1841/1.

"Minutes, 9 November 1844, Draft." The Joseph Smith Papers. https://www.josephsmithpapers.org/paper-summary/minutes-9-november-1844-draft/.

"Minutes and Discourses, 5–7 October 1839." The Joseph Smith Papers. https://www.josephsmithpapers.org/paper-summary/minutes-and-discourses-5-7-october-1839/1.

"Minutes, Discourse, and Blessings, 14–15 February 1835." The Joseph Smith Papers. https://www.josephsmithpapers.org/paper-summary/minutes-discourse-and-blessings-14-15-february-1835/1.

"Minutes, meeting of the First Presidency and Quorum of Twelve, Fox River, Illinois (May 1, 1865)." Council of Twelve Minutes, Book A, 11–12. Community of Christ Library and Archives, Independence, MO.

"Minutes of a Conference, Apr. 6, 1857." *Early Minutes of the Reorganization*, typescript. https://latterdaytruth.org/pdf/101023.pdf

"Minutes of a Conference, Apr. 6, 1858." *Early Minutes of the Reorganization*, typescript. https://latterdaytruth.org/pdf/101025.pdf.

"Minutes of a Conference, June 12, 1852." *Early Minutes of the Reorganization*, typescript. http://latterdaytruth.org/pdf/101013.pdf.

"Minutes of a Conference, Oct. 6, 1852." *Early Minutes of the Reorganization*, typescript. http://latterdaytruth.org/pdf/101014.pdf.

"Minutes of a Conference, Oct. 6, 1855." *Early Minutes of the Reorganization*, typescript. http://latterdaytruth.org/pdf/101020.pdf.

"Minutes of a Conference of the Church of Jesus Christ of Latter Day Saints, held in Voree August 25th and 26th, 1849." *Gospel Herald* 4, no. 24 (August 30, 1849): 106–7.

"Minutes of a special meeting of the Church, 1844 Sep. 8, 10–12." MS 23159. LDS Church History Library, Salt Lake City, UT. https://catalog.churchofjesuschrist.org/assets/aa68abe3-e44f-412b-8eee-e5f1044988f3/0/.

"Minutes of the Annual Conference, April 6, 1860." *Early Minutes of the Reorganization*, typescript. https://latterdaytruth.org/pdf/101030.pdf.

"Minutes of the Annual Conference of the Church of Jesus Christ of Latter Day Saints, held at Voree April 6th, 7th, 8th and 9th, 1848." *Gospel Herald* 3, no. 4 (April 13, 1848): 16.

"Minutes of the Annual Conference of the Church of Jesus Christ of Latter Day Saints, held at Voree on the Sixth, Seventh and Eighth of October, 1848." *Gospel Herald* 3, no. 30 (October 12. 1848): 146–47.

"Minutes of the Annual Conference of the Church of Jesus Christ of Latter Day Saints, held in Voree on the Sixth, Seventh, and Eighth of April, 1849." *Gospel Herald* 4, no. 4 (April 12, 1849): 15–16.

"Minutes of the Annual Conference of the Church of Jesus Christ of Latter Day Saints, held in Voree on the Sixth, Seventh, and Eighth of April, 1849, concluded." *Gospel Herald* 4, no. 5 (April 19, 1849): 17–18.

"Minutes of the Annual Conference, April 6th, 1863." *The True Latter Day Saints' Herald* 3, no. 10 (April 1863): 193–98.

"Minutes of the first Tri-annual Solemn Assembly of the Schools of Preparation." *Zion's Harbinger and Baneemy's Organ* 3, no. 4 (April 1853): 30–32.

"Minutes of the High Council at Voree." October 4, 1846. James Jesse Strang Collection. WA MSS 447. Beinecke Library, Yale University, New Haven, CT.

"Minutes of the Semi-Annual Conference, Oct. 6th to 9th, 1860." *The Saints' Herald* 1, no. 10 (October 1860): 235–39.

Moody, Thurmon Dean. "Nauvoo's Whistling and Whittling Brigade." *BYU Studies* 15, no. 4 (1975): 480–90. https://scholarsarchive.byu.edu/byusq/vol15/iss4/8.

Morgan, William. *Illustrations of Masonry by One of the Fraternity Who has Devoted Thirty Years to the Subject*. Batavia, NY: 1826.

"The Mormon Conference." *The True Latter Day Saints' Herald* 1, no. 5 (May 1860): 101–5. https://latterdaytruth.org/pdf/100724.pdf.

"Mormonism." *Western Luminary* 3, no. 43 (October 26, 1844): 344.

"The Mormons' City." *Daily Missouri Republican* 19, no. 2347 (April 20, 1841).

"Mormontown: The History of a Little Understood Settlement in Pike County, Illinois." MS 23667. LDS Church History Library, Salt Lake City, UT. https://catalog.churchofjesuschrist.org/assets/dd98880f-f402-485f-9ef6-d774bb66cded/0/0.

"Motion from William Marks, 15 January 1842." The Joseph Smith Papers. https://www.josephsmithpapers.org/paper-summary/motion-from-william-marks-15-january-1842/1.

Mulder, William. "Mormonism's 'Gathering': an American Doctrine with a Difference." *Church History* 23, no. 3 (September 1954): 248–64.

"Municipal Court." *Times and Seasons* 5, no. 10 (May 15, 1844): 538–40.

"Municipal court attendance reports, 1843–1845." MS 16800. LDS Church History Library, Salt Lake City, UT. https://catalog.churchofjesuschrist.org/assets?id=c6e85994-9abf-462f-8a99-21b6f8a196b1&crate=0&index=0.

"Municipal Election." *Times and Seasons* 2, no. 7 (February 1, 1841): 309.

"Nauvoo City Council Minute Book, 1841–1845." The Joseph Smith Papers. https://www.josephsmithpapers.org/paper-summary/nauvoo-city-council-minute-book-1841-1845/1.

"Nauvoo City Council Proceedings." MS 3435. LDS Church History Library, Salt Lake City, UT. https://catalog.churchofjesuschrist.org/assets?id=a67c7db2-98d3-43a7-9405-f37832f9c988&crate=0&index=46.

"Nauvoo City Council Rough Minute Book, February 1844–January 1845." The Joseph Smith Papers. https://www.josephsmithpapers.org/paper-summary/nauvoo-city-council-rough-minute-book-february-1844-january-1845/.

"Nauvoo City Council Rough Minute Book, February–December 1841." The Joseph Smith Papers. https://www.josephsmithpapers.org/paper-summary/nauvoo-city-council-rough-minute-book-february-december-1841/.

"Nauvoo City Council Rough Minute Book, January–November 1842." The Joseph Smith Papers. https://www.josephsmithpapers.org/paper-summary/nauvoo-city-council-rough-minute-book-january-november-1842/.

"Nauvoo City Council Rough Minute Book, November 1842–January 1844." The Joseph Smith Papers. https://www.josephsmithpapers.org/paper-summary/nauvoo-city-council-rough-minute-book-november-1842-january-1844/.

"Nauvoo Fourth Ward, Record of Membership, 1842." CR 387 44. LDS Church History Library, Salt Lake City, UT. https://catalog.churchofjesuschrist.org/assets/1e60f152-1878-4bdf-8f0f-96e970172a1e/0/0.

"Nauvoo Mayor's Court docket book, 1841 October–1843 February." MS 3434. LDS Church History Library, Salt Lake City, UT. https://catalog.churchofjesuschrist.org/assets/69ef22bb-90bf-47ff-8fc1-25c60ceb8c2e/0/66.

"Nauvoo Stake High Council papers, 1840 October–1842 November." LR 3102 23. LDS Church History Library, Salt Lake City, UT. https://catalog.churchofjesuschrist.org/assets/54e77dc8-00a7-4996-b3db-413872df5dee/0/52.

"Newel Knight autobiography, circa 1871." MS 19156. LDS Church History Library, Salt Lake City, UT.

Newell, Linda King, and Valeen Tippetts Avery. *Mormon Enigma: Emma Hale Smith, Prophet's Wife, "Elect Lady," Polygamy's Foe, 1804–1879.* Urbana and Chicago: University of Illinois Press, 1994.

"Newspapers of James J. Strang: 1846–1847 Articles." Uncle Dale's Readings in Mormon History. Accessed May 7, 2024, http://www.sidneyrigdon.com/dbroadhu/ia/jstrang1.htm#101447.

"Notice." *Latter Day Saints' Messenger and Advocate* 3, no. 7 (April 1837): 496.

"Notice, 11 May 1842." The Joseph Smith Papers. https://www.josephsmithpapers.org/paper-summary/notice-11-may-1842/1.

Nuttall, L. John. "L. John Nuttall journal, 1876–1877." MSS 790. L. Tom Perry Special Collections, Harold B. Lee Library, Brigham Young University, Provo, UT.

Oaks, Dallin H., and Marvin S. Hill. *Carthage Conspiracy: The trial of the accused assassins of Joseph Smith.* Urbana: University of Illinois Press, 1979.

"Oaths from Nauvoo City Officers, 3 and 8 February 1841." The Joseph Smith Papers. https://www.josephsmithpapers.org/paper-summary/oaths-from-nauvoo-city-officers-3-and-8-february-1841/1.

"Obituary of Elder Wm. Marks." *The True Latter-day Saints Herald* 19, no. 11 (June 1, 1872): 336.

"Officers of the Nauvoo Legion." MS 20447. LDS Church History Library, Salt Lake City, UT. https://catalog.churchofjesuschrist.org/assets?id=a5fa1b03-2dec-4ecc-8317-3779af9424a6&crate=0&index=0.

"Oliver Cowdery diary, 1836 January–March." MS 3429. LDS Church History Library, Salt Lake City, UT. https://catalog.churchofjesuschrist.org/assets/d11962ee-4618-4177-90aa-aa72cedc0f98/0/33.

"On the 6th day of April." *Voree Herald* 1, no. 6 (June 1846): 27.

"Ordinance, 14 May 1842–A." The Joseph Smith Papers. https://www.josephsmithpapers.org/paper-summary/ordinance-14-may-1842-a/1.

"Ordinance, 5 July 1842–A, as Published in the Wasp–B." The Joseph Smith Papers. https://www.josephsmithpapers.org/paper-summary/ordinance-5-july-1842-a-as-published-in-the-wasp-b/1.

"Ordinance, 8 August 1842." The Joseph Smith Papers. https://www.josephsmithpapers.org/paper-summary/ordinance-8-august-1842/2.

"Orson Pratt Letter, November 20, 1852." CR 1234 1. LDS Church History Library, Salt Lake City, UT. https://catalog.churchofjesuschrist.org/assets/45c5a0a7-3ae8-4f5b-a9ff-11434240ca55/0/0.

Ouellette, Richard Donald. *The Mormon Temple Lot Case: Space, Memory, and Identity in a Divided New Religion.* Austin: University of Texas at Austin, 2012.

Pack, John. *John Pack: As Revealed in the Records.* Ann Arbor, MI: The John Pack Family Association, 2012.

Park, Benjamin E. *Kingdom of Nauvoo: The Rise and Fall of a Religious Empire on the American Frontier.* New York: Liveright Publishing, 2020.

Parrish, M. "Kirtland, Feb. 5, 1838, To the Editor." *Painesville Republican* 2, no. 14–15 (February 15, 1838): 3.

Partridge, Scott H. "The Failure of the Kirtland Safety Society." *BYU Studies Quarterly* 12, no. 4 (1972): 437–54. https://scholarsarchive.byu.edu/byusq/vol12/iss4/8.

"Paternity suit of Mary Clift vs. Gustavus Hills, Robert Clift agent for Mary Clift, September 15, 1842." Transcript, box 5, fd. 44, MSS 76. L. Tom Perry Special Collections, Harold B. Lee Library, Brigham Young University, Provo, UT.

Phelps, W. W., W. Richards, and John Taylor. "To the Church of Jesus Christ of Latter Day Saints." *Times and Seasons* 5, no. 12 (July 1, 1844): 568.

"Plat of the City of Zion, circa Early June–25 June 1833." The Joseph Smith Papers. https://www.josephsmithpapers.org/paper-summary/plat-of-the-city-of-zion-circa-early-june-25-june-1833/1.

"Pleasant Vale Branch Report." CR 100 589. LDS Church History Library, Salt Lake City, UT. https://catalog.churchofjesuschrist.org/assets/6911b229-346a-444c-aedb-7b928fd99803/0/1.

"Printing Office, Kirtland Township, Ohio." The Joseph Smith Papers. https://www.josephsmithpapers.org/place/printing-office-kirtland-township-ohio.

"Proceedings, 1841 February–1845 February." MS 3435. LDS Church History Library, Salt Lake City, UT. https://catalog.churchofjesuschrist.org/assets/a67c7db2-98d3-43a7-9405-f37832f9c988/0/.

"Proceedings, 1842–1844." MS 3430. LDS Church History Library, Salt Lake City, UT. https://catalog.churchofjesuschrist.org/assets?id=cef6fb7b-da6f-447c-82e4-107353392a31&crate=0&index=41.

Proceedings of the Grand Lodge of Free and Accepted Masons of the State of New York, One Hundred and Twenty-Ninth Annual Communication. New York: J. J. Little & Ives Co., 1910.

"The Prophet's Death." *Deseret News*, December 8, 1875, 10–12.

"Prospectus of the *Nauvoo Expositor*." M209.05 N314pr 1844. LDS Church History Library, Salt Lake City, UT. https://catalog.churchofjesuschrist.org/assets/ce448652-47a8-4f05-8620-c3670eb9f24f/0/0.

Quinn, D. Michael. "The Council of Fifty and Its Members, 1844–1945." *BYU Studies* 20 (Winter 1980): 163–97.

———. "Evidence for the Sexual Side of Joseph Smith's Polygamy." Comments on Session #2A: "Reconsidering Joseph Smith's Marital Practices." Mormon History Association's Annual Conference, Calgary, Alberta, Canada, June 29, 2012. Circulated paper in possession of the authors.

———. "From Sacred Grove to Sacral Power Structure." *Dialogue: A Journal of Mormon Thought* 17, no. 2 (Summer 1984): 9–34. https://www.dialoguejournal.com/articles/from-sacred-grove-to-sacral-power-structure/.

———. *The Mormon Hierarchy: Origins of Power*. Salt Lake City: Signature Books, 1994.

———. "The Mormon Succession Crisis of 1844." *BYU Studies* 16, no. 2 (Winter 1976): 187–233.

Quist, John. "John E. Page: An Apostle of Uncertainty." *Journal of Mormon History* 12 (1985): 53–68.

———. "Polygamy among James Strang and His Followers." *The John Whitmer Historical Association Journal* 9 (1989): 31–48.

"Record of the Twelve, 14 February–28 August 1835." The Joseph Smith Papers. https://www.josephsmithpapers.org/paper-summary/record-of-the-twelve-14-february-28-august-1835/.

"Records of attendance of city council." MS 16800, box 2, fd. 7. LDS Church History Library, Salt Lake City, UT. https://catalog.churchofjesuschrist.org/assets?id=a116a308-a34f-44c0-b7db-412688cd9bac&crate=0&index=0.

"Records of the Oakland Presbyterian Church, 1819–1871." LDS Film #007896023. https://www.familysearch.org/ark:/61903/3:1:3Q9M-CS4N-WSTM-9?mode=g&cat=4313481.

"Reminiscences and journal, 1845–1889." MS 1504. LDS Church History Library, Salt Lake City, UT. https://catalog.churchofjesuschrist.org/assets/2f9886f6-7a7b-4b26-a038-f402586a9087/0/0.

"Resignation from John C. Bennett, 17 May 1842." The Joseph Smith Papers. https://www.josephsmithpapers.org/paper-summary/resignation-from-john-c-bennett-17-may-1842/1.

"Reuben McBride reminiscence." MS 8197. LDS Church History Library, Salt Lake City, UT. https://catalog.churchofjesuschrist.org/assets/bd605485-a499-4e7d-93e1-2ffbf24ed2e9/0/1.

"Reuben Miller letter." CR 1234 1. LDS Church History Library, Salt Lake City, UT. https://catalog.churchofjesuschrist.org/assets/f60802fa-0a45-4a6e-8fda-0044c8b50620/0/0.

"Revelation, 12 January 1838–C." The Joseph Smith Papers. https://www.josephsmithpapers.org/paper-summary/revelation-12-january-1838-c/.

"Revelation, 19 January 1841 [D&C 124]." The Joseph Smith Papers. https://www.josephsmithpapers.org/paper-summary/revelation-19-january-1841-dc-124/.

"Revelation, 20 July 1831 [D&C 57]." The Joseph Smith Papers. https://www.josephsmithpapers.org/paper-summary/revelation-20-july-1831-dc-57/.

"Revelation, 6 June 1831 [D&C 52]." The Joseph Smith Papers. https://www.josephsmithpapers.org/paper-summary/revelation-6-june-1831-dc-52/.

"Revelation, September 1830–A [D&C 29]." The Joseph Smith Papers. https://www.josephsmithpapers.org/paper-summary/revelation-september-1830-a-dc-29/2.

"Revelation, September 1830–A, as Recorded in Hyde and Smith, Notebook [D&C 29]." The Joseph Smith Papers. https://www.josephsmithpapers.org/paper-summary/revelation-september-1830-a-as-recorded-in-hyde-and-smith-notebook-dc-29/2.

"Revelation Book 2." The Joseph Smith Papers. https://www.josephsmithpapers.org/paper-summary/revelation-book-2/127?

"Revelation on celestial marriage, 1874 February 16." MS 2673. LDS Church History Library, Salt Lake City, UT. https://catalog.churchofjesuschrist.org/assets?id=eaeb2710-5a79-408b-b855-dd087708c604&crate=0&index=3.

The Revised Code of Laws of Illinois: Enacted by the Fifth General Assembly. Vandalia, IL: Robert Blackwell, 1827.

"Rich, Decidedly." *The Warsaw Signal* NS, no. 47, whole 162 (January 22, 1845). Typescript by Dale Broadhurst. Readings in Early Mormon History. http://www.sidneyrigdon.com/dbroadhu/IL/sign1845.htm.

Rich, Joseph C. "Correspondence." *Deseret News* 50, no. 13 (January 19, 1870): 595.

Richards, Willard. "Appendix 3: Willard Richards, Journal Excerpt, 23–27 June 1844." The Joseph Smith Papers. https://www.josephsmithpapers.org/paper-summary/appendix-3-willard-richards-journal-excerpt-23-27-june-1844/3.

Rigdon, Sidney. "The Purposes of God." *Latter Day Saint's Messenger and Advocate* [Rigdon] 1, no. 8 (February 15, 1845): 113–15.

Riggs, Michael S. "'His Word Was as Good as His Note': The Impact of Justus Morse's Mormonism(s) on His Families." *John Whitmer Historical Association Journal* 17 (1997): 49–80.

Ripley, Alanson. "Alanson Ripley Statements, circa 1845 January." Joseph Smith History Documents, [1–4]. CR 100 396. LDS Church History Library, Salt Lake City, UT. https://catalog.churchofjesuschrist.org/assets/512f3b47-15d3-4d7e-ad74-7c2993f73564/0/0.

———. "Keokuk, Lee County, Iowa Territory." *Times and Seasons* 1, no. 2 (December 1839): 24.

———. "Nauvoo." *Times and Seasons* 1, no. 8, (June 1840): 122–23.

Roberts, B. H. *The Rise and Fall of Nauvoo*. Salt Lake City: The Deseret News Publishing Company, 1900.

———. *Succession in the Presidency of the Church of Jesus Christ of Latter-day Saints*. Salt Lake City: The Deseret News Publishing Company, 1894.

Saints. Edited by B. H. Roberts. 7 vols. 2nd ed. rev. Salt Lake City: Deseret Book, 1948

Sampson, D. Paul, and Larry T. Wimmer. "The Kirtland Safety Society: The Stock Ledger Book and the Bank Failure." *BYU Studies Quarterly* 12, no. 4 (1972): 427–36.

"Samuel Akers correspondence, 1843–1846." MS 14413. LDS Church History Library, Salt Lake City, UT. https://catalog.churchofjesuschrist.org/record/5ff3e3d6-365e-455f-8385-35bf7bb7a2ea/0?view=browse&lang=eng.

"Samuel Miles autobiography, circa 1904." MS 5096. LDS Church History Library, Salt Lake City, UT.

Saunders, Richard L. "Officers and Arms: The 1843 General Return of the Nauvoo Legion's Second Cohort." *BYU Studies Quarterly* 35, no. 2 (1995): 139–48. https://scholarsarchive.byu.edu/byusq/vol35/iss2/13.

Scherer, Mark Albert. *The Journey of a People: The Era of Reorganization, 1844 to 1946*. Independence, MO: Community of Christ Seminary Press, 2013.

Sherwood, H. G. "To the Saints Scattered Abroad, in the Region Westward from Kirtland, Ohio." *Times and Seasons* 1, no. 2 (December 1839): 29.

Shook, Charles A. *The True Origin of Mormon Polygamy*. Cincinnati: Standard Publishing Company, 1914.

Shurtleff, Stella Cahoon, and Brent Farrington Cahoon, eds. *Reynolds Cahoon and His Stalwart Sons: Utah Pioneers*. Salt Lake City: Paragon Press, 1960.

Smith, Andrew F. *The Saintly Scoundrel—The Life and Times of Dr. John Cook Bennett.* Urbana: University of Illinois Press, 1997.

Smith, Emma, and William Marks. Signed lease August 25, 1844. Community of Christ Library and Archives, Independence, MO.

Smith, George D., ed. *An Intimate Chronicle: The Journals of William Clayton.* Salt Lake City: Signature Books, 1995.

———. *Nauvoo Polygamy: ". . . but we called it celestial marriage."* Salt Lake City: Signature Books, 2008.

Smith, Heman C. *Duplicity Exposed.* Lamoni, IA: Herald Publishing House, 1911.

———. "William Marks." *Journal of History* (January 1908): 24–29.

Smith, Heman C., and F. Henry Edwards. *History of the Reorganized Church of Jesus Christ of Latter Day Saints.* 5 vols. Independence, MO: Herald House, 1951–1984. Online edition at https://www.centerplace.org/history/ch/default.htm.

Smith, Hyrum. "Affidavit of Hyrum Smith." *Times and Seasons* 3, no. 19 (August 1, 1842): 870–72.

Smith, Joseph. "Letter of Appointment." James Jesse Strang collection. WA MSS 447. Yale University Library, Beinecke Rare Book and Manuscript Library.

———. "Letter to Isaac Galland, Sept. 11, 1839." The Joseph Smith Papers. https://www.josephsmithpapers.org/paper-summary/letter-to-isaac-galland-11-september-1839/1.

———. "Letter to the Presidency in Kirtland, 29 March 1838." The Joseph Smith Papers. https://www.josephsmithpapers.org/paper-summary/letter-to-the-presidency-in-kirtland-29-march-1838/3.

Smith, Joseph, et al. *History of the Church of Jesus Christ of Latter-day Saints.* Edited by B. H. Roberts, 7 vols., 2nd ed. rev. Salt Lake City: Deseret Book, 1948

Smith, Joseph III. "What do I Remember of Nauvoo?" *Journal of History* 3, no. 3 (July 1910): 334.

Smith, Lucy Mack. *Biographical Sketches of Joseph Smith, the Prophet, and His Progenitors for Many Generations.* London: Published for Orson Pratt by S. W. Richards, 1853.

Smith, William. "It being a little stormy to-day, I gladly sit down to commune." *Zion's Reveille* 2, no. 14 (April 22, 1847): 58.

———. "A Letter from William Smith." *New York Daily Tribune* 17, no. 5,025 (May 28, 1857): 5.

———. "To the Church of Jesus Christ of Latter Day Saints." *Zion's Reveille* 1, no. 12 (December 1846): 3.

Snow, Eliza R. *Biography and Family Record of Lorenzo Snow, One of the Twelve Apostles of the Church of Jesus Christ of Latter-day Saints.* Salt Lake City: Deseret News Company, 1884.

"Special Conference, June 25 and 26, '64." *The True Latter Day Saints' Herald* 6, no. 2 (July 15, 1864): 20–21.

"Special Meeting." *Times and Seasons* 5, no. 16 (September 2, 1844): 637–38.

Staker, Susan. "A Matter of Many Wives: Joseph Smith's Courting in Secret Nauvoo." *John Whitmer Historical Association Journal* 41, no. 1 (Spring/Summer 2021): 3–53.
"Statement on Marriage, circa August 1835." The Joseph Smith Papers. https://www.josephsmithpapers.org/paper-summary/appendix-3-statement-on-marriage-circa-august-1835/1.
Stenhouse, Thomas B. *The Rocky Mountain Saints.* New York: D. Appleton, 1873.
Strang, James J. "Extract of a Letter." *Gospel Herald* 2, no. 29 (October 7, 1847): 120.
———. "John C. Bennett." *Zion's Reveille* 2, no. 16 (July 8, 1847): 68.
———. "Message to the Conference." *Zion's Reveille*, 2, no. 12 (April 1, 1847): 52.
———. "Revelation, Given Jan. Seventh, 1849." *Gospel Herald* 3, no. 43 (January 11, 1849): 233–34.
Strang, James J., George J. Adams, and William Marks. "A Testimony to the Nation." *Gospel Herald* 5, no. 12 (June 6, 1850): 92–95.
Sweeney, John Jr. "A History of the Nauvoo Legion in Illinois." Master's thesis, Brigham Young University, 1974. https://scholarsarchive.byu.edu/etd/5155.
Taylor, Samuel W. *The Kingdom or Nothing: The Life of John Taylor, Militant Mormon.* New York: MacMillan Publishing Co., Inc., 1976.
Thompson, Charles B. "An Address." May 26, 1850. *Zion's Harbinger and Baneemy's Organ* 2, no. 1 (January 1852): 4–7.
———. "April 18th, 1852." *Zion's Harbinger and Baneemy's Organ* 2, no. 4 (April 1852): 30–31.
———. "Close of the First Year." *Zion's Harbinger and Baneemy's Organ* 5, no. 2 (May 1, 1855): 24–32.
———. "Covenant, to be taken upon entering the Congregation of Jehovah's Presbytery of Zion." *Zion's Harbinger and Baneemy's Organ* 4, no. 1 (January 1854): 9–10.
———. *Evidences in Proof of the Book of Mormon.* Batavia, NY: D.D. Waite, 1841.
———. "For the *Gospel Herald*." *Zion's Harbinger and Baneemy's Organ* 2, no. 3 (March 1852): 22–24.
———. "The Gathering." *Zion's Harbinger and Baneemy's Organ* 3, no. 2 (February 1853): 15–16; 3, no 6 (June 1853): 46–48.
———. "The Gathering and the August Assembly." *Zion's Harbinger and Baneemy's Organ* 3, no. 7 (July 1853): 55–56.
———. "The Law of Sacrifice." *Zion's Harbinger and Baneemy's Organ* 4, no. 5 (May 1854): 70–74.
———. "The Law of Tything again." *Zion's Harbinger and Baneemy's Organ* 4, no. 4 (April 1854): 56–58.
———. "A Proclamation." *Zion's Harbinger and Baneemy's Organ* 1, no. 1 (January 1849): 1.
———. "The Progress of the Work of the Father." *Zion's Harbinger and Baneemy's Organ* 4, no. 4 (April 1854): 61–62.
———. "Revelation." *Zion's Harbinger and Baneemy's Organ* 4, no. 5 (May 1854): 68–69.

———. "The School of Works." *Zion's Harbinger and Baneemy's Organ* 4, no. 2 (February 1854): 27–28.

———. "St. Louis, Mo., October 1st, 1852." *Zion's Harbinger and Baneemy's Organ* 2, no. 10 (October 1852): 79.

———. "Who is Baneemy?" *Zion's Harbinger and Baneemy's Organ* 3, no. 2 (February 1853): 14–15.

———. "The Word of the God of Abraham, of Isaac and of Jacob to his servants of the seed of the Church of Jesus Christ of Latter-day Saints, Having the testimony of Jesus Christ, Concerning their Organization, in preparation for the Endowments of the Priesthood, and their Regeneration in the Family of Israel." *Zion's Harbinger and Baneemy's Organ* 1, no. 2 (April 1850): 1–2.

Thompson, Charles B., et. al. "Preamble and Resolutions." *Zion's Harbinger and Baneemy's Organ* 3, no. 9 (September 1853): 72.

Thompson, Robert B. "Minutes of the general conference of the Church of Jesus Christ of Latter Day Saints held at the City of Nauvoo, Hancock Co. Ill. on the seventh day of April, in the year of our Lord one thousand eight hundred and forty-one." *Times and Seasons* 2, no. 12 (April 15, 1841): 386–88.

"To all the Saints Throughout the World," *Latter Day Saints' Messenger and Advocate* [Rigdon] 1, no. 7 (January 22, 1845): 108.

"To the Saints in All the World." *Gospel Herald* 2, no. 39 (December 16, 1847): 181.

"Trial of Elder Rigdon." *Times and Seasons* 5, no. 17 (September 15, 1844): 647–55.

"Tribal History." Official Website of the Prairie Band Potawatomi Nation. https://www.pbpindiantribe.com/about/tribal-history/.

"United States Census, 1840." Caldwell Co., Missouri, United States. FamilySearch. https://www.familysearch.org/ark:/61903/1:1:XHTF-MFW.

"United States Census, 1840." Hancock Co., Illinois, United States. FamilySearch. https://www.familysearch.org/ark:/61903/1:1:XHB8-XX4.

"United States testimony 1892." MS 1160. LDS Church History Library, Salt Lake City, UT. https://catalog.churchofjesuschrist.org/record/d41946ae-97f6-42c7-b8ca-747ee67d8dee/0.

Van Wagoner, Richard S. "The Making of a Mormon Myth: The 1844 Transfiguration of Brigham Young." *Dialogue: A Journal of Mormon Thought* 28, no. 4 (Winter 1995): 1–24.

Vidrine, Jacob. "Succession to Brigham Young." *One Eternal Round*. Vol. 19.

Vogel, Dan, ed. *History of Joseph Smith and the Church of Jesus Christ of Latter-day Saints: A Source and Text Critical Edition: Volume 6: 1843–1844*. Salt Lake City: Smith-Petitt Foundation, 2015.

"The Voice of Innocence from Nauvoo, 1844, March 9." MS 15540. LDS Church History Library, Salt Lake City, UT. https://catalog.churchofjesuschrist.org/assets/19559128-fd44-45f1-9142-3e6b22432d1f/0/0.

"Voree and the Prophet." *Voree Herald* 1, no. 4 (April 1846): 4.

Walker, Jeffrey N. "Habeas Corpus in Early Nineteenth-Century Mormonism: Joseph Smith's Legal Bulwark for Personal Freedom." *BYU Studies Quarterly* 52, no. 1 (2013): 5–97.

———. "The Kirtland Safety Society and the Fraud of Grandison Newell: A Legal Examination." *BYU Studies Quarterly* 54, no. 3 (2015): 32–148.

Warren, Catherine. "Catherine Warren statement." In the Valeen Tippetts Avery Papers. Utah State University, Logan, UT.

"We the undersigned members of the ladies' relief society." *Times and Seasons* 3, no. 23 (October 1, 1842): 940. https://archive.org/details/TimesAndSeasonsV3/page/n373/mode/2up?.

Webb, Eliza J. [Eliza Jane Churchill Webb]. Letter to Mary Bond, April 24, 1876 and May 4, 1876. P21, f11, item 9. Community of Christ Library and Archives, Independence, MO.

Webster, Noah. *Noah Webster's first edition of an American dictionary of the English language*. Foundation for American Christian Education, 1828. https://archive.org/details/americandictiona01websrich/page/n7/mode/2up.

Whitmer, John. "John Whitmer, History, 1831–circa 1847." The Joseph Smith Papers. https://www.josephsmithpapers.org/paper-summary/john-whitmer-history-1831-circa-1847/.

Whitney, Elizabeth Ann. "A Leaf from an Autobiography." *Woman's Exponent* 7, no. 11 (November 1, 1838): 83; no. 12 (November 15, 1878): 91.

Whitney, Helen Mar Kimball. "Scenes in Nauvoo." *Women's Exponent* 10, no. 6 (August 15, 1881): 42.

Whitney, Orson F. *Life of Heber C. Kimball*. Salt Lake City: Kimball Family, 1888.

Wildermuth, Ruth. "William Marks after Nauvoo." *Restoration Trail Forum* 5, no. 2 (May 1979): 1, 4–6, 8.

"Wilford Woodruff Journal, 1833 December–1838 January." MS 1352. LDS Church History Library, Salt Lake City, UT. https://catalog.churchofjesuschrist.org/assets/14079217-b2a7-4eff-8b53-1be6c1e9bea5/0/128.

"Wilford Woodruff Journal, 1838 January–1839 December." MS 1352. LDS Church History Library, Salt Lake City, UT. https://catalog.churchofjesuschrist.org/assets/adc523d5-d74b-42ec-930a-557fdc7d05a2/0/5.

"Wilford Woodruff journal, 1841 January–1842 December." MS 1352. LDS Church History Library, Salt Lake City, UT. https://catalog.churchofjesuschrist.org/assets/28b53d73-2ba2-418b-8ef7-dafcc935bee3/0/6.

"Willard Richards letter." CR 1234, box 41, fd. 28. LDS Church History Library, Salt Lake City, UT. https://catalog.churchofjesuschrist.org/assets/8ff92ded-ada7-4ca1-85f5-57767ba3f161/0/1.

"Willard Richards, Letter, Alston, England, to Joseph Fielding and William Clayton, Manchester, England." MS 5946. LDS Church History Library, Salt Lake City, UT. https://catalog.churchofjesuschrist.org/assets/00175dc1-b8e2-4f92-9382-755f6a2add81/0/0.

"William Dawson statement, 1888 December 22." Mary Jean Freebairn collection, 1831–1972. MS 4337. LDS Church History Library, Salt Lake City, UT. https://catalog.churchofjesuschrist.org/assets?id=3cae7dae-2aca-4da6-8342-dd7be350d34d&crate=0&index=0.

"William Marks deed, 1837 August 7." MS 27035. LDS Church History Library, Salt Lake City, UT.

"William Marks letter." CR 1234 1. LDS Church History Library, Salt Lake City, UT. https://catalog.churchofjesuschrist.org/assets/bc8f1245-261e-41f1-a42c-d9d38eb8b411/0/0.

"William White Purchase, Commerce, Illinois." The Joseph Smith Papers. https://www.josephsmithpapers.org/place/william-white-purchase-commerce-illinois.

"Williams Marks power of attorney, 1839 May 7." MS 27035. LDS Church History Library, Salt Lake City, UT. https://catalog.churchofjesuschrist.org/assets/e5952013-482b-4d95-a413-a691885a0cf4/0/0.

"Wilson Law and Others, Affidavit, 4 January 1843, Willard Richards Copy [Extradition of JS for Accessory to Assault]." The Joseph Smith Papers. https://www.josephsmithpapers.org/paper-summary/wilson-law-and-others-affidavit-4-january-1843-willard-richards-copy-extradition-of-js-for-accessory-to-assault/1.

Woods, Fred. "The Cemetery Record of William D. Huntington, Nauvoo Sexton." *Mormon Historical Studies* 3, no. 1 (Spring 2002): 131–63.

Woods, Henry Ernest, ed. *The New England Historical and Genealogical Register*. Boston: The New England Historical and Genealogical Society, 1907.

"Word of Wisdom." The Joseph Smith Papers. https://www.josephsmithpapers.org/topic/word-of-wisdom.

Wyl., W. "Interview with William Law, March 30, 1887." *Salt Lake Daily Tribune* (July 31, 1887).

"Zerah Pulsipher's History." MS 753. LDS Church History Library, Salt Lake City, UT.

Index

A

Abraham (biblical), 90
Adam-ondi-Ahman, xvi, 26–27
Adams, George J., 92, 145, 151, 156, 180
Adams, James, 98
Adams, James M., 141, 146–48, 152, 158–60, 166, 170–82, 220–42
Adams, Polly Marks, 1, 3–4
Adams, Prosper, 1
Adoption, 178, 230
Adultery, 14, 78, 81–82, 86, 92, 94–95, 104, 141–42, 148, 252, 256
Adventist Movement, 181
Akers, Samuel, 135
Albany, Iowa, 171, 237
Aldrich, Hazen, 135–36
Aldrich, William, 188–89
Alger, Fanny, 14, 19, 76
Allen, Reuben, 149
Allred, James, 252, 254
Amboy, Illinois, 189–90, 194–97, 199, 245
Anderson, Blakley B., 203
Anderson, Eliza, 203
Anderson, Mary, 203
Ashtabula, Ohio, 176
authority, 7, 9, 26–27, 47–50, 56, 59, 63, 69, 80, 111–12, 118–22, 126–29, 131, 141, 145, 149, 156, 161–62, 175, 177, 185, 188, 196, 209–10, 215
Ananias and Sapphira, 164
Aurora, Illinois, 152, 177, 228, 230
Avery, Daniel, 67

B

Babbitt, Almon, 51
Badlam, Alexander, 116
Baldwin, Caleb, 37
Baneemy, 157–58, 161, 164, 169–70, 173, 177, 221, 232, 261
Banking crisis, ix, 11, 13, 19–22, 178, 227
Barlow, Israel, 33
Barnett, John T., 58–60
baptism, xv, xvii–xviii, 1, 3–4, 40, 94–95, 151, 176–78, 186, 190, 205, 209, 228, 230

baptism for the dead, 97, 151–52, 200–201
Batavia, Illinois, 165, 224, 259
Beaver Island, 136, 146, 153–56, 162, 178
Beaverton, Illinois, 188
Beloit, Wisconsin, 185
Bennett, John C., 53–56, 62–64, 70, 73, 78–82, 85–87, 97, 99, 142–48, 213, 215, 255–56
Bennett, Mehitabel, 3
Bent, Samuel, 103, 129, 252, 254
Bernhisel, John, 135
Bidamon, Lewis, 187
Bigler's Grove, Iowa, 202
bishop, 16–19, 25, 27, 30–31, 38, 40, 43–44, 57–60, 62, 70, 79, 81, 98, 115–16, 123, 125, 139, 143, 186, 199, 209
Bishop, Francis Gladden, 46, 163
Black Hawk War, 138
Blacks and priesthood, 200
Blackstone, William, 48, 107
Blair, Samuel, 186
Blair, William W., 178, 181–82, 187–90, 192, 194–96, 201–2
Blakeslee, James, 152–53, 158, 165, 182, 259
Bleazard, John, 94–95
Bliss, Daniel, 44
Boggs, Lilburn, 30, 63–66, 155
Book of Mormon, x, xiii–xiv, xvii, 6, 15, 18, 28, 44, 49, 146, 155, 157, 169, 177, 182, 185, 235, 261
Boynton, John F., 6–7, 14–15
Braden, Clark, 88
Brewster, James Colin, 17–18, 46, 159, 177
Briggs, Edmund C., 182, 187–88, 193–95, 213
Briggs, Jason W., 185–88, 195, 198
brothel, 78
Brotherton, Martha, 88
Brunson, Seymour, 49
Bump, Jacob, 143
Burlington, Wisconsin, 194
Burnett, Stephen, 21
Butler, John L., 108, 110
Butterfield, Josiah, 212, 244–50
Butterfield, Justin, 65
Buzzard, Philip H., 141

C

Cahoon, Reynolds, 19, 21, 110, 115–16
Cahoon, William, 21
Caldwell County, Missouri, 19, 71
Campbell, Alexander, 181
Carlin, Thomas, 64–65
Carlton, Joseph, 29
Carrier, Daniel, 252
Carthage, Illinois, 104–5, 108–9, 114, 261, 263
cemetery/burial ground, 58–60, 110, 127–28, 135, 202, 205
Chase, Darwin, 82–83
Chicago & Galena stagecoach line, 139
Chicago, Illinois, 137, 208, 233
Childs, Harry, 161, 163, 167, 223, 258
Church of Christ (Old Standard), 15
Churchill Webb, Eliza Jane, 88
City Council, Nauvoo, x, 53–60, 64–65, 68–69, 78, 84, 99, 101, 107–8, 127, 131, 208, 215, 255
Civil War, 181, 200
Clayton, William, 90, 94, 113–17, 121–22, 190
Cleveland, Isaac, 141
Cleveland, John [Judge], 37
Clift, Eliza, 77
Clift, Mary Ann, 77
Clift, Robert, 77
Clift, Sarah Ellen, 77
Cobb, Rowland, 171
Colesville, xiv
Commerce, Illinois, 37–40, 43, 58
Congregation of Jehovah's Presbytery of Zion, ix, 156, 159, 161, 163, 169, 172, 260
Constitution, United States, 55, 63, 68, 106–7
cornerstone, 38, 97–98, 112, 216
Corrill, John, xvi
Council of Fifty, 102–4, 106, 113–16, 133, 175, 215
covenants, xiv, 22–23, 30, 100, 117, 130, 158, 164–65, 169–71, 221, 223–24, 235, 252, 258–59, 261
Cowdery, Oliver, xvi–xvii, 5–6, 10, 76, 177, 230
Cowdery, Patience, xvii
Cowdrey, Warren, xvii–xviii, 8, 10, 12
Cowles, Austin, 91–93, 121–22, 191, 252, 254
Cutler, Alpheus, 108, 110, 115–16, 118, 129, 175, 203

D

D&C 132 (Plural Marriage Revelation), 90, 106–7, 200
Daily, Moses, 132
Danites, 72–73, 94, 255
David (biblical), 90, 99
Davis, Amos, 57, 68–69
Davis Durfee, Elizabeth, 203
Des Moines, Iowa, 32, 171, 237
Douglas, Stephen A., 63
Douglass, Charles, 152
Durfee, Jabez, 203
Durfee Anderson Muir, Julia Ann, 202–4
Durfee, Savilla, 202

E

Edwards, Thomas, 32
Elliot, John C., 133
Ells, Josiah, 158, 167
endowments, 5, 10, 66, 98–100, 120, 141, 156, 161, 164, 178, 207, 244
Ephraim, 161, 221
eternal marriage, 75, 85, 89, 97–100, 199–202
Everett, Elisha, 77
exaltation, 92, 153, 168, 191, 214, 223, 260
excommunication
    Austin Cowles, 93
    Brigham Young and Twelve Apostles, x, 140–42
    James Adams, 148
    John C. Bennett, 97, 144–45, 148
    John Gaylord, 178
    in Kirtland, ix, 15–16, 178
    Moses Martin, 49
    in Nauvoo, x, 55, 142
    by Nauvoo City Council, 55
    Polly Adams, 4
    Presbyterian, i, ix, 2, 4, 16
    Rosannah Marks, 4
    Sidney Rigdon, x, 123–25, 215
    Stake President, 127
    William Marks, ix, 4, 126, 153, 209
    William Smith, 148
extermination order, 30, 155

F

Far West, Missouri, 19, 25–31, 34, 37, 42, 76, 97, 207, 260
Faulk, Hyrum, 212, 244–50

ferry, 37, 42–43, 46–47, 76, 134–35
Field, Elvira, 152
First President/First Presidency, 6, 13, 26, 31, 42, 47, 49, 56, 60, 62, 82, 92, 98, 106, 111–13, 117–20, 124, 127, 136, 140–41, 144–47, 150–51, 162, 186, 196–99
Flanders, Robert, 211–12
Ford, Thomas, 65, 108
Fordham, Elijah, 49
fornication, 78, 81–82, 104, 141
Forscutt, Mark, 212–13
Foster, Charles, 106
Foster, Robert D., 51, 88, 105–7
Fox, Illinois, 259
Freedom, New York, xvii–xviii, xx, 8
Freemasonry, 26, 73–75, 99, 102–3, 106, 143, 156, 158, 190, 197, 215, 255
Fulmer, David, 129, 252, 254
Fulton City, Illinois, 134–37

G

Galland, Isaac, 32–35, 37
Galland Purchase, 34, 37, 47
Galland's Grove, Iowa, 196
Gallatin, Missouri, 37
gathering, ix–x, xiii–xvi, 4, 9–10, 16, 19, 21, 27, 30–35, 38, 40, 44–45, 52, 54, 58, 70–72, 84, 97, 119, 121, 125, 134, 136–41, 146, 150–51, 156, 159, 161–83, 197–98, 204, 207, 209, 215–16, 221–24, 227–28, 232–33, 236, 245, 251–54, 258, 262
Gaylord, John C., 141, 178, 180, 182, 188–89
Glastonbury, Connecticut, 1
Goodrich, Ira, 152
Goodrich Marks, Sarah, 1
Gould, John, xviii, 165, 224, 259
Granger, Oliver, 16, 26, 37–39, 44
Great Basin, 208
Green, John P., 17, 48–49, 255
Gregory, William, 50–51
Grover, Thomas, 43, 48, 91, 110, 122, 252, 254
Gurley, Samuel H., 187–88, 193
Gurley, Zenos H., 185, 187, 189, 192, 195–96

H

habeas corpus, 53, 63–68
Hale, Jonathan, 8
Halcyon Order of Illuminati, 143
Hamilton, Artois, 110

Hamilton's Hotel, 109
Hancock County, 45, 47, 98, 104–5, 109, 255
Hancock, Solomon, xv
Harris, George W., 45, 252, 254–55
Harris, Martin, 5–6, 15
Harvey, Joel, 29
Hawes, Peter, 105
Hawkins, Lydia Ann, 16
Hawkins, Uriah, 16
Hendrick, James, 45
Herald House fire, 220
Hicks, John, 48–49
Higbee, Chauncey, 79–82, 106
Higbee, Elias, 33, 252, 254
Higbee, Francis M., 102, 106, 108
High Council
    Iowa, 40, 49
    Kirtland, ix, 6, 15–19, 22, 45, 70
    Far West/Zion, 7, 31, 76
    Nauvoo, x, 40–57, 60–62, 68, 69, 73, 76–85, 91–95, 98–99, 111–14, 118–31, 160–61, 165, 168, 175, 177, 194, 196, 200, 210, 215, 244, 251–54, 257, 261–63
    RLDS, 196
    standing/presiding, 7, 111–13, 117
    traveling, 7–8, 15, 61, 112–13, 118, 124, 136
    Voree, 140–44, 146
High Priest, 46, 49, 57, 94, 98, 127, 140, 142, 156, 176, 178, 182, 190, 196, 235
Hills, Gustavus, 77, 94–95
Hodge, Abraham C., 108
Hosanna shout, 103
Hotchkiss, Horace, 37, 84
House of Israel, 154, 169, 221, 235, 260–61
Hunter, Edward, 59, 104
Huntington, Dimick B., 41
Huntington Jacobs Young, Zina, 134
Huntington, William, 252
Huntley, Russell, 178
Hyde, Heman, xviii, xx, 121, 250
Hyde, Orson, 6, 123, 125, 128, 140, 142
Hymns, 5, 44, 158, 186, 190, 196

I–J

Iowa City, 171, 237
Ivins, Charles, 106, 207
Jackson County, Missouri, xv–xvi, 5, 27, 30, 38, 66, 198, 204, 221, 245
Jackson, Joseph H., 88, 107
James, Samuel, 131

Jerusalem, xiv, 157, 201, 204, 250, 254
Jews, xiii, 7, 10, 101, 157, 204, 235, 245
Johnson, Aaron, 48, 243, 252, 254
Johnson, John, 12, 15
Johnson, Luke, 6, 15, 21, 46
Johnson, Lyman, 6, 21

K

Kanesville/Council Bluffs, Iowa, 138, 163–67, 171, 175, 177, 223–26, 230, 236–37, 240, 259
Keller, Alvah, 44
Kendall, Illinois, 165, 259
keys/key words, xvi, 7, 10, 99, 102–3, 120, 158–59, 164
Kimball, Heber C., 6, 26, 98–99, 118, 123, 128, 140, 142, 191, 255
Kimball Smith, Helen Mar, 75
kingdom, ix, xvi, 7, 98, 102–3, 113, 119, 124, 134, 141, 153, 164, 175, 223, 232, 252, 254, 262, 264
kingdoms of glory, 223
Kirtland Camp, 22–23, 25
Kirtland, Ohio, ix, xvi–xviii, xx, 4, 7–28, 34–35, 38–39, 44–46, 51, 70–71, 75, 97, 115, 143, 146, 155, 160–61, 164–65, 176, 178, 180, 189, 207, 215, 234, 243, 260
Kirtland Printing Office, 12, 20
Kirtland Safety Society/Kirtland Bank, ix, 11, 13, 19–22, 178
Kirtland Temple, 8–10, 12–17, 22–25, 51, 97, 161, 191
Knight, Joseph, 45
Knight, Newel K., xiv, 252, 254
Knight, Vinson, 37, 40, 62, 255
Kreymeyer, Christian, 110

L

Lake Michigan, 146, 152
Landers, John, 178
Lanphear, C. G., 189
Lathrop, Asahel, 104, 110
Law, Jane, 88, 106
Law, William, 88, 98, 101–2, 104, 106, 115, 191, 207–9
Law, Wilson, 59, 104, 106, 191, 255
Lawrence, Maria, 203
Lawrence, Sarah, 203
Letter of Appointment, 136

Liberty Jail, 30–31, 37, 63
Lincoln, Abraham, 32
Little, Sidney H., 56, 233
Littlefield, Lyman O., 82–83
Louisiana, Missouri, 28–29
Lucas, Samuel D., 30
Lyman, Amasa, 49, 94, 120, 123, 130
Lyon, Windsor, 60

M

Mace, Wandle, 33
Madison, Phebe, 93
Magnolia, Iowa, 170, 228, 230, 232, 234–35
Manifest Destiny, 135, 164
Manifesto, 130, 169
Manti, Iowa, 175
Marks, Cornwell, 1
Marks, Ephraim, 71, 73–74, 152
Marks, Henry, 71, 73, 87, 256
Marks, Ira Goodrich, 71, 155, 202, 250
Marks, LaFayette, 71, 155
Marks, Llewellyn, 71, 155, 197
Marks McHenry, Lucy Ann, 71, 155, 202
Marks Skidmore, Mary Eliza, 71
Marks, Rosannah Robinson, 1–4, 27–28, 71, 87, 100, 128–29, 131, 202, 205, 226, 245
Marks Shaw, Sophia, 71, 87–89, 155, 202, 250
Marks, William
  1839 Conference, 38
  1841 Conference, 60–61
  1844 October Conference, 126–27
  1846 Voree General Conference, 139
  1847 Voree April General Conference, 145
  1847 Voree October General Conference, 147
  1849 Voree August Conference, 151
  1852 Solemn Assembly, 161
  1853 April Solemn Assembly, 166
  1853 August Solemn Assembly, 169–70
  1853 December Solemn Assembly, 170–71
  1856 April Conference, 182, 235
  1859 October Semiannual Conference, 191
  1860 April Annual Conference, 195–96
  1860 October Semiannual Conference, 196
  1863 April Annual Conference, 197–98
  1864 April Annual Conference, 199
  1864 July special conference, 199
  1865 April Annual Conference, 199
  1866 April Annual Conference, 201
  accepts claims of Strang, 139–40

Index   297

accused of apostasy, 128–34, 190–91, 208–11, 214, 261, 264
agent to bishop, 16–19, 70
alcohol, 2, 55, 57
alderman, 54–65, 69, 99, 127, 139, 210
Anointed Quorum, 98–100, 112, 191, 207, 215
apostle under Strang, 151, 209
associate president to Strang, 151
assumed debts, 21, 25, 45, 84
attends first Reorganization meeting, 189–90
authority over Twelve Apostles, 7–8, 60–61, 112–14, 117–18, 121–24, 129, 131, 136
baptism, xviii, 2–4, 151, 176–77, 190, 205, 209, 228, 230
baptism for the dead, 151–52, 200–201
Beaver Island, 153, 162
birth, 1
bishop under Strang, 139, 143, 209
board of health, 58
board of regents, Nauvoo University, 70
board of supervisors, DeKalb County, 153
burial ground, 58–60, 127
Carthage, 104, 109
charity, 45
city leader, 21, 41, 45, 54–55, 62, 69, 215, 255
coadjutor/guardian to Joseph Smith III, 144–45, 151
commanded to Missouri, 26–27
community affairs, 52, 149, 155, 207, 216
cornerstone laying, 97–98
Council of Fifty, 102–4, 113, 133, 175, 215
crime in Nauvoo, 47–52
death, 205
defense of Rigdon, x, 117, 124–25, 215
donations, 150–51, 169–70, 192, 202
elder, 9
elections held in home, 139
endangered, 101–2
endowment, 66, 98–99, 161, 207, 244
epistle, 78–79, 91–92, 103–4, 109, 154, 167–69, 211–12, 225, 253–54, 260
Evangelical Teacher, 166–67, 171, 225, 260
excommunication, ix–x, 4, 16, 124, 126, 140–42, 148, 153, 209
Far West, 26–31, 207
farmer, xix, 21, 139, 155, 171, 226–27, 237
family, xiii, xvii, xx, 1–2, 28, 31, 38–41, 71, 87–89, 135, 137, 155, 202, 226, 250

financial, 83–84, 149, 155, 169–71, 176–77, 226–29, 231, 234–37, 243
First Presidency under Strang, 144–51
First Presidency under Joseph III, 198–99, 205
Freedom Conference, 8
Freemason, 73, 102–3, 106, 197, 215
friction with Joseph Smith, 101–2
Fulton, 134–37
gathering, ix–x, xiii–xiv, 4, 21, 32–33, 35, 38, 44–45, 70, 121, 134, 151, 161–70, 172–83, 197–98, 204, 207, 209, 215–16, 221–24, 227–28, 232–33, 236, 245, 251–54, 258, 262
grand jury of Hancock County, 104–5
habeus corpus, 53, 63–68
High Council, Kirtland, ix, 15–19
High Council, Nauvoo, x, 40–57, 60–62, 68–70, 76, 81–84, 91–95, 99, 112–14, 117, 119, 121–26, 142, 161, 165, 168, 177, 181, 194, 196, 200, 210, 215, 244, 251–54, 257, 261–63
High Council, Strang, 140–42
High Council, RLDS, 196, 200
High Priest, 127, 182, 235
High Priest, Strang, 140
High Priest, RLDS, 190
home in Fulton, 135, 137
home in Kirtland, 17–19
home in Nauvoo, 41, 55, 71, 88, 101, 115, 207
home in Plano, 204
home in Portage, xix, 2, 8
home in Preparation, 227
home in Shabbona Grove, 139, 155, 165, 189–90, 198, 202, 204, 226, 245
hosts the Twelve in New York, 8
hymnbook, 44, 190, 196
influence, 54, 58, 88, 126, 130–33, 152, 162, 169, 198–99, 208, 216, 262
joins Thompson, 160
justice of the peace, 54, 60, 64, 66, 108, 127, 139
Kirtland Camp, 22–23
Kirtland land dealings, 12–13, 18–23
Kirtland printing office, 11–13
Kirtland Temple, 12–17, 23, 25, 191
leadership, ix–x, 9, 15, 21, 28, 40, 45, 52, 60, 68, 70, 73, 84, 99, 112, 114–17, 135, 139, 161–62, 166, 175, 180–83, 191, 207, 215–16
leaves Nauvoo, 134–35, 244

leaves Strang, 153–55, 175
leaves Thompson, 172–75, 177
legal agent of church, 20–21
letters, x, 117, 121–22, 145–46, 160–61, 163, 165–67, 173, 175–80, 182, 193, 209, 211–12, 218–50, 258–59
liquidation of Kirtland assets, 20–21, 23, 25, 39, 243
loyalty, ix, 13, 66, 70, 72, 103–10, 121, 129, 210, 214–16
marriage to Julia Ann Durfee, 202–3
marriage to Rosannah Robinson, 1
marriage sealing, 100
mayoral candidate, 62
mentors Joseph Smith III, 193–96
missionary work, 165, 169, 173, 192, 199, 221, 233
move to Missouri, 25–31, 207
municipal court, 54–69, 78, 108, 127, 215
Nauvoo burial grounds, 58–60, 127–28
Nauvoo Expositor, 107–8
Nauvoo Legion, 69–73, 106, 110, 215
Nauvoo Mansion, 110, 126, 133–34
Nauvoo temple, 97–100, 115, 121, 169, 202
New Translation of the Bible, 201–2
obituary, 207–8
ordains Joseph Smith III, 196, 208
Order of Enoch, 151
overseer of Strang's Quorum of Twelve, 145
pall bearer, 110
palsy, 198, 245
patriarch under Rigdon, 118
polygamy, ix, xiii, 14, 76, 81, 83–95, 100–101, 104–7, 114, 116, 142, 152–53, 167–69, 175, 192–93, 199–202, 207, 209–16, 244, 256, 260–64
postmaster, 139
praised by Emma, 113–15, 188
Preparation, 165, 167, 170–73, 179, 227, 241, 262
Presbyterian church, 2–4
Prophet, Priest, and King, 100, 103–4, 112, 131, 151, 153–54
priest, 8
prophecy about, 189, 198
public ball, 126
publishing committee, 192, 199
purchase of Montrose, 32
Quincy, 31–32, 38–39

Quorum of Anointed, 98–103, 106, 112, 175, 191, 207, 215
rejected as Trustee, 115–16
reluctance to lead, 52, 117, 135–36, 180–83
removed as Stake President, 126–27, 210
removed from Council of Fifty, 133
removed from Nauvoo High Council, 125–26
reputation, xix–xx, 9, 61, 112, 126–27, 131, 191, 207–8, 210, 214–15
schools under Thompson, 161, 167, 170–71, 225–26, 260, 262
second anointing, 100, 112, 126
Shabbona Grove, 137–39, 145, 148–51, 155, 165, 170, 172, 189–90, 193, 197, 202–5, 219–27, 230–35, 237, 243–44, 259
stagecoach owner, 139
stake president at Commerce, 38, 40–41
stake president at Kirtland, 19, 21, 25, 146, 165, 260
stake president at Nauvoo, 57, 60–61, 69–70, 91–92, 99, 104, 112, 114, 117, 120–21, 126–27, 142, 152, 165, 194, 196, 208–11, 215, 260, 262
statement of loyalty, 129–31
storekeeper, 139
succession, 111–34, 155, 161, 207, 215–16
support of Rigdon, x, 117–19, 124–25, 131, 215
tavern keeper, 1–2, 139
testimony, 65–66, 148, 168, 192, 254–57
Traveling Teachers, 161–64, 166, 171, 176, 260, 262
tried by High Council, 128–30
University of Nauvoo, 70, 132
villainized, 190–91, 209–11
vision, 193, 263
vision by Joseph Smith, 19–20, 210
Voree, 139, 142–47, 151, 162, 165, 219
Voree temple, 147, 150
voted into fellowship in Reorganization, 189
Marks, William, Jr., 71, 139, 155, 197, 250
Marsh, Thomas B., 6–7
Martin, Moses, 49–50
Mason, Elihu, 2
mayor, 53–56, 62, 68, 78–79, 101, 107, 132
McBride, Martha, 88
McHenry, Henry, 71, 155, 202
McLellin, William E., 6–7, 149

McRae, Alexander, 37
Miles, Joel S., 82
Miles, Prudence Marks, xvii–xviii, 175
Miles, Samuel, xvii–xviii, 175
Miles, Samuel Jr., xviii
Miller, George, 62, 79, 81, 98, 116, 191
Miller, Reuben, 141, 144
Miller, Sarah, 79–81
Milliken, Nathaniel, 20
mission work, xv, xvii–xviii, 1, 5, 8, 10, 16–17, 29, 55, 59, 61, 92, 114, 138–39, 146, 152, 155, 159, 161, 165–66, 173, 186–88, 192, 197, 199, 221, 233, 235, 262
Missouri War, 30
Monroe, James, 113
Moon, Margaret, 94
Morgan Harris, Lucinda Pendleton, 46
Mormontown, 32
Morse, Justus, 94
Moses (biblical), 10, 90
Muir, James, 203–4
Mulholland, James, 42
Murdock, John, xviii

N

Native Americans/Indigenous populations/Lamanites, 28–30, 135–38, 154, 157, 164, 221, 235
Nauvoo Charter, 53–54, 62–64, 68–69, 106
Nauvoo Choir of Singers, 44, 79–80, 97
Nauvoo Expositor, 106–8
Nauvoo House, 110, 133–34
Nauvoo Legion, 53, 55, 69–73, 97, 102, 106–7, 110, 215
Nauvoo Mansion, 105, 110, 126, 131, 133–34
Nauvoo Municipal Court, 53–54, 60–69, 77–78, 108, 127, 133, 215
Nauvoo Temple, 77, 97–100, 106, 114–15, 121, 157, 175, 178, 203, 251
Neff Moses, Barbara M., 89
Nephites, 6, 157, 182, 235
New Jerusalem, xiv–xvi, 38
New translation/Inspired translation of the Bible, xv, 201–2
New York City, 176–77, 204, 228, 245
Newell, Grandison, 11
Neyman, Jane, 94
Norris, Moses, 18
Nunda, New York, 1–2
Nyman, Margaret, 79–81

Nyman, Matilda, 79–81
Nyman Miller, Sarah, 79–81

O

Oakland Presbyterian Church, 2–4
Old Standard or the Church of Christ, 15
Order of Enoch, 150–51
ordination, 5, 9, 18–19, 40, 63, 94, 100, 104, 111–13, 131, 136, 139, 142, 146, 151, 153, 156, 159, 161–62, 166–68, 176–78, 186, 188, 190, 193, 196, 198–200, 208–9, 216, 225–26, 259–60, 262
Ourbough, Henry, 50

P

Pack, John, 134
Page, Ebenezer, 148
Page, Hiram, 146
Page, John E., 61, 141, 147, 177–78, 180–81, 209, 230, 233
Parrish, Warren, 13–15
Partridge, Edward, 30–31, 33, 35, 40, 44
Partridge, Eliza, 203
Partridge, Emily, 203
Patten, David W., 6–7
Patten, John, 49–50
Paw Paw, Illinois, 155, 202
Pawlet, Vermont, 1–2
Peck, Washington, 133
Pemberton, Collins, 141
Phelps, William W., xvii, 110, 115, 118, 120, 123, 127
Phinney Foster, Sarah, 88
Pitkin, George W., 66
Pittsburgh, Pennsylvania, 118, 124
Pittsfield, Illinois, 31–32, 39
Plat of Zion, 39
Plano, Illinois, 199, 201, 204, 245
Pleasant Vale Illinois Branch, 61
police, 15, 101, 127, 133, 190–91
polygamy/plural marriage, ix, x, xiii, 14, 16, 75–83, 85–95, 100–101, 104–7, 114–17, 134, 141–44, 148, 152–53, 156, 167–69, 175, 183–88, 192, 199–200, 203, 207–16, 256, 260–61
Pomeroy, Helen, 189
Pool, Betsy, 94–95
Pope, Nathaniel, 65–66
Potawatomi, Illinois, 138

Powers, Samuel, 195
Pratt, Orson, xviii, 6–7, 86, 88, 118, 164
Pratt, Parley P., xvii–xviii, xx, 6–7, 31, 66, 99, 116, 123, 140, 142
Pratt, Sarah, 43, 88
Preparation, Iowa, 165–67, 170–73, 179, 227, 233, 241, 259, 262
priesthood, 14–15, 22, 60, 76, 90, 98–99, 116, 119–21, 136, 139–42, 147, 153, 156–59, 164, 171, 175, 187–92, 195–96, 200, 214
printing press, 12, 20, 43, 107–8, 169–70, 225–26, 245, 262
Pulsipher, Zera, 22
Pure language, 27, 221

Q

Quincy, Illinois, 30–32, 34, 37–39, 64
Quorum of Anointed, 98–100, 102–3, 106, 112–16, 175, 191, 207, 215

R

Red Brick Store, 41
Redfield, Harlow, 42
redress petitions, 38, 152
Relief Society, 86–87, 106
Reorganized Church, ix–x, 158, 178, 182, 185–205, 207–13, 216, 245, 250, 263–64
Reynolds, Joseph H., 66
Rich, Charles C., 252–55
Rich, Joseph C., 59
Richards, Willard, 62, 65, 98, 101, 110, 114–16, 140, 142, 191
Richmond, B. W., xix–xx
Richmond, Missouri, 30
Rigdon, Nancy, 88
Rigdon, Sidney, x, xviii, 11–13, 16, 19, 21, 30–31, 38, 47, 51, 63, 66, 74, 86, 92, 97–99, 113–25, 129–32, 136, 140, 175, 197, 248, 257
Ripley, Alanson, 40, 42, 44, 57
Roberts, B. H., 210–11
Robinson, Charlotte, 2
Robinson, Chauncey, 60
Robinson, Ebenezer, 48, 81, 126
Robinson, George, 31, 73, 176, 228, 231
Robinson, Richard W., 2
Rockwell, Orrin Porter, 63–64, 67, 216
Rockwood, Albert P., 34, 70
Rogers, Chandler, 28–29
Rogers, David W., 32, 46
Rogers, Israel, 182, 191, 194–95, 201–2
Rogers, Noah, 28–29
Rounds, Samuel, 21
Russell, Isaac, 28–31, 46
Rutland, Vermont, 1

S

Sagers, Harrison, 93
Saint James, Michigan, 146
Salt Lake City, 191, 250
Sandusky, Ohio, 155
Savage, Jehiel, 141, 165, 224, 240–41, 259
Sawmill 165–67, 224, 259
Schindle, Melissa, 88
Scott, Isaac, 149, 152
Second Coming, xvi, 5, 38
secrecy, 25–26, 29, 49, 51, 63, 72, 77, 79, 87, 98, 102–3, 106, 117, 133, 143, 152–53, 168–69, 207, 214, 260
seventy/seventies, 22–23, 46, 61, 78, 111, 128, 140, 186, 196
Shabbona, [Chief], 137–38, 149
Shabbona Grove, Illinois, 137–39, 145, 148–55, 165, 170, 172, 189–90, 193, 197, 202–5, 219, 221, 223–28, 230, 232–37, 243–44, 250, 259, 264
Sharp, Thomas, 97
Shaw, Ella, 155, 202
Shaw, George, 155, 202
Shaw, Samuel, 141
Sheen, Isaac, 192, 195–96, 199, 212, 263
Shenandoah, Iowa, 203–4
Sherwood, Henry G., 42, 45, 125, 129, 254
Shiloh, 165
Simmons, Mrs., xix–xx
Skidmore, John, 71
slander, 47–51, 61, 68, 80–81, 121
Smith, Aaron, 138, 140, 143–44
Smith, Don Carlos, 74–75
Smith Bidamon, Emma, 12, 14, 19, 87, 90, 100, 113–15, 126, 130, 135, 187–88, 194–96, 201–2, 245
Smith, Esther, 77
Smith, George A., 59, 116, 130, 140, 142, 188, 191, 209, 255
Smith, Heman, 209, 220, 241
Smith, Hyrum, 5, 22, 30–31, 37, 42, 47–50, 57, 61–62, 65–66, 73, 83, 90–91, 98–100, 105–13, 118, 133, 157, 194, 200, 216, 260

Smith Davis, Inez, 220–37, 240–44
Smith, Jesse Nathaniel, 31
Smith, John, 1, 15, 18–20, 40, 50, 94, 126, 162, 176
Smith, John Aikens, 29
Smith, Joseph, Jr.,
  accused, 63, 65–67, 79, 245
  arrest, 30, 63–68, 108–9
  banking, 11, 13, 19, 21
  baptism for the dead, 201
  betrayed, 191
  board of health, 58
  body, 110, 216
  burden of the church, 131
  character, 255
  charged, 51, 93, 104–5, 108
  complaint, 68, 81
  cornerstone laying, 98
  Council of Fifty, 102–4
  death, 109–11, 114, 126, 133, 157, 161, 179, 183, 194, 198, 207–8, 210, 232, 260, 263
  D&C 132, 90
  Danites, 72–73
  endowment, 66, 99
  escapes from Gallatin, 37
  Far West, 19
  ferry, 47
  financial affairs in Kirtland, 243
  financial affairs in Nauvoo, 42–46, 83–84
  First Vision, 179
  Freemason, 73, 197
  friction with Marks, 101
  funerals, 74, 216
  Galland purchase, 34–35
  gathering, ix, 34–35, 71–72
  happiness sermon, 74
  incarcerated, 30–31, 63, 67, 161–62
  last charge, 160–61
  lawsuits, 19, 21, 63, 65, 81
  Liberty Jail, 30–31, 63
  loss, 71
  marriage sealing, 99–100
  mayor, 62, 101, 107
  Nauvoo Expositor, 107–8
  officiates in Commerce, 40
  ordinance, 68, 78–79
  participates in High Council cases, 44, 50
  plurality of gods, 106
  polygamy, 14, 19, 75–95, 101, 104, 106, 167–68, 186, 192, 200, 207, 212–14, 244, 260–64
  preaches in Kirtland, 5, 14, 16
  preaches in Nauvoo, 80, 101
  preaches in New York, xvii–xviii
  presidential bid, 114
  printing office, 12, 20
  Prophet, Priest, and King, 103–4, 167–68, 260
  publishes Book of Mormon, xiii
  receives golden plates, xiii
  reconciles with Rigdon, 124
  redress petitions, 38
  released, 35, 63–64, 66–67, 108
  revelation, 19–20, 25–27, 90, 126
  ritual, 97, 99
  slander, 51, 81
  Solemn Assembly, 160
  successor, 50, 92, 111–34, 186, 192, 194, 196, 207, 215
  technicality, 66
  theocracy, 106, 153–54
  theology, 71–72
  treason, 37, 63, 66, 109
  vision in Kirtland Temple, 10
  writes to Saints in Quincy, 34
Smith, Joseph, Sr., 1, 14–15, 66
Smith, Joseph, III, ix, 112, 134–37, 144–45, 151, 186–88, 193–96, 199–204, 207, 245, 250
Smith, Lucy Mack, 139
Smith, Mary, 29
Smith, Mary Fielding, 34
Smith, Moses, 141, 144
Smith, Samuel, 110, 116
Smith, Silas, 29, 31–32
Smith, Warren, 102
Smith, William, 6–7, 116, 138, 145, 148, 159, 175, 178, 180, 185, 234
Snively, Hugh, 29
Snow, Eliza R., 15
Snow, Erastus, 131, 188
Snyder, John, 110
Soby, Leonard, 91–92, 102, 122, 124, 252, 254
Solemn Assembly, 160–63, 166, 169–72, 221–22, 226, 262
Solomon (biblical), 90, 99
Spencer, Daniel, 132
Spencer, Orson, 255

Spiritualist Movement, 181
Springfield, Illinois, 65–66
St. Joseph, Missouri, 163, 203, 223
St. Louis, Missouri, 27, 30, 156, 163, 166–67, 170, 221–22, 225–26, 262
Stevens, Richard, 161, 163, 223, 258
Stone, Barton, 181
Strang, James
  angelic ordination, 136, 156, 193
  appoints Marks to building committee, 50
  appoints Marks guardian of Joseph III, 144, 151
  anointed, 146
  baptism, 151
  baptism for the dead, 151
  Beaver Island, 136, 146, 153–54, 156, 162, 178
  brings in Bennett, 142–43, 145
  calls Joseph III into First Presidency, 144–45
  claims, 137–39, 143, 146, 175, 193
  community at Voree, ix
  convert, 136
  death, 154, 175
  endorsed by Marks, 140–42
  excommunicates Bennett, 145, 147
  excommunicates the Brighamite Twelve, x, 141
  gathering, 136, 139, 150, 159, 162
  hierarchical organization, 145
  king, 153–54
  Latter Day Saint, x
  letters from Marks, 145–46, 218–19
  letter of appointment, 136
  makes George Adams his counselor, 145
  makes Marks an Apostle, 151
  makes Marks his counselor, 144
  makes William Smith patriarch, 145
  memorial to U.S. government for redress, 152
  missionaries, 165, 188
  murder of, 154
  Order of Enoch, 150–51
  Philadelphia branch leaves, 153
  political office, 154
  polygamy, 146, 148, 152–56, 169, 185–86
  prophet, seer, and revelator, 138–40
  publications, 138, 141, 144, 152, 157
  Quorum of Twelve, 145–46, 151, 176–77
  reacts to Bennett's excommunication, 144
  rebukes Marks, 150, 209
  recruits Marks, 139, 150
  redress, 152
  rejected by Thompson, 156
  removes Aaron Smith, 144
  revelation, 144, 150, 209
  secret society, 143
  succession, 136, 164, 186
  sustained president of the church, 151
  Tabernacle on Beaver Island, 153
  Temple in Voree, 147
  theocracy, 153–54
  visits Marks in Fulton, 136–37
  Voree, 136
  Voree plates, 138
  Voree Temple, 147, 150
Stout, Allen, 133
Stout, Hosea, 73, 82, 133, 252, 254, 257
succession, ix, xi, 8, 50, 111–36, 158, 160, 164, 175, 183–88, 192–93, 207–10, 215–16
Sweet, John, 29

T

Taylor, John, 28–29, 114–16, 123, 128, 132, 140, 142, 255
Taylor, Leonora, 28–29
Tecumseh, 137
Temple Lot case, 83
Thatcher, George W., 82
Thompson, Charles B.
  affiliates with Strang, 156
  Baneemy, 157–58, 161, 164, 177
  Book of Remembrance, 172
  breaks with Brigham, 156
  Chief Teacher, 158, 160, 221, 262
  claims, 155, 193, 221
  Congregation of Jehovah's Presbytery of Zion, ix, 10, 156, 169
  converts, 155
  covenant, 164–65, 170–72, 224
  endowment, 161
  Enoch pseudepigrapha, 170
  Evangelical Teachers, 166–67, 171
  family, 155–56
  financial, 169–70, 172–73, 226
  Freemasonry, 158–59
  gathering, 156, 159–67, 170, 172, 216, 258, 262
  grand key, 158
  high priest in Nauvoo, 156
  house in Kanesville, 163, 169–70, 223, 262
  hymns and poems, 158

joins the Mormons, 155
Kanesville, 163–67, 171, 223
last charge, 160
Law of Sacrifice, 172–73
letters from Marks, 58–59, 163–67, 211, 258–62
letter to Marks, 173, 241
marriage, 155–56
missionaries, 158, 161, 164–65
Missouri, 155
Nauvoo, 156
Nauvoo endowment, 156
Nauvoo High Council, 160–61
Nauvoo Masonic Lodge, 156
organizes branch at Sandusky, 155
organizes Genessee Conference, 155
polygamy, 156, 168–69
Preparation, 165–67, 170–73, 179
priesthood, 158, 171
publications, 155–59, 162–64, 169–70, 179, 192, 216
pure language, 221
rejected by followers, 173, 175
rejects Strang, 156
revelation, 156
schools, 157–61, 163, 170–72, 221
Solemn Assembly, 160–63, 167, 170, 226
St. Louis, Missouri, 156
Strang, 141, 156, 159
temple/House of the Lord, 157, 170–71, 221
theology, 157–58
tithing, 172–73, 237
wife dies, 155
witness against the Twelve, 141
Three Witnesses, 6, 153
Trail of Death, 138
Turley, Jason, 77
Turley, Theodore, 76–77
Turnham, Joel, 63
Turpin, Jesse, 78
Treason, 37, 63, 66, 109
Twelve Apostles,
 accused by Strang group, 141
 authority, 6–8, 111–13, 117–18, 129, 131
 blessings, 6–7
 campaigning, 114
 chosen in Kirtland, 6–8
 cleanse the church, 82
 cut off Rigdon, 123
 disfellowships Bennett, 62

distrusts Marks, 59
excommunicated, 15–16, 140–42
hierarchy, 6–8, 61, 111
Judas, 101
missions, 8, 19, 61, 114–15
Nauvoo Legion, 69–70
polygamy, 92, 115–16, 169, 213–14
prevents public ball, 126
provision for wives, 47
questions Marks, 128–30
rejects Marks, 139, 215
RLDS, 199–201
second anointings, 112–13
Strang, 146–47
succession, 111–36, 193
Thompson, 156
traveling High Council, 6–8, 112, 118, 124, 136
withdraws fellowship from Bennett, 62

U–V

University of Nauvoo, 53, 55, 70, 77, 132
Van Dusen, Increase, 141
"Voice of Innocence," 87
Voree Temple, 147
Voree, Wisconsin, ix, 136, 139, 142–43, 145–47, 151–52, 162, 165, 178, 219
Voree Plates, 138

W

Waggoner, David, 50
Walker, Oliver, 50–51
Warren, Catherine, 81–82
Warren, S. B., 139
Warrington, Benjamin, 107
Warsaw, Illinois, 97
Washington, DC, 38, 51
Wasson, Lorenzo, 103
Wells, Daniel D., 2
Wells, Daniel H., 47, 59, 104, 108, 132, 255
Whitmer, David, 5–6, 175
Whitney, Newel K., 16, 25–27, 38, 40, 43, 58, 62, 98, 115–16, 123, 125, 132, 191, 255
whittled out, 134
Wight, Lyman, xvii, 37, 66, 118, 175
Williams, Frederick G., 13–14
Wilson, Lewis D., 252, 254
Woodruff, Pheobe, 20
Woodruff, Wilford, 82, 90, 118, 255

Woodworth, Lucian, 105
Word of Wisdom, 8, 60

Y–Z

Young, Brigham, ix, 6, 31, 45, 66, 94, 98, 101, 112–13, 116–23, 127, 134, 139–42, 144, 156–57, 163–68, 175, 183, 185, 188–91, 195, 208–10, 213–16, 230, 242–43, 250, 255
Younger, Joseph, 141, 237
Zarahemla Stake, 50, 186–88, 193
Zion, ix, xv–xvii, xx, 4–5, 7, 16, 21, 27–28, 30, 38–40, 45, 52, 72, 98, 112–13, 156, 158, 161, 163, 169, 172, 196, 198, 201, 207, 216, 251, 254, 260
Zion's Camp, xvii–xviii, xx, 4–5, 207
Zundel, John, 50

Also available from
GREG KOFFORD BOOKS

A House for the Most High: The Story of the Original Nauvoo Temple

Matthew McBride

Hardcover, ISBN: 978-1-58958-016-9

This awe-inspiring book is a tribute to the perseverance of the human spirit. *A House for the Most High* is a groundbreaking work from beginning to end with its faithful and comprehensive documentation of the Nauvoo Temple's conception. The behind-the-scenes stories of those determined Saints involved in the great struggle to raise the sacred edifice bring a new appreciation to all readers. McBride's painstaking research now gives us access to valuable first-hand accounts that are drawn straight from the newspaper articles, private diaries, journals, and letters of the steadfast participants.

The opening of this volume gives the reader an extraordinary window into the early temple-building labors of the besieged Church of Jesus Christ of Latter-day Saints, the development of what would become temple-related doctrines in the decade prior to the Nauvoo era, and the 1839 advent of the Saints in Illinois. The main body of this fascinating history covers the significant years, starting from 1840, when this temple was first considered, to the temple's early destruction by a devastating natural disaster. A well-thought-out conclusion completes the epic by telling of the repurchase of the temple lot by the Church in 1937, the lot's excavation in 1962, and the grand announcement in 1999 that the temple would indeed be rebuilt. Also included are an astonishing appendix containing rare and fascinating eyewitness descriptions of the temple and a bibliography of all major source materials. Mormons and non-Mormons alike will discover, within the pages of this book, a true sense of wonder and gratitude for a determined people whose sole desire was to build a sacred and holy temple for the worship of their God.

Jan Shipps: A Social and Intellectual Portrait:
How a Methodist Girl from Hueytown, Alabama, Became an Acclaimed Mormon Studies Scholar

Gordon Shepherd and Gary Shepherd

Paperback, ISBN: 978-1-58958-767-0
Hardcover, ISBN: 978-1-58958-768-7

How did Jo Ann Barnett—a Methodist girl born and raised in Hueytown, Alabama, during the Great Depression and World War II—come to be Jan Shipps, a renowned non-Mormon historian and scholar of The Church of Jesus Christ of Latter-day Saints? In Jan Shipps: A Social and Intellectual Portrait, authors Gordon Shepherd and Gary Shepherd tell the story of how Shipps not only became an important and trusted authority in a field that was predominantly made up of Mormon men, but also the crucial role she played in legitimizing Mormon Studies as a credible academic field of study.

Praise for *Jan Shipps: A Social and Intellectual Portrait*:

"The person and work of Jan Shipps comprise one of the ten most important factors enabling Mormon Studies to eclipse its parochial past. Authors Gordon and Gary Shepherd have adroitly marshalled the tools of history and social science to lay bare how this unlikely event came to be. This is important reading for any who hope to understand Shipps or the emergence of the field in which she worked. Important also for any scholar feeling that the deck in a competitive academy is stacked against them." —Phil Barlow, Neal A. Maxwell Fellow at the Neal A. Maxwell Institute for Religious Scholarship at Brigham Young University.

"Jan Shipps deserves and the Shepherds are to be thanked for this celebration of her celebrated career. The authors rightly insist this is not a thorough treatment of Jan's life but rather an account of her role in the rise Mormon Studies in the late-twentieth century. It was a watershed time and Jan was a creator of and catalyst to much of the best scholarship which flowed from it. As such, there is much to learn here about Mormonism itself and those who studied it during this period." —Kathleen Flake, Richard Lyman Bushman Professor of Mormon Studies, University of Virginia

Hearken, O Ye People: The Historical Setting of Joseph Smith's Ohio Revelations

Mark Lyman Staker

Hardcover, ISBN: 978-1-58958-113-5

2010 Best Book Award - John Whitmer Historical Association
2011 Best Book Award - Mormon History Association

More of Mormonism's canonized revelations originated in or near Kirtland than any other place. Yet many of the events connected with those revelations and their 1830s historical context have faded over time. Mark Staker reconstructs the cultural experiences by which Kirtland's Latter-day Saints made sense of the revelations Joseph Smith pronounced. This volume rebuilds that exciting decade using clues from numerous archives, privately held records, museum collections, and even the soil where early members planted corn and homes. From this vast array of sources he shapes a detailed narrative of weather, religious backgrounds, dialect differences, race relations, theological discussions, food preparation, frontier violence, astronomical phenomena, and myriad daily customs of nineteenth-century life. The result is a "from the ground up" experience that today's Latter-day Saints can all but walk into and touch.

Praise for *Hearken O Ye People*:

"I am not aware of a more deeply researched and richly contextualized study of any period of Mormon church history than Mark Staker's study of Mormons in Ohio. We learn about everything from the details of Alexander Campbell's views on priesthood authority to the road conditions and weather on the four Lamanite missionaries' journey from New York to Ohio. All the Ohio revelations and even the First Vision are made to pulse with new meaning. This book sets a new standard of in-depth research in Latter-day Saint history."
    -Richard Bushman, author of *Joseph Smith: Rough Stone Rolling*

"To be well-informed, any student of Latter-day Saint history and doctrine must now be acquainted with the remarkable research of Mark Staker on the important history of the church in the Kirtland, Ohio, area."
    -Neal A. Maxwell Institute, Brigham Young University

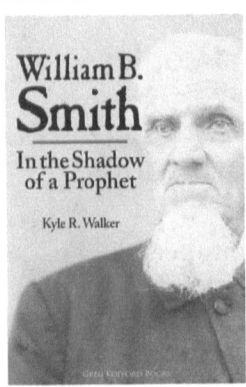

William B. Smith: In the Shadow of a Prophet

Kyle R. Walker

Paperback, ISBN: 978-1-58958-503-4

Younger brother of Joseph Smith, a member of the Quorum of the Twelve Apostles, and Church Patriarch for a time, William Smith had tumultuous yet devoted relationships with Joseph, his fellow members of the Twelve, and the LDS and RLDS (Community of Christ) churches. Walker's imposing biography examines not only William's complex life in detail, but also sheds additional light on the family dynamics of Joseph and Lucy Mack Smith, as well as the turbulent intersections between the LDS and RLDS churches. *William B. Smith: In the Shadow of a Prophet* is a vital contribution to Mormon history in both the LDS and RLDS traditions.

Praise for *William B. Smith*:

"Bullseye! Kyle Walker's biography of Joseph Smith Jr.'s lesser known younger brother William is right on target. It weaves a narrative that is searching, balanced, and comprehensive. Walker puts this former Mormon apostle solidly within a Smith family setting, and he hits the mark for anyone interested in Joseph Smith and his family. Walker's biography will become essential reading on leadership dynamics within Mormonism after Joseph Smith's death." — Mark Staker, author *Hearken, O Ye People: The Historical Setting of Joseph Smith's Ohio Revelations*

"This perceptive biography on William, the last remaining Smith brother, provides a thorough timeline of his life's journey and elucidates how his insatiable discontent eventually tempered the once irascible young man into a seasoned patriarch loved by those who knew him." — Erin B. Metcalfe, president (2014–15) John Whitmer Historical Association

"I suspect that this comprehensive treatment will serve as the definitive biography for years to come; it will certainly be difficult to improve upon." — Joe Steve Swick III, Association for Mormon Letters

www.ingramcontent.com/pod-product-compliance
Lightning Source LLC
Chambersburg PA
CBHW032217230426
43672CB00011B/2586